The Ethical Hack

A Framework for Business Value Penetration Testing

The
Ethical Hack

A Framework for
Business Value Penetration
Testing

JAMES S. TILLER

AUERBACH PUBLICATIONS

A CRC Press Company
Boca Raton   London   New York   Washington, D.C.

The opinions expressed in this book are those of the author and do not represent opinions of International Network Services Inc.

Library of Congress Cataloging-in-Publication Data

Tiller, James S.
    The ethical hack : a framework for business value penetration testing / James S. Tiller
    p. cm.
Includes index.
ISBN 0-8493-1609-X (alk. paper)
    1. Computer networks--Security measures. 2. Computer networks--Testing. 3. Computer hackers. 4. Business enterprises--Computer networks. I. Title.

TK5105.59.T55 2003
005.8--dc21

        2003052467

Visit the Auerbach Web site at www.auerbach-publications.com

About the Author

James Tiller, CISA, CISM, CISSP, is the Chief Security Officer and Managing Vice President of Security Services for International Network Services (INS). He is the author of *A Technical Guide to IPSec Virtual Private Networks*, contributing author to *Information Security Management Handbook 2001–2005*, has appeared in *Information System Security Journal*, and co-authored four patents on security architectures and policy applications. Jim has spent the last decade involved with information security in some form or another. From working as a "white hat" cracking systems, to participating in the development of security technologies and strategies at Bell Labs, he speaks regularly at events and seminars throughout North America and Europe and has been a guest speaker at various universities. You can find him bouncing around the world, or at home with his wife, Mary, daughter, Rain, and son, Phoenix.

Contributors

The original intention was to have several authors assist in the creation of this book. Unfortunately, schedules, pressures, workloads, and unforeseen changes in focus—a regular occurrence over the lifetime of writing a book—limited contributions. However, a couple of individuals accepted my challenge to provide elements of this book and delivered above expectations.

Felicia Nicastro, CISSP, a principal security consultant for International Network Services based in New York, was very helpful in creating elements for policies and procedures, implementation, and the exploitation section. She also helped in reviewing the book several times to keep things on track. She has published several papers and articles, including the paper, "Security Management," and an article on patch management in the *Information System Security Journal*. Her background includes providing security services to major financial institutions, Internet service providers, and various enterprise organizations. Her areas of expertise include security policies and procedures, security assessments, and security architecture planning, designing, and implementation. Prior to joining INS, Felicia was a security administrator at the Associated Press, supporting UNIX and various systems within the organization. Felicia has her B.S. in management information systems.

Tom Carlson, CISSP, a senior security consultant for International Network Services based in Minnesota, wrote the bulk of Chapter 5, Information Security Program. Tom is a certified BS-7799 auditor and is a recognized expert on information security programs founded on the ISO-17799 and BS-7799 standards. His background spans diverse environments including national security, academia, private enterprise, and Antarctic research, encompassing design, development, deployment, and operations. Prior to joining INS Tom worked with multiple government agencies on a variety of mission-critical projects, as well as security solutions for the private sector. His area of expertise is in information security management systems and risk management. Tom has a B.S. in electrical engineering, as well as various certifications.

For My Father

Table of Contents

Foreword

So there I was at my ten-year class reunion, looking around awkwardly and wearing my best suit. Back in my high school days, I was definitely in the nerd crowd, and my discomfort at this reunion was starting to remind me of that fact. I chatted with a small group of friends who had started to grow thinner on top and thicker in the middle. Rick, the track jock who became a forest ranger, asked, "What do you do for a living, Ed?"

"I do computer security work . . . mostly penetration testing," I replied.

"What's that?" asked Mike, a former journalism major who had recently gotten a gig writing for a major newspaper.

"Well," I started, "I hack into computer systems for banks, and then tell them how we got in so they can fix their security holes."

"You rob *banks* for a living?" stammered Mike. "How cool is that!"

As I explained my job, a larger group of former jocks, musicians, cool kids, and, yes, even geeks gathered around. With much excitement, they asked me about the ethics, procedures, and technology that underlie penetration testing. Heck, Mike even asked me to transfer a few hundred thousand dollars into his bank account during my next project. Mike never was much into ethics, now that I think about it.

As my class reunion experience hinted, penetration testing has indeed recently become very popular. In the olden days of the 1970s and 1980s, pretty much only the military, government, and phone companies hacked themselves to find security flaws. They were the only ones with powerful computers storing enough sensitive data to need such services. Today, all kinds of companies, including merchants, manufacturers, and insurance companies, regularly test their own security using penetration testing procedures. Our once esoteric craft is becoming much more mainstream.

Jim Tiller has created an outstanding book that describes in detail the *right way* to conduct a thorough penetration test. As more and more people offer penetration-testing services, our industry needs a baseline of solid practices to help separate the professionals from the charlatans. Jim's book describes such practices, including the policies, procedures, and technical insights that come from years of in-the-trenches experience.

I'm happy to see that Jim addresses the technical issues associated with penetration testing, but he doesn't stop at the technology. There are dozens of books that address just the technical issues. But that's not enough. You could be an unparalleled technical wizard-monster-guru, and completely screw up a penetration test, hosing both your client and your career. Jim's book is special in that it goes beyond just the technical aspects of penetration testing. He also addresses the processes and rules of engagement required for a successful penetration test.

So, read this book, and follow its advice to hone your penetration testing skills. I can't guarantee it will make you more popular at your next class reunion. However, I am sure it will make you a better penetration tester!

Ed Skoudis

Preface

It took some time to decide whether to write this book. A book about the highly technical subject of hacking to have little focus on technology and technique, and simply on value, seemed challenging. No deep discussions on the best tools or how to configure a system to thwart an attack or even case studies detailing how a hack-for-hire penetrated the Bank of China are supplied. Rather, this is a book providing a proven approach to ensuring the value of a test is realized through sound planning, execution, and integration.

Ethical hacking is identifying vulnerabilities through the art of exploitation. Prying open holes in systems and applications helps to determine the state of security within an organization. It exposes weaknesses in operating systems, services, applications, and even users for the betterment of the company and its business.

But this simple prelude introduces some fascinating questions that go well beyond technology and poking around in computers. In the race to see who is vulnerable to what hack, there is a larger perception of value that has become veiled by a wall of technology. It is essential to recognize the distinguishing elements throughout an ethical hacking test to ensure the act of exploitation results in enlightening conclusions and not a collection of misguided intentions.

Security is an incredibly interesting topic that provides the fodder for heated debates. It is commonplace to start talking about firewalls and end up debating the validity of privacy rules and their interpretation in the courts of law. Security is dynamic, broad, and layered in varying perceptions. To discuss one area of security tends to force the addition of another, then another, concept and so on.

Realizing the convolution of the subject in the light of the structure I wish to convey, this book was inevitably going to be an exercise in philosophy rather than technology.

Many look at security very pragmatically: protect information against threats by using firewalls, cryptography, anti-virus, patches, and any combination of technology to keep the bad guys out and the good ones in control. However, security in the digital world is having difficulty keeping pace with computer crime and the people who commit those crimes. Technology has become so engrained in our society that the magnitude of exposure is difficult to fully measure. To criminals, technology is just another tool to get what they are looking for; it is just a different kind of gun, lock pick, or hammer.

In the world of ethical hacking, we're asking people to use the tool of technology in a confined space to make determinations on a much broader perspective of security. Ethical hacking can be an effective method for determining some of the idiosyncrasies of your security posture, but the value gained from the test is directly proportionate to the assumptions and understanding about information security.

Ethical hacking has become a very popular security activity. It seems everyone is looking to hack their networks to see what gaping holes they will find this quarter. Tests are being performed all over the world in many different ways, using different methods, different tools, and very different assumptions of success and failure. It is the "true value" of a test that is going to be investigated, criticized, detailed, and analyzed in this book.

This would inevitably become a test of thought and question, a journey through a technical forest wearing philosophers' goggles, and a challenge with many opposing opinions. Nevertheless, it was clear that although many were traversing the path of ethical hacking, few were mapping the route and most simply followed the beaten trail in front of them or blazed new ones blindly.

There are many books available detailing tools and techniques for performing tests, introducing processes resulting in successfully hacking a system or application, and giving plenty of examples of attacks with amazing results. However, as each new book surfaced it became increasingly clear there was a focus on the tools and techniques to break into systems for an unclear and elusive greater good. It was also apparent that very little strategic information was provided to support the value of such a test to an organization or how to perform a test in a manner explicitly for the benefit of the company beyond listing their security vulnerabilities.

Ethical hacking is obviously different from criminals hacking computers, but the delineation has become thin and out of focus. People assume that acting as a hacker is an accurate example of being a malevolent hacker without consideration for the meaning behind performing the test in the first place.

An ethical hack needs to be aligned with the state of an organization's security posture to gain the most value from the exercise. The person performing the ethical hack will help find the holes and assist in determining the overall risk to assets, but the ingenuity of hackers and their craft cannot be underestimated or completely imitated.

It is fair to say a security consultant armed with experience, tools, and knowledge can easily mimic a hacker and provide insight to an organization's weaknesses. Nevertheless, there are rules, time limitations, access restrictions, motive differences, and consequences associated with assuming the *role* of a hacker to which the *real* hacker is not confined.

A hacker only has to find one hole to meet the objective, whereas the security technology and the people who support it have to defend against all points of entry, even the authorized ones, at times. Always being on the defensive requires intense intellect, diligence, and tenacity, arguably more so than an attacker. The goal is to not abandon these disadvantages and attempt to fully imitate a hacker. Simply approach an ethical hack—as a customer or consultant—fully aware of your disadvantages and limitations, and understand how to best work with them. The apparent differences need to be embraced and used as a benefit and a tool to bring value to the engagement.

The goal of this book is to present information from many perspectives to promote a robust test. I want to shed light on the bigger picture and the associated ramifications of different tactics, while providing added insight to the detailed process that many take for granted. To accomplish this goal, a framework is presented and detailed. It provides a mechanism to demonstrate the relationships between discrete actions performed during a test. Additionally, a framework provides a foundation for managing the entire engagement by establishing a process that promotes the marriage of technical elements with the inherent characteristics of an ethical hack.

Using a framework, the management, supporting processes, technology, and structure of the test within the larger subject of security will ensure the exercise reaches its full potential to offer value to the business. It provides the opportunity to investigate all the test options and determine the impacts to value when used or not used.

The framework is a tool that offers what is possible, presents the potential challenges and how to overcome them, and exposes threats to value as each security ingredient is eliminated from the engagement. To realize the value promised by ethical hacking, the framework focuses on the operational strategies and not on hacking tactics. By evaluating the environment armed with a tool equally as important as hacking tools, the role of security in business success will become a reality.

Acknowledgments

No book is entirely created by a single person. Material taken from offhand conversations, newsgroups, Web site articles, and engagements all appear in this book. This is an opportunity to introduce people who have had an impact, whether they like it or not.

Rich O'Hanley, my editor from Auerbach Publications, was instrumental in helping get this book completed. His trust in me was a constant driver to ensure a valuable project. Anton Chuvakin, Ph.D. was one of the first to review the book in its entirety. His comments were not only inspiring, but provided a great deal of insight to making the book better. Steve Coman, an unwitting influence and a long-time friend, appears in many places in this book. Endless conversations about security on a boat, in a bar, and over the phone or dinner have provided me everlasting impressions of security. Steve always questioned security and the perceptions of it in the business world and from the trenches. Ed Skoudis, the author of *Counter Hack: A Step-by-Step Guide to Computer Attacks and Effective Defenses* not only wrote the foreword, but was incredibly helpful in making sure I was on the right track. Many thanks to Ed for taking the time to review the material and always providing support for the book. Jay Heiser, another unwitting accomplice, author of *Computer Forensics: Incident Response Essentials,* and a friend and former colleague, provided many perspectives of security that will stay with me forever. Many e-mails and conversations (aka arguments) about security helped to formulate some of my perspectives. You can catch some of his writings in *Information Security* magazine. Wayne Selk provided a great deal of assistance throughout the book. He is an old friend from way back and our discussions about security have certainly appeared here. Wayne has been a UNIX expert for years, overseeing large service provider networks, and is a security consultant for Symantec.

The book, *Secrets and Lies: Digital Security in a Networked World*, by Bruce Schneier, founder and CTO of Counterpane Internet Security, Inc., was inspirational. Donn Parker's book, *Fighting Computer Crime: A New Framework for Protecting Information,* sits worn and tattered on the shelf from many readings. His insights into the hacker's mind provided the foundation of many of the perceptions of hackers found in this book.

1 Getting Started

Hiring someone to hack your company goes by many names, such as ethical hacking, penetration testing, tiger teaming, intrusion testing, vulnerability analysis, and even security assessment. In addition, each term has different meanings in different countries or regions. The term penetration testing does not go over well in Central America and some places in the United States, whereas the term ethical hacking is not the preferred term in Western Europe. Tiger team is a derivative of a military term and I have heard it used in Taiwan and Japan, another place the use of ethical hacking, as the name of an act, does not go over well. Nevertheless, the most predominant terms are ethical hacking and penetration testing, and both terms are used quite regularly throughout this book.

The intention of this book is simple: explain and detail the methodologies, framework, and unwritten conventions ethical hacks should exercise to provide the most value to organizations seeking to enhance their security posture.

There is a great deal of respect for other books of similar type, extensive training on the subject, and professional service organizations that provide hacking services. All these convey valuable information pertaining to tools and processes on how to use them. However, it is critical that structure and process combine to ensure all parties recognize ultimate value and a company is not being hacked under false pretenses.

Security is a lot of things combined in many ways that will have varying degrees of impact, good and bad. This is a lesson in value and risk and how they relate to ethical hacking. Within security, one must take into consideration the human element as much as the technical. Additionally, there are the pragmatic issues of value and risk and their effects on business objectives.

There are several areas associated with ethical hacking that have yet to be addressed in their entirety. Following is a list of characteristics of ethical hacking and the gap associated with each. This book provides the framework and structure to address these fundamental issues.

- *Focusing on Tools and Technology, and Very Little on Methodology.* Today, there is a clear understanding of the use and availability of tools to support an ethical hack. Thanks to several popular references, the processes of technically performing a hack are well documented and reasonably well established. However, organizations desperately need to understand the details in the overall processes and how to use the test, and its results, for the betterment of their security posture. This is the ultimate goal behind

1

ethical hacking services but, ironically, remains elusive and a rarity among the greater population of penetration-testing engagements.

- *Interpreting the Results.* When a system is determined "secure" because it has survived a controlled attack, it does not necessarily mean that system is actually secure. The vast amount of assumptions, limitations, and expectations inherent and applied to a test may result in indeterminate conclusions. Moreover, there are situations where the test resulted in voluminous amounts of vulnerabilities being identified making it nearly impossible to weed through the information to find what really matters and measure the risk. Another problem is that results are rarely integrated into the company's security program effectively and usually appear as ad hoc point solutions to solve an immediate need, such as a new firewall rule or another untracked policy statement. In some cases the entire exercise is to simply satisfy executive management that a vulnerability exists, without thought of integrating the results into the practice of corporate security. Few perform proper insightful planning by engaging in a process, resulting in limited scope and value to the company as a whole. Understandably, a test's lack of comprehensive planning is the root cause of the questionable effectiveness of many ethical hacking tests.

- *Protecting the Innocent.* Ethical hacking requires breaking into computer systems or applications to demonstrate the risk of an identified vulnerability. By collecting specific information from the target, an ethical hacker can prove access was successful and reveal the exposure. The result is that highly sensitive information about the target's security capabilities (or the lack of them) is collected and maintained far outside the owner's control. If this information were to fall into the wrong hands, it could be used to perpetrate a real attack against the company. Another risk is the information being leaked to the public or to stockholders who stand to lose their investment if the exposures represent a fundamental risk to the business. Information of this type can result in all types of disasters, including negative portrayals by the media, devaluation, loss of customers, or legal consequences. Also, there are several opportunities for the tester to accidentally inflict harm on intermediates, such as an Internet service provider (ISP), partners connected to the target's network, or customers interacting with the systems or applications under attack.

- *Politics and Processes.* Breaking into a company can represent a substantial threat to the continued employment of several people within the organization. It is essential the test be performed to support the entire company and not an individual. In some cases, the deliverable of an ethical hack was not presented to the people who needed it most to make the necessary security improvements. Politics play a major role in the planning of a test and the creation of limitations and expectations, ultimately affecting the outcome. Establishing a solid foundation of communication, expectations, imposed and inherent limitations, and metrics for the test will help to ensure the company benefits from the experience, not the individual.

- *Testing Dangers.* There are several dangers associated with penetration testing. These range from outages, system or application faults, and the destruction of information to more ominous issues such as information leaks (when questionable resources are used to perform the engagement, possibly sharing critical information with others for status or money) and piggybacking (when a real hacker uses the test's activities to camouflage his attack). Proper teaming and communication protocols will protect both tester and target from inadvertently harboring illicit activities. Moreover, testing engagements are a prime source for teaching people how to break into networks, especially yours. Great care and attention must be paid to the people performing the test and to their ethics and responsibilities.

AUDIENCE

The audience for this book is twofold, each on his or her own side of the "value fence."

Managers of organizations that are looking to solicit third parties (or internal departments) to perform an ethical hack against their networks, systems, applications, and even physical establishments are the primary beneficiaries of this book. Information security administrators, managers, directors, or anyone considering or responsible for obtaining penetration services can gain a great deal by employing a business-value, business-focused approach.

Information about what to expect from all phases of the test, from the first meetings to accepting the deliverable and knowing how to best use the results, are discussed. Elements detailed will help in identifying a good test from a bad one, or finding the value from what was perceived initially as a failure. Most important, organizations seeking penetration services will gain further insight into the appropriate measures and methodologies that should be practiced by a third party. Finally, this book provides guidance in setting test expectations: What are your expectations? What do you think the results will show? Are you prepared for Pandora's box to be opened? Understanding the details of a test will provide unequalled insight, and, most important, business value to any company.

For security practitioners, this book also provides exceptional value. First, by understanding what the customer is reading and digesting the information from his perspective, security consultants can learn more about the impact of his involvement and how to best meet their customer's demands. This book provides a set of methodologies that can be leveraged to protect you and the customer's interests, and ensure that you are providing a highly tuned, valuable service to your customer. Much of the information in this book should not be shocking or new to the majority of the security community. However, the goal is to provide a framework for performing tests and the structured content for all of the processes assumed to be in practice today.

HOW TO USE THIS BOOK

This book is more of a story about the logical, and sometimes illogical, aspects of information security. There are so many nuances regularly overlooked or placed on the back burner because they seem insurmountable or simply do not align with business objectives adding to the bottom line. This story is an opportunity to discuss the larger challenges of information security by using a popular tool—ethical hacking—as a medium for communication. For better or for worse, ethical hacking is becoming a huge component of a security program in the industry, and with it a greater sense of security, or lack of it, depending on your perception.

In Setting the Stage, Chapter 2, we set the foundation of the book by asking the high-level questions about value. We also cover what a penetration test is and the best time to employ such a service considering the state of your security posture and exactly what you are looking to gain. This is also the opportunity to take a quick look back at the history of computer crime and the evolution of penetration testing. Therefore, we also take a close look at the different types of hackers and what level of intensity a company can expect and plan for. And no security book would be complete without some FUD (fear, uncertainty, and doubt) around the state of the industry. Thanks to organizations such as Symantec, Gartner, IDC, CSI, and the FBI, we take a look at the industry as a whole in an effort to support the concept of security.

The Framework, Chapter 3, is a brief overview of the format of a test and ultimately of the book. This is an opportunity to provide a top-down view of ethical hacking and cover the primary methods for exercising a test. It is also the point where the value elements of the test are introduced, setting the stage for much more detailed discussions all founded on value.

Before we can ask the hard questions about the relationship among security, business, and the wedge of ethical hacking, we must establish a common language around security models. In Chapter 4, two common, yet unique models are introduced and then combined to demonstrate the fundamentals of security in the light of penetration testing.

Next, we look at an information security program based on accepted standards. Chapter 5 provides the opportunity to introduce the subject of risk, how to measure it, and see where penetration testing fits in the scope of risk analysis. We discuss management, controls, and measuring the threats and outlining the concepts of ethical hacking throughout the book.

Business Perspective, Chapter 6, introduces the business characteristics, such as the perspectives of security and the objectives of the test, and how to translate those into planning specifics to ensure value. Additionally, we investigate the reasoning for having the test performed in the first place. This is an opportunity to discuss the primary components that will help gain as much value from the process as possible.

Once we cover the business elements, we then move into planning the test. A great deal of information is shared in Chapter 7 and used throughout the book. We cover imposed and inherent limitations that face the test and how to deal with them. Importantly, the type of threat will affect how the test is performed, ultimately affecting the planning cycle.

Performing a test is not as simple as loading your favorite tool and whacking away at networks and servers. Properly preparing technically and procedurally for the test is essential to the value of the test and ensuring the privacy of the targeted company. In Chapter 8, Preparing for a Hack, we take a look at the common practices in addition to the lesser-known preparation techniques. Moreover, how the engagement should be managed is detailed.

Chapter 9, Reconnaissance, represents the beginning of detailing the attack processes. The planning and preparation is complete at this point and we move into action. We cover in great detail social engineering and how to tune the plethora of options to best use this investigative tool within your environment and meeting your goals. The chapter goes on to detail other areas of recon, such as wireless networks, dumpster diving, and combing the Internet for information.

Enumeration, Chapter 10, introduces the first technical phase of the engagement. The act of getting computers, networks, applications, services, and other technology to offer information about how they are configured and running is an art. Tools and tactics are introduced and used as an introduction to the exploitation phase. Again, value and methodology are the key factors during this discussion.

Once a technical picture is created of the organization, a point in the test must be dedicated to simply determining the vulnerabilities. This is where Chapter 11 helps you take different sources of information and convert them into an attack strategy, all based on meeting the goals of the company.

There are many books on exploiting vulnerabilities, but not typically within the framework of a comprehensive methodology. Although penetration testers do this naturally, Exploitation, Chapter 12, helps to map the exploitation of a vulnerability into the planning and, most important, the effects it will have on the final deliverable.

All this would be for naught without a document detailing what transpired during the test. However, we would be grossly remiss if the entire framework of value we established early in the process were not intimately used for the creation of a document. We detail every aspect of a deliverable—where the information came from, how to interpret the test in a manner that takes the goals, objectives, and risks into account—and put it in a format that will make sense to the business and not just the security geeks.

In my experience, the integration of the results from a test is usually limited to applying patches and reconfiguring a couple of routers, at best. Most of this is due to how the test was planned, executed, and the format of the information contained within the deliverable. The Integration chapter takes everything we've covered and provides the roadmap for realizing all the potential value from the test.

This is a story about security, more so than just about ethical hacking. It is about taking a tool, one of many, and applying it in a manner that provides the greatest value from the process. As with any story, the different sections of the framework are intimately related, one feeding off the other to make for a usable collection of information to help you get the most from a test and, it is hoped, from all things security.

2 Setting the Stage

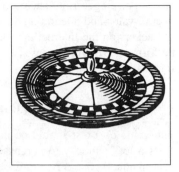

You can compare security, to some degree, to physics. Many different thoughts and disciplines exist in physics, ranging from the pragmatic application of mathematics to the farthest interpretations of quantum mechanics. Ethical hacking has become the pinnacle of thought-provoking security activity that touches on the simplistic nature of security to the wide-ranging and encompassing aspects of managing risks.

Ethical hacking is essentially the act of exploiting vulnerabilities without the darker intentions of an explicit attack. The movie *Sneakers* was one of the first mainstream films that demonstrated the controlled attack. The film begins very late in the evening with Robert Redford and a small team breaking into a bank. After some very technical maneuvering, they successfully escaped with millions of dollars in loot. The next morning Robert walks into the bank and slams a suitcase full of the money on the senior staff's meeting table. It was not until this point that you realize he was not a thief, but rather a security expert proving the vulnerabilities of the bank's security systems by exploiting them.

The pursuit of vulnerability is what people seek, not the negative conclusion normally associated with an attack. For example, a security auditor can explain in detail that the schematics for your alarm system are available on the Internet and, with limited computer resources and ample time, can reverse-engineer the system and exploit its weaknesses. However, no matter the perspective, determining the validity of such a threat and the risk that someone may attempt to exploit it is arguably inconclusive. A security professional performing a risk assessment can apply various metrics resulting in some form of measurement, but these are related to high-level interpretations. Until someone gets the plans from the Internet, performs an analysis, and attempts to exploit the system, the numbers and metrics of the risk analysis are questionable to some degree. In other words, you don't know until you try.

Today, ethical hacking has become mainstream, almost a common occurrence for organizations wishing to test their intellectual and technical fortitude against the underworld. To counteract some concerns behind ethical hacking, many companies use different providers for ethical hacking services. For example, one organization utilizes professional services to test their networks monthly, using a different firm each time. The idea is to get a different perspective, because methodologies differ from firm to firm, not to mention the different habits of the people performing the test.

The Computer Crimes Investigation Unit of the Department of Homeland Security can identify hackers based solely on their technique. How you approach an attack is a fingerprint. Therefore, distinctiveness of each test can be critical to the overall value and integrating the results. One can conclude that, because the number of hackers on the Internet far outweighs the number of ethical hackers available for performing penetration tests, the ability to truly reflect the hacking community is impossible.

PERSPECTIVES OF VALUE

The value of a test should be important, if for no other reason than that it simply costs a lot of money to purchase the necessary tools or hire an outside consulting firm to attack your network. Especially in today's economy, value must be squeezed from every dollar spent and ethical hacking's value is ultimately determined by the applicability of the information learned from the test. A professional services firm may list hundreds of vulnerabilities and hack your network to death, but unless you can translate those results into a meaningful remediation plan, the value of the test must be questioned. Granted, there is value in knowing what vulnerabilities exist, but you can get that information from an off-the-shelf tool. When a professional services company is involved, the transformation of technical results into a sound security plan is the value-add for which you are paying. In addition, for a consultant to perform a test in a manner that promotes value in a sound, business-oriented remediation plan, the engagement must be performed based on business drivers and within a framework.

To ensure value it must be understood by an organization that ethical hacking has a specific use in the scope of a security strategy. Even though the overall security of a company can be assessed without attacking it, the existence of penetration testing as a service is testament to the need for more security, something in the ether between audit and assessment, but with a lot of bite.

Some conclude a penetration test is worthless and provides little value in determining the security of a company's assets. Much of this is based on the idea that most companys' systems and applications are in no condition to withstand an attack, and a traditional security assessment would be as effective. The argument is that more value can be realized faster and safer via a security assessment than attempting to attack the network. Moreover, the dangers related to an ethical hack can introduce problems, whereas a security assessment has none of those intrinsic risks.

Frankly, hiring someone to hack your applications or network of systems is dangerous and fraught with limitless possibilities of failure. However, when planned in a meaningful way and everyone enters into the test with reasonable expectations, the odds of success are in your favor.

WHERE DOES ETHICAL HACKING FIT?

To start this endeavor on the right foot we must first recognize there are two schools of thought on the role ethical hacking plays in the world of information security: a complete approach to security or a part of a much larger security strategy. The two sides of the same coin are founded on how you approach security.

Some see ethical hacking as the overarching umbrella of security. For example, the basis of the rationalization is that if you can expose every vulnerability in a system (a system being a collection of networked computers, applications, services, and data), that system will be more secure with the results of the test used for building a security program. Therefore, the more you exploit a system, the more you know and the more you are aware of your weaknesses—and the impacts if exploited—the more secure you will be. Consider this strategy an ongoing approach to security in the form of exploitation as opposed to observation, with the results being used to generate a security posture based on vulnerability mitigation.

In contrast, some see penetration testing as part of a much more comprehensive security strategy. For example, when performing a risk analysis it is necessary to provide some form of measurement, such as numbers, letters, percentages, or anything that can be used to qualify or quantify various information security characteristics. In other words, you have to measure the value of assets, number and types of vulnerabilities, the likelihood of exploitation, level of impact, and relate this back to a metric to be used to make an informed decision. Penetration testing can be used to build a collection of empirical data relating to the need to know the number and types of vulnerabilities. Moreover, by exploiting those vulnerabilities you can determine the level of criticality they represent based on your environment. When this information is fed into a risk analysis process, along with dozens of other forms of data, a comprehensive evaluation is provided a level of accuracy not previously attainable. At the end, a risk analysis, in combination with a security policy, will be used in the building of a security program.

On the surface, these approaches appear nearly identical. However, in practice they materialize as different methods to addressing security and therefore become different animals altogether. One could argue that the popularity of penetration testing today is founded on the relative low cost and instant gratification of a test as opposed to an exhaustive risk analysis. Moreover, the tests are usually pointed at tactical concerns, such as "What is causing me pain today that I can afford to fix?" A risk analysis is taking the position of "What do I need to do to in order to be secure in relation to my business and operational needs?" The former is a snapshot in time taken over and over, whereas the latter is a discipline supported by detailed information.

One should not be considered better than the other, just different. In this book, the concept of ethical hacking is presented as part of a larger program. It is an opportunity to feed a much larger process in an effort to create a sound security program. Ethical hacking is one of many tools that can be used to evaluate the state of a security program, but is not necessarily the foundation on which one should or can be built. The framework presented herein presents penetration testing as a tool that can be employed to support an overall security strategy, taking into consideration many of the other elements common among many accepted security programs.

So, why is ethical hacking so popular? If you spend the bulk of your book-browsing time in the "Computer and Networking" section of your favorite bookstore, it is very likely the subject of hacking will dominate the security shelf. For those seeking a security consulting company to provide hacking services, get prepared for a slew of candidates, because it seems everyone is lining up to hack your network. Several reasons can be attributed to the frenzy we're seeing, but for me one seems to stand out. Based on hundreds of conversations with companies throughout the United States and most of Europe, many feel they are practicing sound security and have tamed the beast. Now all that is left for them is to test what was implemented and apply a patch or two. Therefore, penetration testing offers the perfect value zone. It is not overly expensive: the cost of a test will typically fit within most budgets and can be easily expanded or contracted to match available funds. Finally, it provides measured results and appears to clearly expose any weaknesses that may exist. Sounds pretty good, doesn't it? If you said yes, most people would be in agreement, or at least the amount of time and investment spent in penetration testing as opposed to other forms of security services would suggest most agree: it's where people are putting the money.

How long will this last? For some it's a novelty, a new toy to add to the list whereas for others it's a serious part of their security program. The reality is information security in the technical world is in its infancy and ethical hacking may become a best practice for the foreseeable future. In contrast, we may look back one day and wonder, "What were we thinking!"

WHAT CONSTITUTES A SUCCESS?

Given that this book is focused on the value of a test, the definition of a successful attack is not only a constant theme throughout the material, but, as we show, it can be much more than simply the systems that were hacked. This is an opportunity to introduce the primary characteristics of a test that can be used to evaluate the overall success of an engagement.

The definition of a successful test can be elusive. Much of a test's success or failure is founded on the goals and objectives stated at the onset of the test. To state the obvious, without planning and some form of goal, there is little chance of determining what was actually accomplished.

There are many metrics that can be employed to rate the success of a test, but the most predominant one is technical exploitation. Having a tester penetrate an online application and gain access to a database of credit card numbers has significant tangible characteristics, which are therefore easy to measure.

Another aspect of a success can be the management of the test. For example, how well was the test conducted? Many organizations establish operating parameters to protect systems, employees, and customers from any potential threat that may come from hacking systems. The most obvious is downtime. Bringing a business-critical system down in the middle of the business day can be a costly mistake. How the information collected about the target handled (e.g., protected) during the test will certainly be scrutinized. If the list of vulnerabilities and how they were exploited were to become public, the test would move quickly from success to damage control.

Some organizations base the success of the test on the deliverable. The quality of the deliverable is paramount to many, understandably so, and even in cases of total technical failure, the deliverable can substantiate a success.

The interchange of value and success will occur in every test. Typically, the definition of success will be associated with meeting a set of specific goals. More often than not, these goals are those vulnerabilities that are identified and successfully exploited. This should come as no surprise because the foundation of the test is typically to hack a target! However, even the exploitation of a vulnerability does not constitute a success. In fact, in some cases, exploiting a hole is exactly what the target does NOT want and success is founded on what can be identified—not broken.

On the other hand, there are companies that insist on evaluating the exposure to attack and are only satisfied if the vulnerability is exploited. Typically, this demand is associated with a specific target, such as a new application, change in the infrastructure, or the addition of new untested technology. Nevertheless, there are many situations where the goal is simple—gain access—and not to accommodate the demand is grounds for failure no matter how well the test was managed, the deliverable quality, or the execution.

NOTE 1: DIGGING FOR THE HOLE

In a meeting with a long-term customer that has monthly tests against their Internet-facing infrastructure, a concern for the potential for someone to hack into their remote access solution was questioned. Up until this point, the success of the test was heavily placed on the deliverable and the identification of vulnerabilities—not exploiting any holes. They preferred to know what the problems were and have us recommend fixes as opposed to potentially causing harm.

In contrast, the next test was to exploit any vulnerabilities in the remote access solution and gain as much information and access as possible. An aggressive test was planned and performed shortly thereafter. The tester gained access to the terminal server (Citrix) by circumventing the poor integration of the Web application, but could not exploit any opportunities to gain access to back-end applications published by the Citrix system.

The result was considered a failure, which was interesting given that all previous tests were based on validation and identification of problems and the quality of the deliverable. Nevertheless, one has to agree with the conclusion. The goal was set, objectives defined, and scope determined, and the target was not met.

Later it was confided by the client that success was expected based on our tester's familiarity with the environment and the remote access solution, which had been in place for over a year. Although knowing a target does not imply success, the point was valid.

Technical attributes of the test are commonly used as the measuring stick for success. As mentioned above, when someone exploits a vulnerability and obtains valued data the vulnerability is defined as well as what was performed to gain access. Both of these elements go a long way in fixing the problem. Therefore, the test's results can be employed and acted upon to reduce future potential harm.

The value of the test is more convoluted, open to more interpretation, and can exist even in the light of a defined failure. If a company seeks to have a new custom application tested and exploited to evaluate the security features of the code, the test may not be considered successful if nothing is exploited. However, the value to the organization may still exist. The value can be as simple as knowing the application was tested and now the company can feel confident in deploying or moving to the next phase of development. Or, the value can be the raw data that was collected by the tester and the tools used to gain more insight into how the application responds to different tactics.

To add to the malaise, the reality is that usually, somewhere in the process, someone is not going to be happy with the test and, depending on who that person or group is, can sway the interpretation of success and most certainly value. The internal politics of an organization can be very convoluted and when a third party is brought in to perform a test it can be the seed of future contention. The administrator of a server that was compromised may argue the test's validity because he is now in the spotlight. It is not uncommon to have entire departments lash out at the test's results because someone else initiated the test and the results were not favorable for them.

Finally, there is the consultant's perspective. If the tester does not exploit any vulnerabilities as demanded by the customer, but the client feels the test was a success, that does not mean the consultant feels the same way. In fact, I know of no tester who wouldn't feel disheartened in some way and begin to question her tactics. It is almost commonplace to talk to disappointed consultants even after a successful test; it is part of a tester's mentality to overachieve and push the limits of the target as well as herself. It is important to consider the consultants' perspectives of success and ensure there is the foundation for future success by their definition. This can be accomplished by training, shadowing on other engagements, or allowing them to focus on tests that require their core skills. From a service provider's point of view, it is important to consider both the client's as well as the tester's feeling of success because both will affect the future of the business.

A QUICK LOOK BACK

Arguably, security is probably the second-oldest profession, and as soon as there was security, someone was trying to break it. One of the early examples was the scytale used by the Spartans in 400 B.C. to encrypt messages for government and military applications. Commonly known as the "Roman Stick," it was an ingenious attempt at security based solely on the secrecy of the length and diameter of a wooden baton. Linen was wrapped around the stick and a message inscribed lengthwise along the surface. When unwrapped, the result was a long list of unintelligible characters. In many cases, the message was secured by messengers using the linen as belts or other utilitarian instruments to further disguise their handling of sensitive data. The security was afforded by the unknown attributes of the wooden baton used during the encryption process. It was also helpful that most people during that age couldn't read. Much later, around 100 B.C., the Emperor Julius Caesar implemented the use of character shifting to hide the true meaning of a message. Confidentiality was maintained by whether you knew the number of letters in the shift and at what point within the message. Even during the time of these simplistic yet effective methods, people were working diligently to crack the codes and obtain the sensitive data.

One of the more interesting stories is the German Enigma machine and the Allies' dedication to cracking the German code. The Enigma was an example of a rotor-based cipher machine. A variety of companies built many such machines, originally intending them to be used for commercial cryptography, but they were adopted by the German army and navy prior to World War II for sensitive communications. Each rotor in a rotor-cipher machine modified the letters of the alphabet. The rotors were mechanically linked so that the first rotor advanced one position with each press of a key.

Its use by the Germans was initially detected in 1928 by Polish cryptanalysts who had been dealing with Soviet and German hand ciphers. In the winter of 1932, Marian Rejewski, a 27-year-old cryptanalyst working in the Cipher Bureau of the Polish Intelligence Service in Warsaw, Poland, mathematically determined the wiring of the Enigma's first rotor: unfortunately, only one of three. In England, during World War II, groups of British and Polish cryptographers were hidden away with the sole purpose of reverse-engineering the Enigma, using only raw encrypted data for cryptanalysis. What was assumed unbreakable was cracked after much time and energy.

In the 1970s there was an underground community committed to making free phone calls. Captain Crunch, a popular cereal, had a whistle for a prize. One day John Draper, who eventually went by the name "Cap'n Crunch," blew the whistle into the phone receiver and gained control of the tone-based circuit-switching mechanisms to make free calls. The whistle created a tone of 2600 Hz, which was a frequency used by the system for call setup. This, of course, was the birth of the Alt-2600 hacking community.

In the 1980s, Kevin Mitnick popularized "IP spoofing," originally identified by Steve Bellovin several years prior as an attack method that used weaknesses within Internet protocols to gain access to systems that were based on IP addresses and inherent trust relationships. Through IP spoofing, one appeared to come from a trusted source but was, in fact, well outside the trusted environment. Mitnick used this technique, along with social engineering, to access systems in order to obtain various application source code for other hacking purposes. Specifically, he wanted the source code for cell phones (the operating system of most cell phones at the time) that would allow him to manipulate phones to access other conversations and greater system access.

The 1990s was the decade of Denial-of-Service (DoS) attacks. DoS attacks were designed to overwhelm computer systems to the point of service failure. This was also the birth of the script kiddie and packaged tools. "Script kiddies" is a term used to describe people who did not necessarily understand the details of hacking but had access to tools that could be easily executed to perform the attack. For example, in 1995 Wietse Venema and Dan Farmer created SATAN (Security Administrator's Tool for Analyzing Networks) and released it onto the Internet. SATAN was a tool designed to scan systems for vulnerabilities and report the known identified weaknesses. Later, it was modified to exploit those vulnerabilities to gain further information. This was the first mainstream example of a free automated hacking tool.

Now, hacks are much more sophisticated and come from many directions and classes of people; the beginning of the twenty-first century will certainly be known as the "identity theft" years. Credit card fraud has become the choice of hackers worldwide, and using information for extortion is a typical occurrence. Also, viruses, worms, and Trojans have wreaked havoc in recent years through intense malicious programming.

Security practitioners knew there were great risks associated with connecting to the Internet in its early years. However, in the face of this new technology, many companies were concerned that security measures would limit the experience and exposure to opportunities the Internet represented. Many chose instead to accept the risks of few or no security measures, which at that time had little historical information to justify their existence.

To try to accommodate some form of security, firewalls were introduced as an opportunity to provide a secure gateway that could at least limit the exposures to threats on the Internet. As this practice evolved, the reliance on firewalls increased to a point where simply having a firewall was more about political correctness than security maintenance. Firewalls today will do everything from scanning for viruses and content filtering to authentication and DoS mitigation. The cost for the increased functionality has been, debatably, security.

Companies were continually attacked even after the adoption of firewalls, mostly due to the advancement of Internet technologies, applications, and protocols, and the lack of sound security policies and fundamental architectures to establish a security baseline.

As the evolution continued, more and more security technologies were introduced to increase security and reduce the onslaught of attacks. Technologies such as virus scanners, Intrusion Detection Systems (IDS), strong authentication systems, and trusted operating systems, to name a few, became new technical point solutions of a security architecture.

As the use of the Internet became more crucial to successful business operations, applications were developed to leverage the Internet to obtain more market share, build efficiencies, or provide greater access to customers and partners. The complexity of the applications increased, and the information being accessed became more sensitive and hence, increased in value and criticality to business operations.

Hackers began to refine their art, taking advantage of the weakness inherent in complex systems and the proliferation of critical systems accessible from the Internet. Meanwhile, due to the poor adoption of strong security practices, organizations were still open to old-style attacks that leveraged well-known, publicized vulnerabilities.

Regardless of the technology, hackers continue to successfully attack systems and, seemingly with ease, access systems to accomplish their goals. There are always the hackers who deface Web sites and bring systems down; however, hackers are becoming more organized, taking advantage of the access for more sinister activities, such as those associated with financial gain.

NOTE 2: FOREIGN INTERNET HACKERS EXTORT DOMESTIC COMPANIES

Making Money from Hacking Computers, a Global Problem

Financial gain of hackers has become a concern for many corporations. Based on information provided by the NIPC, it is well understood that many of the extortions, fraud, and money-laundering activities are coming from Eastern Europe and the former Soviet Union. The FBI has identified several organized crime families that deal in information rather than drugs or prostitution but still use murder and corruption to effectively influence.

The proliferation of attacks from the Eastern European region is due to the fact that many of the countries do not have laws against hacking foreign countries. The lack of comprehensive laws and international relationships makes it impossible for countries such as the United States to retaliate or extradite known criminals. For hackers in the United States, there are many legal implications useful in discouraging attacks within the United States or one of its national partners—if the perpetrator is caught. But without similar restrictions in foreign countries, there is little or no impact on the psyche of the attackers, because they are allowed to perform in the open without limitation or fear of prosecution.

There are several sites based in Europe providing hacking services and proprietary information for sale. This information can be used to extract money from U.S. corporations, such as banks. For example, a hacker accesses a bank's online system and gains all the account and credit card information. The hacker then notifies the bank that if it does not pay $20,000 U.S., he'll publish the information on the Internet greatly influencing the level of trust associated with the company and financial industry.

Not only does this happen to organizations but individuals as well. Hackers based in Belarus have attacked personal computers to obtain or introduce information to use against the owner for financial gain. In an ironic twist, these hackers are fully aware of U.S. laws and use them to their advantage, especially those that pertain to child pornography. There are cases where hackers gained access to someone's personal computer, uploaded pornography, and told the user that if they did not pay the ransom, the hacker would notify the authorities.

The first steps in building strong security are awareness of the vulnerabilities, associating them with the level of threat, and determining the risk to assets. Unfortunately, this is complicated, and the process is hindered by legacy systems, complex applications, multi-access requirements, and sheer cost associated with performing comprehensive security risk analysis.

Knowing what hackers are doing, how they are performing the attacks, and how to stop them can be effective in developing a security strategy. The goal is to use this information to logically invest in security where it needs it the most, rather than implementing technology for technology's sake based on loose promises. For example, if a company invests in a firewall, IDS, virus protection, and comprehensive policies, does this mean their internal systems are entirely protected? No, because there may be characteristics of their networks and applications that represent huge opportunities for hackers, and the implemented technology could be useless in protecting the company from these exposures.

A security strategy is partly technology, but what helps you determine the best practices for management, training, awareness, and technical solutions is knowing the threats to your company and working in a manner that is realistic as opposed to simply throwing technology around. By evaluating the security system as a whole, gaps in the security architecture can be identified, promoting conscious investments in enhancing security.

The need for a process to test the security measures and how well they could withstand an attack became the focal point for many attempting to understand their exposures. Internet System Scanner (ISS), now Internet Security Systems, provided a software package that not only detected vulnerabilities but also exploited them to prove their existence as well as to illustrate the levels of access they provided. It was assumed that the cost of the tool was prohibitive for a hacker to afford and use for malicious intent. Although some of the early adopters were companies purchasing the tool for their own use, it became clear that a specific skill set was required to fully take advantage of the tool. Moreover, this was only one of many tools showing up on the Internet, many of which required extensive knowledge of Linux to operate.

It was at this point that consulting firms began to offer specific security services to their clients to help them evaluate their exposure to hackers and the impact if attacked. What began as a small services opportunity has blossomed into an industry, with hundreds of companies and individuals hacking companies all over the world.

Unfortunately, the result is much the same as what we saw with firewalls nearly a decade before: organizations are beginning to rely on ethical hacking as a security strategy, which may or may not result in increased security.

HACKING IMPACTS

At the risk of stating the obvious, hacking—computer crime—can result in massive financial losses for companies, governments, and individuals alike. The costs associated with computer crime can manifest themselves in various ways, which may range from the obscure to a clear hit to the bottom line.

Digital assets where costs from hackers can manifest themselves fall into four major categories: resources, information, time, and reputation.

1. *Resources*. Resources are computer-related services that perform actions or tasks on the user's behalf. Core services, object code, or disk space can be considered resources that, if controlled, utilized, or disabled by an unauthorized entity, could result in the inability to capture revenue for a company or have an impact on an important process resulting in the failure to meet expected objectives.
2. *Information*. Information can represent an enormous cost if destroyed or altered without authorization. However, there are few organizations that assign a value to information and implement the proportionate controls

necessary to ensure its protection. Data can be affected in several ways that will have a discernible cost related to the type of effect: loss, disclosure, and integrity.

a. *Loss*. The loss of data is relatively easy to measure when compared to disclosure and integrity. Information takes time to collect or produce, requires resources to be managed, and will certainly (to some degree) have value. There are many examples of intentional and unintentional acts resulting in the loss of information. Not having a backup of your data when a hard drive fails is a painful experience we all hope we have to survive only once.

b. *Disclosure*. Nearly every entity that uses information has the potential to be negatively affected by its uncontrolled disclosure. Although the impact of an unauthorized disclosure is one of the most difficult to measure, such a breach is noteworthy because it represents the traditional fear of hacking: proprietary information theft. If someone steals your car, there is a cost that can be quickly determined because of the crime's physical nature. Information, on the other hand, is intangible, and the thief may not perceive content to be as valuable as the owner does; therefore, the disclosure may have little or no impact. Contrary to the assumption of the hacker's ignorance, industrial espionage is the deliberate use of illegally obtained information for the betterment of the competition. In any event, the exposure of critical information could cost a company a great deal of money through competitive disadvantage or the revelation of unwanted information to the public.

c. *Integrity*. Ensuring information is accurate and complete is necessary for any organization. If data were to be manipulated it could become a loss to the owner. This can be as simple as the cost of an item online being $99.99 but represented as $9.99 because a hacker found a way of manipulating cookies to move the decimal point one position to the left. However, there are much more sinister examples that are very difficult to equate with a financial loss. Integrity is the foundation of several forms of legislation. One of the most prevalent is the Sarbanes–Oxley Act that was passed by the U.S. government to ensure that financial reporting is accurate. It can be readily assumed that publicly traded companies use vast computing systems to track financial metrics. Therefore, you can conclude that information security plays a significant role in ensuring the data is accurate and there is a record of changes.

3. *Time*. The loss of time can be related to costs in the form of payroll, not meeting critical deadlines, or an unavailable E-commerce site that would normally produce thousands of dollars in revenue if it were available. Anything that consumes time, consumes money, and expenditures for recovering from an incident can represent the greatest form of financial loss.

4. *Brand and Reputation*. There are many companies who have very recognizable brands, so much so that the color alone will promote images of

the company. For example, Brown . . . UPS. It wasn't until mid-2002 that UPS started to take advantage of their color recognition and started the "Brown" marketing campaign, "What can Brown do for you?" Very smart move on their part. Blue and orange . . . FedEx. Even Coke seems to have taken ownership of the color red.

Reputations of organizations have fallen victim in the face of attacks, many not even remotely associated with information security. I'll spare you commentary about Enron's or WorldCom's debacle or the investment firms with monumental conflicts of interest. However, there are a few who have had problems that can be directly linked to lapses in information security. As demonstrated in Figure 2.1, Aastrom Biosciences, Inc. was forced to defend itself after a fictitious press release stating a merger with another firm sent the stock price soaring. Information security can have a deep impact on the perception of value of a company, resulting in serious ramifications for public as well as private companies.

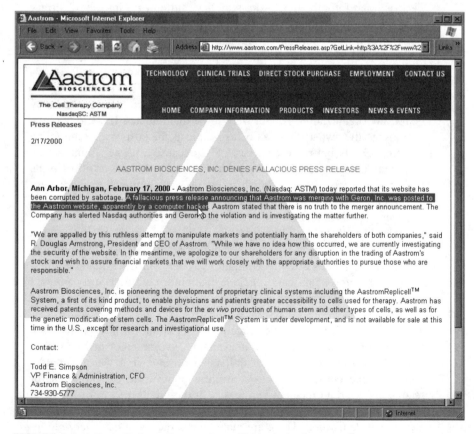

FIGURE 2.1 A Press Release Denouncing a Hacker's Antics

SECURITY INDUSTRY REPORTS

Ethical hacking is exposing the risk associated with vulnerabilities. Of course, some of these are known to exist long before the test and once a system is found with one, it is a matter of exploitation. Therefore, the number, type, and computing services that are affected by known vulnerabilities is a great place to start analyzing just why ethical hacking is so popular.

Vulnerabilities, in the realm of technology, materialize in the form of viruses, poor programming and quality control, poor implementation, poor management, and the proliferation and growing sophistication of automated hacking tools.

Losses associated with viruses remain a pain for customers: 82 percent of respondents to the CSI/FBI 2003 Eighth Annual Security Survey cited viruses as their problem in the last 12 months. Although 99 percent of respondents use antivirus software, 47 percent reported losses of $27.3 million. Viruses and worms represent tremendous threats to the continued security of organizations even in the face of arguably comprehensive controls. In recent papers and articles, there is a clear association with the security state of a system (application, operating system, servers, etc.) and the proliferation and impact of viruses and worms, which are often based on vulnerabilities. Therefore, patch management and system hardening are becoming the next effective layer in a "defense in depth" security strategy. This begins to explain the popularity of vulnerability tools and services, such as penetration testing.

Vulnerabilities are increasing in number and severity. The ability to manage your vulnerabilities and reduce overall exposure is key to the survival of any organization. To do so requires regular risk analysis and appropriate alignment of security management to business needs and exposures. Considering that not all vulnerabilities can be identified, and the ones that can are not always avoidable (e.g., repairable), the effectiveness of a risk analysis in guiding security operational attributes is core to the overall protection of the company's business. Demonstrated in Figure 2.2, from Symantec's annual vulnerability report, the number and severity of identified vulnerabilities is climbing. This is a representation of the threats to organizations globally and the demand for maintaining a security posture.

In combination with Figure 2.2, Figure 2.3 shows that the new vulnerabilities identified are totaling numbers that represent an enormous challenge to companies on a monthly basis. Challenges for companies are gathering information relating to vulnerabilities, determining the impact within their environment, understanding the next steps to remediate, detecting what systems are affected, testing, distribution, and implementation and validation of the appropriate controls.

The eighth annual "Computer Crime and Security Survey," written by Robert Richardson in 2003, was conducted by the Computer Security Institute (CSI) with the involvement of the Computer Intrusion Squad of the Federal Bureau of Investigation's San Francisco office. The CSI/FBI report provides interesting trend analysis on the evolution and impacts of computer-related crime and the associated costs. The report's goal is to quantify the scope of computer-related crimes in the United States.

The CSI/FBI report includes the responses of 530 security practitioners working in U.S. corporations, government agencies, financial institutions, and universities. The number and diversity of the report's sources are very comprehensive, including

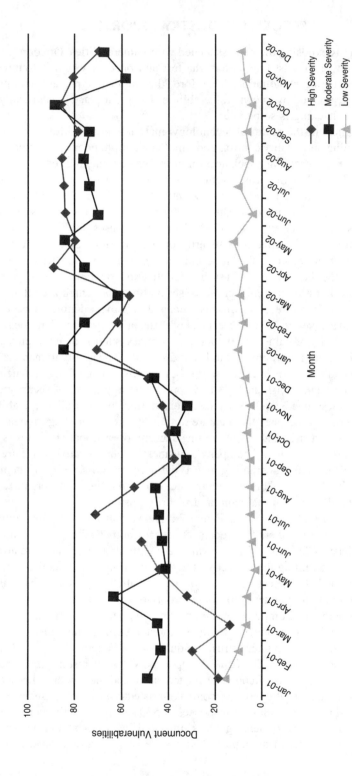

FIGURE 2.2 Vulnerabilities Increasing in Severity and Volume (Symantec, 2003)

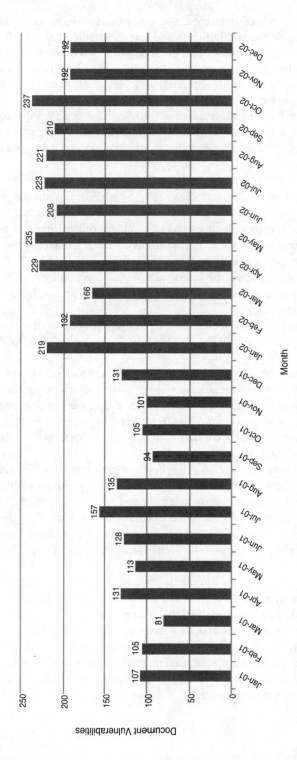

FIGURE 2.3 Number of New Vulnerabilities (Symantec, 2003)

information from nearly all industries, such as health care, retail, manufacturing, public utilities, transportation, high-tech, and telecommunications. As demonstrated in Figure 2.4, the costs of attacks can be staggering, even when only 47 percent reported financial losses. Although these numbers are significantly less than the previous two years, the ability to accurately calculate costs remains a challenge.

So who is causing the most pain? As depicted in Figure 2.5, attacks were grouped into five categories: hackers, disgruntled employees, domestic competitors, foreign companies, and foreign governments. What is interesting to note is respondents to the CSI/FBI survey cited hackers and disgruntled employees nearly equally as the source of attacks.

According to a 2002 Symantec report, 29.6 percent of all attacks worldwide originate from the United States, followed by South Korea with 8.8 percent and China with 7.8 percent. Although the United States represents the largest source of attacks, there are countries with enormous percentages of their population attacking networks and systems worldwide. For example, 26.2 percent of those in Israel's Internet community are regularly hacking companies, followed by 14.5 percent of Hong Kong's and 11.6 percent of Thailand's. Finally, according to the report, 10 percent of South Korea's Internet population is responsible for 8.8 percent of all attacks on all companies!

Attacks on networks can be collected into two groups: opportunistic and targeted (61 percent to 39 percent, respectively, based on Symantec's 2002 report).

1. *Opportunistic attacks* are intent on locating any vulnerable system that exists on the Internet regardless of who owns the system or the specific function. In this situation the victim is not sought out but instead selected solely because of its vulnerability. Usually, these attacks are preceded by a broad scan across the Internet until the hacker identifies a system that has vulnerabilities to be exploited.
2. *Targeted attacks* are directed at a specific organization or entity regardless of the vulnerability. These attacks are based on finding vulnerabilities to exploit specific to that company. The target is identified in advance, with the deliberate intent of gaining access through a vulnerability. Symantec categorized targeted attacks based on two criteria: lack of preliminary scanning by the hacker and the focus on a single entity.

In Figure 2.6, we see that the Internet is increasingly the point of attack, followed by the slight decline in internal systems, and then by a growing remote access trouble. One could conclude that the growth of the Internet as the primary point of pain is due to the massive losses associated with malware, the proliferation of vulnerabilities, and the growing sophistication of hacker tools. Although cited as a much less significant point of problems, the increasing concern over remote access could be linked to the massive adoption of VPNs (Virtual Private Network) and expansion of the corporate roaming user population.

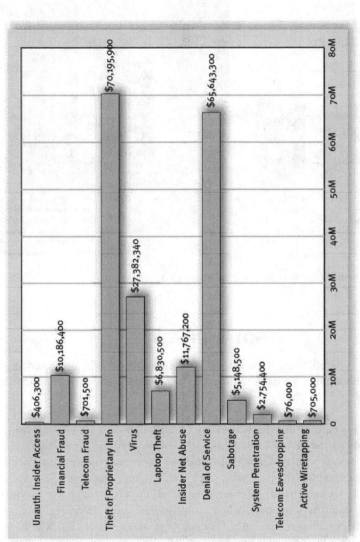

CSI/FBI 2003 Computer Crime and Security Survey
Source: Computer Security Institute

2003: 251 Respondents/47%

FIGURE 2.4 Report Costs of Computer Crime in 2003 (CSI/FBI 2003)

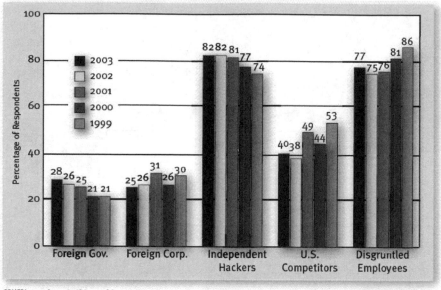

CSI/FBI 2003 Computer Crime and Security Survey
Source: Computer Security Institute

2003: 488 Respondents/92%
2002: 414 Respondents/82%
2001: 484 Respondents/91%
2000: 583 Respondents/90%
1999: 460 Respondents/88%

FIGURE 2.5 Likely Sources of Attack (CSI/FBI 2003)

NOTABLE FACTS

The following is a collection of security-related survey results from the second half of 2003 that I thought provided an interesting perspective and shed some light into dark places.

- Forty-two percent of respondents say security concerns are slowing down implementation of wireless technology. (*NetworkWorld*, June 2003)
- Thirty-nine percent of financial institutions experienced at least one security breach within the past year. (Deloitte Touche, June 2003)
- The first six months of 2003 have seen a 17.5 percent increase in virus activity over the same period last year. (*Sophos*, July 2003)
- The number of wireless LAN (WLAN) hot spots worldwide will more than double by 2005. (Gartner, July 2003)
- Security spending since September 11 has increased on average by only 4 percent; corporate spending for insurance premiums has jumped by 33 percent. (American Society for Industrial Security International, July 2003)
- Nearly half of companies with revenues greater than $100 million tagged poor WLAN security as a major reason why they've held off rolling out

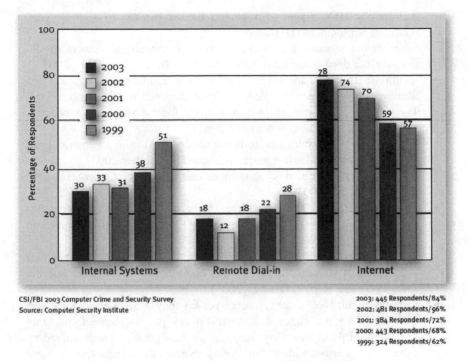

CSI/FBI 2003 Computer Crime and Security Survey
Source: Computer Security Institute

2003: 445 Respondents/84%
2002: 481 Respondents/96%
2001: 384 Respondents/72%
2000: 443 Respondents/68%
1999: 324 Respondents/62%

FIGURE 2.6 Internet is Increasing Points of Attacks (CSI/FBI 2003)

WLANs, or expanding their current wireless infrastructure. (Jupiter Research, July 2003)

- One third of companies say their ability to even know whether they are under attack is "less than adequate," and one third think their ability to respond is inadequate. (Ernst & Young, July 2003)
- U.S. healthcare providers will increase IT spending three percent to four percent annually, driven by a need to meet changes in patient safety and federal regulations. (IDC, July 2003)
- Sixty percent of the firms surveyed no longer bother trying to calculate ROI on security. (Ernst & Young, 2003)
- During the 12 months ending June 2003, 3.4 percent of U.S. consumers were victims of identity theft compared to 1.9 percent last year. (Gartner, August 2003)
- The number of software vulnerabilities has doubled every year since 1999, to 4200 in 2002. (CERT Analysis Center, August 2003)
- Forty percent of IT security execs say they spend IT security dollars on the wrong risks. (Forrester Research, August 2003)
- The number of people banking online in the United States grew by 164 percent between 2000 and 2003. (Pew Internet & American Life Project, August 2003)
- Twenty percent of enterprises will experience a serious (beyond virus) Internet security incident by 2005. (Gartner, August 2003)

- It costs $300,000 a year to manually deploy patches to 1000 servers. (Gartner, September 2003)
- Securing the network from hackers is the top concern of network executives for the third consecutive year. (*Network World*, September 2003)
- Identity theft cost businesses $48 billion from fraudulent use of the stolen data over the last five years. (Federal Trade Commission, September 2003)
- The average cost for a company to recover from a virus attack is $81K per attack. (ICSA Labs, September 2003)
- Ninety percent of security exploits are carried out through vulnerabilities for which there is a known patch. (Gartner, September 2003)
- Corporate security remains the number one priority of IT professionals. (IDC, September 2003)
- At least 44 percent of U.K. businesses suffer one or more security breaches a year, costing £30,000 each on average. (U.K. Department of Trade and Industry, October 2003)
- Sixty-four percent of IT attacks during the first six months of this year were aimed at vulnerabilities less than one year old. (Symantec Internet Security Threat Report, October 2003)
- Almost two thirds of senior IT executives say they adopt security measures to limit liability, and almost half say it is to comply with regulations. Only 37 percent of participants say adopting security measures is prompted by a fear of a security incident that affects revenue, or because experts have long recommended such precautions. (*CIO Magazine*, 2003)
- U.S. businesses lost $300 million from economic espionage in 2002, up from less than $50 million in 1997. (*Optimize Magazine*, October 2003)
- Large organizations spend as much as $350 per employee annually on computer password management. (Aberdeen Group, October 2003)

THE HACKER

First of all, the term "hacker," historically speaking, is inaccurate. In the early days of computing a hacker was someone who investigated the workings of computers for fun and a challenge. Cracker was a term used to identify people who would break computers to use them for free or use system resources. Somewhere between the Internet revolution and the movies, hacker was adopted to describe computer criminals.

It is essential that business and security consultants alike understand the nuances of the hacker society, social status, drivers, and most important, to whom they are attracted. It is important to understand the types of threats in order to truly gauge the risks of an organization. To ensure the value of the test is realized, it is a significant task to contemplate the types of threats that should be mimicked. This is no different from approving an internal attack to test the defensive capability against employees. Employees symbolize a type of threat and having an internal test is plausible to verify the exposure and impacts of such a threat. Not to apply this to the Internet side (or unknown elements) of the equation would be remiss.

In the following sections we take a look at some of the types of hackers, their techniques, and what can be expected from them in an effort to assist in appropriately planning the test.

TYPE OF HACKER

Hackers come in all shapes and sizes; race, religion, and age are all valid variables. First, we dispel some myths and establish a sound basis for outlining hacker types.

A prevalent myth regarding hackers is that they are derelicts with limited education and poor professionalism with nothing but time to wreak havoc on the unwary. Many hackers have been known to be law-abiding citizens but with questionable ethics and a twisted sense of crime. Most of this is due to the anonymity the computer provides. A hacker may not run a red light or shoplift due to the obvious exposure and tangible and immediate reaction of the act, such as a car crash or getting caught walking out the door. Many hackers would be horrified if they had to confront their victims face to face, or witness the results of their actions. This is a critical differentiating factor between hackers and other forms of criminals. For example, in many cases an arsonist will start a fire to watch it destroy property with the simple intent of watching something burn. Similarly, hackers may only gain satisfaction knowing their activity is causing some form of dismay. The most basic example is people who write worms or viruses and launch them onto the Internet: the satisfaction of knowing it causes problems somewhere is pleasure enough.

Hackers rely mostly on impersonal acts and see computers as the tool. In the minds of hackers, computer systems do not physically hurt anyone. In addition, the challenge is a constant theme. There are several motives, discussed later, but all rely on a mixture of challenge and desire.

There are several types of hackers, but we can reduce this to three basic characteristics that we can use to categorize the enemy:

1. Script kiddies
2. Hackers
3. Über hacker

SCRIPT KIDDIES

"Script kiddie" refers to a hacker wannabe who leverages tools created by other, more knowledgeable hackers to perform malicious acts. There are several degrees of damage that can be caused by people who fall into this category. Simply stating that they are less informed and unenlightened by the art of hacking does not immediately insinuate they are harmless. Script kiddies can be grouped into three areas: unstructured, structured, and determined.

1. *Unstructured.* This group is better defined as pranksters or a nuisance that usually includes juvenile acts that are typically not long lasting. Attacks of this nature are usually port scans and minor attacks that fill logs. They have little or no capability of covering their tracks unless the program

they are using does it on their behalf. Recreational hackers, individuals who want to pursue and gain a limited understating of hacking because of the lure and excitement, also fall into this category. In many cases, the damage caused by recreational hackers is limited in scope but destructive nevertheless. Internal employees performing recreational hacking represent the greatest threat to organizations. They may download tools in an attempt to perform a practical joke on their cubicle neighbor and unknowingly have an impact on critical systems.

2. *Structured.* The right tool in the wrong hands can have immense potential and combined with an opportunistic behavior can have measurable results. For example, the Distributed Denial of Service attacks (DDoS) were founded on a handful of tools that were easily installed on insecure systems around the world. Trin00 (tree-no) is one of several server/client-based tools that can be used to construct a hierarchical web of systems for a synchronized attack. By installing Zombies on remote systems, a single hacker can conduct an attack from hundreds of computers simultaneously, overwhelming even the most robust sites. The success of the DDoS attack can be attributed to the explosion of cable modems and insecure PCs residing on the Internet and a comprehensive toolset freely available on the Internet. Therefore, it is no longer simple to say that script kiddies are less of a concern when armed with comprehensive tools.

3. *Determination.* The persistence of an attacker certainly increases the probability of success. If for nothing other than sheer luck, a determined script kiddie will get in eventually. When writing this book, I asked a close friend of mine and respected security professional, Stephen Coman, about determination. He replied,

> *Most of the hacking cases I have been involved with have had to do with a young script kiddy that just wouldn't stop. This one kid in Texas used every attack he could compile until he found a vulnerable system. He nailed something like 200+ systems all over, based only on the fact that he tried everything until he found something that worked.*

Admittedly, the shotgun approach is not the best tactic, but the determination of script kiddies can be more of a problem for security administrators than most of the accomplished hackers out there.

NOTE 3: SOPHISTICATED TOOLS WILL COVER FOR THE UNSOPHISTICATED

Even though a script kiddie's knowledge is limited, the proliferation of complex tools has reached staggering proportions. It requires very little understanding of security or hacking to combine several tools to obtain the desired results. Sub-7 and BackOrifice (BO) are powerful packages that can be easily installed on systems over the Internet to allow unparalleled access and control. For example, ButtPlug is a tool that embeds BO into a common file that when executed will install BO and contact the server (hacker's system) upon completion. Once this life cycle is complete, a completely unknown entity has total control over your computer and the information that it maintains. There are several delivery techniques that range from the complex to simply sending the attachment via e-mail—sooner or later someone will run the attachment.

There are several arguments on the subject of how to categorize hackers and the impacts of script kiddies. The tools are becoming much more complex, yet easy to install and use. It is analogous to giving a bazooka to a 13-year-old kid. Automated attacks were first postulated by Donn Parker, the foremost expert on computer crime, who believes that we'll reach a point in time when you tell a computer program what you need and it will get it—covering its tracks—all this without a shred of skill.

HACKERS

Hackers are the next step in the evolution of an attacker and make up the majority of the people who inflict chaos. Hackers explore computers for education, the challenge, and to achieve a social status among other hackers. They work diligently to obtain resources and compete with their peers to gain recognition and power within the hacking community. There is a strong sense of power in controlling remote resources for their own use and the more systems owned, the more clout in the community.

Again, hackers of any kind are not to be underestimated. These are typically very intelligent people with exceptional skills and logic. It is the latter of the two characteristics, logic, that truly separates hackers from script kiddies. Hacker logic is processing information and forming deductions based on the refusal to accommodate traditional thinking.

The simplest and oldest trick in the book is the Fax Trick. Take two pieces of paper, tape them end to end and start the fax machine. Once the first page is through, tape the leading edge to the back of the previous page; the result is a looping effect and an endless fax. This is an incredibly simplistic example of combining out-of-the-box thinking with technology. The goal is to make a system do what is needed by exploring all the options not previously combined.

As with any classification, there are variances in the characterization that can assist in further defining, and "hacker" as a label is no exception. There are four distinguishing faculties of the hacker: malicious, solvers, hacktivist, and vigilante. Each of these has its own unique idiosyncrasy.

1. *Malicious.* Malicious hackers are people with the sole intent of causing damage, destruction, or disruption of information systems. Writers of malware fall directly into this category, as do people who gain access to sites and corrupt information. Hateful actions are usually based on some opinion of the target or desire to gain a reputation. In some cases, destruction

of systems and data is used as a tool to cover tracks or other attacks. These types of hackers are especially worrisome because they have the skill and no conscience for the ramification of their actions.

2. *Solvers*. There are hackers that gain access to systems to solve a problem they or a friend may have. Many of these attacks are based on changing or removing information to rectify a situation. Examples include obtaining software or code for personal use or changing records to eliminate evidence of other misconduct. Solvers also hack to prove a point and rely on the concept that they hacked a site to prove an insecurity. A report in *ComputerWorld* in December 2000 disclosed that a university hospital in Seattle was hacked by "Kane" in the Netherlands, who obtained 5000 patient records and posted his findings, and a copy of the records to prove his point, on SecurityFocus.com. Through interviews with Kevin Poulsen, Kane expressed that he simply wanted to expose the weakness in the hospital's network.

3. *Hacktivist*. There are several hacking communities that band together for a common cause. Anarchists, racists, animal rights, and environmental protection groups are examples. The sad reality is that the law-abiding establishments with similar goals suffer from the acts of their hacker counterparts. Advocacy hackers can be exceptionally dangerous to certain businesses that support or represent antagonism. Companies that perform testing on animals, mine for resources, or simply write software are targets of hackers of this type. This is an important factor for companies wishing to have an ethical hack performed on their networks. It will help determine the scope and provider of such services based on their methodology, capability, and tenacity. In addition, by stating what represents the greatest threat to your business, the testers can assume the mindset of the proposed attacker.

Another aspect of hacktivism is the use of cyber assets for "positive change" or an activist agenda. As stated on thehacktivist.com:

> The Hacktivist is dedicated to examining the theory and practice of hacktivism and electronic civil disobedience while contributing to the evolution of hacktivism by promoting constructive debate, effective direct action, and creative solutions to complex problems in order to facilitate positive change.

4. *Vigilantism*. One aspect of hacking that you do not see on the news and in the daily paper is the vigilante groups that surreptitiously attack the Internet's lower lifeforms, to use their terms. Child pornography is one of the darker sides of society and as with many social characteristics the Internet has amplified its availability and intensity. There are groups of extremely computer-savvy people who will do anything within their capability to thwart, damage, or stop child pornography. Interestingly, this raises several questions of law and ethics. The FBI has regularly investigated perpetrators of computer crime only to find out their target was a ring of child pornography dealers and forced to arrest the vigilante-hacker trying to put lowlifes out of business. In most cases, vigilantes are

respected individuals in their normal surroundings, but once on the Internet an alternate persona takes over and the need to wage a war against the "scum of the Earth" takes over.

After the terrorist attack against the United States on September 11, 2001, hackers launched several cyber initiatives on their own. For example, the Web site for the Iranian government's ministry of the interior, www.moi.gov.ir, was hacked in retaliation for the terrorist assaults. The presidential palace of Afghanistan, www.afghangovernment.org, was brought down for nearly a month because of endless DoS attacks against it. The FBI's response was a statement reminding hackers that attacking Web sites and infiltrating network systems is against the law, adding Internet disruptions will only hurt America more. Moreover, law enforcement is concerned with vigilantes attacking systems because data used for prosecution can be lost during the attack, canceling the original intent of the vigilantes.

ÜBER HACKER

In German, *über* can be loosely translated to "super." The resulting definition is easy to interpret: "Super Hacker." An über hacker is a person with exceptional skills, fortitude, and a long list of experiences to draw upon for future hacks. These are the elite and nearly unstoppable hackers. To be an über hacker you must have exceptional skills in programming, logic, systems, operating systems, applications, hardware, communications, and protocols along with a strong dose of attitude and unethical behavior. Über hackers are the most feared because of their capability. These are the people that write the tools used by other hackers and are sought by unscrupulous businesses and governments.

With this type of power in the hands of immoral people, the options are vast. Although some über hackers remain dormant and hide in the fog of legitimate professions, there are others who actively use their capabilities to benefit themselves or others. There are two types of super hackers: extortionists and spies.

Extortionists

A growing popularity among the best hackers is using information to pressure people and organizations into paying money to remain quiet or to stop attacking them. The irony is not only do they make substantial amounts of money doing this, but also the payers actually believe the hacker. The usual result is the organization becomes the target of other extortionists. The FBI is flooded with cases that entail organizations receiving demands for money, unless . . . .

Financial institutions, online retailers, and gambling sites are typical targets due to the impact the loss of reputation can have and their access to cash. There are many examples where hackers gain access to a bank's systems and obtain a list of accounts and personal information. Once acquired, the list is sent to the bank, proving their ownership of the information and ability to gain unauthorized access, with a note explaining that if they do not submit $20,000 U.S. they will publicize their acts. In comparison to the potential loss of business and reputation, $20,000 is not a lot to pay, and many companies do so. It is interesting to realize that firms pay the ransom assuming the information will not be released, when in fact the people who perform these acts are obviously not people to trust. The result is other crime communities focusing on the target because they've been labeled a "sucker" and represent free money.

The discriminating factor between über hackers and other forms of hackers (beyond the skills) is they do not perform the attack for reputation or respect: they do it for money. Money is an enormous motivator and can grant hackers a constant influx of tools and the latest technology to support their appetite for knowledge. There are two types: hitmen and terrorists.

1. *Hitman.* Über hackers of this grade are usually associated with a crime organization to support a symbiotic relationship. Much like a hitman that performs deeds for the boss, hackers are called upon to gain information to control people and money — for money. An example is a hacker inserting evidence of an unlawful activity onto a government representative's computer to force him to perform acts for the benefit of the organization. Yes, they are given an offer they can't refuse.
2. *Terrorist.* There are numerous examples of terrorists' activities that do not use planes or chemicals but rather the computer. To date, they have not had the same impact as 9/11 but remain a substantial threat nevertheless. It is assumed, and hoped, that government entities such as the NSA, FBI, and CIA are successful in their counterterrorism techniques.

We see computer terrorism in many forms that range from the benign to the malignant. The government is a prime example of a targeted attack by distributed groups bent on disruption. When a U.S. naval spy plane was damaged by a Chinese jet over China it was forced to land in a less-than-receptive country. In retaliation for spying, several government networks were harshly attacked by Chinese hackers in protest. Organizations that are related to government operations or technology, or public systems (e.g., water, power, transportation), or represent involvement with a community are targets of cyber terrorism. Although this book focuses on ethical hacking—a much lighter subject—it is necessary for everyone to be aware of the desire of some factions to cause damage that can lead to harming people.

Espionage

Of course, there is government espionage using people as much as technology, but that does not relate directly to the common business. Industrial espionage, however, can influence the development and success of organizations worldwide and can turn the tide of competitive advantages overnight.

An example may be the development of a new drug that has required years of research and testing, leading to conclusions and design. A collection of documentation may provide enough summarized information about the research that could catapult another organization's ability to pursue or support a less successful study of the same subject.

NOTE 4: THE VALUE OF SEEMINGLY BASIC MANUFACTURING TECHNIQUES

An interesting story has to do with valves, complicated valves that are used to separate various elements in liquid to extract different types of materials. The applications vary, ranging from medical applications to animal feed. The valves were revolutionary and extremely expensive, starting at $1.5 million to $20 million per valve. What made these valves unique was the overall design, more specifically, the port design. Much as with the centrifugal cylinder compression design of early Porsche engines, there were certain design characteristics that you simply did not want to share with a competitor.

It was important to protect the details about the valve and the manufacturing techniques. This was difficult because it was necessary to share the information with partners for construction and customers to ensure specific design features met their demand. One day a small package arrived with a miniature valve, which had unsettlingly similar properties, for pharmaceutical applications. Compelled to determine if this was simply two companies reaching the same conclusion, or something much more sinister, an investigation was launched to understand the exact flow of data within the small community of machine shops and customers. After an exhaustive process it appeared that one of the design files was taken from a partner's computer system over a year before the package's arrival. Luckily, by that time the design feature was not critical to the newer valves and the experience expedited the new manufacturing process as well as information security practices.

SOCIOLOGY

Hackers are often thought of as pathological loners rather than as members of a community. However, hackers exist within social groups that provide expertise, support, training, periodicals, and conferences. Hacker Michael E. Marotta, known as "The Knightmare," said, "To find 'hacker culture' you have to take a very wide view of the cyberspace terrain and watch the interactions among physically diversified people who have in common a mania for machines and software. What you will find will be a gossamer framework of culture."

The society of hackers is driven by technology, secrecy, and anonymity. The technology provides the catalyst for the community. This theorization draws on Benedict Anderson's concept of the imagined community and on social theories that see movements as dispersed networks of individuals, groups, and organizations that combine through a collectively articulated identity. Anderson names the power of an imagined identity to bind people, who may never meet each other, together in allegiance to a common cause.

Secrecy and anonymity play a fundamental role in hacker society. Hacking demands secrecy because the actions of the group are illegal and exposure would mean certain repercussions. Although the sharing of information is essential to the community as a whole, collaborating to plan or perform an attack is a rewarding if not exciting part of hacking. A byproduct of anonymity is the fluidity of membership and acceptance. Chris Coggins, also known as the hacker Eric Bloodaxe (no relation to the brutal ruler of the Viking kingdom of Northumbria) said about hacker membership:

> *People come and go pretty often and if you lay off for a few months and then come back, almost everyone is new. There are always those who have been around for years. . . . I would consider the hacking community a very informal one. It is pretty much anarchy as far as rule making goes. . . . The community was structured only within the framework of different hacking 'groups.' Legion of Doom would be one example of this. A group creates its own rules and usually doesn't have a leader. . . . The groups I've been in have voted on accepting new members, kicking people out, etc.*

Although a social framework of hackers undoubtedly exists, the community is based on fundamental social objectives and survival necessities. Interestingly, the Internet has become the instrument fueling the diversity and communal actions through increased exposure to communications and anonymity. The building block of society is communication and the first step of the evolution of complex social networks was the birth of written communication. Once a collaborative framework is established, people with similar thoughts, desires, and goals can begin to share information for a common growth. The Internet has provided an insulated construct to facilitate the hacker and ultimately the imagined community.

Motives

Motives are the combination of the characteristics introduced above, social influences, mental capacity, and attitude. It is nearly impossible to provide categorization of the mind of a cybercriminal because of the complexities and endless variations. Donn Parker wrote, "Psychologists and criminologists warn that it is nearly impossible to create a taxonomy of motives because any such taxonomy would be too complex and change continually."

Understanding what drives a hacker to perform illicit acts is difficult to define, probably because of the overly simple concept of human curiosity. Not more than a year ago, my son came downstairs with clumps of hair missing from his head. I rushed upstairs to find my daughter surrounded by hair clippings. When asked why she cut her brother's hair, she simply replied, "I don't know." I'm sure many parents have been faced with the sibling haircut scenario and received much the same answer. Human curiosity can be our strongest asset and when armed with a sharp instrument can be damaging.

Hacker Maelstrom said:

> *I just do it because it makes me feel good, as in better than anything else that I've ever experienced; the adrenaline rush I get when I'm trying to evade authority, the thrill I get from having written a program that does something that was supposed to be impossible to do, and the ability to have social relations with other hackers are all very addictive. For a long time, I was extremely shy around others, and I am*

able to let my thoughts run free when I am alone with my computer and a modem hooked up to it. I consider myself addicted to hacking. I will have no moral or ethical qualms about system hacking until accounts are available to the general public for free. Peer recognition was very important; when you were recognized you had access to more.

The infamous hacker Kevin Mitnick described his motivation as, "You get a better understanding of cyberspace, the computer systems, the operating systems, how the computer systems interact with one another; that basically was my motivation behind my hacking activity in the past. It was just from the gain of knowledge and the thrill of adventure, nothing that was well and truly sinister as trying to get any type of monetary gain or anything."

There are six fundamental drivers for hackers:

1. *Addiction to Computers*. Many hackers have confessed to the addiction and obsession with computers and the feeling that they are compelled to hack. Computers offer a controllable environment that poses intellectual challenges for those who may have difficulty in finding similar stimuli in other areas of their lives. There are examples of hackers with learning and communication disabilities, which cultivate hands-on learning and eventually drive them to computers. Computers also make excellent targets. They do not feel pain or harm people—directly—and therefore are simply a tool to continue supplying their addiction with new, different, and more powerful systems. It is not uncommon for a hacker to have several, if not hundreds of, computers at his disposal.

2. *Curiosity of the Possible*. Very similar to the intuitive knowledge and out-of-the-box thinking, curiosity is a powerful characteristic that intensifies the inquisitive nature supported by the addiction of computers. Curiosity is a strong stimulant that encourages probing systems to simply discover opportunities. In essence, a hacker is motivated by the unknown of the target and of his own abilities. Finding a system on the Internet and speculating how far he can gain access is a primary factor in what provokes many attacks.

3. *Excitement*. In the early years of the Internet, everyday people were becoming online junkies because of the excitement compared to the boredom of real life. Mostly this was based on the anonymity the Internet provided and the freedom to be whomever you wanted to project into the ether. With offline experiences that pale in comparison to the exhilaration of Internet activities, many people hack to facilitate the experience. It is clear, despite social complaints, hackers and their community represent a certain aura and mystique that can be seen in movies, TV, and books, much the same as the phenomena we see around organized crime. We know these people murder, steal, and promote the use of drugs and prostitution, but socially we're drawn to them. Based on this observation, the excitement of being a hacker is related to the perception of becoming part of a popularized and elite group.

4. *Social Status.* One of the more critical encouragements to successfully attack or vandalize a system is gaining acceptance into the community or establishing alpha roles within a smaller group. Some operate independently and in isolation, but for the greater population there is a small support group that judges them based on their activities. The most common version of this is a type of peer pressure. For example, if someone is absorbed into a group, but does not offer any services (i.e., illegally obtained computer resources, software, or tools) in return for learning from the group, they will certainly be excommunicated.

5. *Power.* The ability to take over a system and control resources for personal or communal purposes is a commanding attraction on which hackers thrive. Taking control of a system is a thrill not easily duplicated or attained in their normal lifestyles. An example is a hacker who accessed a PC in someone's home, specifically in the bedroom, and took control of the system and the camera attached to the system. The hacker proceeded to taunt the user and finished by taking a picture of the man using the PC and then showing it to him. You can imagine the look on his face! The goal of this attack was to simply empower the hacker and make a statement to the victim, her social group, and to herself. Power is a formidable motivator.

6. *Betterment of Society.* On several occasions, hackers have been quoted as stating they helped the general computer public by exposing a security hole, leading to the resulting fix reducing future attacks based on that vulnerability. This is also the foundation upon which the hacker-turned-consultant phenomenon was built, something we're now seeing as a very risky venture.

3 The Framework

What is a framework? Moreover, how does it apply to attacking a system? Finally, is a framework a methodology? A framework is collection of measurable tasks, whereas a methodology is a specific set of inputs, processes, and their outputs. A framework provides a hierarchy of steps, taking into consideration the relationships that can be formed when executing a task given a specific method.

For example, this book presents a framework of steps with options within each and they appear as chapters, headings, and so forth. The context within each section of this book introduces methods for performing certain tasks heeding the value represented by other points within the framework. When combined, an entire process geared towards value can be presented.

By formatting ethical hacking in a framework, as opposed to simply a collection of methods and tactics, elements can be easily removed and added to accommodate specific requirements of the test. Of course, the removal of a particular element within the framework can have repercussions when the goal of the entire framework is value.

How this applies to penetration testing is in ensuring the value of the test is realized. Given that a penetration test is part of a larger security program, one must include other characteristics of security to align the test appropriately to the demands driving it. Moreover, a framework highlights each phase, drawing relationships between them to make sure you're on track with the objectives. In addition, each step in the phase helps you take into account the nuances of performing a controlled attack. For example, there are limitations, inherent and imposed, that will have effects on each phase translating into varying degrees of value. Finally, it provides operational structure to the test. Knowing how and when to perform a task is as important as the task itself.

The mission of the framework is to explain the steps, their relation to other points within the performance of a test, and to expose the impact on value when excluding various methods within each. In the simplified Figure 3.1, we see each primary phase of the framework with points within each representing a task or value element. Some circles are larger than others, signifying more potential value. Depending on what tasks are not employed, some downstream elements may not be available simply because the required information or results from previous elements do not exist. Given that the framework is founded on related processes that span phases, the use (or omission) of a process will limit the availability or effectiveness of other processes.

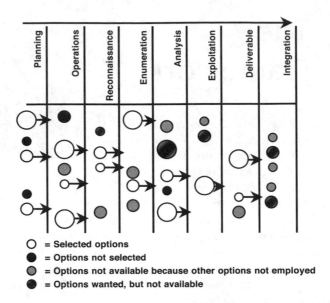

○ = Selected options
● = Options not selected
◓ = Options not available because other options not employed
◑ = Options wanted, but not available

FIGURE 3.1 Determining the Impact on Value Based on Selected Options

Of course, for your specific goals of the test, the unselected or unavailable elements may prove to be of little or no value and therefore the impact is nonexistent. The important fact to evaluate is which elements are needed to meet your goals and understand there may be an inherent relationship to another point within the framework you have not considered or do not want to be exercised. The ability to gain visibility into the affiliation between one phase and another is the value a framework brings to the entire process.

While in its infancy, ethical hacking meant simply attacking a network and exploiting any vulnerability presenting itself; that was the goal—get in. And, quite frankly, this is still the M.O. for many engagements today. The tools have changed, the techniques are much more sophisticated, the knowledge of the consumers is much more comprehensive, but the essence of the test has remained much the same. Technique and tools are important and provide a strong foundation for further evolution, but with regard to security, the environment is too dynamic to base success on technique and tools alone. Racquetball is one of those sports of technique and tools: insightful volleys and a good racquet will win the match. However, the court does not change in size, the lines don't move, the back wall will always be there, and the environment is predictable.

With the absence of continuity, value rests on the shoulders of the tester and the framework that is followed. The ability to assess the situation and make quick determinations based on similar experiences is an attribute of a successful attack by today's standards.

On the other side of the equation is the recipient of these tests attempting to make value decisions based on his impression of a planned attack, an impression fed by security consultants, magazines, friends, and employees and not from extensive experience in being the target of hundreds of tests. I liken it to asking a regular person to purchase food for a restaurant. They know what food is and have an understanding of value and use, but buying 250 pounds of meat, 10 gallons of mayonnaise, 25 pounds of cheese, and 8 boxes of detergent would challenge anyone not familiar with the process.

After performing and being involved with many penetration-testing engagements, there is a theme that begins to surface. People are not fully aware of the options available to them and how to apply those options to their environment. Many characteristics have varying degrees of intensity and requirements, such as information and limitations, that will influence other areas of the test and how they relate to the value of the test in an overall security program.

PLANNING THE TEST

As with anything worth doing, proper planning is essential to performing a successful project. Planning provides an opportunity to evaluate existing business demands and processes, how they relate to a new business endeavor, and to make choices on which characteristics are worth doing and those in which you're not willing to accept risk.

Existing security policies, culture, laws and regulations, best practices, and industry requirements will drive many of the inputs needed to make decisions on the scope and scale of a test. Arguably, the planning phase of a penetration test will have a profound influence on how the test is performed and the information shared and collected, and will directly influence the deliverable and integration of the results into the security program.

Planning describes many of the details and their role in formulating a controlled attack. Security policies, program, posture, and ultimately risk all play a part in guiding the outcome of a test. What drives a company's focus on security, its core business needs, challenges, and expectations will set the stage for the entire engagement.

SOUND OPERATIONS

How is the test going to be supported and controlled? What are the underlying actions that must be performed regardless of the scope of the test? Who does what, when, where, how long, who is out of bounds, and what is in bounds of a test all need to be addressed. Logistics of the test will drive how information is shared and to what degree (or depth) each characteristic will be performed to achieve the desired results. Operational features will include determining what the imposed limitations of the tester are and how they are evaluated during the test.

RECONNAISSANCE

Reconnaissance is the search for freely available information to assist in the attack. The search can be quick ping sweeps to see what IP addresses on a network will respond, scouring newsgroups on the Internet in search of misguided employees divulging useful information, or rummaging through the trash to find receipts for telecommunication services.

Reconnaissance can include theft, lying to people, tapping phones and networks, impersonations, or even leveraging falsified friendships to collect data about a target. The search for information is only limited by the extremes to which a customer and tester are willing to go.

The reconnaissance phase introduces many of the questions surrounding what actions truly provide value to the company. In this section, we examine the reconnaissance techniques, such as social engineering, and the necessary environmental characteristics that must exist to realize value from intense investigation. It is also in this section that the value of a certain type of test is questioned, which exposes the effects of poor planning or a poor understanding of limitations applied to the test.

Reconnaissance offers a plethora of options, each related to one another. However, unlike other phases within the test's framework, each option can be controlled, moderated, and measured to a surprisingly high level of granularity. Therefore, the relationship between the framework, tasks, and methods will become very clear.

ENUMERATION

Enumeration (also known as network or vulnerability discovery) is essentially obtaining readily available (and sometimes provided) information directly from the target's systems, applications, and networks. An interesting point to make very early is that the enumeration phase represents a point within the project where the line between a passive attack and an active attack begins to blur. Without setting the appropriate expectations, this phase can have results ranging from "Oops" to "Do you swear to tell the truth and nothing but the truth?"

To build a picture of a company's environment there are several tools and techniques available to compile a list of information obtained from the systems. Most notably, port scanning is the "block and tackle" of the enumeration and NMap is today's most valuable player. The simplest explanation of a port scan is the manipulation of the basic communication setup between two networked systems using TCP/IP as a communication protocol. TCP/IP uses a basic session setup that can be used to determine what application ports a system is willing to use to establish communications.

Simply stated, port scanning is a way of detecting where a computer responds to requests to make connections. More technically, the TCP protocol has what is commonly known as the "three-way handshake" that is used to start TCP connections:

1. Computer A sends a message called a "SYN" (Synchronize) to Computer B.
2. Computer B acknowledges that message with a "SYN+ACK" (SYN with an Acknowledgement) to Computer A.
3. Computer A sends back an acknowledgement—"ACK."

Obviously, collecting information about systems is the first step in formulating an attack plan. However, information collected during the reconnaissance phase can be added to help build a picture of the target's systems and networks. It is one thing to collect information and it is another to determine its value, and the perceived value in the hands of a hacker. On the surface, enumeration is simple: take the collected data and evaluate it collectively to establish a plan for more reconnaissance or building a matrix for the next phase, vulnerability analysis. However, this is the phase where the tester's ability to make logical deductions plays an enormous role. It is also the reason why great testers (and hackers) are not taught; they are grown.

As mentioned earlier, hacking is an art form, the ability to use rules and predictability to your advantage. Computers, if nothing else, are masters of rules and performing repeatable tasks perfectly (well, most of the time). The talent required to manipulate this rigid environment is rare. To accomplish this, a human's intellect will resolve problems by combining seemingly disparate information to formulate a hypothesis for other avenues of attack. Enumeration is inventorying all the collected information to build logical threads to circumvent the security controls of a network, system, or application.

VULNERABILITY ANALYSIS

There is a logical and pragmatic approach to analyzing data. During the enumeration phase, we try to perform an interpretation of the information collected looking for relationships that may lead to exposures that can be exploited. The vulnerability analysis phase is a practical process of comparing the collected information with known vulnerabilities.

Most information can be collected from the Internet or other sources, such as newsgroups or mailing lists, which can be used to compare information about the target to seek options for exploitation. However, information provided by vendors and even data collected from the target can be used to formulate a successful attack.

Information collected during the reconnaissance phase from the company can provide information about vulnerabilities unique to its environment. Data obtained directly from the company can actually support the discovery of vulnerabilities that cannot be located anywhere else.

As mentioned above, information found on the Internet is very helpful. Known vulnerabilities, incidents, service packs, updates, and even available hacker tools help in identifying a point of attack. The Internet provides a plethora of insightful information that can easily be associated with the architecture of the target.

EXPLOITATION

A great deal of planning and evaluation is being performed during the earlier phases to ensure a business-centric foundation of value is established for the test. Of course, all of this planning must lead to some form of attack. Exploiting systems and applications can be easy, such as running a tool, or intricate, with fine-tuned steps executed in a specific way to get in. No matter the level of difficulty, good testers follow a pattern during the exploitation phase of a test.

During a penetration test the details considered in the planning come into full view and affect the outcome of every action taken by the tester. A sound course of action is needed to translate the planning into an attack to meet the objectives within the specified period and within the defined scope.

The attack process is broken up into threads and groups and each appears in sets of security. A thread is a collection of tasks that must be performed in a specific order to achieve a goal. Threads can be one step or many in a series used to gain access. Every thread is different but may have similarities that can be useful. Therefore, threads can be combined into groups to create a collection of access strategies. Groups are then reviewed and compared to support comprehensive attacks using very different threads in a structured manner.

Each test is evaluated at every point within the operation to ensure the expected outcome is met. Each divergence from the plan is appraised to make two fundamental determinations:

1. *Expectations*. Are the expectations of the thread or group not being met or are the test's results conflicting with the company's assumptions? The objective is to ensure each test is within the bounds of what was established and agreed upon. On the other hand, if the test begins to produce results that were not considered during the planning, enumeration, and vulnerability analysis phases, the engagement needs to be reconsidered or, at a minimum, the planning phase needs to be revisited. Meeting expectations is everything and in the world of ethical hacking it can represent a fundamental challenge when not planned properly or not executed according to the plan.

2. *Technical*. Is a system reacting in an unexpected manner, which is having an impact on the test and the engagement as a whole? Much more granular in theory than general expectations of the test, technical gaps are literally the response of a system during the test. Keeping your eyes open for unexpected responses from systems ensures you have not negatively affected the target or gone beyond the set scope of the test.

The exploitation phase is an opportunity to discuss the tactics of performing the test rather than focusing on the tactics of the exploitation itself.

FINAL ANALYSIS

Although the attack process has many checks and validations to ensure the overall success of the engagement, a final analysis of all the collected data and exploits must be performed. Vulnerabilities associated with the test need to be categorized to determine the level of exposure and to assist in supporting a well-defined deliverable and mitigation plan. The final analysis phase provides a link between the exploitation phase and the creation of the deliverable.

The first goal of the analysis is to take a comprehensive view of the entire engagement and look for other opportunities that may exist, but are not directly observed. The idea is to build a bigger picture of the security posture of the target's environment and classify vulnerabilities to communicate the results in a clear and useful manner.

The final analysis is part interpretation and part empirical results. To define something as critical with little evidence can become problematic when presented to the recipient of the test. However, if there is enough evidence from other threads and groups that prove the vulnerability could represent a substantial risk, it becomes much more palatable and easier to communicate in terms of value and remediation.

DELIVERABLE

Throughout the history of penetration testing there have been deliverables communicating the results of the test in numerous ways. Some are short, only listing the identified vulnerabilities and where to find the patch to fix them. Others are cookie-cutter reports from tools that simply state which port was open, the vulnerability it represents, and where to find the patch. And, there are some that detail every move made by the consultant: how she found a hole, got the etc/shadow, cracked the passwords, and took over your shipping application . . . and, of course, where to find the patch.

Are these examples of poor deliverables? In reality, no. These are simply the results of a technical test performed in conjunction with the demands of the company. Many organizations place so many controls on the test (or the lack of controls) that a comprehensive deliverable is difficult. The only avenue of the tester is simply to state the facts. In addition, ethical hacking has become so commoditized that if a deliverable doesn't drive fear into the hearts of the executives it could be considered a failure.

In contrast, I have seen reports from many companies and individuals that are, in a word, exceptional. They provide insightful commentary, step-by-step details, and rank the vulnerabilities to the best of their knowledge and understanding of the customer's business. They provide measurable levels of risk, raw results from the test, where backdoors are, how they were placed, and how to remove them. Some include status reports and all correspondence associated with the engagement. Finally, how the engagement was planned, what the drivers were, and the overall expectations, the imposed limitations, and their impacts are also included.

It is my expectation that the recipients of deliverables—good and bad—would like to know what a good deliverable should include and ultimately how to translate it into valuable security improvements. The above list contains only a few of the general characteristics of a good deliverable. In the chapter on deliverables, we take a much closer look and discuss sound practices associated with exceptional deliverables.

INTEGRATION

Finally, how to use the test to your full advantage is directly dependent on the proposed integration process. There are several assumptions within this chapter, one of which is that the penetration test actually found something and followed many, if not all, of the previous phases. Another is that the deliverable communicates all the necessary information needed to actually support some form of integration. Of course, the deliverable can be combined with existing materials, such as a risk analysis, security policy, previous test results, and information associated with a security program to enhance mitigation.

There are three distinguishing factors that should be considered during the integration of any test results:

1. *Mitigation.* If something were found that represented a threat to secure operations and was beyond acceptable risk, then it would need to be fixed, to put it bluntly. Of course, there are the easy things to rectify and there are very complicated solutions to seemingly simple problems. Mitigation of a vulnerability can include testing, piloting, implementing, and validating changes to systems.
2. *Defense.* How should you address the insecurities in a strategic manner? What about your networks, systems, applications, and policies that need to be addressed to ensure sound practices are employed to minimize the impact of future or undetected vulnerabilities? Defense planning is establishing a foundation of security to grow on and ensure long-term success.
3. *Incident Management.* Arguably, the core element of security—the ability to detect, respond, and recover from an attack—is an essential part of any security program. Knowing how you were attacked, the vulnerabilities exploited, and the potential impacts aids in formulating an incident response plan. The test provides an opportunity for you to learn about the various weaknesses and attractive avenues of attack. Finally, you get an understanding of critical points in the network that may need more attention than others, and this may not be the perimeter as normally assumed.

So we've covered all the bases, at least the big ones: fix what is broken, establish a plan to protect you from future mistakes and oversights, and prepare for a real assault on your company. This is what you can expect from a well-structured penetration test. Penetration tests can be a valuable component of a security program. They can provide fascinating insights to the presumed security of an organization and the actual security employed. Tests can also assist in defining acceptable levels of risk and exposure and set the foundation for future security developments.

4 Information Security Models

Just about everyone involved in information security has heard the term "defense-in-depth," the practice of building many layers of security into systems, networks, applications, or anything that needs to be secured. Defense-in-depth is creating several controls that are unique, but complement each other to provide effective protection.

Layered security is best recognized in a bank. They have guards, a safe, alarms, security cameras, and locked doors. If one of these were to fail, another corresponding security control would back it up. For example, if the guard is subdued, the alarm should detect the intruder. If the alarm is disabled, the vault remains a formidable challenge.

By applying separate security controls that complement each other, the odds of detecting and thwarting an attack are greatly increased. Of course, security controls that are duplicates or have the same function should be considered a redundancy rather than another layer in the model. Nevertheless, it all comes down to interpretation. Having a Checkpoint 1 and a Cisco PIX, one after the other, can be considered a form of defense-in-depth when in fact they are both firewalls.

If we're to apply this to the framework for performing a penetration test, we must extrapolate this basic rule into a model to demonstrate at what level a test can expose weaknesses. In addition, building a layered model will help in explaining the act of hacking all within the detailed framework.

Two models are introduced here: the different levels, or layers, where one can employ security controls, defense-in-depth, and a security architecture. A security architecture is another set of layers that helps companies classify different aspects of security, such as resources and perimeter. Together, these will help in understanding the framework of a value-based penetration test. These models are combined and demonstrated in Figure 4.1.

The defense-in-depth model is defined in four layers:

1. Computer security
2. Network security
3. Service security
4. Application security

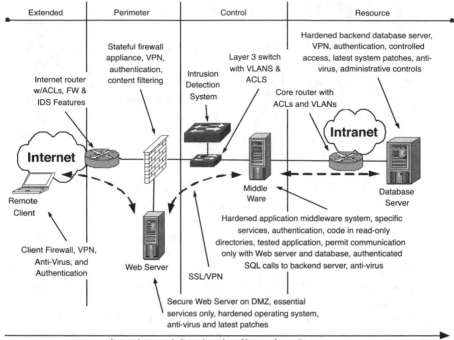

FIGURE 4.1 Defense-in-Depth within a Security Architecture

COMPUTER SECURITY

Computer security includes many diverse subjects, such as controlling authorized (and unauthorized) access, managing user accounts and their privileges, software management, change control, development, and database security, to mention a few. Much of the security is afforded by the operating system responsible for providing the interface between the hardware and the software and ultimately the user. Operating systems come in many types and flavors. Microsoft's Windows is the most prevalent operating system used today for home and business. UNIX, an operating system born in Bell Labs, has many flavors and versions, such as Linux, BSD, Solaris, and AIX, to name a few of the popular ones.

Historically, computers filled rooms and were centrally located with dumb terminals providing access via a serial interface. Security controls were relatively simple. Each terminal was essentially a window into the main system where all the controls were employed. There were no hard drives, floppy drives, or other means of injecting viruses or worms. As users logged in they were provided only what they required to perform their duties; this is typically referred to as Mandatory Access Control (MAC). Security was realized because there was basically one computer with tightly controlled shared access. One person couldn't see or access files another was using unless those privileges were provided by an administrator.

Later, as computers became much cheaper and as common as the TV, people could use them for whatever they wanted. Controls were at the discretion of the user or owner. Of course, businesses saw the opportunity to leverage this inexpensive resource to enhance their productivity. In the early 1980s, Lotus 1-2-3 was the first breakthrough application that engrained computers into the business DNA. Lotus 1-2-3 was the first spreadsheet program where each cell could contain values and formulas to build complex mathematical computations. Something that was previously done by hand and calculators (requiring enormous amounts of experience and time) could now be built into a spreadsheet and shared as a template with which others could work. Accountants became one of the early adopters and soon nearly all financial firms were using spreadsheets to perform difficult calculations.

At this point in time, there were thousands of individual computers operating independently of each other with very little concern for security. Unfortunately, as the technology grew at an incredible rate, resulting in faster connected systems, security remained in the shadows. Now, we see computers of all types connected together sharing information with various levels of sensitivity. To provide some form of security, Discretionary Access Controls (DAC) were employed to permit the system to manage each user's privileges based on the ownership of a file or application. For example, Alice would log in to a system and create or manage her files, which were identified and controlled by the operating system. At that point, it was up to Alice's discretion to decide who would have access to those files and what level of access that would be. Without centralized computing and data stored in different locations, this was the best that could be realized.

With many shared systems and limited controls provided by an operating system normally designed for personal use, how does one control access to information or applications? How do you control what applications are installed and who can run those applications? Moreover, how do you control what the privileges of the application are? How does a company provide comprehensive security in a distributed environment with many different users, systems, and access rights? It can get very convoluted very quickly.

Computer security goes well beyond the user. Applications are the reason for a computer's existence and controlling the type, privileges, and integrity of an application can become challenging. Enforcing licensing rules when you can copy an entire application as simply as you can copy a file can lead to legal ramifications. How do you control the number of applications in use? What if an application license is based on the number of hours or the number of employees permitted to use it?

Much of what has been discussed is based on theoretical security models created by the Department of Defense in the '70s and '80s. Most notable is the Rainbow Series, a collection of color-named standards that included system security models. Trusted Computer System Evaluation Criteria (DOD-5200.28-STD), known as the Orange Book, became the de facto standard for computer security. Security was defined in four ratings (D through A), each with increasing levels of security.

One of the more popular security models is Bell–LaPadula, which defines objects, subjects, and access operations. In theory, the Bell–LaPadula model was an exceptional application of security controls but could not be applied in a cost-effective manner. However, the model still has an impact on system design to this day. Bell–LaPadula has two basic security principles: reading data and writing data. What you were permitted to read and write was directly associated with your level of access. You can write above your level, but not below. Finally, you could read below your level but not above. For example, if you had classified access to a system and wanted to sell information to a terrorist organization but could not send classified information, you would copy the data to a lower level, say unclassified, and send the information. Bell–LaPadula provides the logistics to control this type of threat. Also, when in doubt, information can be considered sensitive, therefore, the ability to write above your security level is provided. However, because you only have classified access you cannot read above your assigned security level. Therefore, it is possible to write something you can't read.

Operating system security, as you can see, can come in many forms and each represents its own idiosyncrasies. At its innermost level, an operating system maintains a kernel, a collection of code that controls every action a system executes. Historically, the kernel was small (typically a few hundred thousand lines of code), containing only the necessary commands to ensure basic operations and everything that was used to support applications, communications, and various customizable attributes was outside the kernel. The implementation of a hardened kernel provided system reliability and integrity. UNIX is a good example of a small kernel to provide core functions; everything else used libraries and other code to support general use.

However, as time moved on, more and more code was included in the kernel to simplify use, increase speed, and support a variety of implementations. The practice of employing a secure kernel, which is responsible for ensuring the integrity of system functions, was lost as features became the driving factors. An example of a large kernel is the Windows operating system. Everything is in the kernel and only applications exist beyond it. The assumption is that everything in the kernel is secure, so if all operations for the computer are placed in the kernel, then the result is a secure operating system. Unfortunately, it makes for a huge kernel (Windows NT is over 4 million lines of code) and makes for a complex system. Because complexity is security's nemesis, a large complicated kernel represents a breeding ground for vulnerability and is susceptible to errors. When everything is injected into the kernel, rogue or faulty code can compromise the entire system.

Computer security represents the last line of defense, and the evolution of simple operating systems has promoted the introduction of perimeter controls we see today, such as firewalls, filtering routers, and other network-related security.

There has been some evolution of computer security to close the gaps: Trusted Operating Systems (TOS), introduced many years ago but that still have not reached mainstream implementation, construct compartments for services to run and users to work. Compartments are internally controlled, logical boundaries in the system other applications are completely unaware exist. Each compartment is assigned a security level and a low security level cannot access system resources of a higher security level. Although a greatly simplified description, an exploited vulnerability within an application or service will only affect the resources associated with the compartment (i.e., memory, disk space).

Trusted Solaris, HP Presidium, and Argus PitBull are examples of operating systems or add-ons that greatly enhance the overall security of a system. Although a great solution, TOS introduced intense system administration and therefore never took hold as a common platform.

Computer security, better yet the lack of, could be considered the flashpoint for the birth of the common hacker. The pains we're experiencing today, the constant focus on the perimeter as the primary security provider, the explosion of viruses and worms, and the constant battle of integrity and reliability, all stem from the poor evolution of computer security. Operating system security will not solve world hunger, but a secure system allows greater investment in access controls, comprehensive network security, and application security with less focus on viruses and small holes that lead to big results.

HARDEN A SYSTEM

Determining what steps are necessary to harden a system can be very frustrating. There are numerous sources of various tactics for securing a system. There are sample configurations and tools that can be used to configure Microsoft and UNIX systems. The following are some common characteristics of hardening a system.

Physically Secure It

Many systems are vulnerable to direct access. For this reason, you should make certain that only authorized people can physically access the box. Everything from turning the system off to installing malicious software can be performed on a system if you can get to it.

Common practices are as follows:

- Install case locks on publicly accessible systems, such as workstations.
- Place critical systems in a locked cabinet (cage) in a controlled facility.
- Avoid the use, or installation, of removable media support such as floppies, CD-drives, and removable hard drives.
- Disable or remove support for external access ports, such as UBS ports, COM ports, and keyboard support when applicable.
- Set up a BIOS password to reduce the exposure of someone rebooting the system and making changes to the system.
- Disable the power switch or use a lockable switch.
- Ensure power supplies are secured and redundant. It is one thing to hit the power button; it is another to just unplug it.
- Provide suitable operating conditions such as raised floors and environmental controls.
- Control access to the computer room.

Installing the Operating System

During the installation of an operating system it is typical to know the role that system will play in the company. When concerned about the security of the system, there are several practices to start you on the right foot.

Setup practices include the following:

- Determine if there is a company-approved configuration or system image that is relevant to the role of the system. For example, a Web server configuration may be very different if it is for Internet services as opposed to an internal development system.
- Install the operating system from scratch. In other words, avoid updating an existing operating system. The result may be inheriting vulnerabilities, viruses, or poor configurations.
- Select the appropriate file system format that reflects the needs of the computer. However, based on today's awareness of security, rarely is a nonsecure file system implemented, such as FAT (File Allocation Table).
- If provided the opportunity, such as during the installation of Microsoft, RedHat, Solaris, and BSD, to name a few, do not install any services by default. Look to enable services rather than disable. Windows 2003 installs with all (most) services disabled by default. Disabling services during installation is a trend many operating systems are practicing to reduce the likelihood of frivolous exposures based on unused system elements.
- Enable interfaces only when they are necessary to complete the installation. This will avoid interaction before it is properly configured. For example, to load a specific module you may need to connect to a different system on the network to collect the application for installation.

Get It Running

At this point you have a half-baked system somewhere between security and doing what you need it to do. However, you're still not ready to start piling on applications. There are some tasks to ensure the system is prepared for more serious hardening.
Cleanup practices include the following:

- The first thing to check and configure correctly is that the system is configured to restart in a manner that is expected. For example, the init.d file in UNIX and startup configuration in Windows need to be reviewed to make sure nothing was added or removed during the final stages of the installation.
- Create an administrative account. In UNIX, it is not a good practice to use *root* for managing the system on a day-to-day basis and the same is true for other platforms. Therefore, using an administrator or *root* equivalent user to log in to a system provides one more layer of security. If necessary, the administrators can "SU" (Super User) up to *root* to accomplish specific tasks. By establishing this practice early on in the process, you can configure the system to not allow people to log in as *root* (locally or remotely), offering greater control over the system.
- Disabling services is a primary phase. During the installation, you avoided installing services, but many systems install some anyway (or are hidden as with Windows).

- Determine application dependencies. Inevitably, some applications are installed to support various system administration. When cleaning the system or extraneous services and applications it is necessary to evaluate relationships in order to avoid rogue processes.

Set System Policies

Now that the operating system is installed and specific services are running, there are administrative configurations that need to be implemented to support moving into a functional role.

Common administration setup is as follows:

- Set up password policies. A handful of accounts may have been created, but now is a good time to set the policy for how new accounts are to be created.
- Assuming more and more elements are going to be added to the system, establish an audit function so you are aware of all changes to the system. With logging enabled, you can look back to system modifications and determine any unauthorized or authorized changes that may have had a detrimental impact on the system's integrity. This is also helpful in troubleshooting initial problems in complex systems. Even authorized tasks can become troublesome.
- Now that you have set user policies and begun collecting system logs, you start constructing the necessary directory structure for the system. Most important, this task includes the creation of directory and file permissions.

Accessing the System

Assuming the box will be accessible over a network, the next phase is to control the type of remote access for users, services, and applications.

The network setup consists of the following:

- Implement access control lists restricting only the protocols that are going to be used on the system.
- Make protocol stack changes. For example, change the number of permitted open connections or shorten the wait time associated with half-open connections.
- Configure the system to accept or deny remote login and remote procedure calls that are associated with execution of remote applications.

Cleanup

Before installing applications and other things that will affect the security of a system the next step is very important and many still don't do it: applying patches. By the time you get the CDs for installing an operating system there are undoubtedly patches for it. There are three types of patches:

1. *Functionality.* A patch that fixes or enhances a certain function of the system. For example, how memory is handled, performance of network connections, or adding more options to an administrative program.
2. *Feature.* A feature patch increases the use of the system, an added feature.
3. *Security.* A security patch fixes a vulnerability in the system due to unexpected conditions the system is in or a misstep in programming.

The simple fact is that patches will exist and must be applied to ensure the integrity of the system. Moreover, this is not a point and shoot and forget solution. As with many things security, you must be prepared to apply patches regularly.

NETWORK SECURITY

It is tough enough to build a singular secure system, much less thousands of them connected together. It places a great deal of stress on the concept of access, which can be well beyond the control of the computer itself. Now, instead of the hacker having direct access to a system, she can sit halfway around the world and attack the system using the network.

Networks are relatively simple. When a computer wishes to establish communications with another it generates a message augmented with a header, containing logistical information about the source and destination, and the entire package is called a packet. Much like an envelope containing a letter with a "to" and "from" address, the packet is then injected onto the network where network devices manage forwarding the packet from one system to another until the final destination is reached. (Of course, there are hundreds of types of networks and protocols that are used to support this communication. We're addressing the security of the communication and the associated vulnerabilities and not the technology specifically.)

When computers communicate, they do so with discrete messages to each other containing parts of the conversation. You can liken it to sending letters back and forth using a different envelope for each page of the correspondence. When the packets are received, they are assembled and passed into the operating system for processing. To get each packet to its destination, routers are used (at least for networks that use TCP/IP, such as the Internet) to investigate the header and forward it to the next router or final destination. Routers know where to send the packet based on routing information typically acquired by routing protocols — protocols that exist on the same network as the data that help the routers and other networking elements to learn the lay of the land.

As with computer security, there are various characteristics of network security. These are summarized in the following list:

- *Transmission Security.* The protection of data as it is transmitted from one location to another.
- *Protocol Security.* The construction of packets and how they are processed and used to transmit information.
- *Routing Protocol Security.* The information that is shared by network devices to work together to support communications.

- *Network Access Security.* Controlling connectivity from one network to another based on protocol specifics.

TRANSMISSION SECURITY

One aspect of network security is the protection of information in transit. Ensuring sensitive data is protected from unauthorized changes or viewed by unauthorized people (or applications) is an important aspect of secure network communications. Security protocols, such as IPSec (Internet Protocol Security), SSL (Secure Sockets Layer), and SSH (Secure Shell) to name a few, provide authentication and encryption to protect information from unwanted interactions.

Information protection during transmission is a concern for many organizations, as it should be. Network sniffers are devices that can surreptitiously collect packets on a network segment for later investigation. In some scenarios, the information contained in the data portion of a packet is in cleartext, meaning that you can read it without any further processing. E-mail is the most common example of cleartext. Text you type in for an e-mail is placed in several packets and forwarded to a mail server and ultimately to the recipient. In many cases, the contents are in plaintext, which is easily captured, viewed, and possibly altered by unauthorized people without the sender or the recipient any wiser.

There are also protocols that usually work in cleartext. File Transfer Protocol (FTP) and Telnet are interactive sessions between systems that are not provided any protection to keep the commands and passwords private. Another example is Simple Mail Transfer Protocol (SMTP) and Post Office Protocol (POP), protocols that are used for the transmission of e-mail. POP is a common protocol used by many to collect e-mail from their mailboxes. It requires a username and password to be entered in the clear. Anyone sniffing the network looking for this type of session would be privy to the information, and use it to collect your e-mail.

Applying authentication and encryption to a data stream will help ensure that unauthorized systems, users, or applications cannot gain access to the information. Although this is not a complete solution nor will it fully protect you, secure communications are an effective and inexpensive solution to a common security exposure.

PROTOCOL SECURITY

Another characteristic of network security is the protocols that are used to support the communication. Transmission Control Protocol and Internet Protocol (TCP/IP) is the most common protocol used today and is the protocol for use on the Internet. A protocol is the standard by which a communication is established. TCP/IP is the foundation for several other protocols and services, like the ones mentioned above. TCP/IP was developed for communication with very little consideration for security. It is flexible and can support a vast array of communications over a huge distributed network.

There are many protocol weaknesses that are associated with TCP/IP. By using illegal packet structures and manipulating the session management the protocol provides, several types of attacks can materialize. Most notably, Denial-of-Service attacks can use basic features of the protocol to bring systems to their knees. In the late 1990s it was the ping flood attack, such as ping of death, teardrop, and SYN floods that would render a system useless because it was so busy dealing with apparently legitimate session requests.

Other weaknesses in the protocol allowed one system to appear as another. This was an especially effective attack when security was based on assumed trust relationships based on an IP address, the unique identifier of a system on a TCP/IP network. IP spoofing was a technique of replacing the source IP address of a packet to make it appear as though it were coming from a trusted source. To demonstrate, a server provides services to a client system on the same network based on its IP address. A hacker sends a packet from a distant network with a forged source IP address that is the same as the client's. When the server receives the packet, it executes the commands assuming it came from the trusted system.

Of course, when the server responds, it will send the packet to the original client and not the hacker, because it is the original return IP address in the communication. The hacker has to accommodate two things for this to work. One, he has to disable the client system so when it receives a packet from the server acknowledging the communication it doesn't respond with a RESET, effectively shutting down the communication.

Second, because the hacker is not receiving the acknowledgments, he must respond in the appropriate timeframe with all the correct information expected by a normal session. This is when sequence numbers within the TCP/IP protocol and their predictability make the attack plausible. Therefore, acting as a trusted system and predicting the sequence of the communication, the server can be told to accommodate changes in the system to permit direct access by the hacker.

There are thousands of protocols available for communications. Some are foundation protocols, such as TCP/IP, whereas others use TCP/IP as a carrier for higher-level operations, such as SSL, FTP, IPSec, and POP mentioned above. There exist vulnerabilities in foundation protocols as well as higher-level protocols that can be manipulated to circumvent firewalls, routers, switches, intrusion detection systems, and systems to support an attack.

ROUTING PROTOCOL SECURITY

Routing protocols are specific communications between network supporting systems that allow the sharing of network information so a group of devices can collaborate on appropriately forwarding data. When routing data is shared among a group of systems communications can be routed based on network availability, performance, and cost of the connection. Figure 4.2 is an example of a large network supported by the OSPF (Open Shortest Path First) routing protocol. OSPF uses "areas" to define borders for summarizing network routes to different regions, as with this example, or departments.

Given that routing protocols provide the foundation of how data is routed from one location to another they are a consistent target of hackers. If a hacker were able to manipulate the routing information in a router, she could reroute information or use it to change her attack vector to hide her original location. Finally, a hacker can

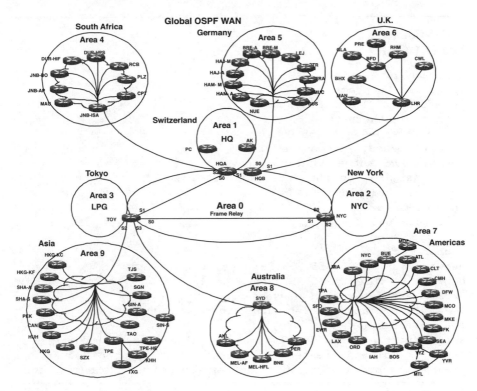

FIGURE 4.2 A Global OSPF Network Design

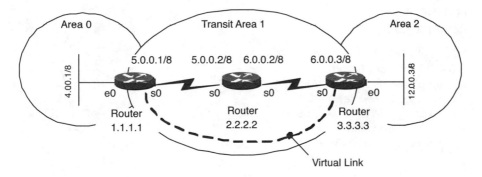

FIGURE 4.3 OSPF Network Design Example Configuration

manipulate the routing, placing stress on a particular section of the network causing a form of denial of service.

There are methods of securing routing protocols. Continuing with OSPF as an example, you can apply authentication to the exchange of information to ensure integrity. Figure 4.3 shows an example of applying MD5 (Message Digest 5) authentication to OSPF communications.

LISTING 4.1
Router 1.1.1.1

```
hostname r1.1.1.1
interface Loopback0
ip address 1.1.1.1 255.0.0.0
interface Ethernet0
ip address 4.0.0.1 255.0.0.0
ip ospf message-digest-key 1 md5 cisco
!-- The MD5 authentication key is
!-- configured on the interface as "cisco."
interface Serial0
ip address 5.0.0.1 255.0.0.0
clockrate 64000
!
router ospf 2
network 4.0.0.0 0.255.255.255 area 0
network 5.0.0.0 0.255.255.255 area 1
area 0 authentication message-digest
!-- This command enables MD5 authentication for area 0
!-- on the router.
area 1 virtual-link 3.3.3.3 message-digest-key 1 md5 cisco
!-- This command creates the virtual link between Router
!-- 1.1.1.1 and Router 3.3.3.3 after successful authentication.
```

LISTING 4.2
Router 3.3.3.3

```
hostname r3.3.3.3
interface Loopback0
ip address 3.3.3.3 255.0.0.0
interface Ethernet0
ip address 12.0.0.3 255.0.0.0
interface Serial0
ip address 6.0.0.3 255.0.0.0
!
router ospf 2
network 12.0.0.0 0.255.255.255 area 2
network 6.0.0.0 0.255.255.255 area 1
area 0 authentication message-digest
!-- This command enables MD5 authentication for area 0
!-- on the router.
area 1 virtual-link 1.1.1.1 message-digest-key 1 md5 cisco
!-- This command creates the virtual link to area 0 via
!-- the transit area 1.
```

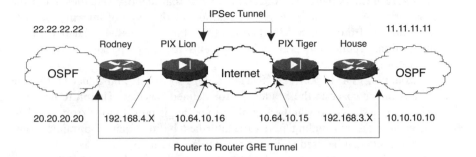

FIGURE 4.4 VPN and GRE Used to Protect OSPF Protocols over the Internet

Based on Figure 4.3, the Listings 4.1 and 4.2 are sample configurations for Cisco routers using MD5 authentication for OSPF.

As mentioned above, protocols may leverage others to accommodate functionality or security and routing protocols are no exception. Virtual private networking offers secured communication using encryption and authentication to protect data in transit. VPNs can be used to secure routing information between devices.

In Figure 4.4, we see two networks that share information over the Internet, including routing protocols. As with typical Internet connections there is a firewall connecting the network to the Internet and an internal router supporting the intranet, in this example, networks 11.11.11.11 and 22.22.22.22. A Generic Routing Encapsulation (GRE) tunnel is created between the two intranet routers, Rodney and House. A GRE tunnel is a very simple form of encapsulation—no security—that effectively simplifies configuring the firewalls and intermediate routers to allow OSPF to pass.

An IPSec VPN is established between the two firewalls, Tiger and Lion, to protect all the communications between the two networks. By combining GRE and IPSec, the OSPF protocol is provided isolation and security while traversing the Internet. The GRE tunnel provides a conduit for OSPF to interact with other systems in a manner that does not influence the protocol's ability to "map" the network. There are various characteristics of OSPF that have the potential to be inadvertently affected by a VPN. GRE has very little overhead, which can eliminate many problems in troubleshooting down the road and IPSec is only concerned with encrypting a very simple IP protocol to support routing services.

When performing a penetration test you can use routing protocols to learn about the network layout, which can be very helpful in creating an attack plan. This can be exceptionally valuable when network mapping techniques and tools fail, but an insecure router is accessible by a tester that has all the routing tables representing internal systems.

NETWORK ACCESS CONTROLS

Network security can also be characterized by applying access controls, limiting the availability of communications between systems or applications.

In TCP/IP headers there are collections of bits that identify specifics about the communication. Application ports are an example of this type of information. The port is a number from 1 to 65535 that identifies the services associated with the communication. Application ports allow systems to accept packets destined for specific services or applications.

For example, POP is port 110, SMTP is 25, FTP is 21, and telnet is 23. The first 10 bits of the space in the header are for defined services. Therefore numbers 1 to 1023 are assigned to standard applications. High ports, those from 1024 to 65,535, are for the responding port to established bidirectional communications. Application ports can be used to limit access to a system.

A firewall's basic function is to look up these ports in the header and determine (based on an installed rule base) if the packet should be dropped or passed through for communications. An internal system may accept communications on ports 21, 23, 25, 80, and 110, but the firewall only permits packets with destination port 80, HTTP from the Internet, another aspect of defense-in-depth.

As you can see, network security is realized through different controls placed on the interaction of systems and the movement of data. A hacker has the opportunity to interact with any one of these attributes to perform an attack.

SERVICE SECURITY

Services are processes that run on a computer to provide common functions for applications, users, or other services. Services fall into two very similar categories:

1. *Operational.* A process that provides a service to applications or users for functionality.
2. *Network.* A process that supports the exchange of information for network services.

The following are examples of operational services used in Microsoft Windows:

- *Security Accounts Manager.* Stores security information for local user accounts.
- *Plug and Play.* Enables a computer to recognize and adapt to hardware changes with little or no user input.
- *Net Logon.* Supports pass-through authentication of account logon events for computers in a domain.
- *Event Log.* Enables event log messages issued by Windows-based programs and components to be viewed in Event Viewer. This service cannot be stopped.
- *Logical Disk Manager.* Configures hard disk drives and volumes. The service only runs for configuration processes and then stops.
- *Indexing Service.* Indexes contents and properties of files on local and remote computers; provides rapid access to files through flexible querying language.

The following are examples of network services:

- *DNS*. Resolves and caches Domain Name System (DNS) names. If this service is stopped, DNS names will not be resolved and Internet services not located.
- *telnet*. Enables a remote user to log on to a computer and run programs. If this service is stopped, remote user access to programs might be unavailable.
- *FTP*. Allows the exchange of files over the network.

Regardless of type, each service is an opportunity to attack a system. Potential vulnerabilities in how services interact with a network, applications, and other parts of the operating system make them the focus of hackers. What makes services so attractive is that many are weak, do not offer levels of security configuration, and can have a huge impact. Services typically have privileged access to other system resources and given the number of services running on a typical computer (a quick check of my Windows XP system reveals at least 42 services running and another 30+ disabled or not started) there is a plethora of options for a hacker.

There are countless examples of service vulnerabilities leading to massive attacks. One could argue that service insecurity is the predominant avenue of attack affecting millions of computers and costing companies lots of money. On January 25, 2003, the SQL Slammer worm became the fastest spreading worm in the history of the Internet. The SQL Server Resolution Service (SSRS) is used by MS SQL 2000 to provide referral services for multiple server instances running on the same machine. The service listens for requests on UDP port 1434 and returns the address and port number of the SQL server instance that provides access to the requested database. Slammer uses the SSRS "Keepalive" protocol to find and infect other SQL servers. SSRS is essentially an SQL ping service that promotes interdomain communications that Slammer . . . well, slammed.

A well-known "problem port" on Microsoft systems is the Remote Procedure Call (RPC) service implemented by default on most Microsoft platforms. The RPC service is used to allow programs on one system to seamlessly execute on another. Although the service and associated protocol are standardized, Microsoft has some customized attributes specific to their implementation, hence certain vulnerabilities are present in only Microsoft's implementation of the service. Recently, the Blaster worm used the weakness in the RPC service to infect systems, making them spread the worm and constantly crash the system. As an added benefit, the worm includes the ability to launch a TCP SYN flood Denial-of-Service attack against windowsupdate.com.

One more point worth noting: security patches were available for both of these vulnerabilities before the worms were released.

Services represent an interesting attack vector for hackers and testers alike. By leveraging insecurities in the service itself or using them as a gateway into the operating system or application, services can represent a substantial threat to company security if not properly managed.

APPLICATION SECURITY

As we climb up the layers of security, applications represent the last step.

An application, especially software, is a collection of libraries, executables, and other utilities used to accomplish a wide variety of tasks. Microsoft Word, the application I'm using to write this, grants me the necessary tools to create text, format, and check spelling (it is hoped).

Applications can come with their own forms of vulnerabilities and weaknesses that could be used by a hacker. Some of these are benign from the perspective of the Internet because they require complete access to the system. Nevertheless, there are applications that hackers attack because they do represent a chance to gain greater access. Sometimes the application will supply the much-needed last step to obtaining the target data.

Software introduces its own set of security concerns. Applications can have errors, better known as bugs, which can not only disrupt operations but can provide a hole through which a hacker can crawl. A software error can lead to massive failures, either on purpose—as in a case of a hacker using an application fault to bring down several systems—or by accident, such as implementing a rare configuration that exposes a bug in the software.

Faults in application development and design are arguably the predominant time consumers of any security professional. Basically, there are thousands of new bugs discovered or reported daily and administrators have to review them and determine if the application is vulnerable to an attack. Administrators must perform some form of analysis to measure the cost of fixing the vulnerability and actually implement some change to rectify the problem. Bugs in applications can have an impact on routers, servers, workstations, databases, e-mail programs, Web browsers, back-office applications, and any system that uses software to perform tasks on behalf of the user or other applications.

Hackers can leverage bugs in programs as a wedge to gain greater access or use it to support other attacks. An example of a hacker using a bug to gain greater access is usually realized by injecting code or scripts, or obtaining data about a system through the error. Buffer overruns are an example where data (such as a command or script) is placed into a field normally used for some other purpose. When the application accesses the field, it arbitrarily dumps the code into memory, the overrun, allowing it to be implanted and execute. There are ample examples of these types of vulnerabilities that can be used by a hacker in many ways. Following are a few examples I collected while writing this chapter:

- There is a bug in Microsoft's Internet Explorer (IE) 5.5 and 6.0 that allows hackers to run arbitrary scripts on a remote system using cookies. IE has an error in how it manages security zones, allowing a hacker to run programs embedded in a cookie. Because the cookies are seen as part of the "Local Zone" they are accepted, trusted, and processed.
- Snort, an open source intrusion detection system employed by many companies, is vulnerable to a DoS attack. Snort 1.8.3 does not properly define the minimum ICMP header size, which allows remote attackers to

cause a denial of service (crash and core dump) via a malformed ICMP packet. It is conceivable that if a hacker knows there is a Snort-based intrusion detection system, he can effectively shut it down allowing him to continue the attack unnoticed or recorded.

- Real Networks RealPlayer version 8.0 and earlier allows remote attackers to execute code contained in the length value of the header, which actually exceeds the length of the header.
- A seemingly harmless feature in MS Outlook 8.5, the "Automatically put people I reply to in my address book" does not check to see if the "reply to" address is the same as the "from" address. With this option on, a remote attacker could spoof a legitimate address and intercept messages intended for others.
- The Microsoft Exchange Server 2000 System Attendant gives the "Everyone" group privileges to the WinReg key, which could allow remote attackers to read or modify registry keys.
- Internet Explorer 5.01, 5.5, and 6.0 allow remote attackers to read files on a remote system via malformed requests to the GetObject function, which bypasses some of GetObject's security checks.
- In Microsoft Windows NT and Windows 2000, a trusting domain that receives authorization information from a trusted domain does not verify that the trusted domain is authoritative for all listed Security Identifiers (SIDs). This could allow a remote attacker to gain Domain Administrator privileges on the trusting domain by injecting SIDs from other domains into the authorization data of the trusting domain.

A good application development policy should define requirements and coding standards. During a code review of an application, the standards and practices can be compared directly to the application architecture in an effort to reduce vulnerabilities at the time of development. When executed correctly, code reviews will uncover many straightforward but dangerous security violations, such as:

- Buffer overflows
- Race conditions
- Tainted input
- Format string issues
- Trust management
- Third-party package connectivity
- Input validation
- Temporary file or memory usage
- Poor cryptography
- Appropriate logging and auditing

Similarly, with an application architecture review, the plan is to identify components and designs that present a security risk. This is achieved by validating trust relationships, ensuring appropriate use of encryption, access controls, and authentication, and reviewing component interdependencies.

Application developers are challenged with writing code that considers all points of attack someone may try to exploit. It is reasonably assumed that it is not an easy task, but certainly not insurmountable. However, what about when the programmers introduce their own vulnerabilities? Some of these are simple oversights, but represent a huge risk to customers of their product. In November 2001, Microsoft SQL Server and Microsoft Data Engine shipped with a null default password on the administrative account. Therefore, if the password was not changed, it could represent a hole. The reality is that good security practices demand setting a new password, so the real impact of such an error is questionable, but the example does demonstrate these errors exist.

There are many more examples that tend to make consumers think twice about the security practices of software vendors. Just as recently as February of 2002, Oracle Database Server version 9iAS installed with several default log-in accounts. The usernames and passwords have been made publicly available on the Internet and could be used by an attacker to gain access to an Oracle server. Depending on the components chosen at installation time, Oracle Database Server version 9iAS (and possibly other versions) includes in its default configuration as many as 160 accounts with known usernames and passwords. Many of the passwords are the same as the corresponding username, making it even easier for attackers to gain access. In this example, Oracle simply did not include the concept of security in their development process. Fortunately, they did not try to hide their blunder and publicized the poor practice.

Unfortunately, very bad practices go unnoticed until it is too late. There are examples where default usernames and passwords were implemented but not documented. They had to be discovered by a hacker or tester. Avaya Cajun switches recently required a firmware update that contained multiple undocumented users with default passwords. Access to these accounts results in developer privileges, allowing read/write access to the switch.

In nearly all of these cases, the software vendor provided patches, updates, or workarounds to accommodate their gross oversight. Applications, software, code, firmware, whatever you call them, are vulnerable to human error. It is for this reason that application security takes an incredible amount of time and energy to accommodate.

SECURITY ARCHITECTURE

At the beginning of this chapter, two models were introduced: defense-in-depth and security architecture. In this section we discuss a common security architecture.

Companies have a competitive imperative to adopt comprehensive technical architectures to support business demands and transformations. By the same token, a security architecture must not only exist but also interact with the business objectives and provide a reference framework that serves as a fundamental guide when new technology and requirements are introduced into the company.

Today, a great number of corporate entities have been forced to integrate their systems and applications with the Internet to remain competitive. In order to reduce costs, gain greater return on investments, or simply keep up with the current of

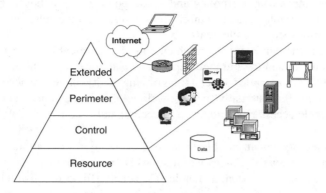

FIGURE 4.5 Example of a Typical Security Architecture

expected services, businesses are integrating the Internet and complex systems into their core objectives. Many of the companies have leveraged the Internet for partner access, remote user access, customer services, supply-chain management, and data warehousing. Physical boundaries and specific chokepoints alone cannot address the multifaceted and dynamic relationships within and among today's businesses. In direct correlation with advances in technology, business demands, and the ever-present competitive differentiator, security has grown inherently more complex in the actual business environment as well as philosophically.

As we move into an age of multi-access, multiple platforms, access technologies, and the increase of regulation and legal requirements, companies are forced to adopt new infrastructure designs, which in turn require a variety of access management and layered security. To accommodate the dynamics of business, technology, and environments, it is necessary to adopt a security architecture that will allow flexibility in operations, in addition to providing a point of reference so that one can make sound decisions when change in demands and environment occurs.

There are several examples and types of security architectures from organizations such as the Department of Defense (DOD), National Security Agency (NSA), Federal Bureau of Investigation (FBI), National Institute of Standards and Technology (NIST; or more specifically, Computer Security Resource Center (CSRC)), Internet Engineering Task Force (IETF), and CERT (formally known as Computer Emergency Response Team). Each ranges greatly in complexity, ability, and, of course, cost. However, there is a consistent theme among all that can be applied to today's Internet-enabled economy.

Commonalities among many of the architectures that are available are four layers that can be identified to promote sound security integration and management of technology, information, and policy (see Figure 4.5).

1. The *resource* layer is where services and data reside. It is the home of servers, applications, databases, workstations, and storage.
2. One of the more critical and complex is the *control* layer, which provides identity and access management services. Moreover, the control layer is the point where policy becomes reality in the technical space. It provides

management with the policy and is the point where policy is bound to data to promote greater authorization across the other characteristics of the entire security architecture.

3. There is the *perimeter* layer, which enforces a logical boundary between the Internet and the intranet, departments, applications, and even users.
4. Finally, the *extended* layer is a growing entity in its own right. This represents the externally facing envelope of influence and security, such as remote access risks, application access, and E-commerce.

For business to remain nimble in today's economy organizations will have to confront many challenges. Enterprises must work much more closely with external entities to maintain a consistent and agile value chain. To accomplish the challenge, companies must successfully manage relationships—internal and external—and the information flow between them. There remains the need to work closely with partners, customers, and various providers, but qualifying that communication and the necessary controls is what a security architecture provides.

One may assume that security can be rigid, but due to mergers and acquisitions, environmental changes, or simply rapid economic changes, security does not have the opportunity to remain static. The Holy Grail of security is a technology and architecture that establishes an environment which remains constant regardless of changing business demands.

Therefore, a security architecture is a policy-supporting overlay that can interact with users, resources, and external influences. To accommodate the desired flexibility, the architecture must be built for general purposes and well conceived. It can provide broad guidelines to allow for conceptual segmentation, encouraging the aggregation of various services and products to function optimally within a layer or interactively with others. It must be deployed in an abstract manner that separates physical from logical, focusing on the latter. For example, each layer could have its own characteristics that can be interchanged with other layers, such as the control layer, whereas some layers represent technology limited to only one specific layer, such as the perimeter layer. Firewalls are traditionally associated with the perimeter, whereas authentication resides in the control layer, and authentication (logically or physically) can exist in the perimeter or the resource layer. Each layer is loosely coupled with the next, allowing for flexibility but reducing redundancy.

Due to merger and acquisitions, legacy systems that may not support a higher form of adopted security measures, and highly complex business requirements, security infrastructures today rarely follow a comprehensive overlying architecture. The result is one of two possibilities or a combination of both: a point solution that focuses on limited control of specific information flows, or strengthening within a layer, instead of the points of interaction with other layers of the security model. For example, many organizations focus on the perimeter by implementing firewalls and realize security in the resource layer by leveraging traditional operating system security. However, the lack of a comprehensive control layer weakens the interaction between the perimeter and resource layers and could represent a vulnerability within an organization.

RESOURCE LAYER

Resources, as previously defined, are systems, applications, internal users, databases, services, printers, local area networks, operating systems, and data. Resources represent what organizations feel are their core technical requirements to make money, or supporting mechanisms for the evolution of the business as a whole. Nevertheless, resources are effectively what you want to protect, control access to, and use to conduct business. In that light, not every resource demands the same level of security. It is not uncommon to have useful information destroyed with little or no impact on the business operations. On the other hand, the slightest unauthorized change or loss of a specific piece of information can be catastrophic.

Accurately determining the resources that exist at this layer is not obvious and is especially difficult for large organizations that have multiple business units with different demands on those resources. Nevertheless, identifying your resources and the value to your company's continued success should be the primary goal of any security manger.

The fact is that resources are money—to someone—and the disruption of that fragile yet complex relationship between business and information systems can wreak havoc. Understanding the resources and their role within the scope of daily business is crucial to supporting a successful penetration test. Although seemingly obvious, this is rarely considered a requirement for a successful test. This assumption could not be more wrong. You cannot gain true value from a penetration test without knowing what your digital assets are and their value to the organization. Without information from a risk analysis there is no feasible method for translating vulnerabilities into an actionable remediation plan. With the pressures of today's economy and the constant demand for more efficiency in business, the likelihood that money will be invested to fix a security hole that cannot be financially justified is just wishful thinking.

CONTROL

The control layer is an opportunity to identify and group systems that manage access to resources. In a perfect world all identification, authentication, and authorization to resources would be controlled by a single system. Unfortunately, we're not quite there yet (unless you read sales collateral for some identity management product vendors). Thanks to legacy systems, different application architectures, and different approaches to applying security controls, the control layer is typically made up of many diverse products.

The result of this scenario is a fragmented security architecture with controls existing at varying degrees of intensity and rarely centralized. The term "fragmented" may seem harsh, but many organizations have several types of authentication systems from many manufacturers and few have centralized management, much less provisioning.

The control layer represents an enormous challenge to nearly every company no matter the variety of applications and systems. Today there are many vendors providing identity management solutions that attempt to integrate most environments to provide a common authentication system in addition to providing access controls in multiple heterogeneous environments. Therefore, we're seeing a trend in many firms on focusing on the control layer to meet security demands in a distributed environment.

Penetration testing at some point will run head on into the control layer. Quite frankly, a good tester will find a way around by seeking other vulnerabilities that will get them through the proverbial back door. For example, when a tester is attempting to access a router he may perform a brute force attack directly against the router, basically entering password after password until the correct one is entered. This may seem archaic but it can be productive and there are many hacker utilities out there that will perform the attack on your behalf: just point and shoot.

An example of working around the control layer is finding a hole that allows access to control layer information. Let's say an NT system is exposed to ports 137 and 139; under certain circumstances you could use tools like DumpSec to obtain the SAM (Security Account Manager) database. Once acquired, you can use offline attack tools against the database, such as L0pht Crack, to get the usernames and passwords, essentially bypassing the control of the targeted system.

The control layer can be considered the most complex and logically structured of all the layers. Therefore, it is no easy task to clearly identify and categorize the control layer within any security architecture, but understanding the layer is essential for establishing goals of the test and establishing the foundation for interpreting and absorbing the results.

PERIMETER

Perimeter security is the most obvious layer in the security model. Basically, it's where your network stops and someone else's begins. It can be your connection to the Internet, the segregation of certain system types, or business units with different security needs. Suffice it to say, the perimeter is usually easily identifiable. However, through the years the actual security that can be employed has come under fire. At the time this book was written, it has become generally accepted that firewalls (the workhorse of the perimeter) are a necessary attribute defining the perimeter.

The perimeter is much more than a firewall and there are other technologies that promote secure communications between trusted and not-so-trusted networks. Intrusion detection and, most recently, intrusion prevention systems have provided another layer of security for the perimeter.

In short, the perimeter has to be labeled as the first line of defense in a suite of protective layers of security. This seems painfully obvious to anyone trained in military tactics, but it is also well known that many companies rely solely on their perimeter for security, fully aware their plan is flawed.

So what does this mean to a hacker—or a penetration tester? Many years ago when firewalls were fresh and changing dramatically to deal with the increasing volume and complexity of Internet threats, there was a practice called firewalking. People would spend their entire hacking or professional careers trying to get through firewalls for the simple purpose of proving it can be done. As each new bypass was discovered the vendors would come up with a solution, then a new bypass was found, and so on. Ultimately, the dedication died off because the sophistication of hackers moved on to bigger and better attacks with greater potential for success and less for being detected. But the practice has become fundamental in attacks; everyone has a firewall (or should), and getting past a firewall is an essential skill. Now we're seeing much of the same evolution in IDS with attackers using techniques to go undetected through the firewall and onto a network.

Many firewalls and IDSs are being tuned more regularly to thwart sophisticated attacks and as a tester and customer of a penetration test this has to be considered for effectiveness. In addition to the entire perimeter architecture and its inherent complexities discussed above, the act of the test can help greatly in establishing the elusive baseline for what should be categorized as an attack and which of those attacks demands attention. It is not uncommon for companies to invest in IDS and get inundated with alarms and start backing off on the sensitivity of the system, usually rendering IDS ineffective. Having a penetration test performed is a unique opportunity to tune perimeter security technology in ways not possible with any other method. This raises the question of why would a firm seeking a test not want the consultant performing the test to know IDS was present? Of course there may be circumstances where not knowing details would be desired, but that's what this book is about—making those decisions logically and understanding the benefits and losses.

EXTENDED

The extended layer is how corporate security is projected out into the ether. The most basic example is customers going to Web sites that have a security policy defining how information collected from online transactions is used. VPNs for roaming users are another example of how corporate security influences information protection beyond the perimeter. Organizations are concerned with the security of their intellectual property, brand name, and various information assets that are accessed and shared in many ways with varying types of users.

Methods for sharing information beyond the perimeter include e-mail, PDAs, wireless messaging (cell phones, Blackberries), and direct access, such as VPNs and dial-up, all with their own forms of insecurity. For example, VPNs are widely considered to be secure and this is true when is comes to the transportation of information, exactly what VPNs were designed to accomplish, although the exposure of digital assets at the termination point outside the perimeter is under question. If a user, say the CFO, downloads the financial spreadsheets of the company onto her laptop while on the road using hotel high-speed access in the room, what is the implied security of that data? The layers of security realized at the corporate head-quarters are exponentially more secure than a lowly laptop.

Of course, extranets can fall within the extended layer of security as can remote users and customers. Communications with business partners and even comparators require a different application of security controls. Beyond technical solutions associated with extended security, organizations have to address legal issues, regulatory requirements, and Service Level Agreements (SLAs). In addition, the ability to identify users and systems of partners on both sides of the network plays a major role in ensuring security measures are enacted in accordance with what is expected and agreed upon.

Extended networks, for many organizations, represent an enormous challenge with regard to security controls. Different partners have unique access requirements, want specific security policies in place, and have varying SLAs and legal obligations, all leading to security mayhem. Not only is this a challenge for organizations that have many partner or customer network communications, but a tester performing a penetration test is exposed to a wide range of imposed borders that are not clearly marked. The result is a virtual line that a hacker is not forced to acknowledge. The line is a thin border between the customer's network and the partner's, representing a potential to accidentally stumble into a system that was not within the scope of the engagement. This plays clearly into the hackers' world: they don't care about legal requirements, agreements, or the scope of some test; whatever meets their needs will be exploited.

There are occasions where the partner networks and communications are included in the scope of a penetration test, but the ramifications are immense. Without proper agreements to protect all parties involved the result could be disastrous.

So, the risks associated with extended networks are severalfold—security in the form of technology, access management, legal agreements, support issues, and so on—not to mention the complexities with which the tester is faced. Therefore, having detailed documentation about the architecture and environment is instrumental in the planning of a sound security model and provides the foundation for making decisions on the scope and scale of a penetration test.

5 Information Security Program

Managing the technical and procedural complexities of information security can become overwhelming for any company. A security program provides the foundation and guidance as to how security is realized throughout a firm and is crucial to the management of security. The lack of a security program is typically reflected by the poor state of security for an entire organization and the tactical nature of security-related activities. For companies that maintain a security program, there is a clear understanding of expectations, processes, and even documents that support the program and ultimately the maintenance of security. To properly prepare for an ethical hack, the existence of a defined security program can be vital in ensuring the test is supportive to the overall program and ultimately the integration of the test's results into the business needs of the organization.

An information security program implements a repeatable and sustainable process to manage overall business risk. Risk management may not be limited to information security, but addresses all risk to which an organization may be exposed. For example, the agriculture industry routinely sells short commodities contracts to manage the risk of market fluctuations, and individuals think nothing of participating in health insurance programs to manage personal risk. Risk management will also vary depending on the risk tolerance of the organization. Shrinkage acceptable to a retail enterprise would be wholly unacceptable to a bank.

The formulation of a security program and the value of a penetration test require that risk first be identified and then quantified in some meaningful way. A well-constructed information security management program allows organizations to readily identify assets, their value, and impact on the business in the event the assets are lost or damaged. Additionally—and inherently—a security program promotes tools and best practices for securing information systems and managing risk to the business information systems.

SCOPE OF INFORMATION SECURITY PROGRAMS

A security program is concerned with preserving the confidentiality, integrity, and availability of an organization's information assets and information should be considered an asset in whatever form. This is a "big picture" approach to enhance the breadth of risk analysis, requiring a multidisciplinary look at risk identification.

Unfortunately, it is common for organizations to consider network- and host-based security programs as sufficient security. In reality, these types of focused programs are subsets of an information security program, dealing with the specific risks involved with the transport, processing, and storage of an organization's information.

A comprehensive security program must also consider, for example, physical security, including physical access controls and physical media handling procedures. Although much attention is traditionally lavished on logical controls such as firewalls and access lists, perceptive hackers are fully aware that information can potentially be obtained through activities such as dumpster diving. Every day confidential printouts and unsanitized magnetic media are thrown out by unsuspecting organizations with stellar network security controls but marginal information security controls. Understanding not only the company's digital assets and logical and physical controls, the expected management of risk based on the security program provides a substantial supporting element to the employment of a penetration test.

Another aspect often overlooked is the organization's personnel. Typically, an organization will be very cognizant of education and experience requirements for personnel, and some industries may require varying degrees of background checks. This only establishes their credibility and suitability to perform their jobs, but does not address information security in any meaningful way. Unless the level or status of the employees is directly related to their roles with regard to information use, access, responsibility, and other security concerns related to digital assets, the role of the employee and the investigative employment process has little measurable support for information security.

A comprehensive security program should be functional role-based, recognizing that individual employees may fulfill multiple or shifting functions within an organization and with each change comes information security considerations that have to be measured.

Role identification allows for the specific assignment of information security responsibilities, as well as the basis for role-based information security awareness training. Perceptive hackers are very familiar with social engineering and skilled at extracting information from trusting and well-meaning employees. If personnel are unclear regarding their responsibilities, unaware of the potential threat environment, and uninformed as to recourse, they no longer serve as an effective layer of defense. When defining the scope of an information security program, it is important to recognize that security is not just a technical problem, nor is there only a technical solution.

Ethical hacking is testing security through the act of exploitation, the exploitation of anything that is assumed to provide a layer of control protecting resources, information, or other forms of assets. A security program defines the necessary characteristics to ensure each layer of security is working in accordance with expectations, in addition to ensuring continuity of security from one layer to another.

Much like the quantum leap of an excited particle, information is afforded security in layers applied in different ways as it is created, transmitted, and stored, moving from one control mechanism to another. Security is ensuring no meaningful gaps between the layers exist.

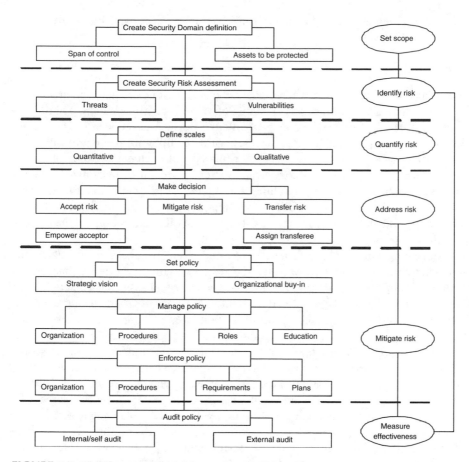

FIGURE 5.1 The Process of Risk Management within a Program

THE PROCESS OF INFORMATION SECURITY

Effective information security is an iterative process (see Figure 5.1). The process must identify and mitigate present risk, as well as allow feedback into the process to mitigate future risk.

When developing an information security program, the instinctive first step is to look at the technical and managerial structure of an organization in an effort to determine the best course of action based on the industry's security demands communicated by best practices, standards, and regulations. However, by beginning at a much higher level, risk, the program will be aligned to business elements and not be influenced by the nuances of technical firefights and dissimilar management practices. By approaching the creation of a security program by using the element of risk, the process is much more efficient and applicable in the end. In addition, by taking a nontechnical, business-level approach to security, the planning of the penetration test will be clearly aligned to the economics of the company. There will be plenty of opportunities to take into consideration technical specifics during other phases in the framework.

IDENTIFY RISK

Identification of risk involves identification of assets, threats, and vulnerabilities. Assets are classically defined as something of value to an organization, and may be tangible, such as hardware, or may be intangible, such as goodwill. Threats are events that offer potential harm to an asset. Vulnerabilities are inherent weaknesses that may allow a threat to occur. Risk is associated with each combination of threats and vulnerabilities. To further complicate matters, threats may be realized by multiple vulnerabilities, and vulnerabilities may be the basis for multiple threats. This results in the fact that assets will face multiple risks, with varying degrees of both probability and harm. Identification of risk is the first fundamental step of the process of information security.

Ethical hacking has become a tool to formulate an awareness of the vulnerabilities that represent a threat to assets. The tester is acting as a threat (hacker), in search of vulnerabilities that will allow the exposure of an asset, such as credit card numbers. In doing so, the test has the potential to reveal the fundamental elements necessary to create a comprehensive foundation to employing security throughout an organization. However, without planning and clear assignment of threat, asset, and vulnerability scope, the test is limited and only helpful in the larger scope. Assignment of threat is related to the type of attack or hacker mindset. Obviously, assets are data, services, applications, or anything that represents a measurable impact on business success. Vulnerability scope, an interesting concept, is the hard definition of a vulnerability and that definition will affect the planning and execution of a penetration test. Is an employee's incorrect answer a vulnerability? That depends on the information provided and the feasible impact on business. A traditional vulnerability is associated with technology; however, when considering the challenge of defining vulnerability scope during your next penetration test don't be surprised at the issues that arise. Nevertheless, the exercise will be invaluable to the success of the test and the integration of the results for the betterment of the company.

When performing a risk analysis the empirical data collected from the act of exploiting a vulnerability will lend more granularity and accuracy to the deliverable and provide clear guidance in implementing acceptable controls in dealing with the risk in accordance with the security program.

Risk Analysis Process

A risk is considered the probability of a threat agent exploiting a vulnerability resulting in damage, disruption, or loss of a system or information. Risk analysis is used to ensure that security is cost effective and relevant to the identified threats. It assists companies in prioritizing their risks and illustrates the amount of resources required to protect against those risks in a proportionate manner. The main purpose of performing a risk analysis is to quantify or qualify the impact of potential threats or to put a value on the loss of business functionality.

Performing an analysis enables an organization to align its security program objectives with its business objectives and requirements. The overall success is based on the amount of alignment these maintain. When an enterprise knows and understands how much its assets are worth, and the level of threat to which they are exposed, the company can then determine the investment that is required to protect them. Therefore, a penetration test can expose vulnerabilities that would be considered high risk for a common infrastructure without a firm understanding of the value of the exposed assets. As demonstrated in Figure 5.2, the process for performing a risk analysis can be extensive. The ability to identify risk, leading to the determination of threats, vulnerabilities, and the likelihood all fall within the realm of ethical hijacking.

The two main results of a risk analysis are the identification of risks and the cost versus benefit justification of the countermeasures. Both are vitally important to the creation of a risk mitigation strategy. The hard question for business owners and IT managers is to determine how much risk exposure an enterprise can afford. For example, if a new Web server is to be implemented, which provides profitable business functionality, steps must be taken to ensure it is protected from an unwarranted attack. At this level, the enterprise must confirm that the level of risk it is exposed to is kept at a minimum and proportionate security measures are in place.

There are many benefits to conducting a risk analysis. It creates a clear cost-to-value rationale for security protections, essentially providing investment guidance when implementing security control measures based on the value and the risk to valued systems and other cyber assets. The results of the risk analysis can also influence the decision-making process when dealing with hardware configuration and software system design. Because hardware configuration and software system design should be standardized across the enterprise, this exercise should occur early, and be revisited on a regular basis. If a risk analysis is performed on a regular basis, it ensures that the configurations and designs are constantly being improved as each new threat is introduced, affecting the level of risk realized. As you can see, a regular penetration test can provide the necessary fodder to support a risk analysis. In fact, this is the goal of a penetration test; however, many have lost sight of this and the results are never integrated into an overall security program.

Conducting a risk analysis can also help a company to focus its security resources where they are needed most. The risk analysis pinpoints the areas most at risk, which the resources can then dedicate their time to mitigate, and revisit these high-risk areas often to ensure the exposure remains constant and controlled.

There are several steps to performing a risk analysis. Typically, the core business functions and requirements are identified to begin the development of a technology map and its role within the framework of the business demands. This initial phase of a risk analysis assists in beginning to understand the value of networking and application assets and lays the foundation for establishing the relationships among business units, partners, and customers that further assists in measuring the value of data. For example, a large organization may have several sites with many or only one department at each site. Each site and business unit has a role within the organization, and based on that role the information systems and data linked to that

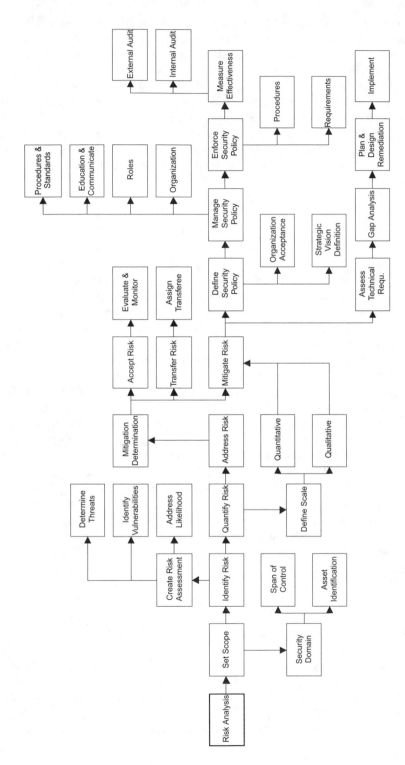

FIGURE 5.2 Detailed Risk Analysis Process

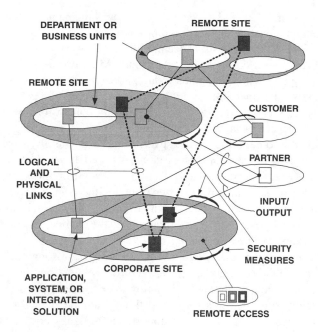

FIGURE 5.3 Breaking the Organization into Logical and Some Physical Components to Initially Simplify the Process

department can be measured to determine the impact of loss, even if for a brief time. Finally, by breaking the company into logical elements (system inputs and outputs) as demonstrated in Figure 5.3, the business requirements can be translated to the implemented technical solutions.

Once there is a picture of the organization structure and fundamental business processes, the analysis can begin to assess the technology related to providing the critical business functions. As the technologies are defined, their exposure to threats and the likelihood of those threats being exploited are determined through a test.

Each area of technology is exposed to different threats based on access, population using the asset, and vulnerabilities within the systems or applications. Then the focus turns to the implemented security measures. The security systems that are currently in place must be identified and assessed. This would include firewalls, intrusion detection systems, RADIUS servers, and so on, any system that has been implemented to protect the company's assets. The security systems are highlighted first inasmuch as mitigating their risks is based on the important role they play in the realization of security. If a major vulnerability has been identified in a version of firewall software that can jeopardize the integrity of the firewall, this is now considered a high risk until that software is patched or upgraded. Finally, the other technical elements of the organization are assessed to determine their exposures and ultimately the data they maintain.

The overall goal is to identify digital assets that are important to the business, assign some form of measurement of value, determine input and output requirements, such as partner interaction, and assess the threats to the data and systems based on vulnerabilities and their likelihood of exploitation.

As you can see, a risk analysis, especially one that covers an entire organization, can be complicated, time consuming, and difficult. Moreover, it is clear why ethical hacking is so popular with companies today. There needs to be some manner by which the impacts of vulnerabilities are gauged to complete the risk analysis. Prior to ethical hacking, this was accomplished by drawing conclusions based on similar companies' experiences or industry standards.

It is impossible to demonstrate the severity of a vulnerability exploited during a penetration test unless the data or systems exposed have a measurable value. However, tests are performed regularly when there is no firm or documented awareness of value. A company having a test performed without an initially defined asset valuation is simply approaching its concerns from the outside in, basing the risk of the company on the exposure to any information and the applicable security measures based on the assumed value of the assets exposed. In these scenarios, it is extremely rare for the results of the test to evolve into meaningful resolutions. The tactical mitigation of vulnerabilities may appear to be effective; however, they are typically the result of point solutions that are not taking the organization's security strategy into consideration. Typically, in a very short timeframe, the applied solution begins to become a problem for management, support, and on-going costs that were never properly justified.

It should not be concluded that this is a poor tactic when performing a test in the scope of a future risk analysis. In reality, many companies have an inherent understanding of what systems, data, and applications are important to the organization's success and therefore the test has some merit. Although, when the results of the test are provided, determining the next steps becomes time consuming because the severity of the attack and the related exposures have to be assessed to implement proportionate security controls. The concern is that by the time a security plan is developed and implemented, there will be new vulnerabilities and new exposures with which to deal. It is for this very reason that companies have a test performed against them only to have another exercise a short time later.

Every organization approaches risk differently. Some feel that an early ethical hack will expose all the threats and be the initiating factor in procuring further investment for a full-scale risk analysis. Others tend to use the test as a measuring device to validate their assumptions made within the risk analysis project. And then there are companies who have integrated regular tests into an ongoing security strategy that provides regular information to stimulate the management of risk. Each of these examples is a valid use of a penetration test. The only difference is the ultimate value to the company in supporting their security posture.

QUANTIFY RISK

Identifying risk in and of itself is of marginal value and the quantity of identified risks may at first seem overwhelming but necessary in defining risk. Risk must be in some way quantified to allow for prioritization. Prioritized risk may then be used as the basis for a risk mitigation strategy such as an information security program, which can include technology investments, people training, or the allocation of a consultancy. In this way, the risk with greatest impact will be addressed first. Also set in motion will be the realization that protection of information requires revenue, and the foundation will be set for enabling the business through logically applied security.

Any quantification scheme must take into account the nature of the organization in order to be of benefit to decision makers. For example, an E-commerce organization may prefer risk to be quantified in dollars per event in order to cost justify controls whereas a noncommercial organization may be comfortable with a relative ranking of high to medium to low. Regardless of the quantification scheme adopted, risk can now be ranked based upon predetermined and consensual criteria.

There are two main methods to account for risk when building a business case.

- *Quantitative*. An analysis based on quantification of data is related to amounts, such as the amount of money or amount of data that can be physically damaged or stolen. These types of assessments are based on the amount of loss. One of the factoring algorithms includes Annualized Loss Expectancy (ALE), which takes the amount of loss times the Annualized Rate of Occurrence (ARO) to equal the loss expectancy. A risk analysis based on quantity can be used to determine financial impacts in the event of an attack on resources.
- *Qualitative*. Qualitative assessments are based on the forecast of loss compared to several calculated factors. Some of the factors include the use of (ARO) and a more ambiguous Exposure Factor (EF). For organizations that have a high market-value-to-asset ratio, qualitative risk assessments are typical.

One of the principal sources of operating risk in the IT environment is incompatibility of technical systems with business strategy. To lessen that risk, enterprises should build a framework to conform their technology decisions to business demands and risk. Because of the rapid pace of business and technology change, enterprises must document the risks and underlying assumptions involved in the arrangement to adjust the relationship as assumptions evolve or prove to be inaccurate.

Inherent Risk

Inherent risks are threats that exist when various, seemingly unrelated faults in networking, applications, services, or systems can combine, representing a significant vulnerability. Security is realized through the application of layers with varying degrees of granularity and focus at each layer. However, the interaction between security systems may not support end-to-end security.

Within inherent risk, there are two control levels, pervasive and detailed. Pervasive controls are those spread throughout the enterprise, or that have the tendency to be throughout the enterprise. Therefore, the level of pervasive control within an enterprise should be taken into consideration at the level appropriate to the organization. Detailed controls are specific to the systems within the enterprise, and the resources responsible for them.

Control Risk

Control risk is defined as the level of potential that a weakness can occur within an enterprise. This level of exposure to harm or loss can be considered material, individual, or as a combination with other existing weaknesses. Control risks are typically not prevented, nor detected and corrected in a timely manner by an internal control system. During the risk analysis process, the level of control risk is usually considered high. This is unless there are relevant internal controls, which have been identified as effective, then tested and proven to operate appropriately. Then the level of control risk can be reduced to a manageable level.

An example of an enterprise with a high level of control risk would be one in which the manual reviewing of system logs is in place. When logs must be reviewed manually, it is extremely time consuming and prone to error or oversight. If an enterprise had an automated process in which logs were effectively processed, this would in fact then reduce the level of control risk.

Detection Risk

Detection risk is the risk associated with the ability (or inability) to detect an attack or event. In an enterprise, detection risk associated with identifying breaches of security in an application system is ordinarily high because of poor monitoring practices or poorly tuned technology.

Handling Risk

Once an enterprise has evaluated and understands the amount of total and residual risk with which it is faced, a method must be put into place that mitigates the risk. There are four methods to eliminate or reduce the level of risk associated with the vulnerabilities and asset valuation.

- *Transference*. There are many types of insurance available to enterprises when it comes to protecting its assets. If an enterprise were to decide that the total or residual risk is too high to gamble with, it can purchase insurance, which would transfer the risk to the insurance company. Transferring risk can appear in many ways beyond basic insurance. For example, if a company is using an outside organization for their Web site, and that company is responsible for the server, data, and ultimately the integrity of the system, the risk associated with the loss of data can be logically transferred to the provider. Of course, the contract and SLA between the two organizations have to support this conclusion, but the possibility exists nonetheless.
- *Denial*. If an enterprise is in denial of its risk or ignores it, this is rejecting risk, which can be very dangerous. Unfortunately, there are more examples of denial of risk than other forms of managing risk. Numerous organizations are regularly faced with substantial losses if a threat is not mitigated, but in today's weakened economy and harsh competitive landscape, the

investment required to address a risk usually is too great for a financially strained company.

- *Reduction.* Traditionally, companies implement some of the recommended or required countermeasures to eliminate the greater portion of risk. Although this is a step in the right direction, there remains the potential of substantial exposure. The most common form of reducing risk is modifying existing technology, or making business-related changes that require the least investment. A simple example is a company using a freeware version of antivirus programs to accommodate the lack of virus controls that represents a risk to the company. Given the dynamics of viruses and the potential for huge losses, an industry-recognized solution—that costs money—is the traditional solution. Companies that base their success on detecting and eliminating viruses, such as Symantec and McAfee, are better positioned to provide timely support to stay abreast of virus evolution, whereas a freeware product, although it may be a good one, usually does not provide the support needed by the customer.

- *Acceptance.* The last approach is to accept the risk, which means the enterprise understands the level of risk they are faced with and the potential losses and simply accepts it. Organizations accept risk every day; we all do in some form. Accepting risk is the assumption that the likelihood of a vulnerability being exploited is low. Each day thousands of people get on airplanes hoping the engines do not fail. This is exactly what companies are doing when they accept risk. In many cases, it is simply a necessary evil for the company and the risk being accepted is traditionally a small characteristic of greater risks that they have accepted in other areas of business. I was meeting with an executive of one of the world's largest financial companies, and when presented with a certain type of technical risk that represented an exposure in the neighborhood of $500,000 to a million dollars, he simply smiled and said, "That's less than a tenth of a percent of other risks I accept daily." Enterprises will typically accept a specific level of risk when the cost-to-benefit ratio indicates that in order to mitigate the risk the cost exceeds that of the risk itself.

Address Risk

Prioritized risk can be used for informed decision making. Decision options include risk acceptance, risk transference, or risk mitigation. Risk acceptance may be justified when probability, harm, or dollar cost is low. Risk may also be accepted when the cost to mitigate exceeds the value of the asset being protected. Risk may be transferred to another with a higher risk tolerance, who in essence then accepts the risk. This is routine in the insurance industry where risk tolerance is raised by spreading risk among multiple clients.

Risk may also be mitigated by deploying control mechanisms that lower probability, harm, cost, or whatever metric is used to quantify the risk. For example, access control strategies mitigate risk by reducing the probability of unauthorized access, encryption strategies mitigate harm of disclosure, and backup strategies mitigate cost by allowing rapid restoration. Whatever option is selected to address a risk, it should be justifiable and supportable.

Mitigate Risk

Risk is mitigated by the selection and deployment of controls. Control starts at the top of an organization through the formulation of a risk-based high-level mitigation strategy. This strategy should outline the conceptual goals of the organization, thus allowing definition of subordinate controls. Subordinate controls may be such things as standards, process and procedure, configurations, and devices, and it is common to have multiple layers of supporting controls. All controls require a management infrastructure to maintain their effectiveness and relevance.

Measure Effectiveness

Information security is a process, not a product, and no environment is static. A mechanism must exist to both evaluate the effectiveness of the organization's risk management strategy, and reintroduce results into the process. Controls deployed today may not be effective tomorrow, but an iterative process allows for adaptation.

The requirement to measure security performance is driven by regulatory, financial, and organizational reasons. A number of existing laws, rules, and regulations cite IT performance measurement in general, and security performance measurement in particular, as a requirement. These laws include the Clinger–Cohen Act, Government Performance and Results Act (GPRA), Government Paperwork Elimination Act (GPEA), and Federal Information Security Management Act (FISMA).

Security services management provides guidance on how an organization, through the use of metrics, identifies the adequacy of existing security controls, policies, and procedures. It provides an approach to help management decide where to invest in additional security protection resources or identify and evaluate nonproductive controls. It begins with the development of metrics and the implementation process and how it can also be used to adequately justify security control investments. The results of an effective security services management program can provide useful data for directing the allocation of information security resources and should simplify the preparation of performance reports.

Metrics are a collection of tools designed to facilitate decision making and improve performance and accountability through collection, analysis, and reporting of relevant performance data. Security services management metrics must be based on defined security performance goals and objectives. Security performance goals state the desired results of a system security program implementation. Security performance objectives enable accomplishment of goals by identifying practices defined by security policies and procedures that direct consistent implementation of security controls across the organization. Security services management metrics monitor the accomplishment of the goals and objectives by quantifying the level of implementation of the security controls and the effectiveness and efficiency of the controls, analyzing the adequacy of security activities, and identifying possible improvement opportunities.

COMPONENT PARTS OF INFORMATION
SECURITY PROGRAMS

Any information security program will consist of component parts, as shown in Figure 5.4, that implement the process of information security.

RISK ASSESSMENT

An information security risk assessment identifies and quantifies risk, thus serving as the basis for addressing risk. The risk assessment process requires creation of an initial security domain definition to set the scope of the assessment by acknowledging the span of control and relevant assets. This corresponds to the security architecture model (extended, perimeter, control, and resource layers) by defining physical and logical boundaries and tabulating assets at risk.

The security architecture definition is used to modularize the security program by implicitly setting the scope of other program components. For example, an established risk assessment security layer definition may be used to establish the scope of an incident response plan. Because boundaries and assets are synchronized, any incident response feedback can seamlessly feed back into the risk analysis process to close the loop. The advantages of modularity in a security program warrant extra effort in the initial definition of risk assessment security domains.

The information security risk assessment is a living document with established ownership and review. It may serve as a vehicle to modularize a security program, offering cohesiveness and flexibility, as well as a vehicle to document due diligence. The value of the information security risk assessment is only as effective as the accuracy and thoroughness represented within.

MANAGEMENT SYSTEM

The information security management system functions to address risk, whether it is accepted, transferred, or mitigated; information security management systems are beginning to enjoy the adoption of internationally recognized standards, and are increasingly being seen as analogous to Total Quality Management (TQM) systems, managing the quality of information security.

One rapidly emerging internationally recognized standard is ISO17799, heir apparent to the venerable BS7799 standard, and focused on ten functional control areas including:

- *Information Security Policy* addressing management support, ongoing commitment, and direction in accomplishing information security goals;
- *Organizational Security* addressing the need for a management framework to create, sustain, and manage the security infrastructure;
- *Asset Classification and Control* addressing the ability of the security infrastructure to protect organizational assets;
- *Personnel Security* addressing an organization's ability to mitigate risk inherent in human interaction;

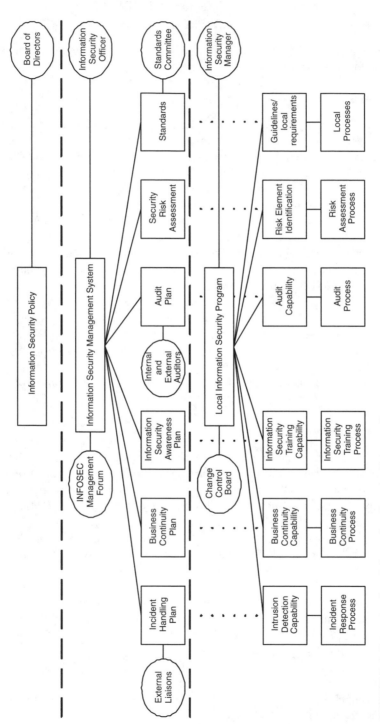

FIGURE 5.4 Example of an Information Security Program Structure

- *Physical and Environmental Security* addressing risk inherent to the organization's premise;
- *Communications and Operations Management* addressing an organization's ability to ensure correct, secure, and repeatable operation of its assets;
- *Access Control* addressing an organization's ability to control access to assets based upon business and security requirements;
- *System Development and Maintenance* addressing an organization's ability to ensure that information system security controls are both incorporated and maintained;
- *Business Continuity Management* addressing an organization's ability to counteract interruptions to normal operations; and
- *Compliance* addressing an organization's ability to remain compliant with regulatory, statutory, contractual, and security requirements.

Security management based upon ISO17799 takes a very holistic look at information security and at all aspects of an organization's ability to manage risk. The ten functional control areas serve as a high-level checklist of things that should be evaluated in the creation of a security program, and the selection of controls.

Security management systems define functional requirements of the security architecture model control layer. Scope and requirements are driven by the results obtained from the risk assessment that is fed by a penetration test. Components typically include security organizations, codified practices, and ancillary support programs.

Security organizations address the individual's role in the security program.

- *Functional Roles* allow assignment of specific security responsibilities such as Information Security Officers.
- *Information Security Management Committees* are chartered with specific tasks such as Configuration Control Boards.
- *Multidisciplinary Management Forums* are tasked with promoting information security awareness throughout the organization with codified practices that refine an organization's risk mitigation strategy to a level of granularity that can be implemented.
- *Policies* express conceptual goals of upper management defining the risk mitigation strategy.
- *Standards* define measurable requirements in support of policy goals.
- *Guidelines* offer best practice advice on how to meet standard requirements.
- *Procedures* furnish step-by-step instructions to create a consistent and repeatable process.

Ancillary programs address risk not addressed by security organizations or codified practices. In some organizations, these ancillary programs may liaise with the security program, but be externally managed. For example, business continuity may stand alone, or security awareness may fall under HR or training.

- *Business Continuity* programs ensure the sustainability of the organization.
- *Incident Management* programs respond to anomalies.
- *Security Awareness* programs educate an organization's personnel on information security issues.

There is no cookie-cutter approach to creating a security management system, each being unique to the sponsoring organization. Any implementation must be justified by identified risk, have the full support of the organization's upper management, and take into consideration existing organizational culture and politics. Buy-in from stakeholders at all levels is crucial to both initial success and ongoing effectiveness.

CONTROLS

Controls come in many forms, including physical devices, configurations, roles, and processes, affecting networks, platforms, roles, and operations. Many controls require subordinate or supporting controls. For example:

- A firewall is a network control device used to enforce network access and service requirements. The firewall requires:
  - A supporting procedure for authorized users and services
  - A supporting role to administer the device
  - A supporting organization for configuration control
- A sniffer is a network control device used to monitor traffic for both network management and anomaly detection.
  - A supporting monitoring policy may be required to mitigate an additional risk of illegal eavesdropping or invasion of privacy.
- Hardening scripts are platform controls used to modify system configurations to minimize effectiveness of common system exploits.
  - A supporting role must track and update the scripts.
- System logging is a control that includes:
  - A device such as a log server
  - A configuration to enable logging on each device
  - A role to analyze the log files

Functional role definitions are a control used to assign and evaluate information security responsibilities and training requirements. If "Information security is everybody's responsibility," an effective system ensures that "Everybody knows his or her responsibilities and is trained to react accordingly."

Procedural controls exist to ensure the process of information security is consistent and repeatable. Standard operational procedures, for example, are controls to standardize the outcome of operations throughout the organization. Controls are an implementation of the risk mitigation strategy adopted by management and validated by risk.

Maintenance Plan

An effective security program must always be considered an ongoing initiative, subject to regular maintenance. Controls deployed today will only meet the current threat environment, and tomorrow is another day. The program maintenance plan validates protection of the security architecture model, addressing both security program review and audit.

Program review should start at the top with yearly reaffirmation of program goals by upper management. Security risk assessments and supporting standards and procedures should be analyzed for continued relevance, and an authorization review should ensure users and services are still justified by business requirements.

Program audit must include both the capability to measure effectiveness of the existing program and introduce the audit findings into the process for program enhancement. For example, regularly scheduled internal or self-audit against pre-established baselines may allow detection of unauthorized changes showing an ineffective configuration control process, or a previously unidentified vulnerability.

Independent or external audits allow unbiased third-party evaluation of an information security program, and may be legally required by some organizations. External audits may be based against a standard such as ISO17799, a legislative requirement such as HIPAA, or "best practice."

RISK ANALYSIS AND ETHICAL HACKING

One of the predominant questions fielded during discussions about security, and especially about ethical hacking, is the delineation between a risk analysis and an ethical hack. We've covered the basic elements of risk analysis and ethical hacking, but what is the role of each in the world of information security? For example, when should a company have a risk analysis performed as opposed to an ethical hack? What scenarios exist that would favor one over the other?

Much of the decision to employ a risk analysis over an ethical hack, or vice versa, is based on interpretation, scale, goals, and cost. The immediate assumption is that a risk analysis would take more time, consume more resources, and cost significantly more than an ethical hack. Much of this is due to the presumed scope. For example, a risk analysis conjures up visions of dozens of consultants weeding their way through the entire organization for months. Whereas, in contrast, an ethical hack seems more focused and has a definite start and end, both of which are very desirable attributes to a CFO.

However, these differences are based on conjecture rather than fact. A risk analysis can be very focused as long as other environmental conditions are not specifically addressed. A risk analysis can be performed against a specific solution, department, or application in a very short period. An ethical hack can become a huge endeavor (sometimes never-ending, like painting a bridge) if the entire target company is to be evaluated.

Another aspect of these two assessment techniques is that risk analysis is collaborative, whereas ethical hacking is independent. During a risk analysis, the environment

TABLE 5.1
Role of Ethical Hacking and Risk Analysis in Evaluating Security

Evaluating Threats and Vulnerabilities	Determining Effectiveness of Security Controls	Establishing Value of Assets
Ethical hacking	Ethical hacking and risk analysis	Risk analysis

is evaluated by cooperating with the company and learning through investigation. In contrast, ethical hacking is typically autonomous, observing through direct interaction. These are two very different assessment tactics. For example, a consultant performing a risk analysis may review the rules on a firewall in combination with the governing security policies to evaluate the controls for a particular application. A tester may scan and probe the firewall to search for any vulnerabilities that can be exploited in the same application. The results may demonstrate the exact same problem, but with different methods and different assumptions of risk.

Therefore, considering that scope and scale are interchangeable and the difference in method, when should one be used over the other? Before that can be answered, it should be made clear that the option to use both types of assessments in conjunction can be very effective (see Table 5.1). A risk analysis determines the value of assets and evaluates their exposure to threats. A component of performing the analysis is evaluating the security controls and how they are employed. Of course, understanding the threats and their level of potential impact is fundamental to the analysis. Evaluating threats is when ethical hacking becomes most valuable. Performing a test to identify vulnerabilities and determining the level of effort to exploit them provides the fundamental information needed to produce a comprehensive risk analysis.

Therefore, using ethical hacking to locate and exploit vulnerabilities provides the threat information to drive the other parts of the analysis. Ethical hacking also helps evaluate the security controls, finding weaknesses in their implementation and use. The risk analysis also evaluates the security controls and uses all forms of information to determine the value of data, ultimately establishing a perception of risk and criticality.

There are situations when using ethical hacking is clearly more effective than performing a risk analysis. Also, there are opportunities to perform a risk analysis instead of an ethical hack to accommodate a specific need or goal. However, no matter how assured you are of the selected task, there typically exist pros and cons for each. Following are some examples of scenarios, the typical assessment type employed, and the pros and cons of each. (Note: The scope and scale are not considered inasmuch as these are interchangeable and cannot be used exclusively to express one type over another.)

Table 5.2 provides a general perspective of the differences between ethical hacking and performing a risk analysis given some basic scenarios. The goal was to highlight the diversity in approach and results. When placed side by side it should be clear there are appropriate uses of one form of assessment over the other. Albeit open to interpretation, if the objectives of the assessment are well defined, selecting a form of evaluation will be much simpler.

Another interesting aspect of these two forms of assessment is they can be combined to gain even more insight as to the controls implemented and their weaknesses. The result is a comprehensive appraisal of potential problems, which directly associates them with the impact as well as a remedy. The most significant difference between ethical hacking and risk analysis is that ethical hacking requires significant planning and alignment of tasks to ensure the experiment in exploitation actually tests the control in question. Whereas with risk analysis, more information is available to the process, promoting broader visibility into the security controls.

Determining one over the other is fodder for extensive debate. A risk analysis can evaluate the full spectrum of contingencies from an internal perspective, however, ethical hacking does much the same from an adversarial point of view. Although very different approaches, with arguably different results and assumptions, one must be very cognizant of how the results are going to be used for the betterment of security. If an organization places a great deal of emphasis on process and procedures, a risk analysis that takes all elements into consideration may provide more value when compared to an ethical hack. For example, a risk analysis may expose poor change management, a root cause for many system vulnerabilities. On the other hand, some organizations place a great deal of value on determining what is possible given the current practices. Therefore, the results will assist in addressing the vulnerabilities and recommend closer attention to security practices, at which point the root causes for the lapse in security will have to be evaluated.

Both are very valid approaches to security assessments and offer the recipient a plethora of insightful information. It is suspected that ethical hacking is popular because it can be controlled and finite, whereas risk analysis conjures images of end analysis. The latter is certainly not a foregone conclusion, nevertheless, ethical hacking is being used when a risk analysis can be much more valuable, and vice versa.

TABLE 5.2
Pros and Cons of Ethical Hacking and Risk Analysis

Scenario:	Assessing Security of Internet-Facing Infrastructure	
Ethical Hacking (Typically Employed)	**Pros:** Identifies technical vulnerabilities Determines exposure to threats Establishes the level of effort required to exploit a vulnerability Provides a perspective of the infrastructure from an unknown entity (i.e., Internet public, competitor, etc.) Technically comprehensive (scan entire networks and groups) Provides information on necessary tools and tactics required to attack firewalls, services (e.g., DNS, FTP, etc.), and other infrastructure elements	**Cons:** Does not consider management practices and security policy Potentially affected by firewall or other chokepoint capabilities Exposure to detection by IDS/IPS or other monitoring Potential for adverse events (e.g., downtime, damage, etc.) Does not provide information or recommendations regarding elements outside of immediate observation Does not take asset value into consideration (Note: this is performed only through the tester's perception, not documented asset classification)
Risk Analysis	**Pros:** Considers all aspects of information security: technical configurations, management, operations, and policy (among others) Does not present a risk to the operations of Internet applications and systems Comprehensive configuration analysis of routers, firewalls, and systems Provides a detailed analysis of risk to Internet-facing systems, networks, and applications based on traditional Internet threats	**Cons:** Vulnerabilities are determined through investigation, not empirical evidence from system interaction Assumes level of effort to exploit a vulnerability Assumes potential vectors of attack (i.e., does not test for alternate routes to assets, but assumes them based on infrastructure Performed based on sampling or light vulnerability scanning (potentially not comprehensive)
Results	**Ethical Hacking:** Itemized list of vulnerabilities found on the Internet-facing systems An understanding of depth attained from the Internet Detailed analysis of exploitation, tools, and tactics used against the identifiable systems Raw data from the test Recommendations for remediation	**Risk Analysis:** Detailed analysis of security policies and practices used to manage the security controls Analysis of security architecture and recommendations for modification Asset valuation and exposure to common Internet threats Recommendations for remediation

Scenario:	Assessing Security of Specific Custom Web Application	
Ethical Hacking (Typically Employed)	**Pros:** Directly tests user data input and potential for processing errors; Evaluates any client-side scripting, applications, or plug-ins; Tests potential performance issues; Can expose technical weaknesses permitting access to private information; Manipulates cookies or other programming attributes to exploit the application	**Cons:** Does not include (typically) access to code or application elements not published or provided; Does not address the planned applications developments; Is not aware and cannot clearly evaluate the infrastructure attributes; Does not address the management, operations, or processes supporting the application
Risk Analysis	**Pros:** Evaluates the supporting infrastructure and can make security recommendations on information flow controls; Access to supporting data, systems, and business data to specifically determine level of impact; Evaluates authentication procedures and interaction with supporting elements; Can clearly determine the impact to the organization in the event of an outage or breach of security; Identifies errors and opportunities for improving application development processes	**Cons:** Vulnerabilities in the application are based on code, process, and previous development phases and not on technical observation; May not address client-side technical elements and make assumptions on remote system vulnerabilities; Does not look for other, unrelated technical avenues for attack; Cannot clearly evaluate the options to threats given various forms of attack
Results	**Ethical Hacking:** Detailed list of vulnerabilities and the level of access attained from exploitation; Comprehensive understanding of software flaws and the resulting immediate impact	**Risk Analysis:** Detailed analysis of the potential impact in the event of attack; Evaluation of software development practices; Security review of the code

TABLE 5.3
Pros and Cons of Ethical Hacking and Risk Analysis (continued)

Scenario:	Assess Level of Risk from Internal Employees	
Ethical Hacking	**Pros:** Perform social engineering from outside or as an employee to evaluate the level of access and impact of an internal resource Can use vulnerability scanning tools to seek opportunities for greater access Directly exploit vulnerabilities (i.e., access secured areas, collect materials from other employee's desks, system access, etc.)	**Cons:** Potentially time consuming Limited to approved social engineering testing options Limited to the experience and capability of the tester Not exposed to defined policies, roles and responsibilities, and management processes Exposed to discovery
Risk Analysis (Typically Employed)	**Pros:** Evaluates the entire infrastructure for potential physical, network, and system (application) access Can evaluate the level of security controls based on business requirements Evaluates the existence of various level of controls and implementation Exposed to the interdependencies related to systems, departments, geography, and partnerships	**Cons:** Does not clearly evaluate the access of a given employee Must address all elements of the internal environment, even if a focused effort Does not test specific applications or technical solutions to determine discrete access
Results	**Ethical Hacking:** A detailed analysis of potential problems from one or a small group of employees Provide technical insights to internal network and application vulnerabilities Can provide specific materials and access available to internal employees and communicate the results	**Risk Analysis:** Detailed analysis of potential threats based on internal controls and configuration Analysis of employee management practices Evaluation of internal controls, policies and procedures, and recommendations

Scenario:	Assess Security of Internal Network or Segment	
Ethical Hacking (Typically Employed)	**Pros:** Provides greater insight to the scope of opportunities to internal employees to interact with systems and other networks Identifies discrete vulnerabilities at all layers in the network (i.e., physical, IP, services, systems, and applications)	**Cons:** Due to the openness of the infrastructure, it significantly increases the potential for affecting business operations Can result in an inordinate amount of vulnerabilities to sift through to determine next steps Assumes internal threats are sophisticated
Risk Analysis	**Pros:** Evaluates the infrastructure through controlled observations rather than explicit testing Not limited to the immediate technical environment and conclusion can be determined based on business-level information Information about vulnerabilities is typically associated with architecture and process (i.e., configuration management, access controls) as opposed to specific vulnerabilities	**Cons:** Does not clearly represent the perspective from an internal system on the network, or someone with specific credentials Does not typically provide specific vulnerabilities about systems or applications based on direct interaction
Results	**Ethical Hacking:** A list of vulnerabilities and how they were identified and potentially exploited Assists in fixing technical issues	**Risk Analysis:** Detailed analysis of the internal architecture and the potential exposures based on observations Assists in addressing the high-level technical concerns in addition to process changes

TABLE 5.4
Pros and Cons of Ethical Hacking and Risk Analysis (continued)

Scenario:	Assess Physical Security	
Ethical Hacking	**Pros:** Evaluates the security controls inherently designed to thwart human threats (See Note, Ch. 9: "The Physicality of Social Engineering") Has the potential to accurately reflect various threats Provides the option of comprehensive control and granularity	**Cons:** Requires substantial planning to ensure the potential threat is replicated Increases the liability associated with exploitation of physical controls
Risk Analysis (Typically Employed)	**Pros:** Determines the level of threat and vulnerabilities through evaluation of security controls Assesses the policies and procedures related to physical controls	**Cons:** Does not assess security based on tested weaknesses Level of threats and vulnerabilities based on interpretation of the controls as opposed to testing
Results	**Ethical Hacking:** Provides a list of vulnerabilities that contributed to the failure of controls Offers a detailed understanding of what is obtainable to a person at various points or stages in the test A detailed explanation of what was performed to thwart the security controls	**Risk Analysis:** Detailed analysis of physical controls, potential vulnerabilities, a collection of threats, and likelihood of exploitation Provides a collection of broad recommendations, including policy and process, to accommodate potential weakness

6 The Business Perspective

To ensure the test is valuable to the overall security program, in addition to being financially effective, the demands of the business must be understood. Moreover, the perception of security by the management and the sponsor of the test needs to be evaluated. What are the goals of the test? What is the scope? What are the limitations and why? Finally, what elements of the test are going to be employed, to what granularity, and are they going to expose vulnerabilities that relate to your security risks? These questions and more are addressed to make certain the test is effective for the business.

You can liken a penetration test and all its options to an amplifier. An amplifier will have several adjustments for bass, treble, mid-range, volume, loudness, and tone, along with many other available tweaks. How you adjust these elements of sound depends on the shape of the room, types of speakers, the condition, such as during a party or a romantic evening, and finally the ear of the listener. Ethical hacking has elements such as social engineering, wardialing, physical security, application testing, and network testing to name only a few. The proverbial room is the organization's technical environment, such as the infrastructure. Types of speakers can be related to the tools available to the tester, each with its own uses and effectiveness. The condition is directly related to the culture of the target company. The social and political conditions regarding information security and the tactics of using ethical hacking are part of the security program. Finally, the ear is business and level of awareness of the nuances of each element of the test.

How the elements of a test are adjusted is based on the completeness of the planning of the engagement and clearly understanding the expectations. Otherwise, it can mean the difference between white noise or Beethoven's fifth symphony at the end of the test.

BUSINESS OBJECTIVES

So what is the objective of the test? Why are you considering permitting someone to hack your network? What do you expect to learn and are you prepared for the results? Do you have the capabilities to address the identified issues? Have you considered the risk of the test and feel that you can identify a success or failure? Finally, is security even part of your business? Is it ingrained in your actions and does it play a role in your organization's success? No, really—don't lie to yourself. Many claim to take security seriously and people who perform ethical hacks will tell you that even the most robust firms fall quickly. But, is this a reflection of poor security practices, or poor planning of the test?

There are many characteristics of security and how security is realized in a company. The number of people responsible for security, their practices, and job pressures will have an impact on how the perception of security is materialized in the systems and applications. Ask yourself, when a new application is developed, is the security group included in the process from the beginning? And if it is, are the recommendations employed? How many times does the firewall administrator get a call saying to open ports 1024 to 45000 to get a new application online, and what happens when she says no? Even though there are more CISOs today than ever before, they typically do not have enough influence to effectively protect the company's interest and meet their mission objectives. As with many things in business, there are always compromises, agreements, and politics that play into the mix. Without a supporting mechanism built into the business, an ethical hack will only be a Pandora's box and not very valuable in the long run.

SECURITY POLICY

It would be a gross omission if security policies were not discussed in some manner, albeit a much talked about aspect of information security and a broadly accepted requirement for a successful security program. Nevertheless, its role in a penetration test cannot be understated.

A security policy is one of the most important components of a successful information security program. Security policies play a critical role in managing the organization's security by defining a desired posture that the organization strives to achieve and maintain. Policies set the bar for the organization's security, and information security management and operations personnel are tasked with driving the organization to that mark.

A security policy is the foundation on which all security operations are built. Without a security policy to define the expectations of the security controls it is effectively impossible to establish a well-fortified security program.

As discussed above, the existence of a risk analysis is key to the value a test can offer to a company. However, appreciative of the fact that an ethical hack is part of a risk analysis, a previous risk analysis may not be available — a chicken-and-egg scenario. It is at this point a security policy takes front stage. A security policy will state the acceptable uses and procedures in maintaining the desired security level. These attributes will help in the planning of the test, shape the tasks to be performed, and assist in evaluating success factors. All of which will culminate into a deliverable formatted to accommodate proper integration.

However, this makes several assumptions about the completeness of the existing policies. A book sitting on the shelf in the IT director's office for the last couple of years does not count. Moreover, what should also be noted is that the structure of the deliverable and resulting implementation plans will be based mostly on the presentation of security within the policy as opposed to measurable risk factors. Therefore, an old or outdated security policy will greatly affect the value of the test.

Unfortunately, many security policies suffer from neglect. Many organizations have security policies simply because other organizations and legal requirements demanded them to be implemented. Unfortunately, many are not maintained, properly communicated, or used as a guide in day-to-day activities. The requirements for a firm to have a policy, politically or legally driven, tend to ensure a policy is created but do not instill a method for maintaining it. Many policies have become paperweights and are referenced only in the event an employee contests being reprimanded for poor and insecure behavior.

Security policies come in many forms, from simple documents to policy applications that work within the environment to ensure they are communicated and applied. Policies are created to describe, detail, and communicate the expected security practices as well as the processes that are to be followed to protect, defend, and recover from attacks. They also help act as a reference for configuring new systems, connections to the network, adding remote users, and integrating new technology or applications.

There are several policy structures that can be leveraged to create a well-organized policy and inherently assist their development. With any comprehensive collection of information, content organization is a key factor of the degree to which the information is integrated and used.

At the most fundamental level, a security policy is comprised of collections of statements, with each containing supporting material. A policy statement generally defines the organization's stance on a particular aspect of information security. The supporting material behind a policy statement consists of standards, guidelines, and procedures that outline specific processes to enforce the policy.

- *Policy Statement*. Policy statements should be clear statements on the particular aspect of security that provide no room for interpretation. They should provide generalized, yet pertinent information on what is expected to be practiced within the organization. Policy statements should avoid justification of the policy, details that are supported by the standards, guidelines, or procedures, or any specific technology associated with the policy. All these characteristics tend to add complexity and open the opportunity to interpretation. Allow the details to be addressed in the supporting statements.
- *Standard*. A standard is the actual definition of the technical nature of the requirement communicated by the policy statement. Standards provide specific details that explain or quantify the policy statement with which they are associated. Standards should be detailed and clear in communicating the requirements of the policy statement by quantifying the necessary attributes of the policy. However, the standard should not include procedures or step-by-step processes on how to implement the policy. The goal is to define the final structure associated with the statement.
- *Guideline*. A guideline is a collection of supporting activities to help associate everyday activities with the support of the policy statement. Guidelines provide general suggestions or recommendations that further

clarify the policy with general details or suggestions for their implementation. Without guidelines, the policy statement and standard would have little meaningful impact on the typical user. To accomplish this, guidelines should provide associated technologies and guidance in various conditions. However, once again, the processes for carrying out the policy should not be addressed within the guidelines.

- *Procedure*. A procedure defines the tasks required to meet the requirements set forth in the policy. Procedures are step-by-step instructions detailing how a particular task is to be performed. These are executed to implement and enforce policy statements, or to measure the organization's compliance with a particular statement for later auditing purposes. Procedures should be very clear on performance of necessary tasks and should avoid any information outside the scope of simply providing the steps to complete and enforce.

Following is a simple example of the policy structure.

- Policy Statement:
    - Users shall use strong passwords on all network systems and elements.
- Standards:
    - Passwords must be at least eight characters in length.
    - Each password must contain alphabetic, numeric, and special characters.
- Guidelines:
    - Users should avoid using personal information that can be easily guessed, such as a name or critical number as a password.
    - Users should seek combinations of words that are easy to remember yet difficult to guess.
    - Users should avoid the use of passwords that are commonly found in dictionaries.
    - Users should avoid writing the password down.
- Procedures:
    - Enforce password policy on NT Domains.
        - Log on to domain controller as Administrator.
        - Run the User Manager application.
        - Select "Accounts..." from the Policies menu.
        - Configure the system's password policy to mirror the organization's password policy.
        - Click "OK" and close the User Manager application.

As we show later, the existence and proper language of a policy regarding penetration testing or evaluating security through the act of exploitation becomes critical to ensure that the value of the test is realized and meets the requirements of the overall expectations of the security controls within an organization.

PREVIOUS TEST RESULTS

There are many organizations that have tests performed regularly with their own set of results, recommendations, and implemented countermeasures. The deliverables from a previous test provide the opportunity to plan a new ethical hack in a manner that is complementary to previous investments. For example, a company may have identified specific vulnerabilities during the previous test resulting in the acceptance of that risk. To continue testing a risk that has been identified and absorbed into the client's acknowledged exposure can be a waste of time. Nevertheless, vulnerabilities change with the ebb and flow of technology. Therefore, assumptions about identified weaknesses should not be made lightly.

Finally, and much more common, is that the testing firm can review the previous test results to test the identified vulnerabilities the customer has assumed have been fixed since the last test. Although this has more of an audit flavor, the services firm can move on to other areas after verifying that the holes were fixed.

The question ultimately arises, "If the vulnerability is still there, should it be exploited?" The answer should be, "No." This is for the simple reason that if the target knows the vulnerability is there and the previous vendor exploited it to prove its viability, then exploiting it again would not only use expensive time, but it is more than likely the customer would not consider that aspect of the test valuable.

There is a tendency for the second firm to exploit the vulnerability identified and used by the previous firm to look for other avenues of attack that may not have been originally investigated. The argument for this practice is the assumption that the exposure associated with the vulnerability was not great enough to attract the necessary attention to rectify because the risk of the vulnerability may have been seen as low compared to other, more pressing problems.

Ultimately, whether the old vulnerability is exploited again is up to the customer's perception of the level of risk the original vulnerability presented and the risks associated with a deeper, possibly more rigorous test that could lead to system failures.

BUILDING A ROADMAP

Today organizations are performing more tests and more frequently with the hypothesis that yesterday's vulnerabilities were fixed and today there may be another set with which to deal. For companies that practice regular tests, there is an opportunity to collect the information for later analysis.

By performing test after test, security managers gain the necessary information needed to successfully repair holes that represent a threat and establish a baseline for future increased security. In addition, as information is collected over a period of time, trends in the effectiveness to control risk can surface. By investigating the weaknesses and strengths, a well-founded business case for further security investment can be created.

Only a handful of companies have started the practice of managing the data collected from tests for the long-term betterment of the company. By breaking the previous results into manageable elements, the company's security officer can identify trends and draw various conclusions on the implemented security controls as opposed to the assumed level of security. This is not always an easy task and one must take into consideration the constant dynamics of security vulnerabilities.

Depicted in Figure 6.1 are the number of vulnerabilities measured without the level of risk identified. Therefore, the figure only represents the effectiveness of the security group to deal with all forms of vulnerabilities.

In this example, a company had tests performed the first week of each month for a year starting in January. The total number of vulnerabilities is the combination of the number of vulnerabilities that were not fixed from the previous test and the new vulnerabilities identified for that testing period.

There are several characteristics worth highlighting. The total number of vulnerabilities increases initially, declines as the year progresses, and spikes in October. The spike can be the result of launching a new E-commerce application, Web site, server upgrade, or even something significant such as a merger. Early in the year, the number of vulnerabilities fixed is significantly less than the total number identified. As the year continues, the delta between the two begins to close suggesting the company is getting more efficient at solving problems. Efficiency is typically associated with enacting better processes, such as patch management, integrating tools, or simply adding more resources to perform the work. In the beginning, the inability to fix vulnerabilities quickly resulted in an enormous amount of previously identified holes and then a slight decline as their effectiveness increased over time. As you can see by the light-grey curve declining over time, this is an average of vulnerabilities that remain from one testing period to the next over the year.

Over time, they reduced the number of total vulnerabilities by increasing their ability to fix them in a meaningful timeframe. Therefore, by the time of a dramatic upward shift in the number of new vulnerabilities late in the year, the company reacted quickly and effectively in short order.

This is representative of a company with very poor security controls early in the year that eventually made the necessary changes to people, processes, and tools to ensure acceptable performance over the long term. In fact, you could assume a new CISO was hired, immediately started having tests performed monthly, and built a team to deal with vulnerabilities, among other security challenges.

Figure 6.1 demonstrates that even the most basic results from tests can be used to support future security-related efforts. Unfortunately, this does not provide enough granular information to address the level of risk for each vulnerability, the overall risk mitigation, or the efficiency of the team to address high-, medium-, or low-rated vulnerabilities. If we recalculate the vulnerabilities by differentiating them by using a weighted value and tracking which vulnerabilities are fixed, we can get more insight as to the activities in addition to the relative state of corporate risk associated with known vulnerabilities.

In Figure 6.2 we introduce the level of severity of each vulnerability and break out which vulnerabilities from each group were repaired or new for the month. With the total number of vulnerabilities, the total fixed, and the total identified from the previous test remaining static, we expose an interesting change in the effectiveness of the security group.

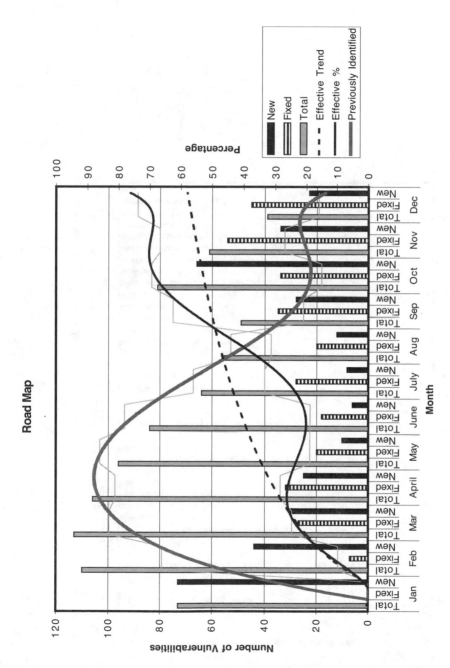

FIGURE 6.1 Determining Effectiveness by Tracking Vulnerabilities and Their Mitigation

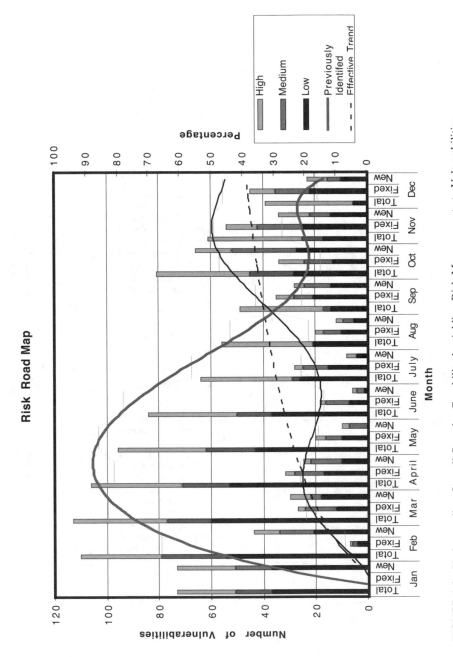

FIGURE 6.2 Understanding Overall Security Capability by Adding Risk Measurements to Vulnerabilities

Now, we see the number of vulnerabilities fixed were predominantly rated low and medium, with a small percentage of the high-risk vulnerabilities actually being addressed. As each month passed, some new high-risk vulnerabilities were being discovered, essentially digging a "risk-hole" for the security team. By comparing the two efficiency trends we can see the security team is much less effective than first expected. Moreover, because we included the level of risk represented by each vulnerability, the effectiveness trend can be translated to the overall ability to address risk associated with known vulnerabilities.

Detailed in Figure 6.3 are the number of vulnerabilities that are low, medium, and high displayed with the delta between the traditional roadmap and the risk roadmap presented. Towards the bottom of the data are the weighted values associated with the risks. In this example, 15 is assigned to low-rated, 30 assigned to medium-rated, and 75 assigned to high-rated vulnerabilities. Of course, any number can be used; however, this scale represents a calculated metric. For example, a medium vulnerability is twice as bad as a low. A high vulnerability is twice as bad as a medium-rated plus a low-rated vulnerability.

Those who have regular tests typically use different providers of the service to ensure the results do not become stale. The byproduct, of course, is that the deliverables are different each time, each with a unique format and how information is presented. This adds to the difficulty of normalizing the data to perform a consistent analysis.

Nevertheless, information about the state of security within an organization can be gathered from historical data. For example, if after six penetration tests the number of vulnerabilities associated with Microsoft that has patches is increasing you should revisit your patch management program. If the same vulnerabilities keep appearing over time, you should investigate the existence and use of a standard system configuration. Penetration tests are not only an opportunity to test the technical resistance to attack, but can provide insights into the effectiveness of existing management controls. The test also supports and becomes part of the security program to ensure the longevity of security investments and maintain the level of desired security within the organization.

The value of comparing test results can assist with operational demands as well as technical. Companies typically have a secure build, or standard configuration, for systems throughout their network, especially ones exposed to the Internet. Previous test results can be used to further tighten the harness on systems through comprehensive change management procedures and reinvestigating the standard builds. Trends in security management can be exposed for good as well as bad practices. All too often good security practices are implemented and used for a certain period until something comes along to challenge the security program. It can be a new application or service to support a business initiative that was pushed through IT and passed over security. Trends in poor practices surface through identifying similar vulnerability types, such as those relating to applications, protocols, or architecture changes. The evidence can be used to support the argument for more security to not only ensure a secure environment, but to protect future investments.

ROADMAP

ROADMAP	Jan	Feb	Mar	April	May	June	July	Aug	Sep
Total # of Vul.	73	110	113	106	96	84	64	56	49
Number Fixed	0	7	27	32	20	18	28	20	35
New Vul.	73	44	30	25	10	6	8	12	28
Previously Identified	0	66	83	81	86	78	56	44	21
Effectiveness %	0.0	9.6	24.5	28.3	18.9	18.8	33.3	31.3	62.5
Delta %	0.0	-2.2	-4.9	-6.8	-0.7	-4.5	-11.3	-11.8	-25.7

RISK ROADMAP

RISK ROADMAP	Jan	Feb	Mar	April	May	June	July	Aug	Sep
Total # of Vul.	73	110	113	106	96	84	64	56	49
Low Vul.	37	54	60	53	43	37	26	21	14
Med. Vul.	14	25	17	18	21	15	5	2	5
High Vul.	22	31	36	35	32	32	33	33	30
Total Fixed	0	7	27	32	20	18	28	20	35
Low Fixed	0	4	12	17	10	7	15	10	21
Medium Fixed	0	2	12	11	4	9	10	7	7
High Fixed	0	1	3	4	6	2	3	3	7
New Vul.	73	44	30	25	10	6	8	12	28
Low New	37	21	18	10	0	1	4	5	14
Med New	14	13	4	12	7	3	0	4	10
High New	22	10	8	3	3	2	4	3	4
Previously Identified	0	66	83	81	86	78	56	44	21
Effectiveness %	0.0	7.4	19.7	21.5	18.2	14.3	22.0	19.4	36.8

Wt. VALUE

Wt. VALUE	Weight	Jan Total	Feb Wt.	Mar Wt.	April Wt.	May Wt.	June Wt.	July Wt.	Aug Wt.	Sep Wt.
	15	555	810	900	795	645	555	390	315	210
	30	420	750	510	540	630	450	150	60	150
	75	1650	2325	2700	2625	2400	2400	2475	2475	2250
	Total	2625	3885	4110	3960	3675	3405	3015	2850	2610
	Weight	Fixed Wt.	Fixed Wt.	Fixed Wt.	Fixed Wt.	Fixed Wt.	Fixed Wt.	Fixed Wt.	Fixed Wt.	Fixed Wt.
	15	0	60	180	255	150	105	225	150	315
	30	0	60	360	330	120	270	300	210	210
	75	0	75	225	300	450	150	225	225	525
	Total	0	195	765	885	720	525	750	585	1050
	Eff %	0.00	7.43	19.69	21.53	18.18	14.29	22.03	19.40	36.84

FIGURE 6.3 Detailed Numbers and Calculations for Risk-Based Roadmap

BUSINESS CHALLENGES

Today companies are facing security threats that will turn into business risks that may include loss of productivity, financial and legal liabilities, loss of network availability, and corruption or theft of data. Furthermore, it may damage the company brand name and reputation and incur loss of confidence by stakeholders.

In spite of the risks to achieve business goals companies understand the need to accomplish several fundamentals to ensuring the success for the overall business:

- Meeting financial and business objectives
- Maintaining and increasing corporate brand value and corporate reputation
- Protecting their network infrastructure investment
- Executing and protecting strategic initiatives (mergers, partner alliances, etc.)
- Providing a friendly and secure E-business environment
- Supporting a remote-based employee environment
- Reducing the time to market for providing new services to users and end clients

The security characteristics include:
- Access to security expertise to deal with rapidly evolving and complex issues associated with ensuring comprehensive network security
- Understanding network vulnerabilities and risks
- Protecting confidential corporate or client information
- Providing global and scaleable security solutions due to the expanding network size, geography mandates, or corporate mergers
- Quickly deploying new security technology or upgrading existing security products
- Providing customized security solutions for their clients' specific needs
- Quickly identifying and resolving network intrusions and misuse of the network equipment (reducing downtime) maximizing uptime and availability
- Training personnel on security
- Meeting industry-specific security requirements or statutes

SECURITY DRIVERS

In 1999, 75 percent of all firms were Internet-isolated. In contrast, by late 2004, 80 percent of businesses will be using the Internet as an integral part of their business processes. As the demand for Internet applications and the use of the Internet as a business medium, the opportunity for adverse security events negatively affecting the core business objectives will certainly increase.

The major drivers fueling the need for security include:

- Increasing network complexity
- Ensuring corporate value
- Lower management investment

- Business consolidation
- Mobile workforce
- Government regulations and standards

Increasing Network Complexity

Networks today comprise a multitude of devices, technology, and applications that are continually being pushed onto the Internet and interacting with customers and partners. The complexities in internetworking systems, and ultimately information, place a great deal of strain on the ability of companies to address core business demands while maintaining secure functionality of these systems. Business systems are more integrated and exchange information over complex networks such as the Internet.

In addition, security is being slowly pushed to the edges of the network, out to the user, to accommodate the growing inability to clearly define a perimeter. More and more companies are leveraging their technical investments to provide a shared environment for their customers, partners, and employees introducing a plethora of vulnerabilities. As the intermingling of users, applications, and networks continues, the line between the good guys and the bad guys is nearly impossible to locate. No longer is the Internet connection an obvious point for security controls when other companies—even competitors—are accessing specific applications within a private network. Penetration testing was originally performed over the Internet to test exposures that were externally facing. As networks become more technically integrated, and in business operations, a test cannot remain a simple attack over the Internet assuming that is where the greatest threats exist.

The increased complexities of an interconnected network and using the Internet have not only exposed businesses to the global online public, but have resulted in a composite of people, applications, and networks where any point within the system is intimately related to nearly every other point. The concept of the weakest link in the chain is truer today than ever before.

Ensuring Corporate Value

Today, many companies are publicly traded on the open market and maintaining shareholder value is significant in business success. In the event of a security breach, the perceived risk of investing in the company will undoubtedly increase, possibly leading investors to look for other avenues to ensure personal gains. The result can be devastating to an organization's brand value, with measurable financial losses.

With the growing dependency on technology to provide critical services over the Internet, companies are forced to ensure the security of those transactions or risk endangering company reputation and ultimately their equity. Protecting assets effectively instills assurance in the investors that the organization can meet their overall commitments.

Lower Management Investment

In competitive markets and industries, the demand to reduce spending on perceived noncritical technology is becoming routine. For many companies, security is not a core business requirement and therefore security solutions usually meet only the observable demands. Therefore, a financially palatable penetration test fits squarely into promoting the need for further security investment based on observed risks.

Nevertheless, the depressed economy during the turn of the century has forced many companies to re-evaluate investments that do not have a positive impact on the bottom line, and security is usually at the top of the list for superfluous items for next year's budget cut.

Business Consolidation

Organizations from all types of industries are seeking opportunities through mergers and acquisitions, and strategic partnerships. Because of the information exchange requirements and the consolidation of dissimilar network infrastructures, applications, and data, there is an increase in the opportunity for security-related issues. Interestingly, companies participating in these activities are acutely aware of the vulnerabilities associated with integrating systems with other entities and the exposure it implies. There is a resounding commitment to protecting information for all parties involved in these network-centric relationships inasmuch as the critical factor of combined success is protecting vital information assets.

Realizing security in a heterogeneous computing and business environment is exceedingly difficult and fraught with obstacles, many of which are expensive and have the potential of stagnating the evolution of business associated with the original merger.

Having an ethical hack performed before or just after a merger is complete can be very valuable for the combined organizations. Gaining visibility into the security control of unknown infrastructures can have a great impact on how they are combined and over what timeframe.

Mobile Workforce

As the demand for distributed operational models for companies increases to meet the demands of customers combined with cost-saving requirements, the result has been the continued evolution of a mobile workforce. A remote workforce needs access to corporate resources to accomplish tasks once provided only to on-site employees. According to IDC, the total population of remote and mobile workers in 1999 was around 35.7 million, and the prediction is to reach 47.1 million by the end of 2003. In addition, 24 percent of remote-capable PCs purchased by businesses with more than 100 employees are laptops. With the acceptance of mobility comes the necessity of securing transactions that leverage the Internet for cost-effective communications, such as VPNs. However, VPNs alone cannot solve the problems of exposing remote workers and data to the plethora of threats the Internet possesses.

The boom of remote workforces and VPN as an enabling inexpensive technology rode in on the coattails of broadband Internet connectivity. With broadband has come the exposure of corporate data on remote systems completely open on a constant Internet connection at home, far from the implemented security controls at corporate headquarters. These factors have resulted in security becoming a major initiative to protect information. Today, after firewalls and IDS investment, securing remote systems is the typical investment for many organizations.

In planning a penetration test, the scale of remote users and their access to assets must be evaluated, although testing a mobile workforce is filled with challenges. In most cases, the applications and services accessed by remote users are tested rather than the remote users and systems themselves. Typically, evaluating the security of remote access systems is realized by performing a security assessment to find vulnerabilities rather than attempting to exploit them. Exploiting remote system vulnerabilities is possible, however, much more is gained by direct observation.

Government Regulations and Standards

In recent years, we have seen the explosion of government involvement in establishing requirements for the protection of information and privacy. The recent proliferation of regulations is mostly due to two factors:

1. Publication of internationally accepted security standards, and
2. Increase in cyber-related attacks on private and public entities.

The advent of security standards has been based on the demand for a doctrine defining the security "best practices" security practitioners have been employing for over a decade. There have been several security standards to take shape, but the tide changed in 1996 when the British Standards Institution (BSI) introduced BS-7799 and then later added Part 2 in 1999. Later, in 2000, the International Standards Organization adopted the BSI standard (Part 1) as ISO-17799 and firmly set the bar for security practices.

Prior to the security standards, professional security service firms had only their collective experience and internally developed methodologies upon which to draw. When customers asked what the best practices were, they were met with a lukewarm answer. After the standards were introduced, companies could easily point to what was considered security best practices.

WHY HAVE THE TEST?

There are many reasons that drive a company to request a penetration test. More companies are seeking ethical hacking services today than ever before. Why is this the case? Many things can be realized by having a test performed. By exposing a weakness it is easier to prove to executive management the need for additional security investment. It can be part of a larger risk analysis or a phase in an application development cycle. A test can be used to validate concerns or tune systems and people to react appropriately to an attack. There are thousands of reasons, each with its own characteristics, that drive companies to look for ethical hacking services.

But why now? Why all the attention on performing penetration tests? One could submit that the awareness of the need for better security has been raised exponentially in the last couple of years, but the demands of running an efficient company have not changed; in reality those demands are greater now than ever before. Thanks to the ever-more-imploding economy, organizations are faced with enormous challenges to keep in step with growing customer demands, intense competition, selective clientele, cost reduction, and investor satisfaction. Now, insecurity can have a great impact on companies' success and many are having to address security head-on to remain competitive within the marketplace. Therefore, today organizations have more operating pressure in addition to addressing a component of their information systems not previously considered during the boom in the mid and late 1990s. Then, technology was seen as the enabler for business to create growth and success. Now that same technology is vulnerable and a potential liability.

Organizations of all types are faced with the dilemma of meeting business challenges and ensuring security. But security costs time, resources, and money, none of which are in great supply. Ethical hacking seems to be providing a guiding light to ensure investments in security are in alignment with what is actually needed as opposed to building a secure empire.

Proof of Issue

One of the predominant reasons for a penetration test is to prove security problems exist and convince upper management that a security vulnerability, which represents a substantial threat to business operations, can be exploited.

In most of the engagements, the driver for the nominal investment is to get more money for more security. It can become a vicious cycle, because security is a constantly evolving animal and at no point are you completely secure. Nevertheless, the popularity of ethical hacking is a sign that security is a concern for many, but they have to prove it.

NOTE 5: PRESENTING ONLY THE PROBLEM IS NOT ALWAYS THE SOLUTION

More often than not, meetings with companies will start by discussing security practices and what should be considered in order to enhance the security posture, only to end up answering questions about penetration testing. In one of these meetings—which seemed to go from one end of the security spectrum to the other—I stopped and asked, "What do you really want?" After a long pause, the Director of IT said, "A penetration test."

I explained this was a completely different approach to security given the goals and objectives shared in the meeting. When I was done, he said, "I have to prove we are not as secure as executive management would like us to be in order to get funding for future security."

Having heard this more times than I could count, I felt compelled to dig deeper. Did they have an overall security plan that the results of the test could be used to support? How secure did the executives think they were? The answers were disjointed because many who are in the position to prove the need for security are forced to act in a tactical manner and not permitted (given the time or resources) to address the larger issues.

Assuming the level of insecurity as they portrayed it, the option for an approach that started with a focused, very short test, followed by an assessment, and concluded by a short-, mid-, and long-term plan—with expected costs and timeframe—seemed to reach an acceptable middle point.

Before the engagement was to start, as an independent third party I had the opportunity to meet with the executives to gather their impression of security. Interestingly enough, they were very pro security and felt that although they performed good practices, there was considerable room for growth. At the conclusion of the engagement, the executives were more interested in the "answer" rather than the proof. If only a test had been performed, I would wager the outcome would have been much different.

The moral of the story is that although on the surface penetration testing appears to be a strong argument for investment, a logical approach that presents the problem and the solution in a meaningful way can go much further.

There is a practical side to the argument. Many business managers are held accountable for various IT investments, many of which need to have a direct impact on business operations. Whether to increase efficiency, to enhance the final product offering, or to stay in step with competition, investments need to show some form of return.

An investment in security is usually considered a business cost to protect other investments. Penetration tests are a comparatively cheap solution to the problem for middle management. They have the potential to demonstrate that security is not only an investment, it is critical to the overall success of the business, hence resulting in more money to support it.

Many tests are performed regularly to make executive management aware of potential risks. On receiving this type of information, they are sometimes more than willing to do what is necessary to maintain the integrity of the business systems and applications. The fact of the matter is many managers are simply too busy taking care of business to maintain the awareness required for sound security. Having a penetration test performed to support better security can be a very positive thing.

Penetration testing offers an opportunity to help organizations invest logically to address critical vulnerabilities rather than investing in technology that may miss the mark altogether. All too often security-specific measures become a fixation for organizations. Some companies have layers of firewalls and have a well-constructed DMZ, but the systems on the DMZ and the internal network are plagued with vulnerabilities. A test can assist in demonstrating weaknesses and present recommendations to modify existing technology to fully leverage their firewall investment.

Limited Staffing and Capability

Only recently have we seen the industry's commitment to security in the form of employing security professionals. Historically, companies have "grown their own" and looked for system administrators or security-savvy people in the IT department to help with security issues. Usually this begins with the implementation of a firewall, which ultimately leads to someone being selected as the "firewall-guy" (or gal). Moreover, the company starts to invest in that person in the form of training, supporting certification, and acquires tools to help them with their security endeavors. In the late 1990s, these employees saw their peers making more money as consultants and left their companies to pursue greater opportunities. The company would usually start the process all over again, sometimes resulting in the same outcome. Eventually, many organizations stopped investing in their security people and sought high-level, experienced security practitioners.

With the demise of the Internet economy, and now in late 2003 with the economy in shambles, many of those consultants are looking for more stable positions with enterprise companies. At the same time, companies are again looking for people with advanced security skills, not only skills in technology, but the business side of security.

So we're seeing a trend in the demand for more security and on some occasions it translates into new staff. Therefore, in addition to creating evidence for more security, ethical hacking provided by an outside firm can be directly associated with the lack of existing employees that have the necessary skills to perform the test. For a company to hire an ethical hacker to simply perform tests against them regularly would be an extreme situation (although I'm sure it has been done). Put aside that the employee would probably get bored, he would most certainly fall into a rut and become predictable. He would become too knowledgeable about the environment and eventually not be as effective.

Third-Party Perspective

Consultants and professional service providers are used because of three basic reasons: they have done it before for other companies and provided similar solutions that can be repeated; they maintain highly experienced people with specialized capabilities; and they can usually come in, get the job done, and leave the company with the ability to help themselves. In the world of security services, especially ethical hacking, there remains one more attribute: an outsider's perspective.

Different perspectives of security, internal relationships, and job stability are all potential obstacles to a sound security solution. In addition to being separated from the day-to-day demands of running a company, a consultant brings the element of independence, not hindered by knowledge of previous projects and technical issues surrounding the company. A consultant can come in and take a fresh look at the organization and make determinations based on his observations.

For ethical hacking services this presents two advantages: it promotes the concept of a hacker trying to penetrate the network defenses, and releases the consultant to look in places that someone familiar with the environment may not simply because she assumes it's secure.

Recently, a company was provided penetration-testing services and during the planning meeting asked that all effort be directed at the partner segment with its own Internet connection. When executives were asked about the regular Internet connection used for Web servers and employee access to the Internet, they stated that it was secure. On the surface, this is an acceptable request and we performed the engagement as directed. However, this leaves the fundamental question of value and completeness of the test.

Therefore, their assumption that the Internet-facing architecture was secure was based on their perspective and not by empirical evidence. It would seem logical to have a test on the second access point because both effectively led to the same core network and systems. In this case, a short test to simply look for vulnerabilities would have been prudent and would require little, if any more investment on their part. Of course, this leads us back to comprehensive business planning, but it does exhibit a tendency to make assumptions based on assumed comfort.

IT'S ALL ABOUT PERSPECTIVE

Look at M. C. Escher's painting *Concave and Convex* and you will quickly understand the meaning of perspective. On the other hand, maybe you prefer the saying, "A picture is worth a thousand words." No matter your definition, everyone seems to have a different perspective about security, especially penetration testing.

Certainly, we all agree on what is being done during the test, but what of the impacts our decisions have on the test? What are the inherent and imposed limitations and how do we work within them to ensure value? What are your expectations of the test and your security program? Setting expectations and understanding the limitations of the test will help ensure proper planning.

OVERALL EXPECTATIONS

Companies that look to ethical hacking for security services have a broad spectrum of expectations. This can be a touchy subject with many topics to consider, ranging from political, technical, financial, and simple naiveté of security. Many companies expect that the penetration engagement will represent a real hack and the results can be directly applied to operations to mitigate any further intrusion. Unfortunately, this is not possible because of the various limitations placed on the testers, such as time and ethics, and the dynamics of technology as well as the mindset and capabilities of the tester compared to a hacker.

Another assumption by test recipients is that the results are comprehensive. Everyone understands that no system is entirely secure and is vulnerable to some form of attack. Considering this, many conclude that a highly paid whitehat hacker should find a hole and successfully exploit it. With the pressure to be successful, a tester may identify a single vulnerability and spend the entire engagement exploiting it to ensure the engagement was successful, from his perspective. However, this begs the question, "What was missed?" It must be not be readily assumed that all the vulnerabilities were identified, much less exploited.

Expectations for the test will set the bar for which the success of the test is to be measured and will become the foundation of imposed limitations. When performing an ethical hack there must be restrictions to avoid seriously damaging equipment, imposing excessive downtime, destroying data, or causing personal anguish of targeted employees. Therefore, establishing limitations for the ethical hack is a standard procedure, but are organizations informed when adopting restrictions on the test or simply embracing fictitious boundaries?

For example, a customer, having just implemented several forms of IDS and network controls, wanted an ethical hack. During the initial conversations, it was stated not to reveal the existence of IDS to the testers. This is where the expectations and value collide.

Notifying the testers that IDS is present would allow them the opportunity to test vulnerabilities surreptitiously using specific IDS evasion techniques, ultimately testing the ability of the IDS in concert with the existence of vulnerabilities. Of course, the byproduct is actually tuning the IDS systems to a controlled, highly sophisticated attack.

The fictitious boundary in this example is the assumption by the organization that real hackers will not know IDS exists and therefore neither should the testers. This is a perfect example of a narrow understanding of the inherent limitations placed on the tester, poor threat profiling, and the inability to use the test to one's advantage rather than within a popular framework.

The prevalent philosophy behind ethical hacking is to attack a system. However, this perception ignores the confines of the test and the valuable role it can play in a security strategy. Simply stated, by forcing an experienced security professional to mimic an attacker greatly reduces the differentiating value of the test.

How Deep Is Deep Enough?

It is a common practice to define the networks and systems that are to be targeted, but it is rare to specify the depth of an attack.

There are two traditional approaches to dealing with the depth of an attack:

1. Specify a system, application, data, or authorization level to be obtained before halting the specific exploit.
2. Do not state any limitation to the depth of the attack.

Many companies communicate that if a certain point is reached, such as obtaining root on a server, to stop the engagement or contact the management team as soon as possible. In nearly every case, the boundary is associated with a system, application, database, or some other attribute of the network that represents a point where the test represents a threat to the integrity of the organization.

In contrast, there are those who simply do not stipulate any depth limitations. No restriction on the depth of the attack represents a poor perspective of the potential value of the test and security practices, not to mention the potential damage that may result.

In both cases, there is no solid reasoning behind controlling the depth of an attack beyond the simple protection of systems. In contrast, the depth of the attack should be directly related to the overall security architecture and the relation to identified vulnerabilities. We see much of this when the target wishes to review the list of vulnerabilities prior to the exploitation phase to gather greater insight as to the potential risks associated with each.

Ask yourself: What is the logical impact of a vulnerability? Is it always necessary to obtain root or was the vulnerability essentially proven long before acquiring root-level privileges? When a vulnerability exists and is exploited are there opportunities to make logical conclusions on the obtainable depth into a system without actually prying the hole open any farther?

When planning for the test, what constitutes a success should be defined. This is important for several reasons, most notably, time. Time is what costs money, typically, not a tool or some product. The time it takes to penetrate a network is directly associated with the cost of the test. Given that time is an element not applied to a hacker and only to a tester, the length of time it takes to actually exploit a vulnerability may be an obtuse investment. Most occasions exploiting the vulnerability are core to gaining the most value from the test. However, there are situations where the evolution of the attack meets a point where you are only stacking up evidence to prove a point that was made hours, if not days, prior. The point of the test is to determine the true risk of vulnerabilities to the company if they were exploited. Once that's met, then going beyond that point can be considered superfluous.

To illustrate this point, consider a traditional network with a firewall, IDS, a DMZ with Web servers, and some middleware connecting them to a database of account information. A tester begins by scanning the firewall and peering into the Web server. He identifies a vulnerability in the Web server that can be exploited through the firewall. He spends a few hours researching and discovers a method that could be used to disable the IDS with a paralyzing collection of packets. This proves to be successful and eventually exploits the vulnerability in the Web server. Now, with complete control of the Web server he uses the poorly configured middleware to inject data into the database. During this process he sees the database is running on a vulnerable version of UNIX. With a strong foundation established in the Web server he exploits the vulnerable UNIX system and with a rootkit obtains root on the system within minutes. As root he essentially owns the system and begins to move around the network in search of other opportunities. He spends several days finding many other UNIX hosts that have the same vulnerability and takes them over with much the same technique. At this point he uses the information collected to move to other networks throughout the company. By the end of the engagement, he has found no less than 15 vulnerable UNIX hosts throughout the network.

At what point was the risk associated with the vulnerability proven? As you can see, this is a very argumentative point. Supporters of the depth of the attack would argue that the process exposed weaknesses in many systems well beyond the initial point of entry. Other could argue that once the first UNIX system was exploited the vulnerability was proven. All the same, many would support that this was a very successful test. However, in the scope of true value, once the UNIX system was exploited, the tester should have noted it and looked for other unrelated opportunities. In fact, the tester's finding that all the UNIX systems had the same vulnerability would have been the first signal to the tester to look for other avenues of attack. Several critical vulnerabilities were identified: the IDS, Web server, and middleware to name only a few and all these were proven in a very short timeframe. As a hacker, this example is a great opportunity to wreak havoc on a company, but as a tester, the goal should be to expose a multitude of threats and use his understanding to project the likelihood of deeper attacks. If the tester were to continue launching attacks into the company from a fortified position, his customer, upon closer inspection, would realize the limited inclusiveness of the test and possibly question the overall value.

ONE-HOLE WONDER

To draw upon the previous discussion, there are occurrences of a single vulnerability being used as a gateway into the targeted network. A hole is found on a Web server in the DMZ and exploited to gain administrative control. Due to the lax security controls of the targeted company, the admin account's password is the same across several critical systems. The tester spends the entire engagement pulling sensitive information from every system for which she has administrative access. The results are collected and presented, having a profound impact on her customer.

But, under closer scrutiny the value of the test is nearly nonexistent. The test has proven the existence of a single vulnerability—a highly critical one—but one nevertheless. The test also proved internal security access methods are lacking a great deal. However, is a penetration test necessary to identify these shortcomings? A brief assessment investigating password management and access controls would have exposed the problem much faster, with less risk to operations, and probably at less expense.

All too often companies that know little about security seek penetration testing as the silver bullet to expose their strengths or weaknesses. When a test is performed using a single point of entry, the results are usually astounding and shocking. This is due to the fact that most companies have fortified borders and no regard for internal controls. Therefore, once in, the game is over. So by using the same argument, the test should be used to identify as many points of potential entry and stop, knowing the network could not withstand the attack.

So how is a company to know how to address these issues when a test is being performed? It comes down to balancing the test with the results being gathered and determining the scope of what you're trying to accomplish. If you want to know how far an attacker can get into your network without concern for the vulnerability, then a single hole will do just fine. This is the best approach for an organization that feels its perimeter and internal security controls are sufficient, but does not go as far as being concerned with internal threats. In contrast, if the perimeter is the foundation of your security, the exploitation of a single vulnerability will be useless.

TODAY'S HOLE

A regularly appearing phenomenon is the "day zero test." Day zero attacks are when a critical vulnerability is discovered and used by hackers in devastating scale before vendors and companies are aware the problem exists. The result is thousands, possibly millions, of systems being attacked in a single day, while people rush to seek a method for stopping the onslaught. Almost no one can prepare for these attacks and the ability to avoid day zero impacts is usually relegated to those who practice sound security.

The problem occurs when penetration testers leverage the timely opportunity to attack a client's network. It happens during an engagement when a day zero attack (at any scale) is realized by the tester and then used. To put this concept in perspective, consider the following engagement. An E-commerce company was seeking a penetration test to determine the overall weaknesses of their Internet-facing architecture. It was well accepted that security of these systems was critical to the success of the organization; virtually all of its revenue was realized from sales directly from the Internet. The engagement was planned for three weeks of testing focused at obtaining customer account information by nearly any means necessary. The customer was security savvy and the engagement would most certainly present a challenge to anyone testing or hacking their network.

Three days into the test ColdFusion announced a vulnerability that could allow attackers to run remote applications, obtain administrative access, and even perform a DoS attack. The vulnerability was substantial and the vendor quickly provided a patch that successfully remedied the flaw. Upon learning of the vulnerability, the testers immediately scanned for ColdFusion and found that all the systems were vulnerable. The testers used the vulnerability to utilize several tools to gain complete access to the systems. The firewall was of no help, the IDS had no signature that would identify the communication as an attack, and the multilayered DMZ architecture was not helpful because of the integration of ColdFusion into the systems. Within a couple of days, the single vulnerability was used to implant several backdoors, distribute tools to collect information, and cover tracks. For nearly the entire engagement the testers continued to leverage the initial hole to gain more control and more access even after the patch was implemented by their customer. The existence of hacker tools and Trojans on the affected systems only added to the difficulty of applying patches and troubleshooting system instability.

The value of this test can be questioned. Anyone running ColdFusion was exposed during that short period prior to the patch being available and applied. The testers used a small window of opportunity to gain control of various systems and continued to use them as a platform for further attacks after the patch was implemented only hours after it became available. The odds of having the same "success" without that initial vulnerability were not in the favor of the testers. But we'll never know, because that was the only avenue of attack tested.

This test provided very little value. In fact, it proved patch management is a critical element of protecting systems and the customer had a strong patch management process. The reality is connecting to the Internet presents inherent risks and the test did nothing to prove any true weaknesses. The customer did the best he could given the circumstances.

7 Planning for a Controlled Attack

At this point, we have investigated the various elements of information security. We've discussed common models of addressing security, the business of addressing security, and how exploiting vulnerabilities can have an impact on the value of the test based on the beliefs within the organization.

Using these discussions as a foundation, we move into planning for an attack. All too often integral components of a test are not contemplated before unleashing the invasion. It is necessary to contemplate discrete inborn attributes common to all forms of testing before you can expect any value from the engagement. To accomplish this we discuss each area in an effort to help you determine what aspects will have the greatest impact on value given your environment.

INHERENT LIMITATIONS

Touched upon earlier, inherent limitations are boundaries that cannot be crossed in the realm of ethical hacking. Many of these are based on the fundamental differences between a hacker and a security consultant. It can be argued that security professionals who interact with the hacking world can closely mimic a hacker; the reality is a consultant is being paid and the hacker has goals well outside the understanding of others. Inherent limitations are those restrictions that are associated with paying someone to perform an act normally practiced by criminals from a completely different culture and mindset. Following are some of the limitations that are intrinsic to the test:

- *Time.* The time a real hacker is afforded to collect information, gather tools, test the waters, get to know people, or any other aspect of hacking that can be used to obtained what is desired is arguably limited to only that person's life expectancy. One could rightly assume time is only a minor obstacle for a hacker and is limited by tenacity, determination, and the state of the target. On one side, time can be an enemy to a hacker because of a missed opportunity, or an ally waiting for the right circumstances to launch the attack. Both of these attributes are negatives to the tester. A tester must perform an attack in a given timeframe against a company more than likely prepared for the test.

- *Money.* It should not be assumed that hackers don't have any money. In reality, depending on the role they may play in organized crime, substantial investments may be made in providing them all the necessary tools and technology to perform their deed. For organized crime, investing $250,000 in a hacker is comparable to investing the same amount in guns or drug refinement equipment. By its very definition, crime syndicates are in the business of crime and invest the necessary funds to make more money. On the other hand, service firms that provide ethical hacking are usually limited by the amount of money they can make in a very competitive industry. Many times they are forced to make strategic investments in tools and people only when necessary and when funds are available. Nevertheless, a typical hacker does not have a great deal of money to put towards attacking others, but resourcefulness, time, and resolve more than make up for the lack of money. Finally, the money an organization is willing to invest in a test will have an impact on the scope and ultimately the inclusiveness of the test. Of course, this is related to time. With unlimited funds, time is not a formidable obstacle.

- *Determination.* Tenacity can play a significant role in how a hacker approaches a target. A disgruntled employee of a utilities company, Vitek Boden, took 48 attempts before he successfully accessed the SCADA system to release one million liters of sewage into the coastal waters off Queensland, Australia. The persistence of a hacker cannot be truly replicated because there are simply different motivators between the attacker and the tester. The tester wakes up in the morning, goes to work, gets a cup of coffee, starts hacking, and at the end of the day goes home with little personal attachment to the engagement. Comparably, strong feelings such as fear, anger, bravado, jealousy, and hatred increase the emotional investment of the hacker resulting in a greater sense of accomplishment in finding the elusive kink in the armor. Without some skin in the game and with limited time, the consultant may overlook an opportunity that may have simply taken more doggedness to uncover.

- *Legal Restrictions.* Regardless of a legal documentation put in place to protect the tester from typical activities that under normal circumstances would be considered illegal, a virtual line remains separating the typical attack strategy from an act of terrorism. For example, there is a sizable step between installing a Trojan on a remote system and releasing a worm on the Internet. There is a difference between a tester identifying a vulnerability that has the potential to shut down a city power grid and actually exploiting the vulnerability. It's doubtful there exists any legal documentation that could withstand the intentional act of perceivable terrorism or complete negligence on behalf of the tester in a court of law. Any attack that has the potential for serious damage or personal harm, or negatively affects other people or organizations, is a line a consultant cannot cross, and traditionally he operates to a point well before the virtual line between acceptable and devastation. Of course, this restriction does not apply to a hacker who may go to any length to obtain her goal. Therefore, the legal ramifications for hacking—at least up until recently—are negligible and represent a minor deterrent to the hacker. The only redeeming feature is that many of the more atrocious acts come with a substantial price if the hacker is caught, reducing the probability of broad devastating attacks, but not eliminating them altogether. Therefore, the tester may have the initial advantage and comfort in knowing he is protected while performing many of the tests, but the extent to which a consultant is willing to exploit a vulnerability is much less than what a determined hacker would do. The initial legal advantage can quickly become an intellectual disadvantage.

- *Ethics*. In every professional's career he is at one point faced with a dilemma that forces a decision based solely on his ethics. It's safe to say that security consultants have ethics in how they work with clients and others in the industry. With the lack of ethics, as with hackers, there are no limitations to the extent they are willing to go to accomplish a mission. Without some form of self-control, the limit is only defined by the readiness to expose one's self to risks. On the surface, risks are being caught and going to jail, but more extreme examples can include the loss of life, as with terrorists. At its most basic element, anything is possible if the attacker is prepared to risk everything, and in a mind with no ethics, there is no logical governance.

IMPOSED LIMITATIONS

The ability to realize the true value of a penetration test is proportionate to the client's interpretation of security and how those assumptions are translated into restrictions placed on the test. Limitations can be introduced by the customer for many reasons that can range from financial restrictions, which force less time and inherently reduce the scope of the engagement, to restrictions based simply on political positioning, personal perspectives on security, or a misguided attempt to focus the test.

Imposed limitations are elements of the test that are not employed for reasons that may not have anything to do with security. In fact, one could argue that imposed limitations have nothing to do with security at all and materialize to simply promote control of the engagement.

Of course, imposed limitations can be very positive controls placed on the test to foster accuracy, organize scope, and manage the force of the test. Usually, restrictions are placed on the engagement to avoid an all-out attack on the network. Without some limitations, the probability of system failure, data loss or destruction, or excessive downtime is imminent. In addition to direct impact on the client, without scope control and management of permitted tasks, intermediates may become overly involved affecting business relationships and introducing legal exposures.

Obviously, the overall goal of introducing limitations on the test is to ensure total mayhem does not ensue. Meanwhile, one has to be careful not to place undue restrictions on the test that may be critical to the value of the engagement. All too often, the planners of the test introduce boundaries that usually make for questionable results and stale deliverables.

Unfortunately, a byproduct of unrefined imposed limitations is oversimplification, resulting in the point where everything is important and cannot be exposed to a test. By segmenting the security into very broad areas a sense of what digital components are critical to the organization can be realized. This is not an uncommon practice for other security-related services, but rarely used as an opportunity to control excessive limitations imposed on an ethical hack.

Again, when placing restrictions on the test the client must consider the implications to the overall value of the test. The only way to accurately distinguish what restrictions are needed and which ones are superfluous, affecting the value of the test, is to clearly articulate what is being tested—what is the point of the test? Again, this is directly related to the assumed threat type and overall exposure to those threats. Even the smallest test that only focuses on one area of the network or a single application can be valuable if the goals of the test are within the scope of overall security needs in relation to the business objectives.

Imposed limitations can have more obscure results that do not readily appear and may remain hidden from view throughout the entire engagement and the final deliverables, ultimately affecting the implementation. Many of these have to do with limiting the tools, technique, and targets of the tester. It is very common for a client to specify what systems are permitted to be attacked and which ones are not, assuming that the attack will not yield any greater insight if the excluded systems were tested. Again, this assumption can be based on the importance of the server's uptime or simply that the client does not feel there are any vulnerabilities and therefore does not permit the test.

At the other end of the spectrum is allowing all systems to be attacked, becoming overly involved in the test, and micromanaging which tactics can be employed. The assumption of the client is that he knows more about the target system and is therefore better positioned to determine when the attack is successful or has reached a dead end. Customers that demand close involvement usually hinder the process by the implication of distrust and disturbing the flow of the tester to work her art. Therefore, an imposed limitation can materialize in the form of customer micromanagement of the test when in nearly all cases it is best to leave it up to the experts.

So what are imposed limitations anyway? Following are some very basic examples that some may consider outlandish and others may regularly practice. The point of the small list is to stimulate thought and introspection about your opinions of limitations that have the potential to affect value:

- No dumpster diving.
- Only test certain IP addresses.
- Do not use ISS.
- No Trojans.
- No vulnerability can be exploited until permission is obtained.
- Only wardial certain telephone numbers.
- No e-mail-based social engineering.
- No Web application-focused attacks.
- Only attack Windows systems.
- Do not use partner information to support an attack.

- Do not attempt to avoid detection.
- Only attack one site.
- Do not attack customer DNS systems.
- No user-focused attacks.
- No DoS attacks.
- No information shall be shared between testers on the engagement.
- No information is to be changed.
- No calling cards are to be left behind.
- Do not attempt to attack ports over 1024.
- Only test services running on specified ports.
- If a password file is obtained, the test must stop.

The list can go on because every permution of attack is unique to each environment, but as you can see, there are some basic limitations that can affect the outcome. A few should stand out. For example, only permitting wardialing on selected phone numbers would seem counterproductive in discovering rogue backdoors. By limiting the numbers called, there is the assumption of security associated with the excluded numbers.

The same holds true for limiting the IP addresses. Best practices for determining IP addresses for the ethical hack is to define entire ranges or networks allowing the tester to seek entities you may not even know exist. Today, many stipulate what IP address to test, when in fact you should only specify IP addresses you do not want the tester to affect at all. Using the practice of defining what IP not to attack rather than those permitted promotes greater value to the test.

Finally, any limitations defined in the planning of the engagement, or even during the test, must be documented clearly. This is to ensure when the results are placed under scrutiny that there is a record of the restriction. This can be especially valuable when the value of the engagement is questioned by someone from the client who was not involved in the planning or execution of the test.

NOTE 6: IMPOSED LIMITATIONS CAN CAUSE PROBLEMS FOR EVERYONE

During the planning meeting of an engagement, the customer made several stipulations on the scope of the test without any explanation. In the positioning of providing services it's fairly difficult to make demands of the person who is paying you. The test was performed and the final deliverable and presentation were given to the CIO and the entire management staff. About halfway through the presentation the CIO made it clear that the work performed was well below expectations and questioned the value of our involvement. When the limitations of the test were conveyed the CIO was still not convinced they would have any impact on the test results and maintained his position. In an effort to make amends and to point out that the limitations did have an impact on the deliverable, we offered a free two-week security assessment. At the end of the assessment the systems that were excluded from the test—which were either directly related to the included systems or on the same DMZ—were in fact wide open and presented an enormous threat to the company. When the manager was questioned about the exclusion of the highly vulnerable systems by the CIO there was no acceptable answer. We were paid for the penetration test as well as the assessment.

It is difficult to completely convey the negative impact of excessive restrictions, especially those founded on poor reasoning with little or no alignment to business needs. However, this discussion is not to ridicule scope management practices to ensure safe and effective tests within the realm of the customer needs. Moreover, planning a test without having restrictions is nearly impossible and determining when a restriction is overkill is not always easy.

The best method to determine the impact of a limitation in question is to understand the desired outcome and value of an approved task. If you and the consulting firm can agree that the approved portion of the test will provide insights similar to the questionable limitation, then there is no need to scrutinize it. However, the imposed limitation may not allow the tester to accomplish a valued characteristic demanded from the test, but not plausible from other approved tasks. For example, a company states that no wardialing is to be permitted, yet there is a concern for people connecting from home with modems. Without an alternative to wardialing, there is little hope in supporting this demand and providing value.

TIMING IS EVERYTHING

Security is constantly changing within an organization. Through the adoption and evolution of technology, practices, management, and the perception of security within the company, the security posture of a firm rises and falls frequently. Many characteristics of security increase, decrease, or simply fluctuate with time. As one characteristic gets more attention, others are certainly going to wane or grow stagnant. For example, many companies start their security with technology, such as a firewall, and as the adoption of security becomes more involved, a security policy is ratified to define a doctrine of security. The typical security policy not only communicates good security practices in use at the time of writing, but also usually includes remedial and tactical security plans, setting the bar for the future of security. Once the security policy is communicated, the company starts the process of meeting those demands and in the process ignores the security policy. As time moves on the security policy becomes disconnected from the company as well as the current security demands placed on the company.

Security is the combination of technology, management, culture, and policy, and it is difficult to do all of them at the same time in the challenging environment of a typical company. Therefore, elements of security begin to suffer and become fragmented due to the lack of attention and ultimately action by the company.

Where a penetration test is performed, the cycle of security within an organization can affect not only the outcome, but also the value of the test. It is not only essential to ensure the test is reflective of the threats the client is concerned about, but the extent of the test, and even if the test should be performed, should be weighed heavily.

When a test is performed against an ill-prepared company, the results are scattered and disjointed, and it is difficult to isolate the larger issues. Typically, the closing presentation and the documentation from the engagement are filled with vulnerabilities, and the recommendation is for an information security management program to be implemented as soon as possible. In other words, "You're wide open and have few effective security measures in place."

So how do you know if you are ready for a test? The answer is simple: "Have you been regularly performing good security practices?" Companies know if they are secure or not, or at least have the ability to predict how well they could withstand an attack. If the answer to the previous question is "No" or "Sort of," you should reconsider having an ethical hack against your network. It is not to say the test cannot be helpful in some ways, but mostly the end result is an unmanageable list of vulnerabilities that will only resurface after being corrected, mostly because it is a sign of a more deep-rooted problem. Vulnerabilities in high numbers are one of the symptoms of an insecurity disease.

Nevertheless, organizations continue to venture into penetration tests aware of the fact they have little if any security in place that could withstand a direct assault. In many cases, the determination to have the test done is based solely on justification of the need for more security. Although this is one of the predominant reasons today for having a test performed, it can only provide limited value to the organization as a whole and is typically used to simply raise upper management awareness.

ATTACK TYPE

Given the scope and scale of the Internet, it is easy to assume that there are huge numbers of hackers out there with varying degrees of intent and capability. No matter the number of hackers, it is possible to reduce their activities into two basic areas that allow us to glean more information about hackers and their targets.

1. *Opportunistic*. An opportunistic attack is the result of hackers looking for vulnerable systems rather than systems with specific information for the taking. Usually this is reflected by the plethora of hacks that follow a vulnerability report and the launch of a worm that uses a vulnerability to spread itself and cause trouble. In all cases, the target was identified after the vulnerability was discovered and then exploited. Typically, these attacks are preceded by a port scan or some form of discovery process that exposes the vulnerability. Although this may seem innocuous, many of the hacks on the Internet can be attributed to this type of attack. Mostly, the result is a denial of service, Web defacement, or temporary loss of data. What can be disturbing is the number of highly effective attacks that are based on using the initial vulnerability as a beachhead to launch a much more devastating attack.
2. *Targeted*. A targeted attack is the assumption that the hacker knows the target and knows what she wants to accomplish. Although this is based on whether the attacker is looking for any type of vulnerability to gain access, as opposed to looking for a specific vulnerability for any type of

company, an arguably indeterminate metric, it does demonstrate the basic approach of a hacker. Therefore, one would rightly conclude that ethical hacking is a targeted attack type.

SOURCE POINT

There are several types of attack that can be employed to help a company determine its exposure. Typically, these are broken into three major areas, each resulting in various conclusions about where the attack is launched.

1. *Internet.* When you hear the term ethical hacking you immediately picture someone hacking into a network from the Internet. In most cases, this is a reality. The Internet is seen as the source for all the pains associated with hackers, even though statistics tell us that equal loss is attributed to internal threats. Nevertheless, in most penetration-testing engagements, the Internet is the source point of the attack. This helps an organization determine its exposure to the plethora of attacks represented by an endless sea of threats.

2. *Extranet.* To function in today's connected economy, most companies maintain some form of connectivity with partners, suppliers, and customers. All of these connections are critical to the successful operation of the business and are sometimes overlooked (arguably on purpose) when it comes to security. However, companies are starting to take a greater interest in the security of their connectivity with their business constituents. Today more and more companies are performing tests against their once-trusted networks to look for vulnerabilities that may exist between partners or between them and remotely connected networks. This is also true when attempting to map a network. On more than one occasion discovery tools are used on these network segments only to find that they can see the entire network of a partner, or even worse, of an old partner that should have been disconnected a long time ago.

3. *Intranet.* Arguably, one of the more complicated aspects of ethical hacking is the internal hack. Discussed in much greater detail in the following sections, internal hacking can range from running hacking tools on the internal network to posing as an employee with all the necessary credentials. Intranet-based attacks can be difficult to perform given the imposed limitations, but in practice it is like a playground for testers. Internal attacks are coveted by testers because many organizations are soft on the inside and there is something very 007 about surreptitiously hacking away at a company within its walls. Let's be honest: it can be fun.

REQUIRED KNOWLEDGE

Planning a test in a fashion that will promote the greatest value can be difficult to say the least. One of the first steps in establishing the rules of engagement is considering what information about the target should be provided to the tester. No matter the scope or scale of a test, information flow initially will set in motion other attributes of planning and ultimately meeting factors for which value will be measured.

Usually some form of information is provided by the target and only in the most extreme cases absolutely no information is offered. Some cannot be avoided, such as the name of the company, whereas others can be easily kept from the testers without totally impeding the mechanics of the test.

Following are some basic definitions of information provisioning:

- *Zero Knowledge.* Zero knowledge is just that: the tester is provided nothing about the target's network or environment. The tester is simply left to his ability to discover information about the client and use it to gain some form of access. This is also called blackbox or closed depending on who is scoping the test.
- *Limited Knowledge.* Something growing in popularity with companies seeking penetration testing is providing just enough information to get started. In some cases information may include phone numbers to be tested, IP addresses, domain information, applications, and other data that would take some time to collect and do not represent any difficulty to a hacker, but are rather time consuming for the tester. The interesting aspect of getting some information and not all is the assumption of scope. Organizations tend to use limited information to define the boundaries of the test as opposed to providing initial data to support the engagement. For example, there is a difference in providing whether a customer has IDS as opposed to providing a list of phone numbers. The former is an obvious attempt to limit the information provided to the tester, whereas the latter is influencing the scope of the engagement.
- *Total Exposure.* Total exposure is when every possible piece of information about the environment is provided to the tester. Prior to the start of the engagement, a list of questions and required items is sent to the customer in preparation for the meeting. At the meeting, reams of documents are provided to help the tester gain as much knowledge about the network as possible. This is also known as crystal box, full knowledge, or open, again depending on who is planning the engagement.

We find out through this journey in ethical hacking that the seemingly simple concept of providing information (or not) will dramatically affect the scope and depth of the test resulting in different levels of value.

TIMING OF INFORMATION

During the planning of the test it may be determined that several pieces of information are provided to assist the tester in finding opportunities to attack the network by saving time in collecting the information, but also help in testing the organization's incident-management capabilities. There is an option to control the flow of information from the company to the tester to keep the test stimulated and reflect multiple types of attack scenarios. In the later section, "Multi-Phased Attacks," we cover the different nuances of information management and larger teams of testers focused on a single target; but for now, the goal is to demonstrate the value of information, how and when it can be shared with the tester, and the advantages and disadvantages of the practice.

Security is realized by layers of controls and checks supported by process and management to ensure an overall secure posture. Layers typically materialize in the form of access controls, user rights, and services offered to the authenticated user, among many other things. All of these are based on information or tools made available to users. Each set of information is related to what controls are required for that layer in the security architecture and the roles associated with the user or an application.

To accommodate the needs for variable controls for cyber assets, for example, many companies employ some form of division of authorization through segmentation of systems, networks, and even applications. A company may have three different types of customers, each accessing similar data from a centralized database but with increasing levels of access. The first type may have purchased a monthly newsletter to be e-mailed and be provided an account on a Web server to modify their profiles regularly to ensure they are receiving information in which they are interested. Another type of customer is someone who has paid for enhanced services and is provided access to an application server, such as Citrix or Microsoft's Terminal Server, to use the application supported by data provided by a back-office database. Finally, there may be customers with hundreds of users requiring dedicated access to the network to get the necessary data directly from the systems.

Given this scenario, there are four different avenues into the network.

- Internet
- Web authenticated
- Application service
- Direct access

Internet

Basic use of the Web site and Internet-facing systems is the initial type of access provided to the public. A public access Web site is posted to attract new customers and provide information about the company and the services offered, such as the newsletter. Without any added information, this is the typical route of a hacker beginning an attack against exposed systems that are offering services, such as Web, e-mail, and FTP, that can be exploited to gain access. As a tester, this can also be used as an initial starting point for the test. The Web site can offer information that can be used during the reconnaissance phase of the engagement, or attempt to directly exploit vulnerabilities in any Web-based applications. The value to the customer is clear, seeing that attacking a system on the Internet as if by an uninformed hacker or script kiddy is the fundamental motivator for having the test performed in the first place.

Web Authenticated

To provide personalized use of the Web and make modifications to their profiles, users may provide a username and password to access private areas of the Web site.

Usually, the customer pays via credit card and receives the necessary credentials via e-mail or other form of communication.

A hacker may surreptitiously obtain a paying customer's identity to make modifications to the profile to acquire valuable data, or attempt to use the privileged access to look for more opportunity to attack the network. Attacks can be based on application code only available to authorized Internet users, or provide the opportunity to inject invalid data into the profile in hopes of unearthing a vulnerability. From the perspective of an ethical hacker, the added support of a stolen username and password would help in identifying any vulnerabilities to which a hacker with the same information may be privy.

The client can realize several layers of value depending on when the credentials were provided to the tester. Fundamentally, the client gains an understanding of the vulnerabilities associated with privileged users. Also, depending on the severity the vulnerability represents in the special area of the Web site, the customer can determine how much investment should be made to rectify it. The reasoning of measuring risk against cost of access and the severity of a vulnerability is based on the likelihood of occurrence. The more people who have access, the greater the likelihood that someone with bad intentions will push the limits. If the cost of a username and password is $30.00 per month, a hacker would be less likely to pay the initial fee without knowing there is a vulnerability worth $30.00 deep within the site. In contrast, if the cost were $2.00, the odds of a hacker with a certain degree of motive would likely spend the money on the off chance of finding a hole with greater potential.

Of course, these assumptions are completely based on the security of the enrollment and payment applications. If a hacker can steal the credentials, the risk factor calculated against the cost and exposure is nullified. However, this is exactly the reason why not providing the credentials to the tester until all other uninformed attempts to access the site are executed is so valuable to the customer (unfortunately, this simply takes more time). Ultimately, when the tester fails to gain greater access, the credentials are then provided to perform a test against the secured portion of the Web site. The customer will have a better understanding of the security of the Web site, the severity and exposures related to an exploited vulnerability, and an initial roadmap to repair.

Application Service

A user may pay more to have direct access to an application to allow more features and information than the limited security portion of the Web site. As with the secured Web site, a user can buy the enhanced version of the service, obtain the credentials, and directions on installing a small client application or plug-in for her browser.

As with anything offered on the Web, a terminal services system may be vulnerable to attack without any credentials. Therefore, the organization may, at first, offer no insight to the advanced services offered in an effort to understand the vulnerabilities to the common hacker. However, much like the Web access example above, once the tester has failed, credentials allowing typical client access can then be used to deduce exposures that correspond to enhanced client access.

The ability to launch an attack against the client's network based on the added privileges can be enlightening for the company. Depending on the application and configuration of the terminal system, it may be possible to collect ample amounts of information that can be used later via a different route, or actually launch an attack from the vulnerable system.

However, what is the potential risk the tester is representing by performing the test? Once again, we can revisit the cost of the service and the identified vulnerabilities to determine the overall risk associated with providing the services online. However, in most cases, the goal is to determine what exposure is related to the authorized customers. Some applications are complex and if manipulated correctly, they can be used against the company, such as destroying data and bringing the system to a halt.

No matter what depth of the attack ultimately acquired by using supplied credentials, the reality is that the test is demonstrating risk related to authorized users and does not clearly reflect what a hacker may do. Nonetheless, some risk is attributed based on the likelihood that a hacker would obtain authorized credentials or gain access to the application through other means. Overall, the test is a viable tactic and by providing the information after exhausting all other avenues of attack, the customer is assured the test was comprehensive and reflective of many different types of threats.

Direct Access

For companies with hundreds of users requiring access to specific information, an organization will typically provide network connectivity in the form of a VPN or frame relay connection to support the volume of traffic and greater number of features offered to a premium client. The goal of the target having a penetration test performed in this scenario is to understand the level of risk associated with many unknown sources accessing their network based on a single connection, one that may have only one level of authentication representing all the remote users. The exposure to an attack is either high or low depending on how paranoid you are about security, the setup of the connection, and the depth to which the remote users and systems are allowed into your network. Regardless of the presumption of risk, having a penetration test performed against the dedicated network and application can be helpful and valuable.

As with any cyber threat, the likelihood of an attack—based on privileged access—is related to how credentials are provided, the number of users provided access, the value of the asset being accessed, and the vulnerability of the system or application. When credentials are provided to a user, especially a user from outside the company's domain or control, such as an employee of a partner, there is an assumed level of authentication prior to providing access. If the identification and authorization of the remote users is weak, and there are thousands of them, the likelihood of one of them attempting to harm your network is measurable, if not substantial.

To perform this phase of the engagement, the tester is made aware of the existence of the network and is permitted to attempt an attack with no specialized access provided. There are many situations where this does not provide any additional benefit simply because the tester cannot gain access to a frame relay network or it would require attacking a customer or partner. However, if the customer network is VPN-based and leverages the Internet, there is a potential for a vulnerability to be exploited to gain access to the network. Although it is somewhat rare and requires some sophistication, an attack on a VPN device could be performed by a motivated and experienced hacker. Given the complexity of the attack without providing direct access for the tester, many clients offer network connectivity to execute the test. A modem is usually the method of choice to allow the tester to access the segment connecting the customers to the client's network, although if a VPN is employed, the tester is provided the necessary credentials to act as a customer.

MULTI-PHASED ATTACKS

Many companies look to have several types of penetration testing performed in parallel or series in an attempt to gather as much insight into their security posture as possible. Usually multi-phased tests are based on source points of the test, information provided to the testers, when the information is provided, and any supporting materials associated with the test, such as a username and password. Multi-phased tests represent a plethora of management and value challenges due to the number of phases or resources working on the engagement, but the value realized from the exercise can be exceptional.

In a multi-phased test, the concept is to determine the security posture of the organization at various levels of access and knowledge that a hacker may potentially obtain. In this scenario, an Internet-based attack is typically performed with zero knowledge provided to the tester, followed by limited access attack, such as a VPN account, dial-up access, or a username and password to a terminal system such as Citrix or Microsoft's Terminal Server. The final step is for the customer to provide the tester with internal access to the network. This is usually accomplished by allowing the tester to act as an employee with all the usual credentials. On some very rare occasions, the client requests the internal tester to act as an administrator within the organization.

There are few situations where providing administrator access to the tester provides any value to the customer for obvious reasons. With administrator access virtually anything is possible, negating the effectiveness of the test. However, for companies who employ separation of duties, this can be beneficial to measure the ability of a single person to perform administrative functions that would normally require more than one employee. Separation of duties is a practice whereby certain tasks require more than one person to accomplish them, thereby reducing the ability of a single person to make illegitimate changes to systems. A very simple concept in theory, but difficult to implement and maintain, especially in companies that have limited administrative or security staff.

In a serially performed engagement, one or more consultants is used in each phase before moving on to the next. In parallel, multiple consultants are used at the same time performing each exercise simultaneously. In each type, the exchange or transfer of information about the client's network to the testers increases, providing more insight to the various vulnerabilities. How this information is shared and used throughout the penetration test can impede or support the overall value of the test and the results will be reflective of the type of threat trying to be replicated. As you can see, this can become very complex and the value of the test rides on the ability of the client as well as the professional services organization to properly plan and execute in accordance with what the test was determined to mimic.

By combining types of attack, such as from the Internet with no information, with limited information, and from inside the target, with how information is shared among these phases, a great deal of insight from the test can be had. The key is determining the information to provide to the testers, when, and in what context relative to the other testers and phases. In a series multi-phased attack, this is fairly simple because when one phase ends another starts, providing a direct correlation to the information timing. In contrast, in a parallel attack the flow of information and when one tester is privy to data collected by another can greatly affect the outcome of the test. In many cases companies will seek a parallel test to shorten the time allotted for the test and avoid the complexity altogether by asking that information not be shared.

So what is the big deal? The fact is that information about a target's network, systems, or applications is key to the entire test. More data available to the testers means more opportunity to find a vulnerability or exploit a weakness. Depending on how you interpret your security posture, level of exposure, and threat signature, you can tweak the test to best reflect the available investment and business demands concerning security.

If a company is concerned about collusion between an employee and an outside hacker, then a parallel attack with sharing information between them is needed. On the other hand, if the client is worried about a hacker targeting her company (starting with the Internet and then gaining employment), a serial attack should be used. Finally, there is a time limit to the test that may demand a parallel test to mimic an attack by a single person (moving from hacker to employee, such as a serial attack), but using multiple testers not sharing information learned about the client's environment during each phase. The following explanation should help in summarizing each of the four types:

1. Parallel shared
2. Parallel isolated
3. Series shared
4. Series isolated

PARALLEL SHARED

Multiple resources attacking the client network from the Internet, with limited access, and internal presence at the same time, and sharing information between them to gain added benefits, is an example of a parallel-shared attack structure.

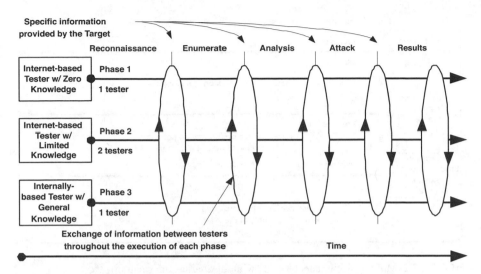

FIGURE 7.1 Impacts of Multiple Attackers Sharing Information Simultaneously

Companies should employ this type of attack when they are concerned about employees collaborating with hackers to obtain information or money. It is worth noting that many crimes, physical and digital, that result in financial losses—typically cash—are the result of insider participation in the planning and execution of the crime. The timing of sharing information can also influence the ability to mimic the threat. In some cases, the information from a previous phase is concealed from the following phase until a certain point is achieved or the second phase has reached a dead end. Previously obtained characteristics about the target are then shared from one tester to another to stimulate the following phase, and so on throughout the engagement. In addition, some clients have placed stipulations controlling the type of information that is conveyed from one phase to another.

For example, the Internet penetration test may be immensely successful in obtaining usernames and passwords to critical systems. If this data were to be utilized during the second, or limited, information phase, the customer-provided username and passwords could be negated, adversely affecting the entire test-to-threat strategy.

One of the more complicated aspects of the parallel-shared method (shown in Figure 7.1) is the direction of the information flow. It may be readily assumed that information is flowing outwardly, such as the internal threat resource sending data to the Internet-based attacker to support the external attack. However, there may be situations where the limited or even the Internet-based attacks can obtain interesting information to assist the internal tester. An example is the internal tester, acting as employee, may not have electronic or even physical access to certain parts of a data center that may store all the electronic commerce transactional data. In contrast, the Internet attacker may have collected information about the system, such as a password or an application hole, that is better exploited internally due to other cyber obstacles facing the outside tester.

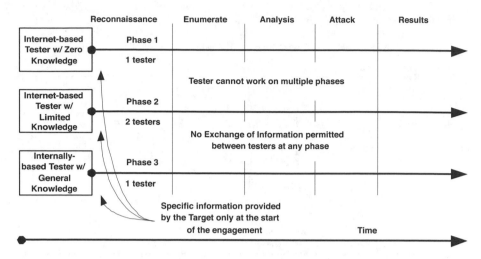

FIGURE 7.2 Multiple Simultaneous Tests without Sharing Information

PARALLEL ISOLATED

There are occasions where the multi-phased test is performed in parallel, but no information is exchanged between the consultants performing the tests. This is much more than limiting information to certain types or withholding data from the following phase; it is not passing along any data from one phase to the next. The typical reasons for executing the engagement in this way are time limitations or the scale of the client's company demands multiple resources and to perform serially would take an overwhelming amount of time and ultimately money (see Figure 7.2).

There are few security reasons to perform a test of this type to mimic a real assault. In nearly all cases, the driving factors are money and time. For those who have or plan to use this type of attack and do not have these driving limitations and desire to replicate some form of threat, the objectives should be reviewed to ensure a real-world scenario is being enacted.

SERIES SHARED

There is always the potential for an attacker to move from a digital attack to a physical one. This is especially true in comprehensive and well-funded attacks, such as espionage or terrorism. Also, there are examples of hackers failing to gain their targets through traditional mechanisms and resulting in physical theft of the information.

On the other hand, it can also include the criminal seeking and obtaining employment at the target company and waiting for the right opportunity to strike. The final attack may be theft or obtaining enough information about the company's security measures and practices to launch a successful attack remotely (see Figure 7.3).

No matter the scenario, there exists a credible threat to organizations of individuals gaining employment for the simple purpose of attacking them later. Given

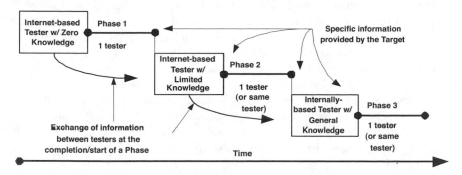

FIGURE 7.3 Sequential Testing Permitting Information to Flow from One Phase to the Next

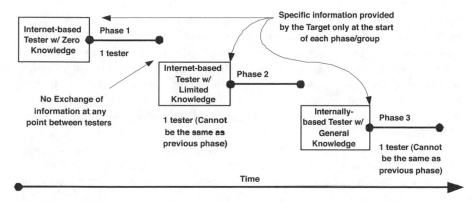

FIGURE 7.4 Sequential Testing without Permitting Information to Flow from One Phase to Another

threats of this nature, some companies will use multi-phased attacks performed in series by one or more consultants or even more than one consulting firm, using the best attributes of each company. The more people and services firms that are involved, the more difficult it is to share information, as opposed to one resource performing the entire engagement. Nevertheless, depending on the timeframe, investment, and number of people and scale of the client, the typical number of consultants is low.

SERIES ISOLATED

Series multi-phased penetration tests where information is not transferred from one phase to another is typically practiced when each phase is considered unique, unrelated, and there is ample time allotted to the engagement. This technique is also leveraged when there is a great deal of management associated with each phase. For example, a customer may want an Internet-based attack to include reconnaissance, enumeration, and vulnerability analysis, but stop at that point to evaluate the discovered vulnerabilities and determine what they consider to be the next step in the engagement based on the findings (see Figure 7.4).

The same milestone management is typically applied to each phase, moving to limited-information Internet attacks and on to internally based attacks. Each phase is measured and evaluated on its own merits and there is no consideration or assumption of collaboration of the assumed threat type. Therefore, the use of this method makes a clear statement about the assumption of threat. By eliminating the exchange of information from one phase to another, it could be argued that an optional intrinsic value of the test is being ignored. Conversely, companies may not agree with the type of threat and actually glean insights from the fragmented attack style.

In fact, there are arguments for and against series-isolated forms of a test. In either case, ensure that the test structure is reflective of the business goals for managing risk.

VALUE OF MULTI-PHASE TESTING

It is safe to assume that information is the key to a successful test, or a real attack for that matter, and managing information in a multi-phased, or even a straightforward, penetration test can directly affect the true value of the test being performed. If the fundamental motive of having a penetration test executed against your environment is to see how well you stand up to a hacker, then you must consider the access and flow of information to maintain a real-world scenario. It is for this reason that imposed limitations can become the catalyst for limited or insignificant results from a test.

Based on the type of threat a company is seeking to replicate and test their network's and system's resistance to certain types of attack, the structure and method of a multi-phased attack becomes a key component of the value perceived at the conclusion of the test.

For example, in a parallel or serial-shared multi-phase attack information shared between the phases at certain times has the potential to increase the realism of specific threats. For example, in Figure 7.5, the gaps represented by the letters A, B, and C close as information from one phase is passed to another. Information feeds, such as 1 and 2, are passed to the Informed, yet External tester greatly escalating their potency in the overall test. As the Informed tester uses feeds 1 and 2 there is an opportunity to feed data to the Zero informed tester (feed 3) making her more effective, and the cycle continues.

There are several reports detailing the level of risk related to internal threats. For example, the ability for any half-baked person to download a sniffer, set up a trigger, and start collecting POP passwords is trivial, but this simple technique can lead to serious problems. Although this threat can be assumed for many companies, one cannot assume the extent of that exposure. Most, if not all, networks use switches, a networking device to segment networks that reduces network noise and enhances performance. One of the many attributes of switches is that packets go only to the destined segment. The result is Mr. Hackwannabe, sitting in the warehouse on a dedicated segment, is typically not going to see traffic between two distant networks. It is for this very reason organizations seek ethical hacking, to determine the level of exposure, but there needs to be more effort on deriving the probability of the attack to evaluate the real impact.

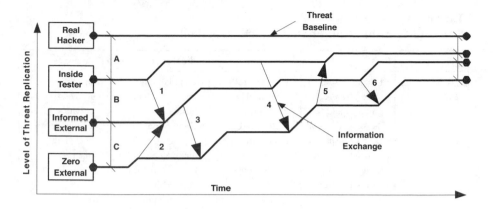

FIGURE 7.5 Impact of Overlapping Information in a Multi-Phased Approach

The above example is painfully simplified and does not demonstrate the innate complexity of attacks, internal or otherwise, but the goal is to provoke thought about the scope of an attack and the criticality of the structure and assumptions made about the attack methodology. Multi-phased penetration tests are an opportunity to test many types of threats by well-planned information management and timing of the phases. By manipulating information flow and when a test is performed, companies can achieve a greater understanding of the security of their environments, and usually in much less time than assumed.

EMPLOYING MULTI-PHASED TESTS

Employing a multi-phase attack has the potential to introduce several types of complexities and costs to the target. Nevertheless, many of these challenges are greatly outweighed by the potential for considerable value of the test. Understandably, complexity is the most prevalent reason for not seeing many of these engagements performed often. But complexity is not the only reason. Companies looking to have tests performed usually have a predefined perception of what they want, leading to a conclusion on the scope and methodology of the test they expect. Vendors of ethical hacking services are more than capable of performing complex tests, but comprehensive testing scares many of their customers.

In an effort to quell some of the confusion about what the value versus complexity can be when considering the use of multi-phased attacks, Tables 7.1 and 7.2 provide characteristics of each to help make a decision.

The easiest approach to a multi-phased test is to compare the scope of the test to the goals and look for opportunities to segment the engagement. If segmentation is a plausible avenue, one needs to investigate the advantages of how information can be used to gain the most value from the test. Although it does require more planning, keeping it simple will go a long way. Isolate the information that is to be shared between testers from the information provided by the target. Clearly define what type of information is needed to represent the threats that meet the objectives.

TABLE 7.1
Pros and Cons of Multi-Phased Attacks (Parallel)

Type	Pros	Cons	Indicators for Use	Challenges
Parallel Shared and Isolated	• Efficient use of time, given each group should be the same duration • Leverages specific skill sets, given the use of different testers for each group • Collects a plethora of security information about the target	• Does not reflect atypical threats, given the exchange of information • Places more reliance on the target's management and White Team	• Time is more important than tactics • Focused on exploiting all (or as many as possible) forms of security vulnerabilities (e.g., people, process, and technology)	• Disruption of business-related activities, given the number of fronts being attacked
Parallel Shared Only	• Can use a smaller number of consultants	• Requires specific types of imposed limitations to control scope and impact	• Desire for comprehensive testing without great concern for type of threats	• Ensuring data security, given the amount of information being collected and shared
Parallel Isolated Only	• Provides for the opportunity for evaluating risk to specific elements • Option to use different consulting firms	• Requires greater effort for any post-engagement risk analysis • Reflective of typical threats specific to each group	• Focused on specific groups without addressing potential relationships • Used to compare different departments with the same responsibilities (i.e., geography, business units, etc.)	• Ensuring data is not shared between the testers

Once the information is identified, determine points within the engagement to provide the data to get the most value. As long as the information is managed appropriately, the opportunity to learn much more with roughly the same investment is considerable.

TEAMING AND ATTACK STRUCTURE

No matter the structure of the attack, an operational protocol is crucial to the success of the test. As with any test there must exist procedures outside the direct experiment to ensure stability, safety, and accuracy of the results. There are risks that must be planned for to address the uncertainties that lie within the test itself.

TABLE 7.2
Pros and Cons of Multi-Phased Attacks (Serial)

Type	Pros	Cons	Indicators for Use	Challenges
Serial Shared and Isolated	• Comprehensive testing process • Leverages one (or limited number of) consultant(s) • More attention on each phase (i.e., clear milestones in the engagement)	• Potentially time consuming given each phase is performed one after another • Requires a great deal of work by the White Team	• Focus on tactics rather than time • Target's architecture's complexity, geography, or organizational structure is diverse • Desire more control over the evolution of the test's threat model • Concern over collaboration of threats	• Dealing with multiple sets of deliverables and perspectives • Requires more upfront planning
Serial Shared Only	• Focuses on the escalation of threats • Gain the perspective of a single-minded individual	• Skills of consultant may not apply to all groups of test (i.e., good at Internet, not good at physical sec.)	• Concern for specific threats, specifically Über hackers	• Target sharing the information with the Red Team that is in alignment with established goals
Serial Isolated Only	• Effective for executive management overseeing diverse environments	• Assumes different threats • Cannot use the same consultant • Assumes no collaboration of threats	• Want greater control over each phase and the injection of specific types of information	• Controlling the exchange of information between testers

The existence of a sound operational plan and controlled communication protocol between all parties helps a great deal to protect each organization and add value to the test. Following is a very simple teaming framework for establishing a project management protocol, which assists in dealing with unexpected events in the engagement—Red, White, and Blue—external, control, and internal, respectively.

Red Team

The Red Team performs the test. Based on the type of test and the level of knowledge their client is willing to provide, they may be involved in the establishment of the engagement with the White Team to make certain expectations, guidelines, and procedures are well communicated. The goal of the Red Team is relatively simple: to attack the target firm within the established scope of the engagement and communicate to the White Team any critical issues that may represent a risk to the target organization. For example, if during a test, a critical vulnerability is identified that could lead to an excessive impact on the target, the Red Team should communicate this to the White Team to express the volatility of the situation and gain permission before exploiting and possibly causing excessive damage or downtime of their customer's network or systems.

In some cases, when faced with the alternatives, there are situations where the engagement is temporarily halted to assist the client in mitigating the vulnerability. This type of redirection can be complicated from a logistical perspective. For example, stopping and assisting in the correction of a critical vulnerability may be beyond the original scope and complicate billing and timing issues influencing the availability of resources or other nuances that may disrupt the engagement. However, the breadth of the vulnerability could render the rest of the test insignificant because the depth of the exposure is so encompassing. It is necessary for the Red Team to provide the following information: vulnerability explanation, testing focus, and mitigation.

- *Vulnerability Explanation.* Detail the vulnerability and the impact that could result from exploitation. This can include characteristics such as downtime, exposure of critical business systems such as billing or transaction systems, customer impact, partner exposure, or the inadvertent disclosure of private or proprietary information previously defined as beyond the scope of the engagement. In many cases, the vulnerability represents a threat the customer intentionally made clear was something he was not prepared to include in the overall test.

- *Testing Focus.* Beyond detailing the extent the proposed attack could have, it is necessary to explain what would be the disadvantages of not performing the test. Penetration testing is a layered approach founded on an initial vulnerability that usually leads to more opportunities to gain greater access. Without exploiting the identified vulnerability there may exist a cascade of other related exposures that cannot be tested. It is necessary for the customer to make a decision to accept the risk of the potential impact to obtain greater insight as to other weaknesses or forgo the test and accept the possibility of other unidentified exposures within the environment.

- *Mitigation.* Finally, for the client to fully weigh the options compared to risk and cost, the Red Team should provide a collection of high-level recommendations for repairing the hole. The details of the recommendations will be limited because it is simply the perspective based on the external representation of the vulnerability.

What may seem like a simple fix from the outside view could result in wide costly modification to the customer's environment. It is at this point where the two companies must address the issue of impact. If the test was being performed with zero knowledge and the client requests help in supporting assessing the required procedures to eliminate the vulnerability, further insight into the customer's network may be required by the Red Team to provide a comprehensive solution. Therefore, if the engagement is paused and the client wishes to address the vulnerability based on the potential risk, the information provided to the Red Team may render the entire engagement ineffectual based on the original intent and structure of the test.

To avoid the situation of providing information to the Red Team and influencing the scope of the engagement, the White Team has the opportunity to identify other security resources outside the Red Team to collect the information and work directly with the company to address the vulnerability. In some cases, this allows the Red Team to continue other avenues of attack, for example, on a completely different location, to maintain continuity of the project.

WHITE TEAM

The White Team is a mixture of customer representatives and the managing staff of the consulting firm. The White Team is the liaison between the attackers and the target providing control over the attack and monitoring the reaction of internal staff to the test. Essentially, the White Team is the field commander managing the test to ensure it remains within the established guidelines. Additionally, the team provides an opportunity to deal with unexpected results. Following are some examples of specific issues where the White Team can become very helpful: piggyback attacks, reverse impact, and detection.

- *Piggyback Attacks.* Some organizations are constantly under attack from real hackers because of their size or what they represent. It is not uncommon for hackers to monitor a target's network, waiting for the opportunity to gain access. For example, in the early days of firewalls, if the firewall was rebooted the system would be completely open to the Internet for a brief time until the firewall daemon was fully operational. Knowing this, many hackers would monitor or attempt to overload the firewall in hopes that it would force a reboot, allowing temporary access to internal systems. Whether intentional or by the grace of good timing, hackers can mask their attack in the malaise of a controlled test. From the perspective of the target organization, it could simply be part of the test. The White Team can monitor the activities of the Blue Team to take the opportunity to simply determine if a monitored event was in fact the act of the Red Team.
- *Reverse Impact.* Stated earlier, the Red Team should notify the White Team if a critical vulnerability is identified and report on the various risks associated with the weakness. The same holds true for the White Team. There are circumstances where the Red Team is unaware of the massive impacts they are having on the target's systems and may continue the operation, potentially harming their customer in ways previously stated as undesirable during the planning of the test. In the event the target is experiencing unmanageable difficulty with the attack, the White Team acts as a conduit to the Red Team to throttle the attack in accordance with the measurable experiences of the Blue Team. In most scenarios, the attack is paused to determine what actually happened before attempting to continue the test.

- *Detection.* Although some tests are performed surreptitiously to avoid detection there are cases where this is not critical to the success of the engagement. For example, a client may wish to test the ability of the technology and internal resource to measure the response to an attack. However, some want to gauge the granularity of the systems and people when presented with a very "quiet" attack technique. During engagements of this type the White Team can provide a signal to the Red Team to let them know when they have been detected and to use other methods. In some cases, the ability to perform the attack without detection is much more valued by the client than actually exploiting a vulnerability.

While working as a security consultant for a large E-commerce firm, assisting with their policies and security program, the firm was brutally attacked. The hacker had effectively gained control of their credit card processing systems and was collecting historical information in addition to live data being entered by hundreds of customers on the Internet buying merchandise.

Although the attack was identified in a reasonable time period, the necessary steps required to stop the attack would have ceased all transactions and had the potential of remaining that way for several days. When faced with this potential loss in revenue the client decided to allow the hacker to continue until another method could be employed to stop the hacker and maintain continuity of customer transactions.

Ultimately, the vulnerability was closed on other systems and the transactions diverted to the more secure applications. However, this did not happen for nearly 24 hours and after the hacker had obtained several hundred credit card numbers along with private customer information.

Even though this event raised ethical questions about the commitment to securing the customer's information, it pales in comparison to more publicized attacks and similar reactions of larger companies in recent years.

Blue Team

The Blue Team is the internal employees who, traditionally, are not aware the test is taking place. If someone knows the test is being performed, it is best to make her part of the White Team. Given the possible vastness of internal resources who are unaware of the test being performed, the Blue Team usually represents a group of employees to be observed more closely who are typically associated with security or IT administration. There are three primary objectives for establishing a Blue Team: incident response, vulnerability impact, and counterattack.

1. *Incident Response.* Organizations have different methods for dealing with attacks and responding to incidents. In some cases, firms seeking penetration-testing services are more interested in measuring the ability of

their security team to react to a threat than the actual attack itself. This perspective represents a divergence of thought behind ethical hacking not usually practiced except for the most security-conscious companies. Companies of this type see the value of internal security capabilities and culture beyond the technical representation of security for their firm.

A standard penetration test, one without focus on true value, will rarely, if at all, offer any visibility into a company's true security posture. Taking into account the human element is a practice many in the security industry would agree is a considerable ingredient of a healthy security posture. Planning a test with an ample amount of attention paid to measuring the psychological impacts has proven to be one of the most valuable aspects of penetration testing.

Many organizations focus heavily on the technical characteristics of an attack, impose restrictions and limitations, and have expectations based on their understanding of security and an attack. Usually the limited understanding of security leads to a company not taking into consideration that technology has proven repeatedly that it cannot withstand a sophisticated attack alone. Culture, the human element of an attack, plays an enormous role in the ability to survive a direct attack by a determined hacker. Firms that seek a greater overall picture from the attack, specifically ones that wish to test the resistance to an attack of all layers of security—physical, technical, and physiological—will reap the most value and overall impact on their security when they focus on the unsuspecting employees.

NOTE 7: INCIDENT MANAGEMENT IS MORE THAN JUST TECHNOLOGY

A very large distributor of computers and networking technology had used internal resources and external security consultants to increase their security for the online ordering systems to begin to better leverage the Internet for purchasing and to cut operational costs. They implemented several layers of technical solutions, ranging from multiple different firewalls and managed IDS solutions, to encryption and auditing techniques. In early 2001, they discovered an enormous amount of goods was being sold to a student in Europe using the cost code of a reseller in North America. With the help of the FBI, they determined that the equipment was being reshipped to an Eastern European country formerly part of the Soviet Union, a country normally out of bounds for obtaining this type of equipment directly from the United States.

Although they had implemented several forms of traditionally accepted strong security technologies, they had no security policies or defined procedures for dealing with an attack. Once the technology failed to protect them they were powerless to stop the onslaught until finally asking for help from an outside source. The attack lasted for several weeks because they were unaware how to thwart the attack. The technical solutions detected the attack and notified them of what was going on, but the method of the attacker and ability to react proportionately to the attack was well beyond their capability.

Once the vulnerability was addressed and the attack was no longer effective, the company contracted a consulting firm to test their exposures through a penetration test. Not realizing technology was not the culprit in the massive failure of security and their inability to react appropriately identified as the ultimate weakness, they simply had the vulnerability of the Internet sites evaluated without considering the lack of human ability that ultimately led to the huge impact of the original attack.

---

2. *Vulnerability Impact.* As with the other two teams, the ability to determine how badly a vulnerability can affect the network's operations falls within the role of the Blue Team. Although unaware of the actual test and forced into a reactionary state, it is up to the White Team to observe the reaction of the systems and people in charge of those systems to gauge the degree of a vulnerability being exploited. If the vulnerability represents a threat to the operations of the business or falls beyond the scope of the engagement, the White Team can notify the Red Team to stop or divert their energy. In contrast, the White Team can query the Red Team to see what type of progress has been made even when the Blue Team has not reacted in any way that would imply awareness of the attack.

3. *Counterattack.* A hugely debated concept is counterattacking. When under attack, a company can attempt to stop it by instituting updated controls, but, in the case of a counterattack, will attempt to inflict damage on the hacker. Usually, this consists of a DoS against the hacker to simply stop him from continuing and providing a window of opportunity to close the exploited hole. There are several issues relating to the counterattack:

   Clear Identification. If a company is under the assumption it is prepared to assault an identified hacker, it must be absolutely certain it has correctly identified the source. Obviously, if it is incorrect the inadvertent attack on an unwitting third party could lead to legal ramifications and poor publicity. Another deterrent is that every owner of systems and networks utilized by a hacker has the right to prosecute if the hacker is located and captured. Therefore, an established company practicing illicit vigilantism could be held accountable for its actions by the same entities.

   Capability. Most companies do not have the necessary expertise to launch an attack, much less one aimed at a knowledgeable adversary. Not fully understanding the ramification of a technical offensive will certainly result in events not previously considered.

   Waking a Sleeping Giant. Let's assume you are being attacked by a hacker interested in you for no particular reason, totally an opportunistic adventure on her part. If a company were to retaliate, it could become the focal point for the hacker and any other hacker looking to topple a company with an attitude.

If an organization does not permit counterattacks by policy or for the above reasons, the Red Team can notify the White Team if they experience subversive behavior from the target.

TEAM COMMUNICATIONS

Creating a communication plan for the White and Red Teams is essential to making sure the groups can communicate in a secure and timely fashion. There is little that can be prepared for the Blue Team because they are simply unaware of the entire process. However, the White Team should present a plan, or an existing communication process at the beginning of the project so the Red and White Teams are assured there is a mechanism for the Blue team to provide information to the White Team.

There are several components to the communication plan beyond membership and contact information.

- *Communication Platforms.* Define the types of acceptable communications that can be utilized by the team members. For example, phones, pagers, PDSs, Blackberry, e-mail, and office and private fax machines are only a few that can be utilized for communications. Of course, this is directly related to the criticality of the information and available security.
- *Criticality Matrix.* Defining a minimum of three classifications of information will help determine what should be shared with whom, how that information is to be communicated, and the timing. Without some form of standard for what type of information should be shared and the processes for each, everything will become critical causing confusion and potential problems (see Table 7.3).
- *Materials and Format.* Based on the type of communication and the platform, there must exist acceptable supporting materials and format of the communication. For example, in the event of a "warning" level communication there should be accompanying data, such as name, department, affected systems, potential vulnerabilities, and so on. Finally, there must be an awareness of the targeted device and the information being sent. If there is a large document that has to be sent to another team, a pager is not going to help. This will affect the type of message, the content, and how that communication will be documented (see Table 7.4).

Initially, the work associated with defining details about the communication structure of the teams can seem like overkill. However, once the plan is established and documented it can be used for any future ethical hacking engagements. Finally, if an adverse event were to pass, knowing who to contact and how based on that event can go a long way in protecting the integrity of the test.

ENGAGEMENT PLANNER

A great number of details have been introduced: subjects ranging from multi-phased attacks to information flow from the target to the testers, as well as between the

TABLE 7.3
Criticality Matrix for Team Communications

Criticality	Description	Communication
Critical	• Represent information of an event, process, or activity that can harm people, business process, or data. For example: – System failure – Denial of service – Law enforcement involvement – Excessive customer complaints – Abusive hacking activities – Identification of a severe vulnerability	• Communication *must* be immediate, and conducted in the following sequential order (all critical communications must be acknowledged and documented): Phone primary contact (office, cell, pager, other) Phone secondary contact(s) Phone primary/secondary administrative contact(s) Fax (private) E-mail On-site visit (if applicable and contact is at location)
Warning	• Information that can assist in avoiding further or more detrimental impacts to business processes or systems. For example: – Excessive system or network load – Noncritical system outages – Identification of potential issues or vulnerabilities in out of scope systems – User complaints	• Communications should be immediate and acknowledged within a four-hour timeframe: Phone primary contact (office, cell, pager, other) Phone secondary contact(s) E-mail
Informational	• Information is relative to the test. For example: – Additional information for the Red Team's next phase – Comments and activities of the Blue Team – Concerns and comments from the White Team	• Communications should be within a two-business-day timeframe and acknowledged: E-mail Status meeting

testers on an engagement. When all these components of the test are considered, the planning of the engagement can become overwhelming. As stated above, many organizations have an ethical hack performed with very little planning. "Just see how far you can get," they say. One of the reasons for basic forms of attack (which ultimately leads to poor value) is that planning an attack can become time consuming and arduous, putting aside the fact that many are not aware of the options available to them.

In an effort to promote comprehensive planning on the part of the company seeking or employing an ethical hack, following are some guidelines and an example engagement planner.

TABLE 7.4
Communication Types and Formats

Communication Target	Format	Type/Content	Security
Phone (Office and Cell)	Voice conversation: • Validate identity • Take notes • Establish plan for alternate form of communication (i.e., send e-mail or fax) Cell: text message (See Pager) Critical: • No speakerphone • Private location or surroundings	Critical: • Full discussion and details • Establish action plan • Establish plan for further meetings Warning: • Full discussion and details • Plan for actions Informational: • Communicate summary and follow up with documentation	Acceptable
Fax (Private)	Document: • Confidential cover page and related contact information • Initial information and followup contact information	Critical: • Limited materials and details • Establish plan for further meetings Warning: • Full discussion and details • Plan for actions Informational: • Communicate summary and follow up with documentation	Limited
Fax (Public)	Document: • Confidential cover page • Message to contact through other means	Critical and warning: • No sensitive information • Establish plan for further communications Informational: • Limited information	None
Admin. Phone/Fax	Document/voice conversation: • Validate identity (if applicable) • Message to contact at earliest convenience or location of primary contact	Critical, warning, informational: • No information • Message for further contact	None
Pager	Message: • Validate identity (if applicable, i.e., auto reply) • Text message to contact at earliest convenience or location of primary contact • State level of criticality	Critical, warning, informational: • No information • Message for further contact	None
PDA	Message/small document: • Text message to contact at earliest convenience • State level of criticality	Critical and warning: • No sensitive information • Establish plan for further communications Informational: • Limited information	Limited

TABLE 7.4
Communication Types and Formats (continued)

E-Mail	Message/Document:	Critical:	Acceptable
	• Text message to contact at earliest convenience • State level of criticality • Supporting documentation • No e-mail lists (i.e., itemize TO: field)	• Full discussion and details • Communicate initial action plan • Establish plan for further meetings Warning: • Full discussion and details • Plan of action Informational: • Communicate summary and provide documentation	

Guidelines:

- Perform a self-evaluation of your goals and objectives. Ask yourself what you expect to gain from the test and how you plan to use the results. Are you looking to address specific weaknesses? Or, are you attempting to seek symptoms of a much larger problem within the security program?
- Consider the scope of the attack and what is "in bounds." Moreover, take the time to evaluate what you have determined is beyond its scope and the potential impact on the objectives. Too much focus of a test is typically the result of budget restrictions or departmental segmentation. With proper planning, both of these areas can be accommodated while still meeting your goals. Of course, too little focus can lead to long engagements that provide little value.
- Ensure all the appropriate people are involved. On paper this appears obvious and simple, but internal politics and departmental rivalries introduce interesting results. There must be an owner, a leader, or primary person that ultimately sets the goals and scope of the engagement. Tests that are planned by committee will typically fail to meet objectives.
- Commit to having a technical expert involved in the process in addition to business managers or executives. All too often, organizations plan and execute attacks without consulting their internal expertise, specifically, security experts. A technical perspective can be very beneficial to outlining the scope and depth of the attack that should be sought to meet executive goals. However, tests that are planned by only technical resources without the dedicated involvement of business management setting loftier goals will certainly affect the potential value of the test.
- During the planning session, ask a lot of questions. However, one must keep an open mind and expect answers that conflict with personal perceptions of security. People typically ask questions they already feel they have an answer for and look to gain the perspective of the interviewee. To ensure the test meets the goals, especially when interviewing a professional organization that performs ethical hacking tests all the time, one must be cognizant of not making any predetermined conclusions.

Nevertheless, it helps to see the options in a concise format to stimulate the planning process and to have some form of documentation to drive the engagement. A sample planner is demonstrated in Table 7.5. Although summarized, the example does provide the opportunity to select characteristics of the test to support more detailed planning. (Note: Some elements in the planner are discussed in following sections.)

TABLE 7.5
Example Engagement Planner

Ethical Hacking Engagement Planner
General Information
Date:___/_____/____Company Name: _____
Team Members

Name	Team (RWB)	Primary Phone	Secondary Phone	Fax (Private)	Fax (Public)	E-Mail	Role/Title

Primary Characteristics of the Engagement (Check all that apply)

☐ Social engineering	☐ Application testing	☐ Identify vulnerabilities
☐ Internet test	☐ Physical security	☐ Exploit vulnerabilities
☐ Intranet test	☐ Wireless	☐ Multi-phased attack
☐ Partner access	☐ VPN	☐ Wardialing
☐ Remote access	☐ VoIP	☐ Wardriving

General Assumption of Threat Type (Check all that apply)

Script Kiddy	**Hacker**	**Über Hacker**
☐ Unstructured ☐ Structured ☐ Determined	☐ Malicious ☐ Solvers ☐ Hackitivist ☐ Vigilantism	☐ Hitman ☐ Terrorist ☐ Espionage

Attack Type Summary (See Information Management Below)

Single	**Multi-Phased Parallel**		**Multi-Phased Shared**	
Information	☐ **Isolated**	☐ **Shared**	☐ **Isolated**	☐ **Shared**
☐ All at once ☐ Incremental	Specific Groups: ☐ All sel. above ☐ Internet testing ☐ Social eng. ☐ Intranet	Specific Groups: ☐ All sel. above ☐ Internet testing ☐ Social eng. ☐ Intranet	Specific Groups: ☐ All sel. above ☐ Internet testing ☐ Social eng. ☐ Intranet	Specific Groups: ☐ All sel. above ☐ Internet testing ☐ Social eng. ☐ Intranet

TABLE 7.5
Example Engagement Planner (continued)

Primary Target Summary (Check all that apply)

Social Engineering	Internet Test	Intranet Test

☐ Entire company
☐ Group (list below)
☐ Department (list below)
☐ Specific location(s)
    (list below)
	☐ All Internet connections
	☐ Specific sites (list below)
	☐ Only certain ISPs
	    (list below)
		☐ Entire company
		☐ Group (list below)
		☐ Department (list below)
		☐ Location(s) (city, state, country)
		    (list below)

Partner Access	**Remote Access**	**Applications**
☐ All partners ☐ Partner access network only ☐ Includes applications ☐ Other (list below)	☐ IPSec VPN ☐ SSL VPN ☐ Dial-up ☐ Other (list below)	☐ Web/Internet ☐ Client-side Internet ☐ Terminal-based ☐ Internal applications ☐ Custom applications ☐ Code review ☐ Other (list below)
Physical Security	**Wardriving**	**Wireless**

☐ All locations
☐ Specific location(s)
    (list below)
	☐ All locations
	☐ Anything that can be
	    discovered
	☐ Specific location(s)
	    (list below)
		☐ All locations
		☐ Anything that can be discovered
		☐ Specific location(s) (list below)
		☐ Public access
		☐ Internal only
		☐ External only

VoIP	**VPN**	**Wardialing**
☐ Data vulnerabilities only ☐ Voice vulnerabilities only ☐ Phones ☐ PBX/Phone systems	☐ Network (WAN) ☐ Partner network ☐ Remote network ☐ Customer network ☐ Specific location(s) (list below)	☐ Numbers provided ☐ Multiple locations (list below) ☐ Single location ☐ Test mailboxes ☐ Seek network access ☐ Seek toll fraud ☐ Other (list below)

General Scoping

Green List (Specifically targeted systems and network elements)		Red List (Systems Red Team must never attack or bring down)		Yellow List (Targeted systems or network elements that must remain on line)	
System:	IP Address/Net:	System:	IP Address/Net:	System:	IP Address/Net:
	__.__.__.__		__.__.__.__		__.__.__.__
	__.__.__.__		__.__.__.__		__.__.__.__
	__.__.__.__		__.__.__.__		__.__.__.__

TABLE 7.5
Example Engagement Planner (continued)

Tools

Permitted:	Client Provided:	Not Permitted:
☐ ISS ☐ NMap ☐ Nessus ☐ Trojans ☐ Open source/hacker tools	Please list:	Please list:

Social Engineering Planner
E-Mail

Specific Group or Dept.: _____ Domain: _____

Imposed Limitations

☐ Single shot ☐ Three strikes ☐ Individual e-mail permitted ☐ Group e-mail permitted ☐ Source masquerading permitted	Length limitation (max. characters:)	Characters_____
	Subject matter focus (if any):	
	Level of intensity (pursuit)	☐ Low ☐ Med ☐ High
	Max. number of exchanges	Number:_____, or ☐ Unlimited

Helpdesk Fraud

Main line number:	___-___-_____	Source Group/ Dept:	☐ Any ☐ Employees only ☐ Partners ☐ Customers ☐ Specific (list below)
Secondary number	___-___-_____		
Alternative number	___-___-_____		
Third-Party Managed Service? ☐ Yes ☐ No ☐ Not Providing Information (NPI)		Max. calls per subject:	Subject:_____ Max. calls____ Subject:_____ Max. calls____ Subject:_____ Max. calls____ Subject:_____ Max. calls____
		Specific subjects not to employ:	

Phone Fraud

Number Range(s)		Target Group(s)	
		☐ Any	
		☐ Discretionary	
		☐ Other (list)	
Max. Calls per Subject	Subject:_____ Max. calls____ Subject:_____ Max. calls____ Subject:_____ Max. calls____ Subject:_____ Max. calls____	Permitted subj: ☐ Any ☐ Discretionary ☐ Other (list)	

TABLE 7.5
Example Engagement Planner (continued)

Max. Calls per Individual	#_____		Specific subjects not to employ:	

External Testing

Dumpster Diving	In use? ☐ Yes ☐ No		Location(s): ☐ All ☐ Discretionary ☐ Specific location(s) (list below)	
	Permitted to follow trash off-site? ☐ Yes ☐ No		Included Shredded Materials? ☐ Yes ☐ No	
	If discovered: ☐ Test concludes ☐ Phase concludes ☐ Continue at another location ☐ Report		Duration of activity: ☐ As long as possible ☐ Remaining work day ☐ Four hours ☐ Two hours ☐ One hour ☐ 15 minute ☐ Depart immediately upon success	
Piggy-Back	In use? ☐ Yes ☐ No		Location(s): ☐ All ☐ Discretionary ☐ Specific location(s) (list below)	
	Once in: ☐ Target all accessible areas (zones) ☐ Discretionary ☐ Specific floors ☐ Area(s) that requires authentication ☐ Specific area(s) (list below)		Duration of activity: ☐ As long as possible ☐ Remaining work day ☐ Four hours ☐ Two hours ☐ One hour ☐ 15 minute ☐ Depart immediately upon success	
	If discovered: ☐ Test concludes ☐ Phase concludes ☐ Continue at another location ☐ Report		Permitted activities: ☐ Target all elements ☐ Shoulder surfing ☐ Material removal from location ☐ Implantation of devices (systems, wireless, etc.) ☐ Disinformation ☐ Report	

TABLE 7.5
Example Engagement Planner (continued)

Location Entry	In use? ☐ Yes ☐ No	Location(s): ☐ All ☐ Discretionary ☐ Specific location(s) (list below)
	Tactics to employ: ☐ All feasible attempts ☐ Focus on guards ☐ Focus on technical controls ☐ Alternative access (windows, vents) permitted	If discovered: ☐ Test concludes ☐ Phase concludes ☐ Continue at another location ☐ Report
	Duration of activity: ☐ As long as possible ☐ Remaining work day ☐ Four hours ☐ Two hours ☐ One hour ☐ 15 minutes ☐ Depart immediately upon success	Permitted activities: ☐ Target all elements ☐ Shoulder surfing ☐ Material removal from location ☐ Implantation of devices (systems, wireless, etc.) ☐ Disinformation ☐ Report

Information Management

Parts 1, 2, and 3 represent staged information provisioning for single attack, or information for multi-phased attacks Information expected at various points within each phase (Check all that apply)	Reconnaissance (Part 1)	Reconnaissance (Part 2)	Reconnaissance (Part 3)	Enumeration (Part 1)	Enumeration (Part 2)	Enumeration (Part 3)	Exploitation (Part 1)	Exploitation (Part 2)	Exploitation (Part 3)
Standard Elements									
Nothing									
Register domain(s)									
Network diagrams									
Internal Testing									
Nothing									
Network architecture									
Documentation									
System types (e.g., OS)									
Policies and procedures									
Access credentials (user)									

TABLE 7.5
Example Engagement Planner (continued)

Access credentials (power user)									
Access credentials (admin.)									
Application information									
Internet Testing									
Nothing									
IP addresses									
Host names									
System types (e.g., OS)									
Network documentation									
Firewall type(s)									
IDS type(s)									
Web account									
Customer Web access account									
Employee Web account									
Partner Web account									
Remote access system information									
Remote access account									
Appication information									
Social Engineering/Physical Security									
Nothing									
Floor plans									
Location information									
Visitor badge									
Employee badge									
Extended access materials									
Door codes									
Policies and procedures									
Wardialing									
Nothing									
Phone numbers									

TABLE 7.5
Example Engagement Planner (continued)

PBX type									
Locations									
System type(s)									
Potential target(s)									
Wardriving									
Nothing									
Locations									
AP type(s)/equipment									
SIDs									
Network access credentials									
System access credentials									
Number of sites									

By using this or similar documentation at the beginning of the planning phase, it will help, at a minimum, to collect your thoughts and perspectives of the test in a single document. Understandably, the example planner is only a summary of probable engagement characteristics and insinuates that much more work is required. For example, the information management section only stipulates the type of information offered to the testers and at what point in the engagement, not the actual data. Nevertheless, this can be a good starting point for planning or the foundation of your own document for future tests. Furthermore, if an organization were to create a similar document and present it to potential professional service companies that perform ethical hacks, it can help determine their capabilities in providing the service.

THE RIGHT SECURITY CONSULTANT

Information security consultants have experienced an interesting evolution paralleled by the expansion of technology and the proliferation of threats to which companies are regularly exposed. Security consultants come in many forms with different abilities and conclusions about security. Much of this is based on their exposure and experience in the security industry and where they have realized successes and failures.

Nevertheless, the skill of security consultants can be categorized in two fundamental camps: technologists and architects. In addition, there are many who have mastered both and are highly valued and respected in their industry.

TECHNOLOGISTS

A natural progression for many in the security field came from their experience with technology and implementing solutions in a secure manner. For some, this started early with their first installation of Windows, UNIX, or a router and they gravitated to securing that system. These individuals have risen through the ranks of security by getting more involved with technology and security-specific applications. Firewalls are a good example where some evolved from installing routers or system gateways to integrating complex firewalls.

As technologists, security consultants continually grew while operating in the trenches of information warfare gaining greater experience and exposure to technical solutions and their vulnerabilities. It is this community we normally see performing ethical hacking services. They have reached a point of technical expertise and security know-how that allows them to manipulate systems in ways others simply cannot comprehend.

Beyond what could be considered network technology excellence are the programmers and specialists. These are the resources that build and maintain secure applications or applications for use in the security industry. In addition, there are specialists in security technology, such as encryption and security protocols such as IPsec, who support the world of security through applied technology at its most fundamental level.

ARCHITECTS

There are security consultants who have moved away from technology, or never fully immersed themselves in technology, and focus on the business of security. Security consultants of this type work on the larger picture of security and are usually the authors of security policies and the minds behind comprehensive security architectures that are supported by the various security-related technologies.

Many architects may have begun their careers with technology, but were immediately drawn to the operational aspects of security. Although usually capable of providing high-level technical services, they are ordinarily not as astute in the inner workings of technical solutions and rely heavily on the technologists to implement what they have architected.

Fully comprehending the totality of security is imperative to establishing a strong security posture and a security program to support all aspects of security. Architects look to the big picture of security and seek out solutions to ensure security is addressed technically as well as operationally.

What is interesting to note is that over their careers many consultants swing back and forth between technology and the pragmatic aspects of security. Much of this is due to simply getting bored with what they are doing or finding interest in a particular technology or process. Both of these attributes are very important to ethical hacking because of the obvious technical nature and the need for understanding the overall effects on security that the test can have on a company.

ETHICS

An understanding of ethics involves learned behavior, problem solving, creativity, invention, awareness, and social structures, among other life attributes. In virtually every event in our lives—in our problems, opportunities, decisions, actions, reactions—ethics make a difference. No matter how you interpret or comprehend your environment, real or potential, we operate within a world based on values and are forced to make determinations, some of which we're totally unaware.

Information security requires a substantial amount of trust, an attribute based on a foundation of ethics. Security professionals are constantly provided sensitive information about a company and their systems to accomplish their task. The devolution of passwords, access information, internal architecture, policies, and processes are needed regularly to assist a company in strengthening its security posture. The entire process inherently places a great deal of trust in the consultant working with a customer. The assumption is that the information obtained by a consultant will result in less of a payoff and a greater risk to reputation if used for personal gain rather than simply working ethically within the margins of professionalism.

This section is simply to communicate what ethics a security consultant should follow and uphold to maintain a certain level of professionalism and to ensure the growth and trust of the industry as a whole. There are several public security institutions that have defined the ethics to be upheld to operate within the security community. The following list is a good basis for understanding what is and should be expected from people performing security services.

- *Perform Services in Accordance with the Law.* There may be situations where a consultant is asked to perform or made aware of something illegal. In this situation it is necessary to abide by the laws society has created. Essentially, it is ethically correct and expected to operate within the boundaries of the law, regardless of personal interpretation.
- *Maintain Confidentiality.* As alluded to above, security consultants are regularly exposed to proprietary information and ethically bound to protect that information. In addition, when in doubt of the level of protection assume the highest form of protection: what is one man's trash is another's treasure.
- *Honesty.* In addition to simple professionalism, given the sensitivity of interacting with proprietary information and all that it implies, honesty must be practiced to ensure continued trust.
- *Conflict of Interest.* Everyone during some point in his or her career has been faced with professional conflict. Typically, this is associated with knowing certain information that if you were involved with another process you may make determinations based on that information. This cannot only lead to personal and professional conflicts but will test the ethical values one may have. Finally, this could have a negative impact on customers, related partners, and the company you work for, possibly damaging reputations and associations.

- *Intentional Acts.* Clearly associated with ethics, intentionally harming or damaging the reputation of clients, employers, or colleagues is unacceptable behavior.

Ethics have an impact on the operational behavior of people and when faced with an ethical "fork in the road" it is best to reference this, or similar, lists to provide basic direction if questioning one's actions.

THE TESTER

It is clear that ethical hacking can provide value to the overall assessment of an organization's security posture and assist in developing solutions that better meet the types of vulnerabilities and threats. However, there is a trend for enterprises, as well as professional service firms, to hire "reformed" hackers. This is a likely progression of the philosophy of ethical hacking. Few understand the idiosyncrasies in performing a comprehensive attack; the processes are difficult to learn, and even harder to practice in the wild, where it matters most. It is only natural to conclude that an experienced hacker would have the necessary skills for performing hacking services. The practice of hiring hackers was commonplace during the early years of ethical hacking when the skills of a traditional security consultant were in defending rather than attacking a customer's network. In a 2000 survey of 4900 security professionals, conducted by *Information Week*, 55 percent indicated they would consider hiring former hackers as consultants for security services. In contrast with today's practices, 68 percent of respondents to the 2003 FBI/SCI report said they would not hire a reformed hacker with the balance of responses equally shared between hiring hackers and simply not knowing.

In addition, for hackers it is an opportunity to meet their personal hunger for illicit activities, but in a legitimized format while getting paid handsomely. People choose various paths in life and the argument for reformed hackers for hire is you cannot hold someone accountable for their historical activities. For example, if a criminal was captured and jailed for several years because he stole a car there is a level risk in hiring that person, although it is understood that he has paid his debt and should be offered the opportunity to re-engage as a functioning part of society. It would be quite a different assumption if he had not paid his debt by realizing the punishment associated with the crime, and therefore one could assume that his attitude would be more volatile based on consequence-free activities. With hacking, there is little punishment associated with these crimes and the latter of the two examples applies. In addition, many hackers who have been caught and released after receiving some form of punishment are typically legally banned from using computers for several years, reducing their availability for hire.

Therefore, how can someone be reformed or prove a new mental state? Interestingly, the motives for becoming a hacker are usually encoded into someone's character and to assume that this can change is a difficult proposition indeed. The traits of a hacker are what many seek, setting the foundation for critical decision-making and ethical challenges for management.

There are several examples of the risks in hiring a reformed hacker. One example is a large government agency hired a known hacker to research potential vulnerabilities within the agency's network. Unfortunately, the hacker elongated the engagement by disclosing only a few vulnerabilities each week, ensuring a regular paycheck. In addition, the "consultant" posted findings on hacker sites to assist others in gaining access. Although this is an ethical issue rather than a technical one, it does raise awareness of the fundamental mindset of a hacker.

Hacking for money is also a fertile territory for training people how to hack. For example, if a services firm seeks to develop these skills internally to ensure they are not using a reformed hacker, they may in fact be training someone how to perform these attacks outside the controlled environment.

The conclusion is not an easy one. There are few tests that can be performed to identify mental traits that could lead to bad experiences or establish strong deterrents to illicit behavior. When choosing a consultant for performing ethical hacking tests, it is critical that the person's social aptitude and goals be evaluated in addition to their technical capabilities.

LOGISTICS

Planning takes time and effort, but it is well worth it. So far, we have discussed planning in the form of establishing teams, setting expectations, understanding the ultimate value of the test, and determining the impacts of various restrictions and limitations. There is another side to planning: logistics. Logistics are the nuts and bolts of an engagement and are a necessary evil to ensure the total operation is a success.

AGREEMENTS

An agreement between the service provider and the customer is a must. Many service provider organizations have a master services agreement that outlines the legal stipulations of the business relationship. These can include warrantees, guarantees, expectations of payment, and other attributes that establish an understanding of the working association. Although usually comprehensive, it is doubtful that standing agreements cover areas directly associated with the risks of hacking a network.

There are several key characteristics of penetration testing that should be evaluated by both parties. Of course, the granularity and the context of the agreement are up to the customer and the provider, but should cover the following in some manner: downtime issues, system and data integrity, get out of jail free card, intermediates, and law enforcement. The following demonstrations, Notes 8 and 9, are only one example of legalese that communicates some form of protection for the services firm and client. Note 8 is a common version that I have seen used several times. (It should be noted that this is specific to testing services and does not cover the entire contractual agreement for consulting services. Moreover, this is an example and should not be used unless approved by legal counsel.

By and Between "Client" and ACME Services Inc.

This Addendum, No. 1, effective as of the _____th day of _____, 200__ ("Addendum"), is hereby made a part of and incorporated into the Statement of Work Agreement, dated _____, and all duly executed amendments and addenda thereto to date (collectively, the "Agreement"), by and between ACME Services Inc. ("ACME") and ("Client").

WHEREAS, the parties wish to amend the provisions of the "Additional Terms of Engagement" section as contained in the Agreement in order to include additional terms pertinent to the Penetration Testing, as defined below, the parties hereto agree as follows:

Client has requested the services of an ACME Project Team ("ACME Team") for a security assessment of Client's network environment. The undersigned has the authority to permit, as further signified by a letter to be supplied to ACME in a form as attached in Exhibit A, and by this signature authorizes the ACME Team to attempt to compromise the devices on the Client network during the proposed security assessment. During the course of assessment, the ACME Team may discover passwords and other sensitive information. The ACME Team will duly report this information to the Client. The Client also agrees to come to the aid of the ACME Team members if the police or sheriff's department should detain them in any manner. The services to be performed under this agreement include penetration testing or other techniques utilizing an "attack methodology" as requested by the Client under this Agreement ("Penetration Testing"). The Client agrees to defend and hold the ACME Team harmless from any liability or damage arising from the ACME Team's performance under this Penetration Testing, including but not limited to claims for violation of privacy laws. Client shall assume responsibility for such Penetration Testing and shall indemnify and hold the ACME Team harmless for all claims, damages, expenses, and liabilities to any third party, which may arise as a result of such Penetration Testing performed under this Agreement.

ACME warrants that all security services shall be performed in a professional and workmanlike manner in accordance with this agreement. ACME makes no warranties of merchantability and fitness for a particular purpose. Client shall remain responsible for the security of its network environment and ACME makes no guarantee as to the level of security Client will achieve as a result of the Penetration Testing performed under this agreement.

In no event shall ACME be liable for any indirect, direct, incidental, special, or consequential damages resulting from performance of the above-defined penetration testing which has specifically been requested by the Client. This Addendum together with the Agreement constitutes the entire understanding and agreement between the parties with regard to the subject matter herein. In the event of a conflict between the terms of the Agreement and this Addendum, the latter shall prevail. All other terms of the Agreement remain in full force and effect.

Accepted and Agreed to by:

ACME Services Inc.:   Client:

_____   _____

Signature   Signature

_____   _____

Print Name   Print Name

_____   _____

Title   Title

_____   _____

Date   Date

NOTE 9: LEGAL DOCUMENT SUPPORTING EXHIBIT A

"Client" has requested a Penetration Test to be performed by ACME Services Inc. ("ACME"). The stated ACME Security Consultants, <Consultant Name> and <Consultant Name—if applicable>, will be performing the following activities related to this assessment:

ACME proposes to deliver Penetration Testing services for Client against Information Technology assets located in <enter location(s)>. This service is structured to assist in identifying vulnerabilities that may be used to gain access to networks and systems processing, storing, or transmitting information assets. The Penetration Testing work includes the planning, testing, and analysis centered about transport, protocol, application, and remote access areas. Work findings include executive-level presentation with documented findings identifying critical security vulnerabilities as well as comprehensive test results and recommended mitigation actions.

This service was requested, scheduled, and approved by <Client Contact Name>, <Title >, who can be contacted at <XXX–XXX-XXXX>. Officers of Client are also aware of this testing and have signed hereunder as proof of this knowledge.

DOWNTIME ISSUES

Even if a DoS attack is part of the engagement, the intentional or accidental shutdown of a system must be addressed. There are many systems in a network with varying levels of importance and in many cases, it is impossible for the tester to accurately identify a sensitive system even when provided all the necessary information to avoid it. Inevitably, some systems will react poorly to being attacked and will cease to function.

Many companies maintain service-level agreements with their customers (internal and external), and when data or services are not available it not only costs the company money to rectify the problem, but there are frequently fines associated with the downtime. It is essential the consulting company understands these risks facing their customer and plans for the possibility of downtime. There are situations where the engagement was canceled because the risk of being held accountable for excessive fines was more than they could bear.

Given the risk associated with a penetration test, both organizations have to come to some form of understanding before starting the engagement. A client must be aware that the professional services company will not intentionally negatively affect any system where possible, but nothing can ensure this won't happen. Difficulty in identifying critical systems and the inability to predict the system's reaction to intense investigation present an unknown beyond the control of everyone involved. The consulting organization must feel confident in their capabilities and methodologies to ensure that systems will not be damaged. Many consulting firms validate, or look for signed consent from the customer, to ensure there are continuity plans in place in the event of a failure.

Without an agreement defining the responsibilities of both parties to address risks associated with the test, the relationship between provider and client can grow very bad, very quickly.

System and Data Integrity

Exploiting a vulnerability is one of several steps in performing a test. Many attacks begin with hackers using a vulnerability to reach far enough into a system to set up a backdoor to return later, much more easily and undetected. Testers employ Trojans for much the same reason.

The major difference is that the tester must notify the client that the backdoor was installed and how to remove it. Anyone working with a firm must address this possibility before an engagement begins. Companies can gain comfort by either stipulating backdoors will not be used or demanding a detailed cleanup is expected to be performed after the engagement is complete. The ramifications of implanting backdoors to bypass security controls represent a huge risk to the client and their use during the test must be made clear.

It should be noted that not permitting the use of Trojans during a test has the potential to affect the value of the engagement. If the goal of the test is to determine the extent to which a hacker can get into the network, one must be aware that Trojans are a common tool used by hackers. Therefore, by removing this option (imposed limitation), the exercise lacks an element of reality. Nevertheless, the risks affiliated with the implantation of hacker tools can outweigh the perceived benefits.

As you can see, implanting backdoors moves well beyond known or discovered vulnerabilities associated with poor security practices of the client and actually introduces security holes based on the actions of the tester. Added insecurities of this type are not the responsibility of the customer to rectify, and the consulting organization should be aware of their accountability to ensure the system's original integrity is restored. Customers, however, should keep in mind that the consulting organization is responsible only for what they implanted and should not be held to implementing changes that may be related to the overall security of the system.

Beyond exploiting vulnerabilities and implanting backdoors, many customers ask for the consulting organization to leave a calling card to prove they obtained access. Calling cards have become a common practice and experienced customers are seeking to add them as a requirement for more detailed evidence that the attack was successful.

In many cases, adding or changing benign information to prove a tester gained privileged access is acceptable and represents little harm or irreversible manipulation of the data. For example, adding a name to a database or placing a small set of characters at the end of sentence on a Web site is usually the extent of a calling card. However, there are cases when entire blocks of information were overwritten and the tester was unaware of the error. For example, a tester may try to inject some text into a file to prove she had write permissions, but does not have read access to see if the changes were made. Assuming the attack was a failure, she moves on to another area leaving the mangled file in her path.

A good practice for leaving calling cards with reduced risk to critical information is for the company to plant files alongside critical data. If the tester only obtains read access, he can communicate the contents of the file to the client, and if he gets write access, he can add information to the file without concern for harming valuable data. An example of a file could be a simple text file (.TXT) containing a simple string, "Roses are Red." The tester can easily remember the contents and can add other text, such as "Violets are Blue," to the file. This may seem overly simple, but the results can be very insightful. For example, if the file only reads, "Violets are Blue," this means that the tester inadvertently overwrote the original file in his attempt to modify the file, demonstrating the type of access attained.

This raises questions of all types. Where do you put the files? What permissions should be set? Are the files easily removed at the end of the engagement? Adding a file is especially difficult when there are a hundred servers and any one of them can be the tester's target. Unfortunately, there are no easy answers. I've seen customers use everything from e-mail to scripts in an effort to distribute and clean up files.

No matter what the final solution, it should be noted that in an attack scenario, modifying data from a remote system with stolen privileges could cause problems. It is necessary for the organizations to discuss preparing, detecting changes, and recovering data in the event of an adverse event.

Get Out of Jail Free Card

One of the more humorous aspects of penetration testing is the "Get Out of Jail Free Card." However, its requirement is anything but funny. Hacking can attract the attention of many people and organizations not aware the hack is a test, such as the FBI. There are also situations where social engineering your way into a building may result in the tester being caught in a less than desirable position.

During the social engineering phase of an engagement, the tester entered a building late in the evening and after talking with the guard, received a visitor badge and directions to the bathroom. Donning a backpack full of hacking paraphernalia, the tester entered the bathroom and started to climb into the ceiling to plant scanners and other network devices to collect information. No sooner did he get started than the guard walked in to seize him and his equipment, and called the cops. The tester presented the letter, on their letterhead, and signed by the executive management. It stated that in the event a person was caught with this letter and detained, to call the included telephone number and verify. Luckily, the guard complied and made the call; some won't.

The "Get Out of Jail Free Card" is an important document to ensure the tester has some form of protection. Of course, the document has to be very clear, dated, and signed with several pieces of contact information; otherwise, it could be used by a real hacker. From the perspective of the tester, this does not provide you a license to kill, but a validation that you were requested to perform the attack as defined. The "Get Out of Jail Free Card" only starts the process of ensuring the attacker is authorized to be performing what he was caught doing. This can get sticky. For example, an ISP may identify malicious activity, shut down the Internet access of the tester, and report her to the FBI. It may take weeks of e-mails, faxes, and phone calls to get the tester or company's name cleared. It is an agreement between the consulting firm and its customer, not with ISPs, law enforcement, partners, and the public.

INTERMEDIATES

During a test, many networks and organizations can be caught in the wake of an attack and possibly be affected by a test to which they did not agree. Also, given that organizations are focused on security issues more so now than ever before, the test can raise concerns for companies that are between the tester and the target. It may be necessary to notify the owners of networks that have the potential of being inadvertently included in the attack.

Partners

As networks have evolved, companies have leveraged them to exchange information with other firms to promote more effective business models and growth through alliances. As with any network, there is an opportunity for the tester to infiltrate the target's network by using an alternate route provided by a partner network. Or, there are conditions when the partner network is mistakenly assumed as part of the client's network and the attack thread results in exploiting a vulnerability in a system well outside the domain of the customer.

Depending on the type of relationship a client has with its partners, it is usually rare for the targeted company to allow or sanction any type of attack on a partner's network. There are some circumstances, however, where the partners are held to a security standard to interact with the client's network and have signed an agreement that will allow the client to validate the security of the connection through exploitation. In these rare cases, an attack against the partner is permitted and the partnering organization is notified.

However, in normal situations, the partner's assets are well beyond the test's scope and infiltrating its network can not only represent legal risks to the client but to the services firm as well. Interestingly, the value to the customer to determine the exposures related to partner's networks is very high, but politically it can be a nightmare.

The difficulty for the tester during the engagement is the possibility of inadvertently attacking a partner's network or system. For customers that maintain business partner systems on their network, this can be especially problematic due to the blending of systems and no specific method for distinguishing one from another during a test.

However, should the client permit the tester to exploit vulnerabilities identified in partner systems on their network? The argument to allow the system to be tested is based on the exposure to threats that may be spawned from the system or application, conceivably affecting the client's security. For example, a hacker may find only a single vulnerability she can exploit and it just happens that the vulnerability is within the partner's system, ultimately allowing the hacker to launch more aggressive attacks against the original target. Moreover, the hacker doesn't care whose system it is; from her perspective it's all the same network with a potential to provide unauthorized access. Naturally, the argument against performing an attack against the partner's systems is the likelihood of damaging or destroying information or hardware owned by a firm that has not agreed to—or is unaware of—the penetration test being performed. If the partner is monitoring its server, it is likely that they will detect an attack, or feel the ramifications if the system is brought down, making for a volatile situation.

If a customer wants the greatest value, the opportunity to test all systems on their network, an ethical hack regardless of owner should be considered. To not permit a test against specific systems solely based on perception could leave a sense of "what if" lingering well after the test has been completed, possibly forfeiting the overall engagement results. This is an example of imposed limitations, which can greatly influence the value of the test. Understandably, there are challenges for the customer to decide if the partner systems are within the scope of the engagement and have the potential of risking the relationship between the two companies. In any case, the relationship, as well as the computing environment, could be strained to a breaking point.

The obvious workaround is to collaborate with the partner and see if it is willing to permit a test against its system. The answer is never a simple one and usually the partnering organization demands more information about the test: what is going to be tested, what are the goals, who is performing the test, why their server is being included, and so on. Some business partners simply state their system is secure and there is no need to test it and, therefore, do not allow it based on their assumption.

In the event the partner does not permit the test and all other avenues have been exhausted, the client should ask them to sign some form of agreement binding them to the potential risks. This is an attempt to transfer risk to the partner and is laden with problems. First, it introduces tension into the partnership, possibly damaging an already strained association. Second, the agreement has to be general in content because no test was performed. There is no way to truly determine the exposure the partner's system represents, therefore leading to a document that states any attack the partner's system may be involved with is the partner's fault and they accept responsibility. It is nearly impossible to accurately predict the risk represented by a partner's system if that system cannot be evaluated.

Partner networks, systems, and applications pose a challenge to the tester in addition to presenting a potential obstacle for the customer to realize the full value of the exercise. In nearly all cases, the imposed limitation of not testing a partner's network or system connected to, or participating in, the client's infrastructure is not based on a security-related decision, but rather a business one. When faced with these challenges, every opportunity should be made to come to an agreement between the two companies to mitigate any risk to either organization.

Customers

Businesses offer a wide range of products and services to customers that may be based on technical integration to provide the product. Some examples of customer interaction are very similar to the partner communications as detailed above. In general, businesses supply several different types of network connectivity for their customers, such as frame relay, remote dial-in access, and VPN on a segmented network, much the way they support partners. Conversely, many companies such as Amazon.com and Yahoo! offer products and services simply over the Internet that are accessed via a traditional Web browser.

There are several types of attacks that can leverage customer connectivity or privileged access allowing the tester to penetrate the target network. The important thing is to ensure the tester does not present a risk to a customer in an attempt to gain access to the target's network or systems. For example, there have been instances of a tester sending an e-mail to a client's customer requesting him to change his password to the provided password. The tester then waited for the customer to change his password and accessed the system with stolen credentials. Exploiting the target's customers should never be part of the engagement.

Although a viable risk to companies that provide privileged access for their customers, the manipulation of a third party that has not agreed to the attack is unethical. For clients who want to understand the exposure if a customer were to attempt an attack or a hacker were to somehow obtain the credentials of a paying customer, they should provide the necessary information to the tester. This is a prime example of a multi-phase, shared attack strategy.

Service Providers

It is common for a company to use a service provider to support various IT services internally or for external customer support. Services can range from simple Internet connections and collaboration tools to applications and managed security services.

An ethical hack can have a multitude of problems on these services with varying degrees of impact. Although each one can be addressed specifically, the best method is to establish a basic approach that can be applied to all types of services, if for no other reason than to build a starting point. This can include:

- *Communication.* Apprise the service provider that the test is being performed and create a communication protocol to support emergencies.
- *Details.* The source IP addresses of the tester, timing of the test, and what falls within the scope of the test are all important elements to share with any provider.
- *Support.* More often than not, service providers can help with collecting information about the test. This is especially true with managed security service providers. They can passively collect information about the test and provide a report on activity.

Without a foundation of understanding the test will have the potential to cause problems. For example, some service providers are very security conscious and when a client is being attacked they become involved either by notifying the customer, or blocking the protocols being used by the tester perceived to be a hacker. Moreover, some provide Customer Premise Equipment (CPE) that they use to manage the service, such as an Internet router, that may become the target of an attack thread. In these cases, the service provider will become aware of the attack and may attempt to stop it.

LAW ENFORCEMENT

As mentioned earlier, law enforcement, specifically the FBI, is getting more and more involved with Internet-related attacks. Usually, the FBI only becomes involved after the attack to help investigate the crime in support of the victim. However, more time is being invested by the FBI and other law enforcement agencies in looking for malicious activities on the Internet. When planning an attack against a company, especially large ones that have historically attracted hackers and may have asked the FBI for support, it is important to make them aware of the test. Not to do so could jeopardize the engagement or the tester. This is especially important if there is an ongoing investigation at the target company, or a customer or partner of the company is being investigated. Notifying law enforcement is not necessary in most engagements, but it should be considered as a gesture of professionalism and awareness that the test could affect others inadvertently involved.

8 Preparing for a Hack

Once the test is planned and tweaked to make certain that process is as valuable as feasibly possible, there remains the practical preparation for the test. Preparing for a test is not as simple as one may conclude. All a hacker may have to do is download his favorite tool and he is off and running. When getting ready to execute a controlled attack there is much more that must be completed long before the first packet hits the wire.

In this chapter we focus on the technical preparation as much as the management of the engagement. This can be very helpful for services providers and their customers alike. For a company seeking penetration-testing services, it can be helpful to know what to expect.

TECHNICAL PREPARATION

Technically preparing to execute a test is arguably one of the most undocumented elements of a penetration test. Everyone has his or her own expectations, favorite operating system, tools, and practices, but rarely are these communicated, much less appear in the deliverable. In this section, we look at some of the common aspects of getting technically ready to run an attack.

ATTACKING SYSTEM

Building a system, or several, to perform an attack is not as simple as some would like you to think, and if they tell you such, I would question their preparedness. The selected operating system, tools, and how the collected data is protected all play an important role in how the test will be performed, ultimately affecting the value of the test.

There are several attributes to building an attacking system:

- *Operating System.* The operating system selected for use as the foundation of an attack can greatly influence the ability to perform certain tasks. These can come in the form of the available tools that can run on the operating system to the actual capabilities of the system to perform as needed.
- *Tools.* Tools are an essential part of performing a test. Tools can range from off-the-shelf products to outright hacker tools. Tools also need to reflect the systems and networks that are unique to the target.

- *Data Management and Protection*. During a test, piles of data are collected to log the various activities and to gather information for the final deliverable. Protecting information about the inner workings of a client and evidence of a hole is essential to maintain integrity of the test and privacy of the client.
- *Communications*. Once teams are established, the security communication between the teams should be afforded the same security applied to the information collected.

Operating System

Every operating system (OS) has unique traits that can be beneficial to the attacker: its flexibility in allowing the user to create scripts, perform rare and known malicious activities, and support the tools required. The availability of the OS and the hardware necessary to run it plays a role as well. Windows 2000 does not require any special hardware and the system requirements are not excessive. Also, it's not too difficult to get a free copy, especially for a determined hacker. On the other hand, OSs such as HP-UX, Solaris, VMS, IRIX, and XENIX usually require specialized or very expensive hardware, are difficult to obtain, and do not offer substantial advantage to a hacker.

Linux is usually the choice for many hackers as a general-purpose system because it is free, easily obtained, and powerful. Linux is a very capable and strong OS that is incredibly customizable, and for the price, it can't be beat. Linux has been modified to run on telephones, PALM Pilots, and even gaming consoles, to name a few applications. Companies such as TiVo, WatchGuard, Cobalt, IBM, and many others use it as the foundation of some of their products. This is a testament to Linux's flexibility, stability, and power.

But why do hackers and testers alike use Linux? You can liken it to a driving enthusiast and cars. A new Yugo off the line is fine for people driving to work or dropping off the kids at school; it's functional and gets you from point A to point B. A Yugo may be functional but is usually difficult to modify as a high-performance car because it was not originally designed at the factory with those characteristics. A car enthusiast looks for a car that can be manipulated, added to, and modified to accommodate desires. A specialized car may apply to the basic rules to work within the fabric of roads, highways, and parking lots with an accelerator, wheels, and brakes, but beyond that, anything is possible. Linux is that car and the computer simply provides the necessities to interact with the rest of the digital world.

Given that Linux provides so much power and adaptability with almost no cost, it is perfect for hackers to create tools for attacking systems. Therefore, it is the logical starting point for testers.

One of the desirable features of an operating system is to allow the user to accomplish tasks that a traditional system would simply not allow. An example of this is the TCP/IP protocol stack. The protocol stack is what the operating system uses to manage communication with other systems. It is what builds the packets, assembles them, applies attributes and flags, and is responsible for managing the virtual connection between the network card and the upper-level services and applications. In Windows, the stack operates based on a set of rules as defined by the creators at Microsoft with few options for modification. However, Linux's stack is wide open and free for anyone to change to make it function according to a new set of rules that permit the manipulation of the communication. Therefore, a remote system abiding by the standard rules can be affected by a rogue computer that does not. Programs can be written to take advantage of a willing and able protocol stack to build packets to which unsuspecting systems fall victim.

In some scenarios, having an operating system similar to the one being targeted can be an advantage as well. Because Microsoft is everywhere and is arguably the most used operating system in the world, it is also a desirable platform to launch attacks against other similar systems. It is not used because of the flexibility, but rather the similarities it has with the target system. It is much easier to leverage existing flaws in a system than it is to try to mimic them in a different operating system.

Tools

Tools can be defined in many ways. However, in general, a tool can be anything that is used to perform an automated function. Everything from standard applications, utilities, scripts, special-purpose programs, and protocols can be used as designed or pushed to their limits to exploit a system. Tools, in the context of performing a test, are usually designed to perform a task with the intention of identifying or exploiting a vulnerability. Other forms of standard software or utilities can be used to expand the attack or collect the necessary information.

Ping, telnet, and nslookup are standard utilities used to gather various information, support an attack, and determine vulnerabilities. For example, nslookup is typically used to gather domain name information from a DNS server. If used with the "ls –d" command option a DNS server could return all the aliases and their IP addresses assigned to a particular domain. The information collected could be very useful to an attacker, but the fact that the DNS server was not configured properly to avoid such a command demonstrates to the hacker the general awareness of security. Telnet is a very old utility permitting interactive sessions with a system. In most cases, a telnet daemon (telnetd) is running as a service on a remote system and supplies the client with a command-line session to perform various tasks as if sitting at the terminal. There are some applications that use telnet to publish simple character-based programs to a user community. Telnet has an interesting feature in that if you provide it with a target port, it allows human interaction with a service normally used only by applications. For example, the command, "telnet pop-server.domain.com 110" provides an interactive session with the POP service. By using a very basic and common utility, a hacker can directly manipulate a service that thinks it is receiving requests from a system.

Beyond utilities are software packages designed specifically for testing system security, such as ISS's System Security Scanner, a popular tool used by many testers and hackers alike. Off-the-shelf products contain collections of exploits and vulnerability scanners that are employed by a simple menu item checkbox. They can be configured to simply seek out opportunities, or actually attempt to exploit the vulnerability. Some even have DoS capabilities. In the wrong hands, commercially available products can be harmful, even destructive. In addition, the wrong hands could be someone with noble intentions who simply does not know the power of the tool. One of the more common mistakes companies make is purchasing tools for internal use and providing them to local administrators that may have little or no experience in penetration testing. Examples of such a practice have led to enormous amounts of downtime, or the assumption of security because the tool did not find anything because it was improperly employed.

Then there are hacker tools. Some are mainstream such as NMap, LOpht, and Nessus, which have deep roots in the hacking community and have been recently popularized by the legitimate security community. LOpht Crack was a free hacker tool from many years ago that would crack passwords contained in a Windows system. Now, the tool is part of a suite of products offered by @Stake, and used as a standard administrative tool for many organizations to test password integrity.

Usually, the hacker tools that become popular and used by the average administrator do so because they are well written, easy to use, easy to find, and easy to install. In addition, these types of tools are usually not destructive and help with the identification of a vulnerability rather than simply prying it open to gain access. On the other hand, there are tools designed for that very purpose, some with incredibly devious intentions. Some are very small programs designed to take advantage of a specific vulnerability in only one type of application and even specific versions.

The more specific the tool or the deeper underground you have to go to get it usually translates to more difficulty in compiling, installing, configuring, and using. It takes someone with strong skills and tenacity, but the result is a tool that can provide exceptional access to a system.

Obtaining, compiling, and using a tool is only a small part of the total equation. During an engagement it is how the tools are used, to what degree, when they are used, and the techniques they were involved in that make for a successful test. Tools have nearly become the proverbial monkey on the back of penetration testers. This is due to some customers being overly concerned about what tools are used, placing a great deal of emphasis on the value of the tool rather than the capabilities of the tester. Much of this can be seen based on the reliance of reports that are generated by a tool. With the introduction of ISS's System Scanner, a detailed report on each identifiable weakness was considered acceptable. Unfortunately, these reports were just that, a report on the vulnerabilities that were identified by a computer without concern for the overall state of the security. Automated reports either led to the assumption of security, or raised awareness around a specific vulnerability, which may have had little to do with any true threat. Undoubtedly, tools play a critical role in a penetration test, but the value of the test is realized by the capabilities of the tester in using the tools.

Using hacker tools can represent a threat to the tester, the system, and ultimately the client. Given the popularity of many underground hacker tools in the corporate environment, the creators will build a Trojan into their software. They can also contain worms or viruses, but usually they are programs that give surreptitious access to the system. SATAN, which does not contain arbitrary code to implement a Trojan or virus, is nearly impossible to find.

One scenario is that of a system administrator responsible for maintaining several Web servers on the network. Left without any comprehensive security utilities, he looks for and finds a free tool on the Internet that looks for vulnerabilities. He installs the hacker tool and runs scans on his systems. Regrettably, the tool also carries a Trojan Horse program that upon installation looks for an Internet connection, contacts the creator, and sends sensitive files that could be used later to hack the network.

One of the more interesting and devastating ways hackers infiltrate people who use tools is to distribute a modified library necessary for compiling many of the tools. A library is a collection of code used to support common functions within programs. For example, it may contain basic code to access the hard drive or network card, or provide utilities that perform other simple functions. The creator of a tool uses these standard libraries to avoid having to rewrite code. However, there are libraries out there for hacker tools that are usually modified versions of the originals to accommodate the hacker community. Some hackers modify the code even further to perform some other task in addition to the expected one called upon by the program. By doing this they can infect many different hacker-related programs that may use their modified library.

Data Management and Protection

One of the more overlooked aspects of technical planning is establishing security controls for the sensitive information being collected from a target's systems and networks. If the engagement is supported by the company providing detailed information about its environment, the tester may have loads of proprietary information that could be useful to other companies or individuals. In addition to information and documents given to the tester, there is data collected during the various phases of the engagement. Raw data from systems, files collected from servers, screen shots, and detailed maps of the network may be obtained throughout the test. Finally, the consultant may generate information to assist in the overall project: attack plans and strategy, concepts, and miscellaneous communications with peers that could be useful to a real hacker.

NOTE 10: THE HUNTER BECOMING THE HUNTED

Many years ago, a customer requested a very comprehensive attack on the company. It included outside threats, partner and customer threats, and internal employee threats. Several consultants were assigned to the engagement to operate together to collect as much information as possible to determine the overall security of the client's operation. One of the consultants worked his way into the office, found a quiet cubicle, connected to the network, and started browsing around. In addition to looking around and running a sniffer, he attempted to gain access to a Solaris server presumably in the data center. The attempt could be considered premature because there was little information about the server, or the entire network for that matter. Unfortunately (or fortunately, depending on your perspective), the administrators of the Solaris system immediately detected the intrusion and identified the system performing the attack. Being security savvy themselves, they decided to hack the attacking system to get more information about who was on their network and trying to gain access into one of their core systems.

The consultant was running a default installation of Linux and was vulnerable to a multitude of attacks. Within minutes, the administrators obtained root access to the consultant's laptop and proceeded to download everything from the system. Once they felt they had enough data, they deleted a handful of critical system files and shut down the system. After reviewing some of the collected documents, they quickly determined the company by which they were being hacked. The administrators stormed up to their boss's office and presented the findings. As you may imagine, this was embarrassing to the consultant and the organization he represented, but no real harm was done—at least on the surface. Much of the data collected by the administrators was from no less than five previous penetration-testing engagements, detailing vulnerabilities, organizational structures, systems details, vulnerabilities that could not be fixed, system versions, competitive data, and finally sensitive information obtained from various servers and workstations. Luckily, the administrators returned all the collected information and it's doubtful that they would use it for an attack. Nevertheless, this clearly demonstrates the need to protect client information, especially on an attacking system.

Protecting information from a would-be hacker requires the same planning for any system maintaining sensitive data. However, unlike a traditional server, the attacking system may have huge security holes because closing them would have an impact on its usability as a tool for testing. Some solutions are to mount a dedicated, removable hard drive or solid-state storage device that can be easily secured or removed if an attack is detected.

Ultimately, encryption is the best solution. Public-key cryptography, such as Pretty Good Privacy (PGP) that employs asymmetrical encryption, can be used to protect data. One method is to generate a key pair for each of the White and Red Team members with an administrative key. An administrative key is a master key that can be used to decrypt anything encrypted with a private key originally created with the administrative key. It is a protection mechanism so that someone with a private key cannot encrypt sensitive data and delete the key, rendering the information useless. In addition, many applications support split administrative keys, requiring two or more people to be present so the master key can be used. Each member of the Red Team can use a fob or key card to store his or her private key to be used only when data needs to be encrypted.

The end result is a private key maintained on a secure device separate from the attacking system that is used regularly to encrypt the collected information. To support an understanding of trust and access, the existence of an administrative key provides emergency access to the encrypted data in the event the tester quits, is hit by a truck, or anything that would hinder access to the data by authorized users. This is only one example of protecting information on an attacking system. However, no matter the solution, it must be robust and effective, assuming any and all possibilities of exposure to a threat.

Finally, information having nothing to do with the engagement may be saved by the consultant on her system. Data may be from previous engagements, e-mail communications, employment data, or anything else that someone would want to keep on a computer. An attacking system should be devoid of personalized data that could be used to identify the tester, or used against the consultant (or her company) or previous customers in any way. It is all too often that a system is compromised by a hacker, Trojan, or virus possibly resulting in exposure of sensitive information.

One example is a consultant that modified her laptop to perform penetration tests. Ironically, this is necessary for many because a dedicated "hacking system" is not provided by many firms. When she traveled from engagement to engagement (as many consultants do), she gained access to the corporate network through a VPN. Her computer was loaded with hacker tools of all types, some installed, others lying dormant waiting to be used. One of the tools installed included a basic keyboard-capturing program that after a few days would quietly send the recorded keystrokes to the hacker. Because the VPN was accessed daily, the hacker had all the information needed to gain access to the corporate network and her laptop. It wasn't until several days later the activity was discovered and her passwords changed. But there is still no clear way to identify what the hacker could have accomplished with her stolen privileges and access to previous customer information.

There are several options to a tester to limit exposure. Following is a list of common practices:

- *Baseline a Standard Build.* Build a system from scratch, test various functionalities, and monitor the system for abnormal activity. Once comfortable with the final configuration, build an image of the computer on CD. At the end of every test, you can quickly get back up to speed by cleaning the system and installing the tested image.
- *Bootable CD.* Historically, there have been testers that build a complete, fully functional operating system on a bootable CD. When a test needs to be performed, the system can be booted from the CD and tools can be run from an unwriteable platform. Knoppix is a perfect example of this practice. You can easily download a CD image off the Internet, burn it onto a CD, pop it in your computer, and have a standard build for performing tests. (Albeit, there are many elements missing and it only provides the basic tools, but it proves it can be done.)
- *Modified Storage.* The results of most tools can be directed to a storage device of choice. In addition, depending on the sensitivity of the tool, the disk can be writeable, but not readable. Therefore, you can pipe the results of a tool onto a storage device that cannot be read from the computer, a Trojan on the system, or remote attackers. Moreover, when data is not being collected or logged in some fashion, the device can be unmounted (or unplugged) to add more protection.
- *Dynamic Encryption.* There is a plethora of utilities available that will encrypt files as they are written to a file system. By storing the key on a

removable device (such as a fob plugged into the UBS port) data can be quickly stored while ensuring privacy.

Data protection goes beyond storing data securely. It is also the practice of protecting information in all forms: e-mail, documentation, and even spoken information about the test.

- *E-Mail.* Obviously, any e-mail containing information about the target must be encrypted and signed. This is incredibly simple, but not practiced as often as one would hope. There are forms of leakage, such as e-mail between colleagues that get inadvertently included in an e-mail to someone well outside the domain of awareness. Therefore, all communications regarding any vulnerability, exploit, or tactic must be protected. This is critical because if someone knows you are a tester and you ask a specific question, there is the opportunity to draw conclusions about the target's weaknesses.
- *Documentation.* When it comes time to generate the documentation for delivery, it is imperative that the computer used to perform word processing and analysis is completely devoid of hacker-related tools or unnecessary software. It would be devastating if the final analysis—detailing everything about the target's insecurity—were to fall into the wrong hands. When the documentation is complete it should be encrypted and stored on an unlabeled CD.
- *Codenames.* How many times have you been out to lunch at a restaurant near several organizations, such as a popular downtown spot, and overhear a business-related conversation? The potential to disclose private information about a company in a public setting is huge unless you and everyone with you is careful about every word spoken. Therefore, using codenames to represent private information, such as the names of people and companies, is a good practice. Also, this applies to the aforementioned modes of communication. Using codenames in e-mail and documentation can go a long way in adding another level of privacy.

Without a doubt, protecting the private information about a company and the test results is of the utmost importance. Regardless of perceived overhead or cost to protect information, not doing so would be gross negligence.

ATTACKING NETWORK

The source of the attack and the networking technology employed have the potential to shape the results in ways that can lead to improper conclusions. Attacks sourced from the Internet are the most likely places to start and are susceptible to configurations that can influence the outcome of certain attack threads.

Most notable is network address translation (NAT), which is used to convert Internet routable IP addresses to a private IP space. In some configurations, all the privately addressed systems on the attacking network are masked through a single external IP address. NAT can impede the ability for some tools to function as expected or make them not work at all. Moreover, if the target site is using NAT, as many do, there are more opportunities to receive inaccurate responses from remote systems.

Firewalls are a common element on networks and if an attack is being launched from a network with a firewall providing connectivity to the Internet for the tester, the results may be artificial. Many firewalls will respond on behalf of a remote system; this is especially true for ICMP messages, fragments, and session management, such as cookies used in Web browsers. In addition, firewalls are usually where NAT is employed, adding to the complexity.

Just about any device, other than a router to provide the basic connection to the Internet, will affect the protocols and tools being employed in some manner. Therefore, the attacking network is typically connected to the Internet without a firewall or NAT employed to ensure the access is clean and unencumbered. In addition to controlling the type of access to the Internet, the type of service provided by the ISP is next in line to be evaluated. Some service providers only provide NATed IP space to their customers; therefore a NAT system is modifying the traffic long before the tester's traffic reaches the Internet.

Bandwidth can become a concern as well for the tester. The last problem a tester wants to be faced with is poor response or intermittent connections caused by the Internet connection or an intermediate. Depending on the technology being used, the Internet connection may be prone to drops or wide-ranging levels of available bandwidth. For example, some cable providers allow 344 Kb download, but only 56 Kb upload. During the attack, it may be necessary to upload a large file very quickly to avoid detection; an asymmetrical connection may become problematic.

Finally, the configuration of the attacking network must be reviewed for collateral exposures. There are many examples where the connectivity being used to access the Internet is provided by a medium, protocol, or architecture that lends itself to exposing others to the hacking activities. Using cable Internet providers as an example, the network is shared for each segment, so everyone in a neighborhood can see what other computers are doing and can, in turn, be affected by the attack.

If the tester is stationed at an office, the Internet connection may be provided by the building management, which may have a dedicated network for the entire building to provide Internet access through a single connection. When performing the test from a shared network, there is the potential to consume a great deal of the bandwidth or worse, inadvertently bring down the system in an attempt to attack the target.

The simplest way to avoid any of these problems and more is to seek out a clean, dedicated Internet connection that is directly accessible only to the attacking system(s).

Attacking Network Architecture

We've discussed some of the attributes concerning the network and systems used to perform a test. In an effort to pull all these characteristics together, consider the following example. As demonstrated in Figure 8.1, an attacking network architecture can be fairly simple, yet security cannot be underestimated.

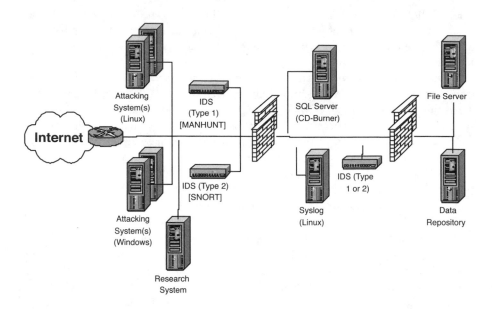

FIGURE 8.1 Example Attacking Network

The goal is to create an environment that is assumed completely insecure and a target for attacks. However, the network and controls must be flexible enough to permit nontraditional activities so the tester can perform complex system interaction with the target without concern for intermediate devices.

Simplicity, flexibility, and security may seem like an oxymoron, but it is a must to accommodate the needs of the tester and to ensure ample security for the target's information assets.

As you can see in the graphic, there is an open connection (i.e., no firewalls or filtering devices) between the tester's main systems and the Internet. Although there are arguments for having some security controls when interfacing with the Internet, if the systems are cycled (e.g., rebuilt) for each test and the information collected is managed appropriately, the risk to the tester and target are minimal. It is also assumed that the Internet connection will only be active during tests. A tester can accomplish this by simply unplugging the connection or applying sophisticated configurations on the router. No matter the practice used to control Internet access, given the network is designed for testing only, other means for day-to-day Internet access should be provided by a separate network altogether.

As discussed above, different operating systems should be employed to accommodate tools in addition to using systems that reflect the target's environment. Although it is not necessary to use, for example, a Windows platform against a Windows system at the target, the option can be helpful to the tester. All the systems that are going to be used for testing purposes should exist—even if only temporarily—on the exposed segment. Initiating an attack from another network should be avoided. Following are some basic reasons for testing from a specific point:

- By sourcing the attack from a set of known IP addresses, the target can easily identify traffic from the tester.
- By sourcing the attack from a point deeper in the network, the potential exists for exposing internal systems to undesirable traffic.
- If the test is performed from different locations that do not have supporting systems, the likelihood of exposing the target's data increases.
- In the event a different ISP is used that is unaware of the tester's activities, traffic may be blocked or reported to authorities.

The inclusion of intrusion-detection systems on the testing network segment are for two reasons: assisting in collecting data about the test, and identifying any unauthorized traffic. The IDS can be configured to simply log activity sourced and destined for the tester's systems and alert to any other suspicious traffic. Two different IDS systems are represented in the graphic only to convey there are different types of IDS with varying degrees of detection and capability. Given the technical capacity of the testers and the value of information that can be collected, having two systems can be very helpful in avoiding any gaps in detection and information collection.

In addition to the IDS and testing systems, a separate system is provided for Internet research. Not only is it helpful to have a different system to prowl the Internet, but also the testing systems may be performing automated tasks that may not allow the tester to perform other activities or simply add efficiency to the engagement. The most prominent reason for the dedicated system is to avoid polluting the testing systems. When searching the Internet for tools or information, the potential for unwanted information being shared or inadvertently being absorbed (i.e., cookies, code, plug-ins, spam, etc.) by the system is a nuisance that can be easily contained and rectified.

Moving a step deeper into the network, a firewall (or some protective device) can be implemented to create a semi-secure environment, or DMZ, for basic support systems. The DMZ is a staging area for data collection. For example, data collected by some tools can be enhanced by the use of a comprehensive database. Exporting information to a system that has additional security controls adds a layer of security for sensitive information. Moreover, systems in the DMZ may contain source code for tools to allow the tester to quickly modify programs to accommodate specific requirements, compile them, test, and put into use without concern for having the necessary libraries on the testing systems. Another helpful attribute is having the ability to collect log information from the IDS, attacking systems, router, or anything that may help collect information about the activities. Not only is this helpful to demonstrate to the target company the activities performed, but it provides a minimum level of forensics in the event tactics are disputed. Again, an IDS on the DMZ can be helpful in identifying unwanted activities on the dedicated segment.

There are a number of reasons for employing a DMZ, but fundamentally the role of the segment is to provide support for the testers in a manner that does not require the testing systems to perform tasks that are not explicitly required for the engagement.

Finally, another set of firewalls is implemented to tightly control data flow between the DMZ and outer networks. In fact, the innermost network should not be permitted to interact with anything beyond the DMZ and the firewall should only permit traffic sourced from the internal network and not from any other external devices. The DMZ is there to support the testing segment and therefore if the tester needs something from the internal network, it should be staged in the DMZ. Given that the DMZ is providing data collection services for the testing network, it may be necessary for internal systems to pull the data to begin analysis or start creating the necessary documentation. The internal network is simply for performing tasks associated with the consultative characteristics of the engagement, but not with the testing elements.

Albeit a simplified example of an attacking network, the fundamentals of segmenting systems with specific roles apply. Networks designed for performing ethical hacks can range from one system connected to a cable modem to hundreds of devices with complicated custom applications to support the process. The most important aspect is to allow the testing systems unfettered access to the Internet and to perform only what is needed to identify and exploit vulnerabilities. There needs to be a secure area to support those systems, and a highly controlled segment for nontesting activities. As long as these attributes are represented in some fashion, the security of sensitive information can be realized while allowing the tester the freedom to perform his or her task.

MANAGING THE ENGAGEMENT

Up until this point, we have covered much about the business and planning regarding ethical hacking, but there is the management of the engagement itself that must be considered. Of course, each services organization goes about managing an engagement with a client in its own way, and in many cases, customers look for these elements when collaborating with a service provider. In this section, we cover some of the basics that should be expected by a customer seeking services

Many of these characteristics of management are general in nature but can take on more importance when ethical hacking is the service of choice. An example is a kick-off meeting to establish the details of the engagement and outline processes to be practiced during the engagement. However, there are many things to consider, such as what information should be shared during the meeting considering information flow controls. In addition, project risk management takes on a new flavor when dealing with technical aspects that are difficult to predict or control.

PROJECT INITIATION

At the beginning of an engagement, many assumptions and associated expectations need to be solidified to ensure the engagement runs as anticipated and the deliverable is in alignment with those expectations. To accomplish this, a kick-off meeting is typically held between the customer and services firm. Following are some of the subjects during such a meeting: identify sponsors, building teams, schedule and milestones, tracking, escalation, and final approval.

- *Identify Sponsors*. It is necessary to identify and collect contact information from all the people involved in the engagement. In addition, roles and authority should be assigned at this point to set the foundation for discussions about escalation, risk management, and change control. It is also necessary to determine who from the company is providing information—if any—for the engagement and a short list of materials to expect. This is important to ensure the planning session and the entire engagement is successful.
- *Building the Teams*. As described earlier, the establishment of Red, White, and Blue Teams is essential to forming the basis for a successful engagement. Nearly every aspect of planning, managing, and closing an engagement is based on the formation of the teams. Without defined teams, the members, contact information, authority, role, communication protocol, and expectations, the ability to perform a test without complication is greatly diminished. Understandably, the White Team is the most important because of the duplicity of interaction and responsibility during the test. It is highly recommended that the following people (roles) be assigned to the team:
  - *CIO*. At least one executive member of the customer organization needs to sponsor the White Team. This is for two basic reasons: executive sponsorship and involvement ensures that all disputes, actions, tasks, and other engagement issues are controlled by a business owner with final say in any decision, and to ensure that the test is approved by a business owner.
  - *Firm Management*. Management representation from the consulting firm must be intimately involved. Although a seemingly obvious statement, consulting management needs to be aware of the engagement well beyond the resourcing, cost, and general requirements. They have to be the organization's liaison for the project to ensure the tester is performing in alignment with expectations.
  - *Client Technical Advisor*. A respected and knowledgeable technical representative from the client's stable is highly recommended to be part of the White Team. There are situations where results from the attack may appear to be causing major problems in the client's environment, when in reality they are not. On the other hand, a technically savvy resource aware of the testers' actions can quickly rectify problems when they do appear.

NOTE 11: WHITE TEAM PROBLEMS AFFECTING THE TEST

Recently, a friend of mine, we'll call him Steve, was working with a customer in preparation for a test. The technical advisor (an administrator part of the White Team) from the customer was involved in the planning sessions.

No sooner were the meetings over when the administrator secretly began to make sweeping security changes to the network in an effort to thwart the inevitable attack from Steve. Moreover, because the administrator participated in the planning of the engagement, he knew exactly where to focus his efforts.

Unfortunately, as with many uncontrolled changes to a network and systems, the result of the administrator's actions began to take its toll on the performance of applications and introduced several access issues throughout the enterprise. It was about this time Steve started the test, successfully attacking the network from a remote location on the Internet.

It was assumed by the White Team that all the user complaints and poor performance were the result of the attack and asked that the process be halted. They began to investigate the problems. Initially, Steve was blamed for their problems and faced serious issues, one of which was having to repair the faulty systems. Convinced it was not his doing, he spent time on the customer's site in search of an answer.

In short order, he discovered that many critical systems, routers, firewalls, and applications were modified the day before the test started. Moreover, it was not difficult to determine who made the changes. Steve was cleared of all wrongdoing, but the engagement was never completed.

- *Shadow Consultant.* In some situations, the consulting firm will provide more than one resource on an engagement at no cost. This can happen for two reasons: the extra consultant was not billing and therefore was available to learn or support the engagement, or the services company provided the additional resources to ensure the success of the engagement to establish a partnership with the customer in hopes of future business based on the initial engagement. Both practices are very beneficial to the client and represent no threat to the integrity of the test. If a services firm does provide additional resources for no fee, a client should look to add her to the White Team. This practice is exceptionally valuable to the engagement for many reasons:
  - *Technical Representation.* Having a second pair of technically savvy eyes on the outside as well as the inside of a test helps to identify problems before they become a reality. This is also true in the event something unwanted occurs and the extra consultant can quickly support the correction of the problem leaving the tester to continue in other areas of the test.
  - *Customer Relations.* Beyond supporting trust and partnership with the customer, the consultant can work closely with the client during the test to provide a level of comfort to the customer that the test is being monitored and controlled to meet expectations. Being aware of the primary consultant's activities and possibly his technique, the second consultant can work with the technical representative from the client to manage the technical aspects of the test.
    NOTE: The only negative attribute that can occur from having a supporting technical role in the engagement is information sharing. In zero knowledge tests, information and the access to information can be key to the overall value of the test. If a blind test is being performed, it

should be stipulated what kind of information should be shared or characteristics of the test acknowledged between the tester and the supporting consultant on the White Team.

- *Schedule and Milestones.* As with any engagement, there is a need to identify a timeframe and goals during the engagement. With ethical hacking this can be a curse and a gift. In some ethical hacking engagements, there is a tendency to perform certain tasks for a predetermined duration at a specific point within the engagement. This is helpful from a project management perspective: knowing on day one you will perform 24 hours of wardialing and beginning on day four you begin wardriving. Therefore, the ability to manage resources and activities is much clearer in a well-formulated project plan. However, the problem arises when other tasks, ones less independent of each other, are segmented. For example, when performing wardriving the attack may employ social engineering to gain limited access to a building to get a better signal or to the network itself. Social engineering is typically seen as a separate task when in reality it remains a constant throughout the engagement.

  The goal of establishing milestones is to remain general in nature and avoid artificially introducing limitations in the test. Throughout my experiences, this is one of the most imposed limitations that companies seem to interject without greater thought to the overall value of the test. I was recently told by a customer that we would have one day of social engineering because it should not take any longer to explore all the people-related vulnerabilities. The reality is that people represent a substantial vulnerability and it cannot be effectively measured in a single day. Therefore, to conclude that many tasks and tactics performed during a test can be neatly proportioned throughout the engagement to support management's desire to control the process is fruitless and will most certainly affect the potential value of the test.

- *Tracking.* Tracking the project can be difficult depending on the type of engagement. This is especially true in multi-phased attacks where there are several consultants working simultaneously to gain access of various types. Once the milestones are set, and the proposed timing is agreed upon, establishing a framework to track the engagement, as well as communication between the customer and firm, become essential to the success of the engagement. Every customer should be presented with a project plan that includes processes for tracking the success or failure of any given event. In addition, if the task is a failure, a detailed explanation should be expected.

- *Escalation.* Ethical hacking is fraught with the potential for failure and damage of all kinds, some of which can last for months if not years after the conclusion of the engagement. In typical situations, the escalation process is to control the risk of damage and to alert those involved of the potential for an adverse event. Therefore, project management is needed to support the tester and the client. It is good practice to have a project manager integrated into the White Team, working with the tester as a sounding board to validate concerns and activities throughout the engagement.

Moreover, an escalation plan must be established to ensure the communication protocol created with the teaming methodology is properly utilized. During the engagement planning meeting the customer should expect a minimal baseline for managing undesirable results. The escalation plan should include a description of general events associated with systems, networks, applications, and personnel that represent an adverse impact on business operations. Without an unambiguous collection of metrics that define a bad situation it would be impossible for the teams to interact appropriately to ensure overall value of the engagement. In its simplest form, it is agreeing to a vocabulary to ensure there is a common understanding of what is a good attack (i.e., a test that results in security insights) and a bad attack (i.e., a test that destroys data or affects system integrity).

An example of a plan would be the identification of systems where someone on the White Team should be notified if an attempt is made to access them. The system can be identified by an IP address, network, or role within the organization. Once the White Team is notified, they can provide guidance as to whether the attempt should be made, or inquire about the type of vulnerability that is the target for the proposed test. Albeit a simple explanation, the details behind the plan can become overly complex or simplified to a point where the test is rendered useless. In some cases (all too common), the White Team simply says not to pursue and move on to the next task at hand, not considering the possible success of the test and only concerned with being the person to approve an attack that results in a critical system being brought down. In a case where the process is overly complicated, the test begins to slow and ultimately stops because the red tape has grown so thick that nothing can be tested without some form of approving committee. All too often, the resulting committee is not knowledgeable enough to make a logical choice or once again fearful of supporting an action that could be harmful.

In addition to establishing a process to preclude a perceived event, the plan must include what to do once the attack has resulted in damage. In some cases, a company has an incident management program that can be reviewed and augmented to support recovery of an adverse event caused by a test. In that light, a plan must demonstrate the ability to identify the attack properly to ensure it is the consultant and not a real hacker, isolate the event, and ultimately stop the tester from continuing.

- *Customer Approval.* Last, the target company has to give the "go" signal. Once everything is planned and processes established, a starting date must be agreed upon.

DURING THE PROJECT

It is one thing to establish a plan for managing a project and all the features of the test; it is another to enact them. During the engagement, there are several things that need to happen—regardless of adverse events—to ensure everything is going as planned. Following is a set of items that should be performed during an engagement: status reports, scope management, and deliverable review.

- *Status Reports*. Regular status reports are essential for two basic reasons: monitoring and value.
    - *Monitoring*. Reports provide everyone with a list of activities that have been performed, the results, and the planned activities for the next reporting timeframe. This ensures that everyone is aware of the activities the tester is performing and highlights any actions that are out of scope or communicating incomplete phases. Reports can also help to determine if the test is moving along as expected.
    - *Value*. One of the most important elements in hiring an outside firm to perform any service is knowing there is actually work being performed. This may seem painfully obvious, but when clients are paying hundreds of dollars per hour, they should know what they are paying for. Unlike buying a product, where you can touch it and realize value upon payment, services are soft investments and value is based on tasks performed and the final documentation. A clear and detailed status report ensures the company sees value in the service.
- *Scope Management*. It is very common for a change in the scope of the engagement to ensure the original intent of the test is met. This may include an observation by the tester, or the company decides that a critical network was omitted from the original scope of work. Given the existence of the White Team, it is very easy to communicate the required scope changes and expand or contract the test. However, unlike traditional engagements where divergence from the plan is clear and added tasks can be itemized easily, ethical hacking represents a challenge in both cases. For example, adding social engineering towards the end of an engagement may have an impact on the results of previous attack threads and may consume an unidentifiable amount of time. When the attack is multi-phased or includes internal attributes, the scope is easier to define and manipulate due to the delineation of duties and activities. The most notable examples of scope changes have to do with what is considered a target. Customers may reduce the number of networks previously slated as targets or reduce the number or type of systems to be attacked.
- *Deliverable Review*. Reviewing a deliverable during the engagement sounds like an oxymoron, but as information is collected and attacks are performed, the deliverable can start taking shape. This is also helpful when the company wants a preview of the documentation in addition to the status reports. During the engagement, the deliverable is an excellent opportunity to perform research on the overall state of the results from the test. This is especially true during the enumeration and vulnerability analysis phases where having the information clearly documented in a single source can assist in unearthing vulnerabilities. Finally, reviewing

the deliverable's accuracy during the engagement establishes the foundation for quality.

CONCLUDING THE ENGAGEMENT

Once the engagement is complete and the deliverable is finalized, there must be some form of closure to summarize the project and transfer materials and knowledge about the engagement in a final presentation. This is an opportunity to share accomplishments, lessons learned, and recommendations. It is also a time to close any remaining items or issues that were spawned during the project to formalize the next steps and remediation.

As a customer, you should expect the presentation of the deliverables and all associated documentation collected from the test. In addition, there should be a summary of events—positive and negative—and an outline of tasks executed during the test. Most important, a clear understanding of the vulnerabilities, their ramifications, and initial recommendations on rectifying the holes should be communicated. There should be a discussion of any adverse events and remedial actions taken, a detailed list of tools used and where, and any remaining digital components in the computer or networking environment. As with traditional forensics, digital or otherwise, Locard's Principle applies. Introduced in 1910 by Edmond Locard, the theory "a criminal always leaves something at the crime scene, or takes something away" would insinuate that once the engagement is complete, there remains evidence that the tester was in the client's networks and systems. Therefore, it is important that there is a clear understanding of the tools employed so any remaining elements which could cause problems later, are identified and removed.

9 Reconnaissance

Defined by Webster's as "A preliminary survey to gain information; especially, an exploratory military survey of enemy territory," reconnaissance is, in essence, to know your enemy. This can be translated into two areas, one for the organization and the other for the penetration tester.

For the organization to properly work with the consulting firm to develop a comprehensive plan for the test, it needs to have an understanding of the viable threats to the company, the know-your-enemy part. Not all hackers are the same and although you may think you can hide in the vast space of the Internet, the odds that you attract some form of attacker is high. I don't care if you make hotdogs, beer, coat hangers, shoelaces, or those annoying little stickers on the edge of DVD cases, you will catch the attention of someone sooner or later; it's inevitable. And for those who deal with money, valuable assets, proprietary information, or any other aspect of business that has obvious value, you have much more to worry about. Knowing the types of hackers out there will help in determining the best approach.

For the consultant performing the test, it is an investigation of the target organization to gain information to learn more about it to formulate an attack. In addition, the process itself can be very valuable to the company. Having someone perform an aggressive search on the Internet and other areas where information can be obtained can offer a great deal of insight as to exactly what is available to the common person and a hacker. There are organizations that provide these investigative services simply to help companies understand what type of data is floating around the Internet about them and help them realize what the potential risks are.

Reconnaissance, in the scope of a penetration test, can be any activity from pinging hosts to digging in the trash. It is all about what can be gained by simply looking around, to put it bluntly.

The process can be extremely valuable to the targeted company in addition to assisting in refining the scope of the test. It will guide the tester in knowing what tactics, such as social engineering, partner information, and network discovery, are viable and permissible. Based on the company's primary goals for the test and where it feels the most value can be obtained, reconnaissance will help resolve the types of threats leading to a closer replication of a real attacker who is interested in the target company.

Hackers will use anything to their advantage and will stop short of personal harm to accommodate their goal. This section introduces the use of information collection techniques to hone their attack. The following is an introduction to some of the technical as well as the nontechnical approaches used to obtain information. This is not the modus operandi of script kiddies and they would never practice these techniques because of the humanized and close interaction with the target. However, hackers have breached this physiological limitation to increase their success.

In this chapter, we discuss reconnaissance in three primary categories and the elements within each. However, what is important to appreciate is that all three categories are related and although each element within a category is unique, they can be interconnected during the engagement and leveraged at different points in time. Moreover, and this is where companies get discombobulated, any of the primary categories and their elements can and should be used throughout the engagement. Reconnaissance, when an approved factor in the test, is a constant, a common denominator in penetration testing.

The three categories are social engineering, physical security, and the Internet. To add even more entanglement in the definition of these categories, physical security and intranet reconnaissance are close cousins to social engineering. However, in the interest of clarity, I've broken these subjects down into different categories.

SOCIAL ENGINEERING

Social engineering is the oldest form of attack to obtain data. It practices coercion and misdirection to obtain information. Social engineering can take many forms, ranging from telephone calls to e-mail to face-to-face interaction. Additionally, the degree of interaction is a variable common among all forms of the attack. For example, a determined hacker may apply for a job that allows access to the establishment for on-site reconnaissance. Hackers may assume the identity of employees or their colleagues to lure others into providing information. While performing a test where social engineering was approved, the consultant researched a doctor known for managing medication testing for pharmaceutical companies. After assuming this person's identity, he contacted several hospitals that were helpful in obtaining patient records and system access privileges to perform the fictional tests, all over the phone.

NOTE 12: THE PHYSICALITY OF SOCIAL ENGINEERING

Many characteristics of social engineering are overlooked or are misunderstood. However, when employed carefully, the results can be astounding. The potential value of social engineering is founded on two basic philosophies: the human element of security and the inherent validity of the test. As many know, people represent the greatest threat (intentionally or unintentionally) to security controls. It can be as simple as someone opening an e-mail that contains a virus, or exceedingly sinister such as sending proprietary information to competitors. People can be influenced easily or forced into situations due to financial strains or political affiliations. Money can be a considerable motivator for illicit activities. For example, when applying for security clearances, the financial stability of the applicant is weighed very heavily. Considering the human element, the second basic characteristic of social engineering is how the tactics can accurately reflect potential threats. Moreover, social engineering directly tests the controls in a manner that the controls were designed to do: control people. The physicality of the test—the testers and the controls—represents a common denominator that reduces (or eliminates) the opportunity for disputing the results and offers substantial value.

On the lighter side, a hacker may simply send an e-mail hoping for a response. E-mail is a potent medium that can be used to extract information. It is easy to obtain names of certain employees and deduce an e-mail address. With very little research on the Internet, you can find subjects that interest a certain individual and establish communication on a common theme. An example is finding a network administrator and his conversations on various newsgroups to determine his physiological profile and willingness to share information. Through e-mail interaction, you may be able to gain insightful characteristics about the internal network and realized security.

A more prevalent approach used by hackers, and thankfully growing more difficult due to security awareness, is calling a helpdesk and asking for a password reset on your account. However, even with good security practices, such as asking for a Human Resource (HR) ID or your mother's maiden name, it remains a simple barrier for a minimally skilled hacker to overcome.

In this section, we're going to introduce several of the elements within the scope of social engineering. Each element can be employed to varying degrees of intensity and can stand completely on its own. This is an important detail. This means that a company can be very specific about the type of social engineering and even, in most cases, limit the acceptable depth of the test. Granted, each element of elimination and reduction of granularity can potentially reduce the value of the test. Although this is true for many of the tactics used in penetration testing, other areas do not allow for such precise control. Finally, with this control, social engineering can be used as a surgical tool to extract the necessary information to determine the level of risk precisely where the exposure is expected.

Of course, to make this a reality you need a firm understanding of the nuances of the different elements to have the desired effect. The delta between knowing and not knowing is equivalent to a surgeon with a scalpel compared to a child with scissors, and with much the same consequences.

Recently, there has been an interesting twist when employing social engineering: getting caught. To level the playing field and to get more of the tester's skin in the game, companies are stating that if the tester is caught, all testing stops. When a company seeks social engineering as one of the tactics to be used against its employees it insinuates a concern for risk associated with people and an assumption of an aggressive attacker. Therefore, if a real hacker were to be caught, the level of risk would be greatly diminished given that the threat was not realized.

Under greater scrutiny, this makes perfect sense from the company's perspective. One of the primary drivers for employing social engineering is to evaluate the human factor and the ability to thwart an attack of a specific type (i.e., the type of hacker and his determination). Consequently, if the avenue of attack were unsuccessful and the tester discovered, the test would be nullified.

The value to a company is hidden from plain sight. Does this mean that the company is secure? Not entirely. Is this the best approach for all situations and all elements of social engineering? No. Does this force the tester to proceed with care? Absolutely, and this is where the value to the company lies. By placing greater risk on the shoulders of the tester, in the form of a lost engagement, it brings the social engineering phase of the test much closer to reality. For example, if a hacker were discovered, he'd probably go to jail, a substantial price to pay. When a tester is discovered, there is little or no ramification and the test moves on. No risk equates to poor alignment of the test to the reality of the stresses a real attacker must overcome to perform similar tasks.

However, for companies seeking social engineering and considering using this type of control, be forewarned that it does not apply to all environments and should be used only when social engineering is used as a primary component of the test.

In the following sections, we highlight five elements of social engineering: e-mail, helpdesk fraud, prowling and surfing, internal relations and collaboration, and corporate identity assumption.

E-Mail

E-mail can be a powerful persuasion device for hackers and con artists alike. E-mail has become a basic element in society and is considered crucial for many companies to run a successful business. People have grown so accustomed to e-mail that they rarely question the integrity of the content or source. To add to the malaise, many people don't understand how e-mail is routed from one desktop to another, and eventually the technology and science take a back seat to magic, leaving people to assume if the sender is dad@aol.com, it must be from Dad. Given that the general public is trusting of their e-mail, the direct access to people the service provides, and the relative obscurity of the communication itself, e-mail is used over and over to spread worms, viruses, and just bad information.

In many cases, people can distinguish among e-mail that was sent directly to them, part of a distribution list, or when they were simply caught in the spray of a shotgun blast. We're all used to some spam leaking into our inboxes, but e-mail used for social engineering is usually much less obvious because it is specifically engineered to get you to believe it by sounding and looking familiar, a tactic that is astonishing simple to perform.

In addition to communicating in a familiar tone and looking like it should, an e-mail designed to fool the recipient is typically asking for something the addressee is permitted to provide or the owner of the desired information. If a hacker were to send an e-mail to someone in maintenance asking for remote access privileges, it could raise some questions about the validity of the request. However, if you send the same e-mail to the remote access administrator, the request's subject matter will be familiar, possibly lowering the guard of the administrator.

Of course, today most people are less naive when it comes to suspicious e-mail, especially after the ILOVEYOU and Anna Kournikova viruses that promised interesting sexy subjects with a much more sinister result. Nevertheless, people still attach a great deal of trust to e-mails and their content and this is especially true when the sender's address is recognizable, such as that of a friend, co-worker, boss, or family.

It is a trivial task to make an e-mail appear as though it came from a known source. This can be especially powerful when sending an e-mail to someone from his or her management requesting the updated design for an executive presentation about the changes to security controls that are in progress. (You would be shocked to know that this actually works!) A consultant performing a penetration test sent an e-mail posing as the CIO of the target company to all the network managers asking such a question, resulting in ample information routed back to the tester.

E-mail can be used in combination with other types of social engineering to simulate gathering information. When working on an engagement several years ago, the reconnaissance phase supplied ample information about a scientist working with the target organization to develop several products. To get more information, I called the office of the scientist looking for whom I needed to e-mail to get the information associated with the development at the target site. Once the address was known, a falsified e-mail was sent appearing to come from the scientist asking for the data and referencing the receptionist (my name) to add validity to the request.

The thorniest aspect of e-mail fraud is ensuring the mail is routed back to the tester. It is not critical that the true sender, the identity the tester is assuming, receives the response, because by then the tester has the necessary information. However, this can become important when a conversation thread is established between the tester and the target. If the true sender were to be involved, the conversation would assuredly break down and the tester exposed. From a technical perspective, there are several options to ensure the mail is routed back to the tester. For example, e-mail programs should compare the "reply to:" address to the "from:" address, but many don't. Therefore, the recipient simply hits "reply" and inadvertently sends the e-mail to "hacker@yahoo.com" and not to the assumed "boss@mycompany.com." Another tactic used is hacking into the mail server and getting the account information to send and receive using an intermediary's account. No matter the tactic, using e-mail for social engineering is popular, relatively simple, and can have positive results.

There is an endless array of e-mail that can be sent to trick people into offering information that can be helpful in other areas of the test. These can range from obtaining remote access phone numbers, information on applications in use, and collecting data on security management protocols, such as getting passwords updated. Companies employ several different types of control measures to ensure a person's identity prior to providing a password. A well-constructed e-mail can help gain insights as to how new passwords are provided or other application and network access is managed.

Note 13: Trusting E-Mail

While on a penetration-testing engagement for a group of hospitals that permitted social engineering (e-mail only), I took advantage of several configuration missteps in their Microsoft Exchange 5.5 system (did I say this was a long time ago?) that permitted me to e-mail employees from what appeared to be an internal address. I started by sending specific e-mails to individuals asking them for some information regarding a recent medical research project that I had learned about from various Web sites. All the responses conveyed they didn't know what I was referring to, but were very helpful in providing other contact information to help me find out. Totally uninterested in the research project, but intrigued by the responses, I started a disinformation campaign throughout the company. I sent regular e-mails to entire departments in remote locations discussing the new HIPAA compliant application, its use, and procedures for setting up accounts. Within a few days and a couple of e-mails, nearly 20 percent of respondents provided security-related information permitting access to internal systems. It was fascinating to see how people completely trusted their e-mail and acted on instructions that would be questioned if asked face-to-face. Even now, when e-mail is as fundamental as the phone, people still tend to trust official-looking and sounding e-mail to the point of self-deception.

E-mail can also be used to implant a Trojan that can allow the hacker to access the recipient's system later. BackOrifice, Netcat, and Sub7 are a few examples of popular remote control tools that permit a hacker to gain access to a remote system undetected. Although many of these applications are blocked at the firewall, they can provide an opportunity to get internal access once a system in the DMZ is exploited.

Finally, the information in the e-mail header can be valuable. It can reveal the server or servers used in the transmission of the e-mail, their IP addresses, version of the mail system, and the version and type of the target's e-mail client. All of the information can be used later to launch an attack or simply add to the pile of other data collected during the test to review during the final analysis.

Value

The value of an e-mail-based social engineering test to the target company can be limited depending on the type of information obtained, the security awareness of employees (or security culture) and, in some cases, the technology employed, and fundamentally, if the company is concerned that people are going to pony up sensitive information. Before agreeing to e-mail fraud tests, ask yourself, "Do you trust your employees and do they have access to information that can be used against you?" The first part of the question is founded on personal perception or experience, but the latter part must be assumed to be "Yes" because most companies have open internal security controls. If you answer "No" and then "Yes," you are a good candidate for e-mail-based social engineering.

Because many of the successful e-mail attacks are based on subject and content, there are no technical solutions that weed out fraudulent e-mails because they simply look and read like any other e-mail. In this case, the awareness of the employee (which can be very difficult to prepare for) takes a primary role in the security associated with e-mail.

As mentioned above, e-mail can be a strong ally for a hacker. Given the comfort of people using e-mail, assumed integrity and trust of e-mail in today's society, combined with the simplicity of the technology, it presents a favorable tool to an attacker to gain information at very little risk of detection or identification.

To summarize, having the penetration test include fraudulent e-mails can be very valuable for the following reasons:

- *Inexpensive.* The process of creating and sending e-mail is fairly simple and consumes very little time and effort.
- *Knowing What's Available.* With a small collection of e-mail sent to various employees, the company can quickly surmise what people are willing to provide information and the level of effort expended to obtain it.
- *Security Culture.* Obviously, the tester will keep all e-mail replies for documentation purposes. This will help the company see empirical evidence on how people respond to e-mail threats. This can also help with determining who was listening and who was sleeping during the last security awareness class.
- *Information Type.* In the event information is obtained during the test, the company can determine the sensitivity of the data, possibly leading to more internal security controls and training.
- *Impact.* Unlike other areas of penetration testing and social engineering, there is little negative impact on the company, operations, or the physiological well being of employees—it was just an e-mail.

Controlling Depth

So you decide to permit e-mail fraud against your employees, but how can you control the depth and granularity to get the most from the test without overly stressing people and systems? The answer is fairly straightforward. Following are some options that can be employed to implement various controls:

- *One Shot.* Only permit a single e-mail to be sent. This ensures that no conversation is established, limiting the infection of the tester in the employee community. This is an especially valuable control tactic if you are concerned about overloading or alienating employees. It also ensures not a great deal of time will be consumed. Finally, many conclude, if you can't get the information with the first e-mail, then an acceptable level of control has been met. Although I personally do not agree, it does make for a palatable option for companies who may be on the fence about permitting such a test in the first place.
- *Three Strikes.* This is an extension of the above example: a company may only permit three e-mails to be used in a thread. The primary driver is to see how much can be obtained, assuming three e-mails should do the trick.
- *Illicit Content.* A more obvious control metric is to limit the type of content. For example, no profanity, immoral comments, or personal attacks should be employed to force extraction. Although I've seen this used before it is entirely unethical.
- *Subject Matter.* When coercing someone there is the potential to use language that can be too aggressive. The best way to implement this type of control is to create a basic template of acceptable tone.

- *Length*. Another method for controlling content, in addition to depth, is limiting the number of words permitted in the e-mail. By stipulating that an e-mail will not exceed 200 words, there are few options for elaborating and possibly negatively affecting the target employee.
- *Subject*. Last, and probably the most obvious, is to simply state the acceptable subject. For example, by only allowing the tester to send e-mail requesting access to related information, the scope of the attack can be controlled. This is an example of finding who may be exposing the company to the greatest threat. For some organizations, this can be recent, unpublicized merger or acquisition information, or product manufacturing techniques.

HELPDESK FRAUD

One of the more common types of social engineering is calling the helpdesk as an employee in need of help. The traditional subject for help is with passwords and getting new ones. The only problem with this tactic is that helpdesk employees are usually trained to follow a protocol for providing passwords and many do not include furnishing them over the phone.

A communication protocol is essentially a predefined list of questions and actions executed by the helpdesk attendant and the caller to ensure authentication. In many cases, there are several options for the helpdesk employee to deal with different scenarios. For example, if the caller cannot retrieve e-mail to get the updated password, the helpdesk may be directed to use voice mail.

However, nothing ventured, nothing gained, and many social engineering tests still include calls to the helpdesk seeking to obtain unauthorized information, and they still get results. Either someone does not follow protocol, or is simply fooled into thinking he has the necessary information to prove the identity of the caller. In some cases, success was based on misdirection and controlled confusion in the conversation, such as introducing elements that were not considered in the protocol forcing the helpdesk employee to make a decision based solely on opinion and assumptions.

Beyond trying to get passwords, which can be difficult, obtaining remote access phone numbers or IP addresses of VPN devices can be helpful as well and many helpdesk employees do not see the need to authenticate the caller for seemingly useless information. In the reconnaissance phase, the tester may learn the target is using an application that requires a customized client to gain access. A quick call to the helpdesk can get the client e-mailed to a remote account to be used later to gain access.

Nevertheless, helpdesks are typically prepared for controlling the provisioning of information and applications, but it is for this very reason that they can be a lucrative target for social engineering. They get calls asking for similar information all day long and expect to provide answers using the protocol, which can be weak. In addition, for large helpdesks or companies that provide helpdesk services for many companies, there is usually a high degree of rotation of employees, resulting in unfamiliarity with the protocol introducing even more opportunities to glean information. In some scenarios, the helpdesk employee may grow nonchalant about giving out passwords and simply give it to the tester on the phone.

Even though the test can be time consuming and may not result in any information, the value of the test to the customer can be tremendous. The test can not only validate the security, or insecurity, associated with the helpdesk, but in the event critical information is obtained, the ability to translate the results into a functioning mitigation strategy is clear.

NOTE 14: GOOD HELPDESK PRACTICES GONE WRONG

There are several examples that clearly demonstrate good practices gone wrong when applied by people who perform them because they have to and not because they need to or care.

An example was calling the helpdesk to get a password reset. We needed to provide an HR ID, which was obtained by e-mailing the employee acting as the HR helpdesk. After talking to the helpdesk, the new password change was going to be e-mailed to us via the real employee's address. Unfortunately, we were not in a position to trap that message, and if the original employee were to receive the e-mail it would raise concern.

Therefore, we asked if there was an alternative method for providing passwords. The helpdesk explained that, while on the line with us, they would call our office phone number listed in the employee profile and leave the password in the voicemail box. This is a practice based on PIN access controls on voicemail systems, further processing your identity. At first, this appeared to be more volatile and increased the risk of exposure more than the original e-mail method. However, the helpdesk asked a crucial question, "Can you verify that the correct number is 312-555-1234?" We responded, "No, that is my old office number. Here is my new number, 453-555-4321. Also, could you please change the number in the system, it appears to be out of date?" "Sure." "Thanks."

The new number was to our cell phone and we quickly changed the voicemail message and awaited the call with our new password. What was even more surprising is the helpdesk walked us though the password change process, providing an Internet-sourced URL to perform the task.

There were several breakdowns of security on this call: the assumption that HR IDs are difficult to obtain and the helpdesk *provided* the number to verify, opening an opportunity to give a different number as well as ask for a change laying the foundation for future password changes. Also, there was never a concern that the new number was in a different area code!

The test assesses two factors with helpdesks: the communication protocol used by the employee and the overall awareness and capabilities of the helpdesk attendant, both of which can be reviewed and augmented to reduce the exposure. For example, if a tester introduces several complexities in the call to render the standard protocol useless, such as the laptop was lost, using a borrowed cell phone, or must access the network while abroad using a kiosk in a coffee shop, the helpdesk may make determinations on what to do in the lack of any structured solution. At this point, a simple line can be added to the protocol saying, "Call the helpdesk manager."

The test can also help with training employees on how to handle situations that seem harmless but can inadvertently reveal proprietary information. For one customer, the test resulted in modified call routing to ensure people with a specific problem speak only to those experienced in dealing with security-related issues. Many helpdesks employ this type of call management, but if an employee is not clear on the process he may be tricked into providing information or changing a password to help the caller.

Managing a helpdesk can be challenging, especially those that support multiple companies with dissimilar protocols. Moreover, working on a helpdesk can be taxing because the fundamental goal is to help people, therefore the mindset of the employee is to help as much as possible. Security can become an obstacle in supporting users effectively, but with proper training, comprehensive call routing, and supportive protocol the caller can be helped without presenting opportunities to a hacker.

Value

Several characteristics of this test offer substantial value:

- *Protocol*. Based on the information collected and the tactic used, the protocol used by the helpdesk can be modified to address similar real attacks in the future.
- *Services*. If a separate organization is providing helpdesk services for your company, the test will expose any weaknesses in their support. If the SLA associated with the service includes security elements, the results from the test will provide ample evidence that its practices are not meeting the needs of the company.
- *Exposure*. As with e-mail fraud, the data collected can be insightful as to the type of information available to a common hacker. This can help reduce exposure and focus controls on the helpdesk practices.
- *Inexpensive*. The reality is that tests against the helpdesk are very similar to e-mail attacks and require minimal effort. It simply takes some time to develop a strategy and compile the information.

Controlling Depth

In an effort to manage the granularity and impact of making several phone calls to unsuspecting helpdesk employees, there are several tactics that can be used by a company to control the tester and manage the depth.

- *Group*. Only permit the tester to appear to be from a certain group, department, or community within the company. For example, permitting calls that seemingly come from a remote sales community can help determine the type of information available to that group.

- *Subject.* As with e-mail, controlling the subject of the call will focus on specific areas of call support. Password resets, software downloads, tools, and access requests are typically high on the list.
- *Number of Calls.* Controlling the number of calls is directly related to the size of the helpdesk (i.e., number of employees working) and the subject. For example, the helpdesk group that handles password resets may only comprise four people. Therefore, controlling the number of calls will reduce the time and refine the approach.

PROWLING AND SURFING

Shoulder surfing is gaining information surreptitiously while possibly engaging in another subject. A good example is watching someone type in her password while talking about what they did over the weekend. This obviously requires close inter-action and proximity to the target and exposes the attacker to being identified in trying to get proprietary information. There are many themes to this type of attack that range from watching people perform tasks to listening in on conversations. Essentially, this is social awareness and seeking the opportunity to gain information through observation.

When social engineering is permitted in the form of someone snooping around the office, this type of attack can provide plenty of information about the practices of individuals within the organization. However, the true value of the exercise can be scrutinized. The value of the attack is determined by the culture of the organization. If a company usually has visitors moving in and out of the office regularly, the test provides an opportunity to see what is available to someone with bad intentions. Conversely, if employees are not used to strangers walking around there is a good chance the tester will be questioned. Nevertheless, regardless of the culture, prowling has the potential to provide insights to a company's internal human security posture, but only in certain cases.

There are several factors that can be used to determine the success or failure of an internal attack of this type. Does the target have a security guard who controls access? And if so, was the tester given temporary access privileges? When the tester is given access, such as in the form of a fake worker, the value of the attack is solely based on the assumed trust of employees of the company. Therefore, the security of the internal network is founded on the access made available to the staff.

The value of the test appears in two forms based on the structure of the test. For example, if the tester was "hired" as a low-level employee who should not have been able to obtain critical information from a protected area of the office, then the internal controls need to be reviewed. In addition, the hiring and training practices of the target should be investigated as well. This is based, once again, on the assumption of trust of the employees.

What is important to understand is that the information collected is typically not in a digital format; this is not someone going into a network from an internal point and hacking (that is internal testing, described later). The test is designed to reveal physical access to information, such as printed receipts, customer lists, contact lists, and other material that may be lying around the office. Therefore, the documents collected do not weigh as heavily as the access to the information, and this can be complicated based on the original formulation of the privileges provided to the tester.

If a company does not differentiate employee's physical access to various areas of the building, then the test's value is founded only on the awareness of the staff. This may seem awkward, but the structure of the test has a direct impact on the conclusions that are made about security. The information collected is not as important as the type of access given to the tester. Granted, the materials collected from the test help determine the exposure of proprietary information to an employee, but when reviewed in the light of security, the larger issue becomes trust.

As a result, the target company will only see value if its staff is in question. Usually, this is associated with companies that have a high rate of employee turnover or they suspect internal fraud of some form. But many organizations gain little value from this type of test because of the assumed trust of internal resources.

Because value is ultimately realized by access, the target may not provide any privileges to the tester, leaving him to his own capabilities to get inside the office and browse around. When compared to the previous example, this test can provide greater insight to the internal and physical security of the target company. However, much like the previous scenario, the goal of the test needs to be articulated. Without an understanding of what is being tested, there is little chance of the results of the test being integrated to thwart a future attack based on a similar strategy.

In contrast to the earlier example, the data collected is of greater importance than the access attained. The assignment of value is also determined by the type of internal access controls that may be founded on employee role, visitor access, or other physical access management. If a company employs internal access controls, such as you need a class "E" employee badge to access the fifth floor, it is usually assumed that documents and other data are inherently secured from physical exposures. However, if information is collected by a tester on the third floor that is the same as what could be found on the fifth, then the classification of the information offers a great deal of value to the client.

Ultimately, two factors weigh heavily on internal surfing. The access type provided to the tester, such as visitor, employee, or nothing at all, places a virtual fork in the road on which direction of the value of the test will prevail. Of course, the division of physical access controls based on the roles within the organization will add to the assumed value of the test. Second, the value of the test is based on exposure of information or the level of assumed trust of the employees. Rarely do these two meet or overlap. One will always become the driving factor of value and is usually based on the type of access provided to the tester.

No matter the perceived value gained from the test, implementing controls to mitigate the threat represented by the test can be cumbersome. As with any type of security, the human element remains the constant variable. However, customers who have permitted the test, in both forms—starting with no access privileges and moving to employee impersonation—have typically invested in comprehensive physical access controls based on employee role and data classification. Unfortunately, once the test moves to a computing environment, such as internal network access obtained by using an open station, the physical division of the target is wiped away because the two control measures are typically not related.

If they are related, as with government offices or secured facilities where computer access is directed aligned with the physical controls within the building, these two elements will be of great value. For example, if the tester is provided a minor employee position and manages to gain access to a computer system in a controlled zone, even if only physical access, the company will have a much greater understanding of physically related vulnerabilities. Of course, if the tester gains access to the system in the secured zone, it will only add to the concern of control in the digital arena.

As with many types of test within an ethical hacking engagement, the goal of the test needs to be defined and the scope must be aligned properly to ensure that the goal is not overshadowed by a loophole in the planning. The result from misalignment is a seemingly successful test that proves a weakness in areas that are not of value to the customer.

INTERNAL RELATIONS AND COLLABORATION

Collaboration between hackers and internal employees is one of the more advanced and dangerous aspects of attacks. Simply stated, this is when a relationship (personal, technical, or superficial) is built between an outside influence wanting to gain access and an internal representative assisting in collecting or divulging critical information. Collaboration may start when a disgruntled employee makes anonymous slanders against the company or people he works for, attracting others who may want to gain access to the company's systems. When solicited for information, the employee typically sees this as an opportunity to cause damage without being directly associated with the resulting attack. He gets to cause damage and chaos without the need for specialized skills and minimizing risk, and the hacker gets the desired access.

There are several forms of collaboration between an internal resource and a hacker. In some cases, the employee may not know what she is contributing until it is too late. On the other hand, it can be a deliberate attempt to assist an attacker for financial gain or personal vendetta against the employer.

Many crimes are the result of collaboration between two or more motivated individuals: one who has the knowledge and another who has the capability and resources. In Donn Parker's book, *Fighting Computer Crime: A New Framework for Protecting Information*, he states five fundamental attributes for a computer crime defined as SKRAM: Skills, Knowledge, Resources, Authority, and Motive are all required elements of an attack. For a single person to have all these elements is typically rare, but collaboration between internal and external individuals can easily overcome the inadequacies in one or more areas of SKRAM. Undoubtedly, collaboration represents one of the greatest threats to companies no matter what industry and the ability to detect or thwart the tactic is challenging.

It is very rare for this type of tactic to be used in a traditional penetration test due to the complexity and time consumed to obtain any meaningful results. In addition, the timing of the test is critical to draw an internal employee into collaborating with a hacker. Even so, organizations that suspect such an activity is occurring will typically permit focused communication on a specific employee.

A company that had this concern hired a penetration tester known for his social engineering capabilities, a former FBI agent, to digitally follow and communicate with an employee using newsgroups and chat. In a very short timeframe, the employee asked the consultant posing as a hacker-for-hire to attack the company's network to collect credit card numbers he could ultimately sell on the Internet. The employee's stake was to tarnish the reputation of the company and all he had to do was provide some detailed information about the internal workings and vulnerabilities of the applications used. Once the communication was logged and the data collected, the company's management was informed and the employee was prosecuted.

The common company does not permit such activities unless there is reasonable suspicion an employee is planning an attack on the network. In addition, there are many legal challenges associated with the test that need to be clearly understood by the company and the investigator to ensure there is no assumption of entrapment or exposure to liability of the company. As with every other aspect of ethical hacking the type of threat should dictate the tactic employed by the tester. Arguably, this type of test cannot be performed by a typical security consultant, nor should it be, and the growing involvement by law enforcement in digital security provides many options to companies that are concerned there is a plot against the organization's assets.

CORPORATE IDENTITY ASSUMPTION

An advanced technique in ethical hacking, typically only employed in very aggressive tests, is identity assumption. This tactic goes well beyond sending an e-mail appearing to come from someone else or making a call posing as an employee. Assuming someone's corporate identity is effectively stealing that person's distinctiveness within the company to collect information or to perpetrate a crime using their privileges. Of course, we're not talking about ripping someone's eye out and using it to bypass a retinal scanner (not possible anyway because the eye would lose specific attributes during the removal, rendering it useless), but it is possible to take on the digital attributes of someone else to gain information.

This can be accomplished by combining several different types of attacks. For example, gaining control over the target's voice mail and e-mail is usually enough to convince others within the company that you are who you claim to be. For hackers who have no limitations, they may attempt to slow down the real person they are trying to impersonate, such as canceling credit cards, phone service, or other more aggressive forms of harassment.

A company never requests a services firm providing ethical hacking services to steal someone's identity. If the customer is attempting to determine the exposure to fraudulent people, it is much easier to assign a new identity and validate it throughout the company via an announcement of a new employee. However, on more than one occasion, the opportunity to appear as someone else in the corporate culture has presented itself, and when the White Team was notified of the opportunity, the majority agreed to the test. Unfortunately, the resulting test does not provide any benefit to the engagement. Once the opportunity to take over someone's identity is identified, there is no fundamental reason to exploit it; nothing further can be truly gained. If the target employee has executive privileges and can access any part of the company, physically and digitally, value could be perceived in leveraging the identity to gather proprietary information. But this can be assumed with risking harm or negative exposure of the test.

The reality is that a determined hacker—or better yet, a technically astute criminal—can assume, if only for a short period, someone's identity to get what he or she wants. Unfortunately, there is no easy or effective way to replicate the act to determine susceptibility to the threat. The first challenge for an organization is to determine if it is a target for such a sophisticated attack and if it is a risk it is willing to accept. If it is a target, such as a research and development firm, and it is not willing to accept the risk, then the test can be valuable. But what is the test? It is clear that performing such a test can introduce severe issues and challenge the ethics of the tester. This is where the final analysis phase provides the greatest value. Once all the information about vulnerabilities and successful exploits is identified, you can run scenarios against the results to determine the level of exposure of various threats that could not be directly tested. This takes imagination and is open to a vast amount of interpretation, but if there is a concern for an advanced type of threat, such as identity assumption, it is plausible to validate the existence of environmental conditions that would support such an attack.

A customer should be aware of this opportunity and expect results formatted to support further conjecture of attack vulnerabilities inherent in the outcome of the test. In addition, providers of penetration-testing services should seek viable attack scenarios to raise company awareness. The risk in performing such a task is possibly adding complexity and appearing as introducing unnecessary fear, uncertainty, and doubt. However, if all the characteristics are present that represent an opportunity for a certain type of attack, it should be communicated.

PHYSICAL SECURITY

It may seem odd to discuss physical security in a book about a subject typically associated only with cyber security. Nevertheless, the fundamental goal of an ethical hack is to mimic an attacker's tactics given the number of available options. One of those options is the physical security employed to protect information.

There is traditional physical security, such as doors, locks, alarm systems, windows, enclosures, foliage, guards, fences, and gun turrets. OK, maybe the last one is extreme, but physical security can be anything to stop someone or something from infiltrating a secured area. However, to test physical security directly could become cumbersome or the act of exploiting may result in damaging something, such as breaking glass.

There are situations where basic physical security can be easily tested. In the following sections, we're going to discuss basic observation, dumpster diving, wardriving and warchalking, and theft.

OBSERVATION

It was difficult to decide whether observation would be a subject that would fall under physical security. Observation is such a broad subject and can be employed in nearly every aspect of ethical hacking, but it seems to appear more often when attempting to interact directly with the target. By simple definition, observation is learning about something or someone by watching the activities to formulate conclusions about habits, processes, or other exploitable characteristics. There is no direct attack based solely on observation, but information attained by watching something can help with other attacks.

As an example, a particular company used a document-shredding service rather than shred documents on its own. They had locked cabinets with small openings to insert documents or other materials to be shredded later. On the surface, this appears as a secure solution to protecting sensitive material. However, after standing outside the building to observe the shredding service collect the documents, it was learned that all the documents were collected in trash bags outside before loading them into the truck and leaving. Once the method and the type of bags used were learned, it was relatively simple to fill our own trash bags with useless paper (we used newspapers) and switch them at the opportune moment, leaving undetected with the sensitive materials.

As many companies do, a company provided a smoking area outside behind the building with magnetic access badge controls. After watching the smokers' activities for a couple of days, a pattern would appear, typically starting around 10:00 a.m. We started sitting at the smoking area five minutes before each time there were going to be several people outside smoking. After a short time the employees were used to our presence and piggybacking our way into the facility became trouble-free. In addition to gaining access, the employees' familiarity with the testing team provided even more freedom once inside the building.

Again, watching and learning from the target is usually the prelude to an attack. It can either provide information on the best time or place to attack, or integrate into the process to become part of the group.

DUMPSTER DIVING

In the old days, dumpster diving was the primary tactic used by thieves to get credit card numbers and other personal information that can be gleaned from what people and companies throw away. Dumpster diving is simply taking what people assume is trash and using that information, sometimes in combination with other data, to formulate conclusions or refine strategies.

This is especially sensitive for companies who may throw away copies of proprietary data or seemingly benign data which in the hands of a hacker can provide substantial information. Simple but useful information ranges from phone numbers and e-mail lists, to communication bills that have the service provider name and account details. A bill receipt containing account information can be used to help authenticate a hacker calling the service provider to access design features or IP addresses for locating logical areas where the exact target may reside.

The value to a client for permitting this type of ethical hacking tactic is high, because the level of investment to reduce the exposure is minute compared to the information that could be collected from everyday trash. Even with sophisticated word processors and a computer on everyone's desk, people still print volumes of documentation, sometimes several times, to share with others or read later, only to throw it away without concern for the sensitivity of the data. It's not uncommon to find network designs, equipment purchase receipts, phone bills, human resource information, internal communications, configuration documentation, software doc-umentation, project plans, and project proposals in a trash can. On one occasion, a team was swimming in a dumpster and found the deliverable from a previous penetration test performed by a competitor.

Beyond providing value to the customer by exposing an outlet of proprietary information, is the question of how the data should be used within the context of the attack. Moreover, when should dumpster diving be permitted within the scope and timeframe of the test? The reasoning of the question is based on the proximity of the attacker to the target. Most hackers do not want physical contact and the implied exposure of going through trash. The ability to go to the location, at the right time, and get information from the garbage insinuates a certain type of hacker with specific motivations. Therefore, one must ask what the value of the test is considering the relative ease of mitigating the exposure.

The answer is somewhat simple. If you shred your trash—or think you do—then the test is a good opportunity to see what type of information is being leaked. Many companies destroy documentation to mitigate the risk of exposing information, and therefore the test is inherently valuable. Conversely, if the company assumes there is little risk of disclosing proprietary information, the test must be heavily weighed against the perceived likelihood that someone would rummage through its trash.

Ultimately, what is being tested is one characteristic of security: is proprietary information out in the open, sitting in the trashcan for anyone to collect? Beyond this is the assumption of risk associated with that exposure, which is left up to interpreting the type of hacker one may attract considering the level of jeopardy he would have to place herself in to exploit the vulnerability.

Wardriving and Warchalking

Wireless is a communication technology rapidly being adopted by organizations. It is inexpensive, easy to deploy, reduces the cost of installing wiring, and provides a great deal of flexibility in offering network services to users. Unfortunately, the propagation of a wireless signal offers hackers the opportunity to join networks designed for private or paying users.

Hackers can simply install a wireless adapter in a laptop and drive near buildings in an attempt to receive signals leaking from internal wireless networks. In the past, this was not entirely a straightforward attack and required modified drivers, special wireless adapter chipsets, and specialized software on the system. Conversely, to support the growing adoption of wireless networks, many vendors have provided similar tools to offer easy roaming capabilities for the typical user. For example, with the release of Windows XP, it is possible to install an off-the-shelf wireless network adapter and immediately be provided with a list of accessible wireless networks.

In addition, there are applications that are specifically designed to discover wireless networks, such as NetStumbler (see Figure 9.1), that provide ample information about

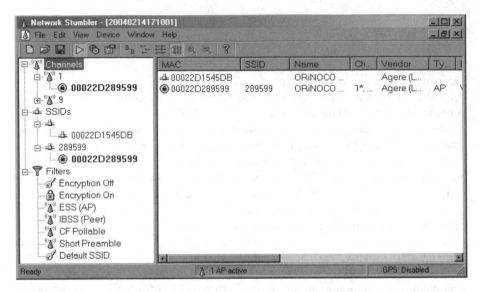

FIGURE 9.1 NetStumbler Provides Some Initial Information about My Wireless Network

the network. It is trivial to load NetStumbler on a laptop and start driving around waiting for something to pop up on the screen.

Typically seen as a passive attack, wardriving is an opportunity to identify networks that allow easy access. However, the attack can quickly turn from obtaining free access to the Internet to collecting data from the wireless network that may contain passwords, files, and sensitive communications.

Warchalking is that act of marking areas that provide access to wireless networks. Depicted in Figure 9.2, symbols, along with information around the symbol, provide enough information to tell others where the access can be attained, the bandwidth, if the network is using encryption, and if it is open (or accessible). There are sites where you can download a key or guide for hackers to ensure the format of the mark is consistent.

With a standard set of markings that convey the necessary information, it demonstrates the popularity and global intention of hackers to find and use wireless networks.

Warchalking can be as simple as a mark on a wall, sidewalk, phone pole, or just about anything. Walk down the street of any major city and you are bound to come across a symbol sooner or later. Given the propagation of the wireless signal, warchalking is not limited to streets and alleys. In some cases, the signal can reach far out into the water; a bay or harbor can become a relaxing place to launch an attack.

Given that wireless networks can be implemented with almost no understanding of networking technology, many are wide open to attack. Of course, wireless networks can be configured to be more secure, but this requires experience and know-how when implementing. Moreover, installing a secure wireless solution is not simply placing passwords on access points or configuring the device not to publish the ID of the system, it includes the physical characteristics of signal propagation.

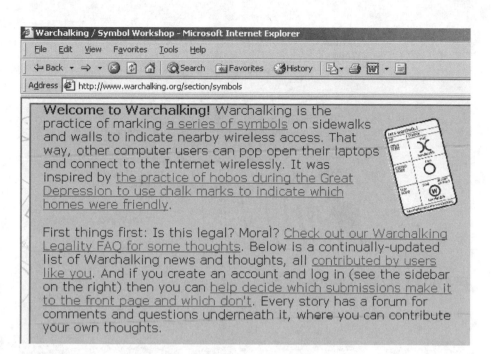

FIGURE 9.2 Standardized Symbols for the Hacker Community

Knowing how signals are affected by windows, walls, and buildings will help physically design the network to minimize susceptibility to attack. Characteristics in radio frequencies, such as gain, reflection, refraction, diffraction, and scattering will play a role in the design of a secure wireless network. The combination of these characteristics is demonstrated in Figure 9.3, where we see the signal wrapping around a building. Given these physical attributes it is feasible for an attacker to sit well out of sight while participating in a network.

Without this type of understanding, people continually install wireless systems for large companies completely unaware that the signal is reaching well beyond the physical location.

In Figure 9.4, the wireless signal is projected far into a harbor by a local business, seemingly unaware that anyone can use its network to access the Internet for free or to hack its network from an innocuous location.

Warchalking is not limited to marks on walls and buoys, there are many sites dedicated to mapping locations all over the globe and in nearly every city. At the time of this writing, the site www.wifimaps.com was populated with more than 122,905 unique wireless networks discovered in the United States, with only 22 percent implementing wireless security, such as encryption. It is shocking to think that 78 percent of networks discovered by simply driving around with a laptop and NetStumbler are wide open for access. The site provides maps of wireless points submitted by individuals. One, known as "blackwave," had submitted over 80,000 locations. In Figure 9.5, we see a compilation of points in the entire database.

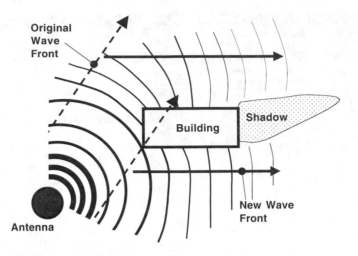

FIGURE 9.3 Physics of Wireless Signals

FIGURE 9.4 Access Can Be Anywhere the Signal Goes

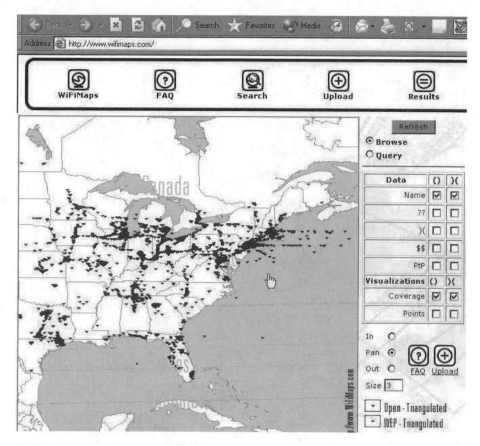

FIGURE 9.5 A Nation-Sized Warchalking Map

And much like any map, you can zoom in on interesting locations to collect information about a specific city, town, or street. What is especially interesting is that you can collect specific data about a particular network and simply go to that location to get access (see Figure 9.6).

Customers who have wireless networks and allow wardriving as one of the tactics used in the test usually gain a great deal of value from the activity. Wardriving is one of those tests where there is no hidden negative or lack of value to the targeted company.

However, there are some who would conclude the attacker's proximity to the target would introduce an unacceptable level of risk. Although the very nature of wardriving does require close interaction, the anonymity of sitting in a car across the street is more than enough protection.

Wardriving is one aspect of ethical hacking that is strongly recommended for companies that employ wireless networks. Nevertheless, companies that do not permit wireless networks in their organization should still allow the test. In many cases, employees or network administrators may get their hands on an access point and plug their network connection at the desk into it to have their own personal

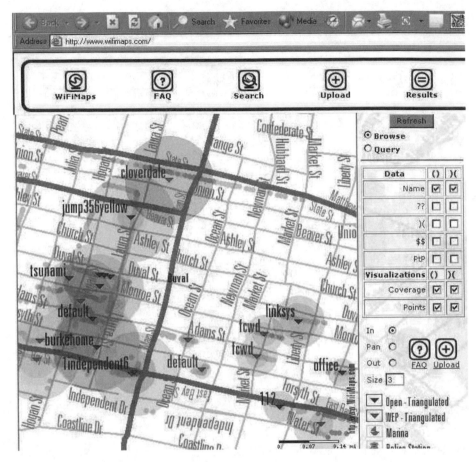

FIGURE 9.6 Zooming in on a Couple of Blocks in Atlanta

wireless network, just because it's fun. For years, rogue hubs and modems would pop up throughout networks because someone decided to add a couple of computers or access his system from home. Wireless network simplicity and low cost have introduced another technology easily implemented, difficult to detect, and fraught with security issues.

In summary, without a doubt, wardriving is an excellent opportunity to learn about the security of existing wireless networks and the possible identification of new ones. Because the ability to find them and exploit them is relatively effortless, the likelihood of being attacked over a wireless LAN is high, effectively outweighing the cost of the test.

THEFT

When in doubt, take it. Dumpster diving is a version of theft depending on the environmental conditions and location. However, theft by this definition is removing documents, manuals, process charts, network diagrams, computer disks, and other valued material that has not been discarded. Examples include everything from physically stealing laptops and computers, to badges and cell phones.

Theft materializes in several ways during a penetration test and is usually coupled with the customer requesting a specific goal or target. This stems from the customer assuming that without setting a physical objective, the ability to gain value from the test is unlikely. Only in rare cases is this true and in most scenarios, actually stealing something introduces substantial risk.

However, a customer maintained a valuable database and wanted to test the exposure to physical threats. Therefore, the tester coerced his way into the building and stole the server most likely to have the database. Unfortunately, the database was not on the box he selected, but it did prove physical access and the ability to leave with an item, both of which are the main drivers for having such a test performed.

The value a company can gain from having someone steal something is very specific. The target has to be something of value and clearly identified to the tester. Otherwise, the risks of stealing it would outweigh the test.

INTERNET RECONNAISSANCE

Without a doubt, the Internet represents the largest, most accessible collection of data and more often than not, you can find interesting information about someone or a company. With very little effort, an adversary can learn a great deal about a targeted company by simply performing research on the Internet. As data is collected, a clear picture begins to emerge that can be used to develop an attack strategy. In the event a zero knowledge test is required, investigating the Internet for more information is essential to starting the test. When you have nothing go on but the company name, you have to start somewhere.

Following are several discussions about features of the Internet that can be leveraged to collect valuable information about the target. Granted, there are many more options than are listed here that are available to hackers and testers alike looking for information, but this demonstrates what can be acquired with traditional sources and techniques.

GENERAL INFORMATION

Information abounds on the Internet and people are typically the primary culprits of simply sharing too much of it. Whether on purpose or by overlooking someone else's best interests, data is regularly exposed on the Internet. In this brief section, we're going to discuss two typical areas of investigating the human element: Web sites and newsgroups.

Web Sites

There was a time when posting a Web site was for nothing more than entertainment or to offer basic information about a company. Since the explosion of the Internet in the late 1990s, Web sites have become an intrinsic part of doing business. The best evidence for this is no sooner is a company name mentioned, than it is adorned with a ".com" in a browser to see what it is all about.

Given the demand for a comprehensive Web site that is useful and informative, many companies unwittingly fall victim to placing too much information about the company. For example, you may see personal information, work history, and activities (even pictures) of executive staff. This is helpful in gathering more useful data about the company and the people who run it. The proliferation of press releases, news articles, success stories, services, documentation, partnership, locations, and other data being posted is useful when learning about how the company operates.

Web sites are notorious for posting seemingly useless information assumed to represent no threat to the company. However, by using other investigative tools on the Internet, more information can be collected about the target. The type of information usually of great interest is learning something about their security technology or something that should only be shared with employees, such as remote access configurations.

Putting information on a company Web site is standard for today's business and to stop doing so would be ridiculous in many people's eyes, however, this does not mean you have to be liberal.

So far we've discussed investigating the target's Web site. However, other companies and organizations may have been more lax about posting information. Partners, customers, and consulting companies are prime candidates for posting information that a company may not want public. It is not uncommon to read a network solution case study and quickly conclude that only three, maybe four companies fit the profile.

News stories, successes, press releases, acquisitions, events, and other information on a partner's Web site have the potential to expose information. Keep in mind that a hacker isn't going to get the keys to the kingdom from a Web site, but even the most seemingly useless information, when compared against other data, can actually become the proverbial key.

Newsgroups

Newsgroups are online forums in which people discuss thousands of different topics supported by a collection of servers participating in Usenet. The opportunity for hackers to learn about various companies is based on employees or former employees having discussion about the company's assets, security technology, vulnerabilities, or other information that can be used against the company. It is also a tool that can be used by the tester to search for similar information.

In other phases of reconnaissance, e-mail addresses and names of employees may be collected. Those can be used to search multiple hacker-related newsgroups to see if people have been discussing security issues with individuals outside the organization. In addition, testers can search many newsgroups of different subjects to see what other type of discussions people are having online that may pertain to corporate proprietary information. Traditionally, http://groups.google.com has been the search engine of choice and early on www.dejanews.com was a great source for peering into online discussion. Many employees will use normal e-mail signatures that contain contact information or the target's domain name in their e-mail reply address, providing one more element to search for within the newsgroups.

The reasoning for performing a search on newsgroups is to look for internal resources or people that have worked for the company in the past who may be offering sensitive information that can be used against the company. Alternatively, it also provides an opportunity to look for discussions between groups and people who may be planning an attack. Albeit very rare, there are occasions when performing reconnaissance on newsgroups and hacker communities that you may find more than you expected.

In most cases when an employee is identified as having online conversations the subject is usually of a personal nature. In some cases, the subject can be more technical, having the potential to expose a missing piece of data for the tester that normally would be considered benign by the employee.

While performing newsgroup reconnaissance against one company, an employee's conversations were isolated and investigated. Along with multiple messages about video games and computers, there were several recent discussions from the employee seeking help in properly configuring Checkpoint Firewall-1 to establish remote user VPNs. The main problem he was having was the authentication was being blocked by Rule 0, the rule that is automatically applied based on selected options prior to the user-configured rules being applied. In his haste to make it work, the employee (later to find it was the firewall administrator) removed many of the default security settings and made several rule adjustments to simplify and troubleshoot the firewall. In later discussions, it became clear that the firewall rules and security options were never reconfigured to meet normal operating standards, which left an opportunity to penetrate the DMZ network.

Again, these situations are somewhat rare, but a brief test to look for activity on newsgroups has the potential of exposing interesting information about the company based on employee activity.

The next question is value. The perception of value to a company permitting this reconnaissance tactic is directly proportional to the level of fear associated with information leakage. Large companies that have enormous brand recognition, have a high rotation of staff who are exposed to sensitive data, or may have recently laid off thousands of employees typically gain the most benefit.

The irony is that less is more. For a tester to come back and say she found nothing is good, very good in fact. Having the test performed does more in helping the CSO sleep than it helps in mitigation. However, if something of interest is identified, it opens an assortment of problems. Putting aside any legal problems (especially with global companies) there is the question of how to stop it. What controls, if any, are in place to accommodate the newfound information hole? Obviously, the focus is honed in on the perpetrator, a natural reaction. But, one must acknowledge that this is usually the symptom of a much larger problem and may extend well beyond traditional security or technology.

Given the process does not take long and can provide valuable information—or the lack of it—it is recommended that any zero knowledge test include newsgroup investigation.

TECHNICAL RECONNAISSANCE

Up until this point, we've discussed the human element. Gathering information on Web sites and from conversations on newsgroups usually translates to poor information management by people. Now, there is the technical element: what can be learned from what computers and applications are offering. As we show later, there is a fine line between getting what is being offered from a system and interacting with the system to gain information. Finally, there is the delineation between collecting data and pulling data from systems and the tactics to do so. If you're not careful, the act of collecting information can be perceived as exploiting a weakness. It is very important to differentiate between the two, especially if you are a tester or a company not wanting anything exploited.

Ping Sweeps

A common and very old technique of discovering systems is using ping sweeps to look for active systems. Ping is a simple utility that creates an ICMP message requesting the receiving system to reply with a similar message. If an IP address is entered and a reply is returned, it is assumed the system is active and available for attack. Many penetration tests start by performing ping sweeps to see what IP addresses are "alive" at the target site. However, because this is an old technique and there have been several variations of DoS attacks based on the ICMP protocol, many companies do not allow ping requests into their network, resulting in mixed conclusions. Also, sequential pings, especially those coming from the same source IP address (the tester's system), can trigger alarms in IDS systems exposing the existence of a possible attack. Overall, the use of ping sweeps is a questionable technique for identifying systems, but there are some situations where the results provide useful information about the target's network.

Frankly, the most effective use for ping sweeps is after the tester has established a home base within the network. A tester may take over a system that has access to the internal network, and sweeps provide a quick and simple opportunity to see what's out there. Moreover, every system has the ping utility (unless an enterprising geek deleted it) so it makes a good starting point for a tester on a compromised system.

Scans

Scanning a network can take on many definitions depending on to whom you are speaking. Some may conclude that a ping sweep is a scan of the target network, whereas others may define it as interacting with each identifiable system's services. Scanning a network is usually making requests to systems and networking elements to determine what services they are offering, or filtering, to gain a better picture of the landscape.

The difference in the definition of a scan is based on the level of interaction the scanning system becomes involved with the remote system. Scanning also assumes the systems have been identified, up, and accepting connections. This assumption is based on the results of a ping sweep or a very light scan that makes simple requests to various IP addresses that would typically not respond to an ICMP request. For example, you may scan a network for very common services that may respond when ICMP is blocked.

There are three different characteristics of scans, starting with light passive scans, moving to active scans, and ending with interactive scans, each providing different results and increasing the exposure of discovery for the tester.

Passive Scan

The goal of a passive scan is to determine what application ports are open on a remote system. During the communication setup, the scanning system sends a SYN packet to the target system (or systems) on a specific application port looking for a reply. If the reply is an acknowledgment, the port is open and the service is accepting connections. If the response is a reset, this usually means the port is closed or filtered. And, if there is no response, and other ports may be responding, it typically means the port is being blocked.

The scan supplies basic information about the target. At the end of the scan, the attacker knows what systems are responding, in what way, and the services being offered. However, the type of service being offered is only assumed at this point because the service was not queried. For example, port 443 may be responding, but a custom application could be monitoring the port and not a traditional SSL service associated with that port. A good example of this is that some VPN devices use port 443 to establish a VPN and not the typical UDP port 500 assigned to ISAKMP for IPSec VPNs. In addition, an initial passive scan only sends SYN packets to the lower standard application ports, 1 to 1023. Another application may only be answering on a high port. An example is some companies force a Web server to listen to port 8080 and not the traditionally assigned port of 80 for HTTP services.

Considering the mildness of this tactic, many testers scan all the ports (1 to 65535) in search of a high port that may be open and offering services. The down side to scanning all the ports is the increased exposure of detection by the target's Blue Team, because nearly every IDS and administrator would notice many requests for service at excessively high ports. In addition, the tester would only perform this type of scan if she knew the system was up and responding and there was suspicion of high ports being active. If the system is not responding to any requests, it may simply not exist or be heavily blocked by a firewall and therefore an exhaustive scan would be a waste of time.

Another advantage to the tester of using a passive scan is it can expose systems that will not, or cannot, respond to ICMP requests. A firewall may be blocking all ICMP requests or allowing them into the network and not out. In any case, the use of ICMP to discover systems is burdened with inefficiencies. A scan that sends requests to typical ports, such as 21, 25, 53, 80, 443, and 110, can reveal a system's status when ping fails. Once the system is identified as being up and responding, the tester can employ a broader scan to look for other open ports.

Active Scan

An active scan is the next step in the communication process we started with the passive scan. In the passive scan the reply, if received, is dropped and no acknowledgment is sent back to the server (in some cases a reset packet is sent back to close the half-open port on the server to lessen the likelihood of discovery). In contrast, during the active scan an acknowledgment is returned to the server to complete the connection. This is practiced to test the ability to establish communications with the remote system, effectively proving the service is valid. The reasoning is some systems ghost open ports, such as a firewall or load-balancing system, which can confuse a hacker.

Presenting false open ports is also practiced by honeypot systems that are designed to attract hackers to not only lure them away from the real systems but also keep them busy until they are discovered and ultimately blocked. By completing the connection with an acknowledgment, the service is assumed to be open and valid. (A point worth noting: the reference to honeypots using this technique is reflective of a poorly configured honeypot system and any hacker above script kiddie would interpret this as a bogus system.)

Beyond proving the port is active, the tester has the opportunity to close the port and move on to the next system, effectively reducing her exposure to detection, or to begin the interactive phase for more aggressive scanning.

Interactive Scan

When interacting with the target system, as mentioned above, there is a fine line between interaction and exploitation. By connecting to the service and exchanging commands and responses, the tester can learn a great deal about the system and possibly test the application listening to the port, but the more the tester pushes the service the closer he or she comes to being detected and moving from discovery into exploitation.

Assuming the connection with the service is complete, the tester has the option to send commands to the service as if coming from the traditional client application to coerce the service into responding with more information. An example is port 80 providing HTTP services. A browser on a remote system automatically makes the request to port 80 and once the basic TCP handshake is complete, sends a GET command, to which the server responds by sending the main HTML (or other Web-based file) to the requester, in this case the browser. When the browser receives the file, it is displayed — pretty simple. A realistic example is a tester connecting to port 25, an SMTP server, and collecting banner information or other data that can be used to identify the version of SMTP being used. The point where the interaction takes on the look and feel of an exploitation is when the tester initiates several SMTP commands, such as MAIL FROM, RCPT, and DATA. By performing these commands with invalid data, there is the potential to discover not only more information about the system's configuration, but to identify any weaknesses or vulnerabilities.

In reality, the use of each one of these levels during system discovery represents a timid approach, but may be necessary given the scope of the engagement. If the engagement is founded on the tester not being discovered, some of these tactics may expose him unless they are executed with care. For example, lightly tapping on the door of a system may alert the Blue Team, whereas an outright exploit that is quick and effective may slip under the radar for a short period. It is a balance between the tester's assumptions and the security of the targeted systems. It may be more advantageous to connect to a service, learn that is it susceptible to attack, and then exploit the system if the opportunity presents itself. However, if the target company does not want the test to move into the exploitation phase without approval this could be a problem. Usually, the various levels of investigation are employed when the test is focused on identification of vulnerabilities rather than exploiting them initially.

The act of scanning a network, no matter the depth used, is an essential part of ethical hacking. Unless the attacker, or tester, knows exactly what is running on which systems (which can be the case in some scenarios) a scan will be needed to discover characteristics about the target network and systems.

10 Enumeration

Collecting information about the target company from the Internet, climbing through trashcans, walking the halls, or talking to friends is considered passive information collection because there is little direct interaction with the target. During the reconnaissance phase the tester looks for information that is readily available, collecting data that can provide greater insights when combined, and setting the foundation for an all-out attack.

The enumeration phase takes on a much more aggressive collection tactic by interacting with systems and networking elements to gather as much information as possible. This goes beyond scanning systems and introduces the attack elements of the test.

Remember the fine line mentioned in the previous chapter? This is crossing it by aggressively pulling information from systems to see what is being offered as well as starting the initial process for building a plan for attack.

An enumeration may be as simple as running a port scanner that makes requests to remote systems to determine if a port is available and responding, a continuation of the technical elements of reconnaissance. The next step is to interact with the service being offered or to work a way through filtering routers and firewalls to peer deeper into systems. For example, NMap has a multitude of options that can be used to squeeze much information out of a system.

However, there is a nontechnical objective. The goal is to begin the process of analysis of the data collected. By using information from the previous phase with the data collected directly from the target's network, you can build an accurate picture of the network and applications. This will help prepare for an attack and refine the vulnerability analysis phase.

ENUMERATION TECHNIQUES

So, you need to extract information from a network and dig your way past firewalls or other filtering devices to see what's on the other side. Thanks to TCP/IP fundamentals and protocol weaknesses, certain packet types can be used to collect information systems typically do not offer readily. (It should be noted that several sources were used to gather this information, most notably a paper authored by Fyodor, creator of NMap, in 1997.) Although many of the techniques are old, they remain useful given that they are based on protocol weaknesses, a protocol used by most systems. However, as the awareness of such tactics is raised, vendors implement changes to accommodate their responses to these types of scans. The goal is to demonstrate that it is possible to dig deeper into systems and networks to gather useful information as opposed to simply scanning a network to see what's being offered. Also, keep in mind that there are hundreds of tactics that are introduced here that will be more effective given today's heightened security awareness.

- *Connection Scanning.* At the most basic level, the TCP connect function is used by a system to interact with various ports. By sending a connect to a port you can determine if the port is "listening." A service typically accepts connections to specific TCP ports to establish communications with a remote system. In most operating systems there is a single process running that manages initial connections and will pass the request to a running process. The advantage to this is you rarely need permissions to establish an initial connection. Unless the port is controlled by an inter-mediate device (e.g., firewall) that authenticates the session, the system will usually respond to the request (if the port is active). Once the session is established it is up to the service to authenticate, but by then we know the service is running. The problem is, of course, that people are very aware of these types of probing and controlled services will be aggres-sively filtered or monitored, both leading to detection.
- *SYN Scanning.* Briefly described earlier, during a session initiation the source system sends a SYN packet requesting a connection on an inter-esting port. If the port is active and accepting connections the service will respond with a SYN/ACK, effectively acknowledging the connection. When the SYN/ACK is received you immediately respond with an RST (reset) to tear down the connection. The advantage is that some filtering devices, especially ones that do not monitor sessions, may let this get through. The downside is that in the early 1990s, when DoS attacks were growing in popularity, the SYN flood was a common type of attack. There-fore, many security devices will immediately pick this up as an attack.
- *FIN Scanning.* Opening connections or performing a "half-open" scan, such as the SYN scan, can be noisy and draw attention to the process. As mentioned, most security-aware devices will not allow this type of activity and most certainly log it as an attack. FIN (FINish) packets, on the other hand, have the potential to bypass several types of controls if not config-ured properly. First identified and documented by Uriel Maimon, the technique is founded on a TCP RFC requirement that if a closed port (one without a corresponding service) receives a FIN packet the response will be an RST packet. If an open port or listening port receives a FIN packet it may not respond at all depending on the type of OS employed. There-fore, this technique can be used to bypass firewalls and routers to gain a better understanding of operating systems and, in some cases, what ports are potentially in use.
- *Fragment Scanning.* There is an option in TCP to fragment the packet into smaller packets forcing the system to accept all of the packets to reassemble the final packet for processing. Therefore, to scan a system behind a firewall or through another box acting as a gateway, you can break up the probing packet into tiny little ones in an effort to confuse

the security systems. This is an old technique and many security systems will catch this in a second. However, over the past couple of years hackers have been sending fragments at certain intervals to slightly overlap the session state table of firewalls and IDSs, but not so long that the targeted system gives up. Therefore, a fragment is sent through the firewall and to the target computer. The computer may wait X seconds for the next packet before dropping the session. In contrast, the firewall may only monitor the session for Y seconds. By setting the interval to less than X and greater than Y, the technique has a better chance of going undetected. Keep in mind that today's firewalls or IDSs usually queue the fragments before sending, but there is always a chance for a misconfiguration.

- *TCP Reverse IDENT Scanning.* The IDENT protocol is used to identify the owner of a connection. By sending the system a port pair, the IDENT service will respond with the owner of the connection and ultimately the owner of the process. Originally identified by Dave Goldsmith in 1996, the IDENT protocol will disclose owner information even if the original port used is not associated with the service being queried. The reality is that most systems do not run IDENT because why would you run a service designed to provide information? Nevertheless, some custom applications may require the protocol for various purposes, but IDENT will be blocked and logged. Therefore, this technique is best used on internal systems, or when there is a clear path into the internal network.

- *FTP Bounce Scanning.* The FTP protocol uses a control connection and a data connection to support the entire session. The control connection is for commands and other user interaction, whereas the data connection is specifically for data transfer. An interesting protocol feature is that the data and control connections do not have to be to or from the same system. Therefore, it is feasible to connect to a system and send data to any other system: this can be bad. However, this can provide an opportunity to use an FTP server to proxy scans on behalf of the tester by manipulating the control and data channels. For example, you connect to an FTP server and use the PORT command to declare a listening port on a target system and then run a LIST forcing the control channel to request data from a remote system on the port specified. If the port is listening, the system may respond; if not you'll receive a data error. To test the next port, you specify the new one and run LIST again. Keep in mind that several things have to break down for this to be successful, but it is plausible nonetheless.

- *UDP Scanning.* Up until this point all the scanning was founded on TCP, a connection-oriented protocol that may offer information about the state of a port. UDP, on the other hand, is connectionless and is not required to acknowledge a session. Even though UDP scans will not receive a reply from a remote port, in the event there is no service listening some systems will send an ICMP message stating the port is unreachable. Therefore, one can conclude the nonresponsive ports are open. Of course, when you rely on ICMP for penetration testing you're going to be disappointed because nearly every firewall and router will block ICMP messages making it look like all the ports are open. The one true advantage to UDP scanning is finding high UDP ports associated with known vulnerabilities in services or even a Trojan hiding on a previously compromised system.

- *ACK Scanning.* Sometimes you may want to know the type of filtering devices between you and the target. Is it a stateful firewall monitoring all the sessions or is it a router just performing port filtering? By sending a packet with the port defined and the ACK bit set, a router will typically pass the packet and you will receive an RST from the system. If the gateway is a firewall, you probably won't get anything in return.

There are many variations on this theme. However, it is necessary to know there is a technical objective and a nontechnical soft objective to collecting and using data during the enumeration phase. The goal is to get as much information as possible, even if it means digging with an axe, for the tester to move to the next phases. You can consider this the past opportunity to investigate systems and applications to start the attack process. It is also the end of an engagement where a company does not want vulnerabilities exploited, or a stopping point to get approval for attacking identified weaknesses.

SOFT OBJECTIVE

Enumeration is focused on the act of investigating various characteristics about the target's technical elements by interacting with operating systems, applications, services, and anything that can be used to gain more data about the target. Moreover, the enumeration phase is the last opportunity, prior to developing an attack plan and performing the exploitation phase, to take a comprehensive look at the reconnaissance data combined with the technical information obtained from the target's environment.

Therefore, at the completion of the enumeration phase, the tester has a collection of data from querying the technical environment in addition to other forms of information collected from the reconnaissance phase. With an initial picture of the technical landscape combined with other evidence the tester can begin to make assumptions and various conclusions about the target's security posture.

As with many things, this happens subconsciously for a professional ethical hacker who is completely unaware he is performing a viable comparison. Although seemingly obvious, without a commitment to perform the task at a dedicated point within the engagement there is the potential for poor conclusions affecting the exploitation. When the tester makes a concerted effort to analyze the data in preparation for the following phases, many assumptions prove to be correct and supportive throughout the entire process.

Given that the next phase is investigating known or potential vulnerabilities with the collected information, it is necessary to look at the data in a manner that will expose vulnerabilities that are not directly identified. An analogy would be to compare the process with how astronomers locate and classify black holes or dwarfs. By observing color shifts, celestial movements, and looking for certain elements that are produced by massive gravitation they can make determinations about something they cannot see or directly measure. In great contrast, a tester does not have a set of mathematical equations and templates to work from and must use intuition and experience, a defining factor in great testers and hackers alike.

Dedicating time to look for "black holes" can be very valuable. It makes up for the lack of time to fully investigate all opportunities. Eventually, the analysis will promote effective research during the vulnerability analysis phase. Enumeration and vulnerability analysis are inherently linked and a security consultant performing a penetration test will not only go back and forth between the two phases regularly, but will return to this point for more guidance in later phases.

LOOKING AROUND OR ATTACK?

The enumeration phase is pretty straightforward and there is not much need to explain the concept in great detail. The most fundamental characteristic to remember is enumeration is somewhere between collecting available information and attacking a target. For example, introduced above, active and interactive scanning are used to pull information about the target system by sending packets to the target system in an effort to determine the status of the system and what services it is offering.

It is necessary to be able to make these determinations during and after the engagement because some clients may perceive the enumeration of systems as an unauthorized attack. For companies wanting to be more involved in the process and concerned about system integrity or overly adventurous testers, the value of delineating between an attack and enumeration can be immeasurable when faced with negative side effects of the test.

It is important to consider the potential impact on systems and networks when aggressive tactics are used to survey systems. For example, a firewall may permit fragmented packets to pass, allowing the tester to query the targeted server undetected. But there is the potential for the server to react in unexpected ways, causing service or total system failure. In many planning meetings before an engagement, companies typically focus a great deal of attention on the potential negative impacts of the exploitation phase. This is natural considering the tester is prying open holes trying to gain access and computers and applications may fall victim to their own inability to withstand the attack. However, it is very rare to question the enumeration phase of the engagement, which potentially has the risks.

If this is a cause for concern when planning a test you should investigate the tools and tactics used by the consulting firm. Of course, you'll have to feel comfortable in your knowledge of possible side effects and discussing these with the Red Team.

NOTE 15: IS IT SCANNING OR EXPLOITATION?

During a penetration test, the consultant was performing a minor ping sweep followed by a targeted port scan that included only the lower TCP application ports. Using only the basic features of NMap, the consultant did not employ stealth scanning or any other specialized protocol manipulation that had the potential to harm the targeted systems.

Only hours later the White Team was notified that the tester was attacking the network, a phase of the test not approved at that point in time. The company's management was furious and insisted the scan was actually an attack, effectively going beyond the scope and risking an outage.

After the test was stopped, it took several meetings to explain the difference between scanning and attacking a system. However, it became exceedingly clear that there is a very thin line and it's very much open to interpretation. If a scan manipulates packets to get to a system, isn't that exploiting a vulnerability in the protocol and filtering systems? Well, the reality is when compared to pulling 100,000 credit card numbers from a database a scan looks pretty tame.

The lesson to be learned is when a test is only employed to identify weaknesses that may be approved for exploitation later in the engagement (or never) it is critical for everyone involved to appreciate the concept of enumeration. Yes, some sensitive organizations may interpret scanning as exploitation, but the reality is you have to investigate systems to know what the real and risk-laden vulnerabilities are, otherwise you'll never get off the ground.

ELEMENTS OF ENUMERATION

Moving from passive scans and information collection into an aggressive, interactive information-gathering technique provides a number of opportunities to obtain valuable characteristics that can be used to begin the development of a comprehensive attack plan. There are many different types of technology that can be pulled from and within each type there are layers of system interaction that represent their own insecurities. Depending on the system type, such as a server, router, switch, remote access system, or phone system, there is data that can be pulled to be used later during the vulnerability analysis phase. Following are some examples of data and system types:

- *Account Data.* There are some applications and even services that have the potential to expose user and system account information. In the hands of a hacker, knowing user account names and if they are logged on can be very valuable when executing an attack. Microsoft publishes available shares to anonymous remote queries. If not configured to eliminate this threat, a tester can execute a simple command to enumerate the shares offered by that system.
- *Architecture.* While performing enumeration, the tools and techniques used have the potential to expose traces of the logical architecture. By evaluating the response of systems to a given request, it is possible to make assumptions about how the network is configured. It is not uncommon for several networks to be scanned resulting in identical data on a specific set of IP addresses. After further investigation a multi-homed server is revealed that is connected to more than one network. In addition to determining the number and types of systems, it is possible to identify

network elements. Although many firewalls can be configured in "stealth" mode, that is, all packets directed at the firewall are simply discarded and logged, it is still trivial to determine the type and configuration of the firewall (but not without exponentially increasing the risk of being discovered). There are many Internet-facing architectures that employ multiple layers of firewalls performing different tasks, such as the first layer providing NAT and the second filtering traffic. By investing remote IP addresses with different methods, the response can provide insights as to which systems are performing what security services, and based on that information a picture of the environment will begin to surface.

- *Operating Systems.* Thanks to tools such as NMap it is possible to identify the type of operating system and version of a target system. This is especially valuable for a hacker to begin to formulate an attack strategy. Although OS fingerprinting is typically considered a passive scan and usually falls into the reconnaissance phase of an engagement, there are aggressive forms of scans and system interaction that can be used to gain much of the same information when tools like NMap do not work. Less accurate and certainly not automated, by manually collecting information from various services running on a target system, a tester can make assumptions about the version of the operating system. For example, if a Microsoft Exchange 5.5 SMTP service is running you can readily conclude that the software is running an older version of NT, such as NT 4.0, but not before NT 4.0 service pack 3. However, as expected, the ability to determine intimate details about a Microsoft system is not difficult by any stretch of the imagination, simply because there are only so many variations. In contrast, UNIX systems can represent an enormous challenge in attempting to determine what version or even flavor the operating system is. Certain distributions of Linux have unique characteristics helping the identification process, but remain challenging because kernels can be compiled in many ways and the use of modules can skew the results. In addition to Linux, there are simply so many derivatives of UNIX operating systems the tester has to make some broad conclusions about the specific version. For example, BSD, Linux, Nokia IPSO, and even Inferno will respond very similarly when investigated using the same technique. In most cases, the operating system version and type is identified by other related attributes associated with the system, for example, a known application that can exist only on a handful of systems types.
- *Wireless Networks.* Wireless networks offer a plethora of opportunities for attackers. First, if there are no access controls placed on the network, anyone with a wireless adapter can join. Moreover, if it is wide open, not only can the tester learn about the internal network and all that it implies, but it conveys a sense of insecurity for the entire organization. Based on this interpretation, more aggressive tactics may be used that, in order to not be detected, would normally not be employed or the tactics would be considered too basic for the typical network.

Beyond conclusions made about a company based on the security applied to a wireless network, the access can be used to learn more about the inner workings of the target's network. If the wireless network falls within the scope of the engagement, the tester has the option to launch an attack through the wireless access. If the wireless network is out of bounds but physical security is included, then the access can be used to learn enough information to support the Internet-based attack.

The latter example may seem like an oxymoron. If the tester has access to the wireless network then an attack should be a viable avenue to demonstrate a vulnerability of substantial magnitude. Why would you simply learn about the network to try to manage an attack from a more difficult source point on the Internet? This is why planning is so important. The network may be under development or there may be a temporary addition to the network to accommodate a specific project. During the planning this may have been the unspoken reasoning of the customer in limiting the attack. It could have been the consultant's own recommendation based on the same information, concluding an attack via the wireless network would not be as valuable because it is temporary or in transition. On the other hand, learning about the internal operations and infrastructure could be construed as "cheating" on the part of the tester. It is at this point information falls into admissible evidence. For example, the tester may have been investigating wireless opportunities and stumbled across an open network. In the deliverable and final presentation the information obtained from the network may be presented to demonstrate the weakness, but the information may not have been used for exploitation.

- *Applications.* Applications can be a great source of information. They maintain data and sometimes manage their own access controls, which may be substantially weaker than what other systems may provide. Furthermore, applications can tell a lot about the target company: preferred systems, services being offered or used internally, critical to business, and types of data one should be looking to find. For example, if a tester finds AutoDesk is being used extensively in an organization, it would be a natural conclusion that once access to an internal system is realized, DWG files could represent sensitive material. If it is a graphics company and Adobe Photoshop is in high use, the tester would look for PSD files containing proprietary graphics. About three years ago a large sports club was redesigning its logo. The investment was enormous: changing uniforms, gear, posters, shirts, beer coolers, you name it. The goal was to keep the new logo secret until the final version was approved by the owners. A hacker broke into the company's systems, lurked around and stumbled across the new logo, and immediately posted it all over the Web. The company lost the valuable contract and the logo was changed once again. Finally, once the applications are identified, the consultant can start collecting information about it to support the search for known vulnerabilities. If it is a Java, CGI, or .NET application, the tester can start searching the vendor's site for security holes as well as other sites dedicated to exposing weaknesses in certain code design.

- *Custom Applications.* Applications that are created and supported internally are notoriously insecure because it takes a great deal of effort and time to integrate security capabilities in an application. Also, custom applications are usually created to reduce the cost of buying an off-the-shelf product, adding to the conclusion that little investment was made to secure the code. A more common attribute of internally developed systems is that the original creator did not document the solution and has left the company. From that point forward, others had to support the continued management, adding features and options as the system expanded with business demands. To add to the malaise, the people supporting the application may not be familiar with the language the original system was written in because the creator wrote in a code she was intimately familiar with, leaving the developers left behind to figure out how to simply make it work, much less secure it. Custom applications provide Greenfield opportunities to a hacker and testers alike. It's open territory to test different avenues of attack using all types of techniques. During the enumeration phase, the goal is to collect as much data about the application as possible. This typically requires interacting with the application directly to see what it does when bogus data is entered in a username or password field, or data entry fields, or any opportunity to input something that could force an error. You can also pull parts of the application out for later analysis. Web applications are a good example of this. If the Web server is not secured properly, a hacker can copy CGI, Java, or other program elements from the Web site and review them offline later to look for vulnerabilities in the code.

PREPARING FOR THE NEXT PHASE

Because the next phase is to perform research on the identified vulnerabilities based on the information learned during the enumeration phase, the final collection data must be broken into two distinct elements to move forward. As described earlier, there is the technically related information, which makes up the bulk of the data from the phase's activities, and conclusions based on the combination of technical details and reconnaissance information. By combining the two there is the opportunity to identify additional systems and networks that may have been overlooked by traditional scans and system inquiries. Usually, after the enumeration data is combined with other data from the previous phase, more detailed technical information typically surfaces

However, once the analysis is complete and the tester feels he has identified all the plausible areas of interest and can make some conclusions about the state of security and begin defining an attack scenario, the technical components of the enumeration data are once again separated and used as inputs for the vulnerability analysis phase. Again, as depicted in Figure 10.1, the technical information can be as simple as a list of listening ports and their corresponding services. Data can also include identified operating systems and versions, applications, patch levels, code versions, and firmware versions.

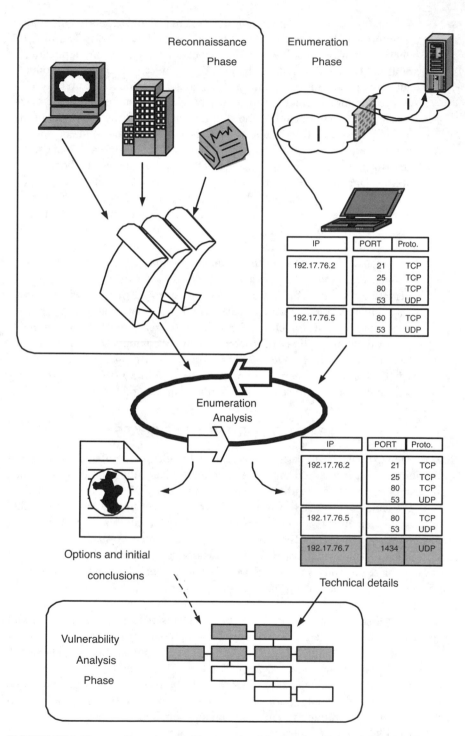

FIGURE 10.1 Process Overview for Enumeration Moving into Vulnerability Analysis

11 Vulnerability Analysis

During the reconnaissance and enumeration phases, we identified the scope of the target systems, topology, systems, platforms, applications, and services. We gathered all the information we could about the nature of those systems, and with that information in hand, we move into the vulnerability analysis phase. The purpose of this phase is to take the information obtained and compare it with known and potential vulnerabilities in order to move forward with the next phase, exploitation.

However, some companies prefer not to move on to the exploitation phase and would rather have the vulnerabilities documented and deal with them based solely on initial interpretation of the vulnerability, as opposed to the level of risk associated with each, which is determined by the exploitation phase. It is not uncommon for companies to have several tests performed, stopping at the conclusion of the vulnerability analysis phase, waiting for the right timing to permit the exploitation.

The goal of performing a vulnerability analysis is to take the information obtained from the enumeration phase, in concert with the reconnaissance data, and compare it to known issues, such as incidents, vulnerabilities, or announcements from other entities that have found a weakness in a product, protocol, or process.

The method is relatively simple: investigate known issues about applications, devices, and systems discovered at the target to determine options for an attack. As with many things, applying a methodology supports efficiencies in performing a task, even the easy ones. Knowing what types of data are collected and their source can assist in finding opportunities for attack much more quickly, as well as any associated tools that may exist to help in performing the exploitation.

In searching for a viable vulnerability, the tester needs to look for holes that promote plausible avenues for attack specific to the company's environment and the planned structure of the test. Obviously, a vulnerability associated with an operating system the target is not employing will not be very helpful. In contrast, a potential problem associated with a service the organization is running may be helpful in exploiting to demonstrate the exposure related to that vulnerability.

More importantly, the feasibility of the exploitation is directly associated with the limitations imposed by the targeted organization. For example, if a vulnerability permits malicious code to be installed on a server, but the restrictions of the test do not permit a Trojan to be used, the vulnerability is not immediately considered as an avenue for attack, but will most certainly appear in the deliverable. However, there may be other options that can be investigated to support an attack leveraging the same vulnerability.

There is a logical method for analyzing data and there is the pragmatic approach. During the soft objective within the enumeration phase, we tried to perform an interpretation of the information obtained in an effort to expose weaknesses that were not directly observed. However, the vulnerability analysis phase is the pragmatic mechanism of comparing the information collected with known problems. For example, a tester may discover a Windows 2000 server with service pack 1 installed. Armed with this information the tester can look for known vulnerabilities that were not fixed until service pack 2, or any of the security patches released after service pack 1. In addition, the scan may have revealed a specific service running on the system that has a known vulnerability. Moreover, there may be recent incident reports that map directly to the target's environment that the tester can duplicate to gain access. Most of this information can be collected from the Internet or other sources, such as newsgroups, mailing lists, or word of mouth that can be used to compare information about the target to seek out options for exploitation.

WEIGHING THE VULNERABILITY

As each potential vulnerability is identified, the tester must weigh it against the planned scope of the test to ensure the attack does not exceed the limitations agreed upon at the onset of the engagement. In situations where a plausible attack presents an exposure well beyond the scope, such as a DoS attack, the Red Team should communicate the issue to the White Team so a decision can be made on how to pursue. This is especially important when a vulnerability raises an immediate concern and represents a measurable risk to the customer or hinders the test in some way.

For holes that represent a substantial threat to the company, the Red Team is obligated to notify the White Team. The difficult part is deciding at what point a vulnerability is deemed an avenue of attack for the tester or a likely point for exploitation by a real hacker—an immediate threat. In some cases, this is painfully obvious, such as when a tester finds a system that has been previously compromised. The fact that the system remains in a terribly poor security condition reveals the company is likely unaware there is a problem. Of course, it would be inappropriate to use the system's troubles to perform further exploits. In the event a compromised system is identified, the White Team should be notified as soon as possible and any testing in that area of the network postponed.

NOTE 16: HACKING AN OLD HOLE IS BAD BUSINESS

Several years ago, there was a penetration tester that was very popular in the community because he gained access into nearly every company in an amazingly short amount of time. He worked from home and engagements would be passed to him through e-mail and conference calls. Based on his success, I decided to visit and watch him during one of his engagements. Almost immediately, I realized he was just scanning for previously compromised systems. During that time, before IDS and when most networks were completely open, it was common to find a Trojan, such as NetCat and BackOrifice. So, his technique was to seek out systems in peril to exploit. The only value that could possibly be interpreted in this case is that the company was ultimately made aware of the susceptibility to such an attack (he would not tell them the Trojan existed prior to testing), but the exposure knowingly forced upon the company totally canceled out any perceived value.

Having said this, some vulnerabilities are much less obvious, lending themselves to interpretation of the testers whether they should notify the White Team or exploit it based on the level of immediate exposure to the company. During the planning session, many companies will stipulate some form of definition of the exposure level. Interestingly, this is associated with managing the depth of the attack as opposed to monitoring the risk of being attacked by a real hacker. For example, the company may state that if the tester can exploit a vulnerability that permits access beyond the second firewall, then stop because there is a risk of affecting customer services or enough has been proven about the hole to justify its level of risk.

The practice of setting limits is common and can be helpful to all parties. However, very rarely is the definition of what should actually be exploited by the testing team questioned. It should be noted that some organizations that use penetration testing regularly have learned about this gap and go on to build an approval process between the vulnerability analysis phase and the exploitation phase. Nevertheless, more planning sessions are concerned with the depth of the test as opposed to the level of risk (or criticality) of an identified hole. If this is not considered, the tester may exploit a gaping hole, which has the potential to damage systems or data, go beyond the scope unintentionally, and may offer no true value. The company would be much better off knowing about the vulnerability and having the chance to fix it.

Luckily, the end result of planning for depth usually satisfies both areas of concern, even if unknowingly covering critical vulnerabilities. When the tester's depth of attack is controlled, a gaping hole will not be exploited because of the engagement scope. Unfortunately, much of this is based on the interpretation of the tester and the definition of depth during the planning process.

What is important to note is that companies which do not define the level of depth must establish an acceptable appraisal of a vulnerability that is to be tested as opposed to being notified immediately of its existence. Having a concern over the level of severity a vulnerability represents is healthy, but has the potential to influence the value of the test in the form of poorly founded imposed limitations. This brings us full circle back to the overall timing of the test. If it is done too early, every exposure will be labeled as a significant risk and must be dealt with immediately, resulting in no valuable testing.

If you are planning a test and have not considered the weight of a vulnerability and do not want to inject an approval phase, following are some basic vulnerability types that you should be notified of upon detection by the Red Team:

- *Trojans*. If a server is scanned and a well-known port used for a Trojan is identified, the White Team should be notified and the system identified. Even if the tester's assumptions are wrong, it is still of great value to the company.

- *Today's Hole.* Discussed in detail earlier, if an advisory is publicized during the test and the Red Team discovered your company is vulnerable, the White Team should be notified.
- *Huge-Hole Syndrome.* If the tester finds a problem with a server, application, or something so pervasive that to exploit it may render many security controls useless, the company should be apprised of the situation.
- *Too Many.* It is not uncommon for a tester to find hundreds of vulnerabilities, each offering an opportunity to attack the company on every level, from network nodes and services to operating systems and applications. Upon discovery, the White Team should be notified and must consider postponing the test until a foundation of security controls can be applied.
- *Hacker Tracks.* If a tester finds evidence of hacker activity—historical evidence or current activity—the White Team is notified and the test immediately stopped. The best action on the part of the testing organization is to assist in forensics and help clean up the insecurities.

In the event there is little planning to deal with weighted vulnerabilities, several methods exist that testers can use to make a determination about a vulnerability and whether to tell the White Team or exploit it. Most notably, the tester can evaluate the overall impact by researching the vulnerability, the sophistication of the available tools, the scope of the target's vulnerable systems, and their importance to the organization. For example, a tester identifies the target as using 72 Microsoft IIS Servers for E-commerce, a primary form of revenue generation, and a vulnerability is discovered that allows hackers to take over control of the system and all its resources by sending a small command to the HTTP daemon implanting a Trojan. Moreover, there are three tools available on the Internet and detailed instructions with several IP addresses of compromised systems. Given the importance and scale of vulnerable systems and that the likelihood of attack is high, the tester must consider the situation harmful to the company and notify the White Team.

As mentioned briefly above, there are the rare occasions when a vulnerability falls beyond the scope of the approved attack strategy, but is so pervasive that performing other aspects of the test becomes more difficult or constantly leads back to the unapproved vulnerability. Situations like this are usually based on overzealous, misdirected limitations placed on the tester. To demonstrate the point, a company may state that no operating system vulnerabilities are to be exploited during the test. However, as the tester starts various forms of attack threads, which may begin with an application weakness, they ultimately lead to an operating system exposure that can be used to obtain the password file. The question begins to arise, "Is it an operating system problem or should the application hole be scrutinized?" The answer is, technically, "Both." Therefore, the limitation stipulated during the planning phase affects the efficiency and possibly the actions taken by the tester.

As stated throughout the book, the typical goal of an ethical hack is to demonstrate the impact of a vulnerability by representing a viable threat, such as a hacker. Understanding the vulnerability, the tester can better weigh the opportunities to realize the desirable results.

SOURCE POINTS

Many sources of information can be leveraged to gain more insight into the possibilities for performing an attack based on the data gathered from previous phases. Each source is categorized into three unique groups: obtained, Internet, and vendors, which can be used to properly align the findings to the vulnerabilities, furthering the likelihood of exposing attack opportunities. Each source of information can help to better understand the practicality of exploiting the hole.

OBTAINED DATA

The most conspicuous source of information about a potential vulnerability is the company that is being targeted. During the reconnaissance and enumeration phases, specific data about the network and applications in use may provide the necessary information to launch an attack. To put this in perspective, assume a scan was performed that resulted in finding five UNIX servers with port 1234 opened and responding to requests. Not sure exactly what this means, the vulnerability analysis phase is used to investigate the existence of a potential hole. Earlier, during the reconnaissance phase, the tester found references to a Web-based application for data processing. To expound on the example, customers going to the Web site are instructed to download a Java plug-in to interact with the application and a set of installation and use documentation. Taking all this information into consideration, the tester may know some tactics to exploit Java-based client-side code. Without the information from the company, the tester wouldn't know what to do next with port 1234 and divert attention to other areas. Armed with nothing more than a hunch, the Java application can be downloaded and used to pry open a service port normally bypassed.

Custom applications are the primary culprit in using information from the company, against the company. All too often companies offer ample information about the use of their application to ensure that users are happy and, therefore, the companies are not getting tons of support calls. It's common to find extensive documentation about an application developed by a company on its Web site, in effect providing the instructions for pulling apart the application.

NOTE 17: THE NEEDLE IN THE HAYSTACK

While collecting information about a company, one system had a Visio file depicting a high-level network diagram of a network. It was a collection of simple lines and system icons that had no specific information that was readily usable. Therefore, I saved the file, and continued the test.

After performing several days of reconnaissance on this client, I was left with piles of general information: DNS entries, telephone numbers, open ports, operating system versions, applications that were in use, partner information, typical customers, and some ideas on the structure of the Internet-facing architecture. Each pile of information was evaluated and then compared to other interesting points of data in other piles.

Once the data was reviewed in its entirety, the Visio drawing made perfect sense. The file was a diagram of their partner network, which used an application I identified earlier in the test. Combined with the other information, it clearly showed there were several network interfaces in the system and several development servers appeared to be on the same segment.

Knowing exactly where I wanted to go and where to start within the network provided me with enough information to launch an attack against their central systems, something I wouldn't have considered before. Using the development systems with the half-baked application code and the multi-homed server, I gained access into the application's database. To prove the level of access, I made myself a licensed doctor (sports medicine, if you are curious) and had nearly a hundred patients with three office employees.

The application being developed had complete control over the information in a critical system and the multi-homed system provided the gateway. Without putting together seemingly limited information, the attack would have never even gone down that path. Quite frankly, I was initially concerned about even getting any access into their network.

THE INTERNET

Conducting a penetration test without using the Internet to research information is like attempting to find a treasure without a map. The Internet can be a powerful tool for performing research about a target's networks and systems. Today, vulnerability information is easy to come by because of the focus on security issues. This has not always been the case. Vendors were not communicating their weaknesses, people who found holes did not have a forum to communicate them to the public, and hacker activity was not being monitored. To know what was going on in the security industry, you simply had to be in the know. Companies that were hacked rarely knew it and when discovered it was typically a well-kept secret.

With the advent of SecurityFocus, CERT, DSheild, ISAC, and other information services, anyone can quickly obtain details about vulnerabilities, incidents, and advisories. With practice, you can recover an amazing amount of information without a significant amount of time and effort.

Armed with the open system ports, types of operating systems, and applications in use, all the tester needs to do is compare what was found with information on the Internet. There are hundreds, if not thousands, of sites that provide security information helpful for investigating potential avenues of attack.

Information about security issues can come in many forms. Following is a brief description:

- *Advisories.* An advisory is the official publication of a vulnerability. A watchdog group, vendor, consulting firm, or even a hacker may have found a condition within a computing environment that will permit some form of unauthorized access, disclosure of private information, or be an avenue for DoS. Upon discovery, the information is typically shared with a small group of people, such as the creator of the software in question, to work on a solution—secretly. If other, less scrupulous people were to know of the vulnerability's existence hundreds, if not thousands, of companies would be affected. At some point in time, usually after a patch or workaround is identified, an advisory will be published.

- *Vulnerabilities.* A vulnerability is the documentation of a problem, potential or measured, that may not have a viable fix or the creator of the software has not acknowledged its existence. Think of a vulnerability announcement as an unofficial advisory, or the discovery of a layered exposure. For example, a vulnerability may be several unique environmental elements that when combined have the potential to cause harm in some form. In some cases, the vulnerability has been proven in a lab, but not in the wild. Overall, there is room for interpretation on what the difference is between a vulnerability announcement and an advisory.
- *Incidents.* A completely new dimension to security information and assisting in the development of an attack plan is the publication of incidents. An incident is after the fact, and most of the information is associated with the event. CERT will regularly publish advisories followed by incidents explaining any nuances to the exploitation. This is best demonstrated when Nimda was released in late 2001. CERT posted several advisories and then incident reports would surface that explained other routes for exposure and what you should do to protect yourself. With Nimda it was first a server-focused worm concern; then, someone was infected via browser access. Using that new information an incident report was provided that explained the new threat characteristics. Incidents offer great information to the tester. Knowing the architecture and overall posture of a company, the incident reports may provide the one detail about a specific situation that can be directly employed against the target.

Below is a short list of security information sites:

- The CERT® Coordination Center (CERT/CC) (http://www.cert.org/)
- Internet Security Systems' X-Force (http://www.iss.net/security_center/)
- @Stake (http://www.atstake.com)
- Counterpane (http://www.counterpane.com)
- SecurityFocus (http://online.securityfocus.com)
- Computer Incident Advisory Capability for DOD (http://www.ciac.org/ ciac)
- The Common Vulnerabilities and Exposures (CVE) project (http://cve. mitre.org)
- Attrition (http://www.attrition.org)
- BindView's RAZOR (http://razor.bindview.com)
- Australian Computer Emergency response Team (http://www.auscert.org.au)
- Forum of Incident Response and Security Teams (http://www.first.org)
- Federal Computer Incident Response Center (http://www.fedcirc.gov)

- Bugzilla Bug Tracking System (http://www.bugzilla.org/security.html)
- ANSI CGI Program Security Advisories (http://www.ansi.co.jp/tech/cgi/security/advisories/)

The above examples are legitimate sites that maintain data for the betterment of the security community. However, there are many more sites dedicated to sharing information and tools within the hacking community, which may provide specific information and tools. Usually, the first thought that comes to mind when discussing hacker sites is the latest and greatest information on a vulnerability and a tool to exploit it. In contrast, it is a great place to begin to find old vulnerabilities and tools about which other sites have simply forgotten.

A tester may identify an old version of Solaris, or even a new distribution running an old version of a service (who knows, maybe for compatibility issues). Sites that offer information may not maintain historical data, links to information may be old or broken, or the information may be stale. In contrast, hackers hang on to everything. It is surprisingly easy to find an old tool designed to exploit a bizarre, forgotten-about hole in a matter of minutes.

In addition to the grouping of source data, there are focal points of information on the Internet:

- *Read the Manual.* More often than not, there is an attribute about an application or system that is vulnerable to attack based on installation practices supported by the vendor. With the Internet, many companies provide manuals and installation guides online for anyone to download and read. Based on the information in the manual, a tester can make some conclusion about the potential vulnerabilities of a target system or application.
- *Default Installs.* Upon installation of an application or operating system, the user has the opportunity (typically) to choose the default installation. To accommodate the user and the use of all the features of the software, the installation process may install and activate every possible option, some without the knowledge of the user. For example, there was a time when if you installed FrontPage Extensions on a Linux server running Apache, the system would reveal passwords, allowing remote unauthorized modification of the Web site. A tester may identify an application in use, install it in a lab, and investigate what vulnerabilities may exist assuming the administrator performed a default installation.
- *Default Passwords.* Most systems require the entry of a password during installation. This is most common with operating systems, but can also be seen in large, complex applications such as Oracle. There are scenarios where the system will create a user and default password on behalf of the administrator to support the smooth, error-free installation of the product. Although helpful to the vendor to ensure its product installs correctly, the result is typically that the default username and password are never changed. Once a tester learns of this flaw, the default user name and password can be tested.

- *Hidden Accounts*. A more sinister activity is when a system creates a username and password during installation that is hidden from the administrator performing the installation. There have been many occurrences of systems being implemented and maintained in a secure manner but still being accessed by attackers because they are using a backdoor. Typically, these credentials are integrated into the system to run services at a privileged level within the system. Unfortunately, there is no method for identifying the existence of the rogue user account and removing it. The Internet, once again, is a great place to find information specific to an application or system to help find opportunities.

- *Protocol Standards*. Invariably, someone will find a weakness associated with a version of a protocol that can be used to circumvent security measures. Of course, there is a fine line between protocol vulnerability and service vulnerability. Is it a weakness in the protocol, or a vendor's attempt to customize the communication? Nevertheless, the IETF is a good place to look for conversations regarding the security of a given protocol. During the creation and promotion of a protocol, someone will find a hole in the protocol and raise concern. If it is a relatively new protocol and is being used by the target, there may be an opportunity to test the person's theory. For example, during the creation of the IPSec protocol, and well after it had been adopted by many product companies, several vulnerabilities were identified within IKE that had the potential to expose all the data within the VPN. A tester armed with insights from the creators and contributors of a protocol could launch a sophisticated attack if the target's environment supports such a tactic.

Knowing where to look and how to find certain data, a tester can learn all she needs to know in a matter of hours to gain access to your network. The scary part is that hackers can do the same thing.

NOTE 18: NASTY TOOLS AND THE DIFFICULTY IN FINDING THEM

Recently, I was in our U.K. office and looking over the shoulder of one of our penetration testers while he worked on a problem for a customer. A newly implemented Linux system providing Web services was acting strangely and we were brought in to find out what was happening. The customer already assumed the system had been hacked and placed it on an isolated network. The goal was to find the vulnerability and how it was exploited before the customer rolled out 1000 more servers just like the pilot. After a couple of hours looking through the system and the Internet, it was determined the hacker (or better described as a script kiddie) managed to use a sophisticated tool to modify the kernel remotely providing total control over the system, nearly undetectable. Information from the Internet was critical in finding data to explain the anomalies found in the system in addition to understanding the tool and the exploited vulnerability. We assumed a script kiddie because the system was being used as an IRC server and nothing more, when in fact it had the potential to be much more valuable to a hacker who owned the system and knew how to use it more effectively. Knowing the consultant, I expect the tool will be used on the next penetration-testing engagement for customers who have a similar weakness. I feel for them already — this attack is very nasty indeed.

VENDORS

Vendors, those that design, build, sell, and support the hardware, software, and systems that we use, are a useful source of information. They operate in an environment of extreme competition, where competitors can gain dominant market position by immediately seizing upon the slightest misstep. The competitive situation is so intense that vendors must make calculated decisions about which features to put in their products and which bugs to fix before the next release.

In the midst of a marathon sprint, the customers expect security features to be built into products as an intrinsic attribute rather than a feature. Customers expect the creators of the business-enabling features in their $50-million-dollar enterprise solution have built in the security required for its safe and robust operation. However, everyday normal users, security testers, and parts of the "underground" community are finding bugs, quirks, and behaviors that can be used to exploit those systems.

Luckily these bugs are being reported to the vendors in various ways, sometimes through trouble tickets, other times with anonymous e-mails, and other times just sent to a public e-mail forum such as Butraq. This starts the cycle of vendors finding security-relevant bugs in their products and setting about their internal resource allocation process to decide when they can fix them.

Fixing security bugs for the vendors is a multistep process. First off, they have the hard-core business of rewriting broken code in a more secure way. Experience has shown this is a difficult task, and sometimes it actually introduces errors. In the popular open-source package OpenSSH, code was added to detect an attack on the checksum or cyclic redundancy check as defined in ISO 3309. The code had an intricate but exploitable bug that allowed remote administrative control of UNIX hosts running particular versions of OpenSSH. A patch was written to address the flaw, but after installing the fix, there was another vulnerability introduced, requiring another fix. Even security fixes have bugs sometimes.

After fixing the code, vendors release alerts to their user communities regarding the new bugs. Sometimes these are mailed to lists of users with support contracts. Other times they are posted to public forums. These are sent to alert the public of serious issues, provide advice for workarounds or fixes, and help just make the world a slightly better place.

Alerts

As vendors learn of a hole they will provide a fix or workaround (it is hoped) and send an alert to the public by using their Web sites and sending the information to the major security portals for greater distribution. Alerts are a great tool for penetration testers to locate precise data about an operating system, application, or service the customer is using. Therefore, the tester may identify a Cisco router, PIX firewall, and Solaris running Apache and the logical first step is to look for known vulnerabilities associated with the systems. What makes this action so valuable is alerts and notifications of vulnerabilities are well archived providing ample data to search for a likely candidate. The unfortunate fact is many people do not stay as up to date on patches and fixes as they should, giving the tester opportunities to collect several different types of data for each element of the customer's network.

Service Packs

Service packs are major updates to code to fix a number of problems discovered after the release of the application. However, and this is more of an aspect of Microsoft platforms, if a change is made to the system (even something as simple as adding a printer driver at times) the service pack must be reapplied. The reapplication of the update is necessary because there may be attributes associated with the change you made to the system that may effectively "roll back" the system to the original vulnerable state. Knowing many companies fail to apply updates to their systems, it's more likely that they do not reapply the updates as well.

The most common negative affect of service packs and security patches is when they are not implemented. Through the enumeration process the tester may be able to discover the target system is at service pack 3 when in fact service pack 4 is available. All the tester has to do is look for all the changes that were made associated with the latest update and test the system's resilience to attacks against the holes that may remain.

REPORTING DILEMMA

As you can imagine, there is the foundation for conflicting interests between the people who find and report alerts to the public about system and application vulnerabilities and the vendors of those products. Does the vendor know about the hole? Should the person or group that finds the bug report it to the vendor privately first to avoid a massive wave of attacks? Or, does it really matter because it has been proven over and over again that patches are usually not applied?

There is an understanding within the professional community that when a weakness is identified in a firewall, for example, the vendor of the system should be made aware before posting on the Internet. If Bob were to find a massive hole in Check-Point, a very popular firewall for many different types of organizations—large and small—and post it on the Internet without concern for companies using the product, there is an enormous potential for hackers to attack targets indiscriminately or provide them the one missing link in obtaining valuable data. Bob could single-handedly promote chaos. Of course, if Bob is a hacker, this is expected, but if he is a member of a professional group or organization with the mission of finding vulnerabilities, there is an obligation to the vendor to offer a fix for the problem before pandemonium consumes the Internet.

However, problems can arise when the vendor ignores or disputes the vulnerability. Moreover, the vendor may listen and acknowledge the vulnerability, but do nothing to accommodate a fix because the cost is too great, the resources are not available, or for some reason the issue just gets shelved. You cannot assume a hacker will ultimately find the hole and release the discoverer (Bob) from the responsibility of dealing with a shortsighted vendor simply because hackers may not be interested. The vulnerability could last for weeks, months, or even years depending on the development cycle and the characteristics of the vulnerability.

Note 19: Reporting Problems Is Not Always Easy

About two years ago, a consultant found a major flaw in a firewall product of the company he was working for at the time. He not only found the hole, but also wrote a comprehensive tool to demonstrate the massive weakness to the development group of the firewall. With some assistance, he managed to get an audience with the development group only to be completely blown off.

After a couple of weeks, the tension grew between the consultants and the product house, ultimately resulting in a crescendo of heated debates with no compromise on either side. As the months passed, there was a growing concern among the consultants that the vulnerability could greatly affect the company's success, placing them squarely in the middle: on one side, supporting customers, and on the other, working for a company ignoring a major problem with its product.

Finally, the consultant, a penetration tester, was on a gig where the customer was using over 100 of the firewalls in question. In a matter of minutes, he used his tool to take over the firewalls and configured VPN access allowing him full and unencumbered access to internal systems from the Internet. At the completion of the engagement, the report clearly outlined the vulnerability with the firewall and the tool used.

The client became immediately concerned when a consultant of a product company found a major hole in their firewalls and, understandably, claimed "foul" and a conflict of interest. As the issue flew up the food chain in the company, it resulted in a firestorm that only fueled the existing smolders of discontent between the two groups. The hole was ultimately repaired and the consultant left the company about a year later to pursue other opportunities. Was the consultant at fault? Was the development team the real problem? I'll let you be the judge.

So what is the result? It usually comes down to ethics meets frustration. Bob will typically start to share his concerns with counterparts and other organizations not only to validate the problem further, but gain more momentum with the vendor as a larger group. As more and more people become involved, the likelihood of the information being leaked increases and the stress to answer the call for a fix rises for the vendor. In most cases, the vendor complies and realizes the situation will be exposed one way or another, leading to work for the vendor, and they would be in better political shape for providing a fix before or at the time of announcement.

12 Exploitation

It could be argued that the difference between a penetration test and vulnerability scanning is the act of exploitation. A vulnerability scanning (or analysis) service is engineered to identify vulnerabilities and determine a level of risk based on the potential of the vulnerability without regard for other environmental conditions on the network that may enhance or cancel out the vulnerability altogether. Without pushing the limits of the vulnerability, the actual risk associated with the vulnerability will remain conjecture. By exploiting the vulnerability, a company can determine the impact of not rectifying the problem as opposed to assuming the level of risk is bearable given a specific vulnerability.

There are vulnerabilities that represent an enormous security risk no matter the network or security architecture in use because it affects something core to the overall security, such as firewall, IDS system, service, or operating system. In these situations, the need for fixing the problem is clear because the threat to system integrity is obvious. However, these types of vulnerabilities are becoming more and more rare in the wild and today they typically have to do with DDoS attacks or worm propagation that takes advantage of a widespread vulnerability or inherent weakness in an application.

By exploiting a vulnerability in a specific type of environment unique to the client's business needs and architecture, the scale and scope of the threat can be determined. There are thousands of vulnerabilities that are identified monthly, weekly, and even daily sometimes, but not all of them have the same potential in every network. A small overlooked vulnerability may have the potential of exposing valued cyber assets in a matter of minutes, whereas in a different network it may be completely harmless. Of course, in both cases, it depends on the type of access permitted to the system or application. A system deep within the network that has no user interaction and lives on a completely segmented network may be very secure and therefore does not typically require regular security management. In contrast, a system in the DMZ that provides services to the general Internet public is exposed to all types of threats that can exploit even the most hidden vulnerability.

Exploitation is identifying the vulnerability and using it to gain access, acquire information, or establish a foundation to launch other attacks. In this chapter, we take a closer look at some of the tools, protocols, and services that are common targets for exploiting vulnerabilities. In addition, the timing and type of exploitation are discussed, introducing situations when exploiting a vulnerability is actually going too far. The goal is to communicate different perspectives on exploitation and test the theory fundamental to ethical hacking.

INTUITIVE TESTING

One of the more interesting and thought-provoking aspects of penetration testing is not exploiting the vulnerabilities that are discovered. What makes it worthwhile for discussion is the assumption that each vulnerability must be pried open to demonstrate value. This concept introduces challenges of performing a penetration test in the first place. If you can tell there is a security vulnerability that poses a risk to the client, why then go through a penetration test when it can be solved directly. The issue is not all vulnerabilities can be quickly surmised, and the ones that can be determined as high risk without exploitation are identified well into a test. Although this does raise the issues of penetration test's value to a customer, the reality is that the service is designed to exploit vulnerabilities to determine the exposure. If customers simply wanted to know what the vulnerabilities were, they would employ a test: a simple but factual conclusion.

Nevertheless, the value and focus of the test must remain paramount during planning and execution, therefore drawing conclusions about a vulnerability may be necessary to stay within the bounds of the engagement as well as demonstrating without exploitation that the risk is real. In most cases, this has to do with sampling, or attacking a specific system that represents the majority of the systems on the target's network. If a UNIX system is vulnerable to allowing a tester to collect passwords, and other systems on the same network are configured identically, it can be assumed that they are vulnerable to the same attack. Even though there may be more valuable passwords on the other systems, the fundamental goal has been met.

Intuitive testing can also be linked to the depth of the attack. Some tests become focused on getting passwords because they represent the keys to the kingdom. If only one vulnerability is used to gain the information from system after system, the value to the customer is questionable. This goal is to expose and rate as many vulnerabilities as possible to provide a clear picture and the various levels of risk related to them. The goal is to draw logical conclusions to support the advancement of security for the company, not to bore into the network and systems, collecting everything in sight because the tester obtained a few choice passwords.

Intuitive testing allows the target to gain as much value from the attack thread while promoting the search for other vulnerabilities. The primary argument against this type of testing is the assumption that why would a hacker not go for the throat than spend more time looking for other avenues of access. This conclusion is founded on the assumption that a tester can and should duplicate a real threat. Moreover, this is an example of not using operational disadvantages to gain more value from the test. Nevertheless, the pragmatic reasoning is not all hackers have the ability to identify and exploit a vulnerability obvious to a tester. Therefore, if other vulnerabilities exist, which may have less impact on the network, there is a potential they may be used by a hacker who did not discover the other, more effective, hole.

There are many situations where information is obtained that would allow a hacker to run freely over the network, for example, a password. It can be readily assumed that once a tester obtains the password, leveraging that data to continue to access other systems does not provide any additional value to the client. A basic and evident example is that there are other scenarios where the tester can simply determine with the information that these actions are possible, without actually exploiting the other vulnerabilities.

The best way to communicate the decision point for the tester to make a conclusion and move on to the next opportunity by ending the attack thread is when the attack is not based solely on a vulnerability. An example could be a misconfigured firewall allowing access to a vulnerable service running on a server. The vulnerability allows a hacker to run an application remotely, such as a rootkit that can be used to obtained root privileges on the server. Once the rootkit is successfully installed, it can be readily assumed the tester can get deeper into the network. Practicing this technique promotes some basic areas that can be valuable to the tester as well as the target. First, the vulnerability can always be revisited by the tester if no other attack thread is as successful. The odds of the rootkit and vulnerability remaining on the system for the duration of the test are high, so there is little concern of the opportunity being lost. In addition, the tester can avoid spending valuable time and effort leveraging that one set of vulnerabilities to gain singular access, when that time can be spent looking for another, which could be potentially broader and more effective in the long run. Consequently, combining the fact that the initial attack thread remains for use later and there is the potential for a better route of attack, the advantage of moving from one place to another without committing to a single point is obvious for the tester. Second, the company realizes value because the tester is taking a comprehensive approach to the test. If the original threat is not revisited due to lack of time or it becomes unavailable sometime during the test, the fact that the rootkit was implemented is more than enough information to show value to the customer.

EVASION

In an attack, one of the goals of the hacker is to remain anonymous by avoiding detection using specific techniques to thwart any detection strategies the target may be employing. Understanding that many of the goals and tactics used by hackers should be included in the methodology of a penetration test, evading detection is typically high on the list for testers, although not an absolute requirement.

Although there exists a value to the company for the tester to avoid being discovered, there is the increased likelihood that a vulnerability will not be discovered or the attack will not be as successful if the tester is attempting to work far below the radar. One of the inherent limitations to ethical hacking is time, and the process overhead of remaining undetected can consume valuable time. Moreover, the act of attacking surreptitiously reduces the options of the tester and ultimately the number of vulnerabilities identified and exploited will typically be less than if the test were done freely.

Conversely, if the test is partly designed to determine the level of detection capability of existing technology and people within the target organization, then evasion must be a high priority for the engagement. The difficult part is few customers seek a test to simply determine the ability of their technology and employees responsible for identifying attacks on the network. Therefore, the need to ascertain incident response capability is secondary at best, but the surreptitious element is not reflected in other aspects of requirements, such as time or information provided to the tester. Without an equalizing characteristic integrated into the plan when covert actions are required, the value of the overall test will be in jeopardy. If a customer wants to test the detection and response of their Blue Team, the tester should be afforded more time or more detailed information about the target to offset the impacts on process in attempting to remain unnoticed.

There are several ways for a hacker, or tester, to be detected attacking an organization.

- *Intrusion Detection System.* IDS is one of the more popular security technologies being implemented to assist in the identification of possible attacks on the network. IDS can exist as a network device, monitoring the network for malicious packets and communications. It can also run on a server that is being used for other services. Host-based IDS monitors the system and many of its basic actions in an attempt to discover unauthorized activity. There are a couple of other variations based on this theme, but most types of IDS detect attacks in one of three basic ways.

- *Signature Analysis.* Many attacks have a predictable format, timing, and structure in that certain communication types and responses are symptoms of an attack. For example, if a hacker telnets into port 80 on a Web server and enters a command never issued by a browser upon connection that will allow remote access to the Web server, the IDS may have a signature in its database that tells it there is an attack using a "push" attack against the server. The ability of the IDS to identify the attack is based on the availability of the signature, which provides the attributes of the communication to isolate the attack, and comparing all communications on the network to that signature. A signature is a rule simply stating if there is an application level request that is known to be used as part of an attack, then the administrator needs to be notified or the event logged.

- *Protocol Analysis.* As an IDS system observes interactions between systems on the network or residing on a host, signatures are used to identify application-level activities. The same holds true for IDS-based protocol analysis, which looks for questionable activities in the protocol itself. For example, there was a DoS attack from several years back called a FRAG attack. The packets sent to the target system were constructed in a manner that when reassembled in memory of the receiving system, the packet data would overwrite portions of the other packets sent causing the system to fail. In this simplistic example, a weakness in the protocol (permitting illegal offset values) was used to attack a system ill prepared for such an onslaught. An IDS system that used protocol analysis would have detected the faulty packets, if it were provided the signature, of course.

- *Anomaly Detection.* One of the more advanced features of some IDSs, and a focal point for many vendors today, is the ability to look for something outside the realm of a defined "normal operation" assuming attacks are out-of-the-ordinary activities. By defining a standard acceptable operating envelope, the IDS only has to look for divergence from the expected procedures within the communication. There are several types of anomaly detection.

> – *Anomaly Signatures*. At the most basic element, anomaly signatures are standard policies for normal operating procedures. Details are built into the system to reduce the configuration requirements of the customer and provide something that can be customized. An anomaly signature is simply a predefined envelope of typical operations that are legitimate in the majority of situations.
> – *Statistical Modeling*. A much more complex aspect of anomaly detection is making a determination as to whether the traffic being detected is an attack on the network. By collecting information about the communication, the IDS can make a determination based on legitimate traffic that has minute characteristics that make it stand out during analysis. For example, a communication session being monitored by the IDS is valid when compared to an application or protocol level, or anomaly signatures. However, when compared to all the traffic patterns collected from previous communications from the suspected host, the content of the communication is dramatically different, raising even greater suspicion about the session being monitored.

- *Observation*. By monitoring system activity, log files, and system status a hacker can be detected based on the reaction the environment has to a typical interference.
- *Evasion*. Oddly enough, when hackers attempt to subvert detection, they typically use tactics that are known, and therefore raise suspicion. Sending packets with limited Time to Live (TTL), with excessive time between each to bypass IDA but not lose the attention of the target system, injecting malicious data through URLs that may not be detectable, or using invalid characters, are only a few examples of evasion techniques that have the potential to expose the attacker. Nevertheless, a company has to be aware of these issues and configure its system to assist in identifying surreptitious activities. In many cases, these have the potential, more often than not, of setting off false alarms, and ultimately getting turned off for that reason. However, on internal networks on demarcations between partner networks, these can be viable options.

THREADS AND GROUPS

The concept of a thread or a group of threads to track the success and tactics of the exploitation is a common practice for those who perform penetration tests regularly but may not be obvious to others who are not as familiar. During a test, it is nearly as important to track your actions as it is to execute them in a proper order and format. Techniques are becoming more and more specific as attacks become increasingly sophisticated. As time moves on and the attacks become more popular, a tool is typically created and the threat goes mainstream. The less-experienced testers will walk through portions of the framework presented here, but typically fall into a loop of "look" then "attack," verify success or failure, and move on to the next vulnerability. The goal of many tests is to determine the impact of a vulnerability, therefore, each exploitation attempt must be documented, including the results (even if they seem benign), time of test, and targeted system, application, service, or user. The concept is that you always learn something even if you do not get any response from a remote system. At least you now know at that point nothing is responding, which in itself is information.

Purely mimicking a hacker, as many attempt to do, does not take advantage of all the opportunities associated with a controlled attack. For example, as information is obtained from the target system, it can be compiled with other activities, such as social engineering, wardialing, wardriving, or physical security to support the overall goal of value. A hacker also does this, but internally where he can make quick determinations about what he has learned and can focus on the fruitful events rather than obstacles. In contrast, the tester is performing an overall evaluation, so all information can be used for "good" and not to simply attack the first hole that presents itself.

Taking into consideration the philosophy of a well-planned attack and leveraging the actions to promote a comprehensive perception of the target's security, attacks during the exploitation phase can be broken into two categories: threads and groups. Introduced above, threads are a single collection of linked actions with a focal point and a traceable path. Groups are combinations of similar or seemingly unrelated threads to meet a greater goal. The entire concept is founded on a methodical approach to penetration testing aligned with the limitations and expectations set during the planning. In addition, by breaking the attack into manageable units, the plan can take into consideration restrictions and obstacles the target may have for the tester.

When considering the following discussion on these two items, keep in mind they don't necessarily default to technical attacks. For example, wardialing can begin with scanning numbers for valid numbers, moving on to limiting the scope to numbers that provide tone, attacking a select few to see what is plausible. A group may be combining the results from the thread that led to five systems responding to tone to support the social engineering efforts that may be under way. The discussion below is best communicated using a technical example penetrating various levels of security by using similar, but not identical, processes. With each layer of security a different challenge of attack is introduced changing the method used to get to the same point as a previous thread.

THREADS

By its simplest definition, a thread is a related set of actions leading to a conclusion. The conclusion can be an exploited vulnerability allowing the implantation of a trophy and obtaining sensitive data, essentially proving the impact of the vulnerability found on a system. In contrast, a thread may end in a hard stop. For example, you may get past the router, firewall, and into the inner working of an E-commerce server, but no opportunity presents itself to gain the treasure one is seeking.

In Figure 12.1, there are seven threads as an example. Threads 3, 4, and 5 are peering into the DMZ gaining information about a Web server, E-commerce server, and a DNS server. To get to this point, the tester had to reckon with the outer router and firewall. This may have included IDS evasion tactics, port manipulation in the

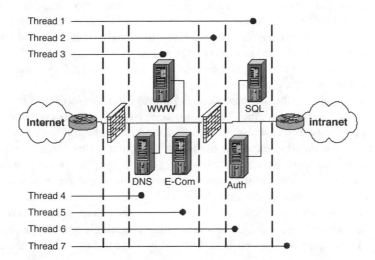

FIGURE 12.1 Each Attack Has Its Own Set of Hurdles and Targets

packet structure, overlapping data streams, or other technical attributes that allowed access to these systems.

Thread number 2 reached into the network far enough to access the firewall and in the process the tester learned more about the Internet-facing infrastructure. Typically, the inner firewall is hidden by aggressive ACLs, rules on the external firewall, and the configuration of the inner firewall. For example, many internal firewalls will only accept packets from the DMZ servers and specific NATed address coming from the internal interface of the outer firewall. The number 2 thread may be difficult to employ because of the various measures taken by the outer router and firewall, and is considered a significant milestone in the attack.

Threads 1 and 6 take the attack to the next level by interacting with the servers on the protected layer behind the inner firewalls and before the internal network. However, it should be noted that to accomplish this task (for the purposes of this demonstration) the same tactics used in thread 2 may not fully apply. In other words, to get to the SQL and authentication servers the tester would have to traverse the outer router and firewall while having enough structure left in the thread to penetrate the inner firewall. If thread 2 tactics were used, the inner firewall might thwart the attack.

Finally, thread 7 makes it into the internal network. This could be achieved by several different tactics including false packets, manipulating one of the servers in the DMZ or inner servers, or simply taking advantage of poor security practices. Attacks that penetrate into the internal network are typically founded on gaps in the layers of applied security. These usually leverage a small opportunity in an element found in one of the outer systems and pry it open to gain greater access. Once on the internal network there are several opportunities to move deeper quickly. As with the threads 1 and 6, 7 may not be as successful if it were to use the exact same tactics because the circumstances facing the tester change at each layer.

Threads are a basic form of attack. They use information available to move through each layer of the security infrastructure with little consideration for the success or failure of previous threads exercised in the past. It is the act of attacking a set of systems with the intent to go as far as one can while meeting the planned objectives. This method promotes the search for more vulnerabilities, but does not ignore the need to exploit an opportunity.

Mentioned above, threads provide an opportunity to perform attacks surreptitiously. By their very nature, they're focused and typically quickly employed allowing the opportunity to pick away at the target systems without a total commitment to the attack and possibly exposing the tester. Effectively, this can also mimic the reconnaissance and enumeration phases. By peering into the target's network at specific points and with varying tactics, information is learned and collected to formulate a better plan as the tester moves deeper into the network. Moreover, because each thread is a unique set of tasks potentially employing different tools there is the opportunity to spread the attack out over multiple sources in addition to lengthening the time between packets, ultimately dipping farther under the radar.

GROUPS

Groups are a representation of two concepts. Each thread is independent, but may leverage an aspect of a previously used thread to branch off and logically jump a layer. For instance, a thread resulting in a deeper attack, such as thread 7, may diverge from a previous attack by branching from a point well before the layer required to be bypassed. To continue with the example given so far, thread 5 gains access to the E-commerce server and thread 2 makes it to the inner firewall. However, the success of thread 1 is based on a Trojan implanted in the E-commerce server thanks to thread 5 (confused yet?). Thread 2 showed us (1) the inner firewall exists, and (2) possible points of entry into a deeper network. One could assume thread 1's success was based on tactics used from 2 and 5, although the point of divergence was at the E-commerce server where a new attack strategy was used to gain access to the SQL server. So a minor mixture of tactics and information gleaned from other threads are used in combination with a new tool to jump over the inner firewall.

Also, threads can be completely combined taking successful attributes from each thread and formulating a group of tactics to meet the final attack goal. Thread 7 in the previous example made it the farthest, penetrating into the internal router behind all the security measures.

In Figure 12.2, threads 1, 2, and 5 are combined to get to the SQL server, as explained above, and threads 7, 3, 6, and 2 are combined to wreak havoc on the internal network. Notice elements from thread 2 are integrated into the attacks for both groups A and B. This can be information learned about the inner firewall or Trojans left behind in servers in the DMZ, or the inner servers that have provided the much-needed launching pad to gain ultimate access to the internal network. Groups are the crescendo of the attack. They take everything gained and apply it to make the push into the target's network. Think of threads as a beachhead and groups as the full-on assault moving to capture the capital city.

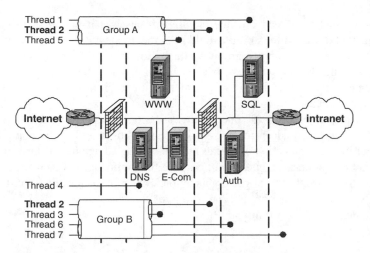

FIGURE 12.2 Threads Can Be Combined to Build Highly Successful and Aggressive Attacks That Are Fast Moving and Productive

It is not uncommon for hackers to use several systems to work their way closer to the target and launch an attack while having the information returned to them through a collection of several different systems. They start by taking over a system, such as your home PC, always on and connected to a cable modem. From that vantage point they start doing the same to others, using each as a launching pad for the next. In the meantime, they set up another set of systems that will pass information through a similar chain of computers to collect the information they seek. When they get to a point where they feel comfortably hidden, they launch an attack against the target, usually using a very specific attack they have planned for quite some time. It would not make much sense building a maze of camouflage to simply start pounding away at the front door. No, at this point they know exactly what they want to do. As each zombie is taken over to launch the attack, this can be defined as a thread or a specific attack with an achievable goal that can be used later. The group is the use of all the commandeered systems to launch the final wave of the attack. In this example, a growing threat from hackers is used to further define the line between thread and group.

The advantage to the organization using this tactic under the influence of the framework will gain value in the information collected from each thread: which ones were successful, which were not, and the threads that were combined to finally build a successful attack. At the end of the test the record of threads and groups can be analyzed to determine the likelihood of such a threat becoming a reality. Given the success of each thread, the exposure to each threat can be measured and ultimately assigned a value of risk. In turn, that risk level will become an input to determining the urgency for repair. Furthermore, and arguably the most valuable aspect of threads and groups, is that each thread combined to build a group is evaluated to determine what repairs to the systems should be implemented first. If a thread is a critical factor in the success of the group that allowed the tester to own your $250,000 per hour server, such as thread 2 in the previous discussion, it would seem clear that the mitigation of that vulnerability would have the greatest impact on the mitigating success of the group B and/or group A attack. To fix the vulnerability in the inner firewall may not be the cheapest, but when compared to the reduction of overall risk, the cost can be logically spread over all the vulnerabilities that led to the success of the other threads.

The exploitation phase of many penetration tests is performed with all these elements raging in the deep recesses of the tester's mind and rarely compiled into a comprehensive explanation of threats and risk balanced against business demands. This is not to insinuate people do not practice this philosophy in some manner and the value translated to the target organization. But, more often than not, the focus is mainly on the final attack and the results of the group, rather than focusing on the combination of several threads.

OPERATING SYSTEMS

Attempting to attack the operating system is one of the most common tactics tried by a penetration tester or a hacker. Inasmuch as systems typically host all the information the organization is trying to protect, they should be the most secure aspect of the infrastructure. Unfortunately, this is not always the case and is usually the most vulnerable because they have to provide so many options to users, services, and applications. Anyone responsible for securing a system or a host of systems is most likely the member of several mailing lists that announce new identified vulnerabilities. With the number of different versions and types of operating systems, properly patching them all is often not achieved, nor is it typically accomplished in a timely manner.

WINDOWS

Microsoft has always designed its Windows operating system with user friendliness in mind. No other platform caters to ease of use as Windows attempts to do. Unfortunately, what Microsoft gains in usability, affects the level of attainable security. Recently, Microsoft realized it must find a method to maintain usability and allow security to coexist on their operating systems. Windows XP definitely can have a higher level of security associated with it, yet the system comes standard with low controls to provide greater options to the user. For example, by default an XP system using a wireless network card will begin to participate in any wireless network that is identified. Until service pack one was released, this would happen without confirming the inclusion in an unknown network with the user; it would simply join in the "trusted" network.

On the other hand, Windows 2003 provides a more secure approach by making services that could be potentially exploited executed under a nonprivileged account. This inherently makes execution of code through an exploit much harder to obtain.

A Windows administrator must be aware of what needs to be done to the system before it is released to production to ensure it is at a level acceptable to the organization and its business function. Older versions of Windows, which are still highly prevalent in production today, may never reach that higher level of security.

During a penetration test, usually the most vulnerable systems identified are those running a Windows operating system. (Of course, Microsoft is the most pervasive OS out there.) Although Windows has generated a large amount of new vulnerabilities, sometimes on a daily basis, the security patches are provided, and the administrators have the opportunity to reduce the level of risk by applying them in a timely manner, although this does not address the incompatibility issues that arise on occasion with patches and custom applications. An ample staff would need to research, analyze, and patch all of the vulnerable systems, and that is usually where the process breaks apart due to budgetary constraints.

It does not improve the effectiveness of the results of the penetration test if 50 systems were exploited by the installation of a rootkit when only one patch needed to be installed to eliminate the risk. The key point here is that if it is obvious a patch installation would reduce or remove a threat, there is no need to drill down farther on additional exploitation using the vulnerability as a starting point. This is time that could be spent identifying additional exploitations within the Windows operating system.

UNIX

There are many flavors of UNIX today, especially with the growing trend of Linux operating systems. Solaris, HP-UX, and AIX are three that have been around for a long time. They were also designed with security in mind, often making them not as user friendly. A user or administrator must understand the inner workings of a UNIX operating system to properly and effectively work with it. Because security was incorporated into the development of UNIX systems, they were not often as privy to vulnerabilities. However, as of late, more vulnerabilities have been identified on UNIX systems, with no prejudice to the flavor of operating system. Although Solaris can be secured in a relatively easy manner, most of the time these steps are not completed, and the system remains vulnerable due to poor implementation practices.

The most common exploit on a Solaris system is due to unnecessary services being left enabled after the standard installation. These services are usually enabled by default, but the administrator did not take the time to disable the unneeded services. Exploiting a Solaris system is easy in this case: all the tester needs to do is run a tool against the server, identify what services are open, and then attempt to exploit them via known means.

PASSWORD CRACKERS

Password crackers have been used since the inception of penetration testing to accomplish just what the name implies. They are a tool that when run against a user's password makes an attempt to find out what it is. Basically, it is a program that can decrypt passwords, or otherwise disable password protection. L0pht crack is a common Windows SAM-encrypted, password-deciphering tool used today, and there is a plethora of other password cracker tools on the Internet for basically any type of operating system and application. These tools are now used to give administrators the opportunity to reveal forgotten or lost passwords, or check that the password policy is being enforced.

Tools that are developed to help users and administrators can often be used in a negative manner as well. A password cracker tool uses different methods to achieve its objective: some use word lists, phrases, or other combinations, including numbers and symbols to find out what the user has set as a password. The tool itself enters word after word at a very high speed until the correct password is identified. Password crackers operate on the theory that eventually, given enough time, combinations, and permutations, the tool will eventually determine the password. Once a password is "cracked" it allows the tester (or hacker) to assume the user's identity, thereby granting them access to all the data they are normally permitted to access.

An emerging trend is what is called algorithmic-based attacks. With a password cracker that performs such a task, typically a system would have to be compromised and a set of programs run in order to determine the algorithm used by the system. Once the algorithm has been obtained, the passwords are reverse-engineered very quickly.

Ironically, more password cracking tools focus on Microsoft Windows and its applications; however, any system can fall vulnerable to a password cracking tool. During a penetration test, the password cracker tool is often used against password files on systems to determine the level of password security followed throughout the organization. In some cases a hacker may have stolen one user's identity by guessing her password, only to allow him to download a password file on a critical system, run a password cracker against the file, and then gain root access to the entire network, allowing him to cause even more destruction.

ROOTKITS

A rootkit is a collection of tools, or a program itself, a hacker installs on a system once she has gained initial access to that system. Even though the hacker must first gain access to the system before she can install a rootkit, these still pose a high threat to system administrators because of their ease of use and the amount of destruction they can cause.

A rootkit allows a hacker to come back to the compromised system at a later time, or to run services remotely on the system without being detected. This is done by installing a backdoor daemon, stemmed from the rootkit itself, which usually runs on a different port than the typical service they utilize. Rootkits typically contain such subprograms as network sniffers, log cleanup scripts, and Trojan backdoor daemons within the tool. The rootkit uses binaries, which it replaces, making the hacker invisible to monitoring tactics and system administrators.

During a penetration test, a tester will install these on a system to see first if they are able to install them, and second, whether they are noticed, and how often they can come back and use the utilities installed within the rootkit. A tester may first install a password cracker tool to gain a user's password and identity on a system, and then use that access to install the rootkit.

One of the most popular rootkits is the Linux rootkit. This rootkit has undergone massive changes throughout history. Stemming from April 1996 with version 1, these massive changes have morphed into rootkits such as the T0rn rootkit and the lion worm. The most common method of identification of a rootkit is by utilizing a file integrity checker such as Tripwire to identify system changes.

APPLICATIONS

Applications can open a system up to a plethora of vulnerabilities. This is due to two main reasons: the application itself is not configured securely, thus allowing a hacker to gain access to a system through the misconfigured application, and the system itself is not secure, thereby making the application run in a nonsecure manner. During a penetration test, three main types of applications are assessed for the level of threat they expose the organization to: Web, distributed, and customer applications.

WEB APPLICATIONS

Three popular Web server applications used in many companies today are Apache, IIS, and iPlanet. There are various exploits that can be tested against each Web server application during the penetration test. One would be to attempt to exploit a vulnerability through the CGI scripts. The CGI scripts present a large opportunity for exploitable bugs in the Web server. Scripts can present two security vulnerabilities: they can leak information about the host system itself, helping a malicious user to break in, and scripts that process remote user input, such as contents of a form or a "searchable index" command, may be vulnerable to attacks in which the malicious user tricks it into executing commands. Even though CGI scripts typically run on the server as the user "nobody," that user still has enough privileges to mail out the system password file, examine the network configuration, or launch a log-in session on a high-numbered port. Whisker, an open source tool, is often used to scan Web servers for CGI script vulnerabilities.

Another popular tactic in attempting to exploit a vulnerability on a Web server is to try to execute a command through the HTML directory itself. For best practice reasons, all HTML pages should reside in a separate directory with limited user access permissions. No other files, programs, or applications should reside in that directory. A tester may attempt to enter in a random URL with specific attributes to exploit the Web server. These URLs typically include suffixes such as .exe, .sh, or login.pl. This would permit the tester to execute potentially destructive commands remotely. During the penetration test, the configuration of the Web applications is analyzed, examining user permissions and directory structure of the Web server itself.

ActiveX is another area of concern with Web applications. There have been several instances allowing code execution on another user's machine. Although this is not a common method of attack, there are still viable security concerns with ActiveX and workstation builds should have their browsers set with security in mind.

DISTRIBUTED APPLICATIONS

Distributed applications include those that permit users throughout the company to access them in order to do their jobs properly. Typically, distributed applications are those that include a database, mail, or collaboration server. A database server may contain sensitive HR information about the employees within the organization, and another that contains highly sensitive financial data on the organization itself may be used by finance. During a penetration test, tests may be focused on trying to exploit applications from within the network directly between two departments. All testing that occurs during an ethical hack does not necessarily have to be based on external or Internet access to the systems. Two departments that need to transfer data to and from each other need to ensure only those permitted can do so, along with ensuring no one within the organization can see this data. For example, HR and finance may need to share certain aspects of the same internal database system. HR may need to access employee data, whereas finance would need access to payroll information. There are two highly sensitive data threads that need to be heavily controlled in regard to user access. During the penetration test, not only does the tester ensure that HR and finance cannot access each other's data, but that other departments, such as the helpdesk, cannot access anything residing on that database. A tester finding the database server can attempt to exploit a vulnerability either by attempting to gain a user's password, or using a password cracker, and then accessing the system to retrieve the highly sensitive information.

CUSTOMER APPLICATIONS

Customer applications are those to which the organization's customers need access, either through a partner agreement or an end-user agreement. An example would be a banking company that provides its customers access to their account information over the Internet. Typically, the Web server the user accesses first is only the front end, with the back end being a database server housing the user's entire pertinent account information. A typical exploit for a tester to do in this scenario is attempt to exploit a vulnerability on the database server through a variety of means.

With the increasing demand of the need for database servers to support Web applications, they can be implemented in a manner that is not secure. If a Web server is accessible from the Internet and queries a database server to retrieve customer information, the Web server and database server must be in constant communication. However, even though they must communicate often, they must be separated securely. The Web server and database server should not be on the same network, instead, separated at a minimum by a firewall. One sure test during a penetration test will be to attempt to access the database server from the Internet, and attempt to retrieve customer information directly. A secure configuration would ensure the traffic between the two devices is configured so that any traffic coming from the Internet to the Web server resides over HTTP(s) and then when the Web server queries the database server, it must transfer to the database protocol (e.g., MySQL TCP 3306), and all traffic from the Web server to the Internet is only over HTTP(s). This ensures that the Web server cannot be used as a stepping stone to get to the database server maliciously.

WARDIALING

One of the earliest forms of attack was using the phone system to gain access to a company's assets. Several years ago this was an extremely successful method for attacking remote systems because prior to VPN technology most if not all remote access was provided by modems on servers or terminal devices on the company's network. Even though VPNs have become the standard for remote access using the Internet, there still exists an abundance of modems used for remote access services. In addition to modems owned and maintained by customers, dial-in remote access services provided by service providers such as AT&T, WorldCom, and others use virtual modems to provide connectivity into a Frame Relay connection that typically has a PVC (Private Virtual Circuit) into the customer's network. There are organizations that have modems for backup in case the primary line goes down, or alternate access to critical systems for maintenance purposes. Many companies buy products with maintenance agreements that require dedicated vendor access via a modem. To add to the risk of attack, many of these systems have default usernames and passwords, some not changeable!

A case in point is a printing services company provides large digital printers for their customers. The printers are connected to the network and have a phone line attached to allow the vendor to track the use of the printer and status of the system. Based on a flaw in the printer, the modem provides PPP (Point-to-Point Protocol) and IP services to the remote system, and not simply terminal access to the required information. Moreover, the printer has a hard-coded username and password to access. Therefore, once a hacker knew the telephone number he would have complete network access through the printer. In fact, the vulnerability still existed at the writing of this book.

Finally, there are users who install modems in their computers at work to have personal remote access from home. It is not uncommon for employees to install a modem, a digital line splitter, and install PCAnywhere. All they have to do is call the main number, enter their extension, and off they go. If a hacker were to learn of this, the potential for access would be substantial. No matter the reasoning for their use, modems exist all over the place and if not configured properly can wreak havoc.

To perform a wardialing test, all the tester (or hacker) needs is software, a modem, a phone line, and a list of numbers to dial. The test simply involves dialing numbers in search of a system that may be exploited in some manner to gain access. However, without some precautionary measures, the test can be fraught with problems.

- *Randomize.* You may recall the movie *War Games* where Matthew Broderick places a phone on a computer receptacle and starts dialing thousands of numbers sequentially: 123 to 0001, 123 to 0002, 123 to 0003, and so on. It did not take long for phreakers to start the same practice and eventually the phone companies caught on to this practice. Now, if many numbers are called sequentially, the phone system will generate an alarm. Moreover, some phone switches are configured to look for random fast dialing of numbers in an attempt to find people abusing the phone system.

- *After Hours.* Because the test uses an automated tool and the goal is to find a computer system and not a human, wardialing is best done overnight to avoid interrupting people at their desks and causing a general nuisance.
- *Take Your Time.* Even though many wardialing applications can operate several modems simultaneously and dial thousands of numbers in a very short time period the test is still performed over several days to avoid detection by the target as well as the phone company. As with dialing numbers sequentially, the phone system will generate alarms when many numbers are dialed from a single line.

A typical wardialing session is performed in steps and leverages the tool's functionality and automation as much as possible. These steps can be performed in a single dialing session, or broken up into phases performed over several days. Much of this depends on the amount of phone numbers that need to be dialed. In some cases, a number is dialed, the target determined, some form of investigative procedure is performed, and if configured to do so, the tool can begin to attack the remote system in an effort to gain access. However, wardialing tests are predominantly performed in stages that are used to reduce the number of valid phone numbers and isolate target systems. Steps can include the following:

- *Number Scanning.* The first step is to determine which telephone numbers are connected to computers, fax machines, modems, or simply do not answer. Usually, these numbers are logged as one of these systems and busy signals are retried until an answer is received or the preconfigured number of tries is exceeded.
- *System Type Scanning.* Once all the different systems are identified they are categorized and the investigative process is focused on specific numbers. For example, the tool may have discovered 37 fax machines in the pool of phone numbers, 6 of which are fax modems that may be able to provide terminal access if the tool can negotiate a modem protocol rather than a fax protocol.
- *Banner Collection.* For every number that answered with a modem tone, there is the possibility that the system will provide a banner communicating the type of system and status.
- *Default Access.* There are some situations where the system is configured to allow access simply based on a username or group name without a password. This is sometimes used to accommodate maintenance access or poorly configured systems.
- *Brute Force.* When a username and password combination is required, this is the act of testing as many passwords as possible. Typically this is supported by a collection of commonly used passwords passed to the remote system sequentially until one of them works. Another aspect is simply defining the scope of characters to use and the assumed length of the password and allowing the system to step through each until the password is cracked.

There are several types of tones that can be received by a phone call, such as a fax machine, modem, or a modem acting as a fax machine. Tools that are designed to perform wardialing are typically capable of determining the type of tone and will attempt to convince a fax modem to switch to a terminal mode to promote access. Once a tone is established a protocol can be employed for traditional communications that support applications such as telnet, terminal emulators, or remote desktop (e.g., Citrix, PCAnywhere). At this point the remote system is identified and the attack ensues.

NETWORK

In performing a penetration test, it is important to attempt to exploit the network devices that are critical to the overall security posture of the organization. This includes the network infrastructure, the routers and gateways between the Internet and intranet, intranet and extranet (client networks), and internal gateways to more secure networks.

PERIMETER

The perimeter of a company's network is responsible for protecting the network behind it from external entities. This can be the Internet, intranet, or extranet. Firewalls are the most popular way to ensure the perimeter of any network is secure. During a penetration test, firewalls are often closely examined in order to ensure a high level of threat does not exist due to a misconfigured firewall. One tactic is to ensure compartmentalization exists on the firewalls. Each interface on the firewall should be assigned a security level. The DMZ, which houses Internet applications, and an internal segment, which contains the server holding company-sensitive data, should not be connected to same interface of the firewall. This design flaw is easily detected, because access to and from the DMZ and internal segment would not pass through the firewall, allowing all services through. Another exploit usually identified during the penetration test would be to ensure that any service not needed is prohibited through the firewall to another segment. Usually HTTP(s) should be the only service permitted inbound to the Web servers in a DMZ. If an exploit were attempted from the Internet, and the tester identified that not only was HTTP accessible, but also such vulnerability-filled services such as NTP, SNMP, and even FTP, this would be considered a high-level threat to the company.

NETWORK NODES

Routers are devices to gain access to networks. During the penetration test, the tester needs to ensure that at a minimum the following characteristics have been implemented on the routers. Do the routers inspect traffic on the TCP/IP layer with packet filters, and do they drop any malformed or fragmented packets? Has NAT been implemented to hide IP addresses for all systems, or at least the critical systems? A security vulnerability within a router is allowing source routing of a packet, which is enabled by default on some systems. Meaning, if a hacker knows the company's network is a private range of IP addresses, it can't route over the Internet, but the hacker can traceroute to the edge device and then sourceroute the packet to attack the private net from the Internet. How is access to the routers permitted? Is it username/password based, or two-factor authentication, such as through the user of SecurID? If the answer to any of these is "No," then the tester has a multitude of tests to perform in order to attempt an exploit against a router within the network infrastructure. Perhaps the edge router has a modem attached to it, which has been left enabled. During the wardialing exercise, access to this router would be identified, and then the process of attempting to gain access would be followed.

SERVICES AND AREAS OF CONCERN

There are many opportunities for hackers to infiltrate your networks and systems by leveraging weaknesses in applications, operating systems, and services. This section provides a brief introduction to some of these areas of concern and typical vulnerabilities associated with them. Some of these application and service exploits have been available for a number of years; others were discovered fairly recently. Hackers have the time, patience, and resources to discover these vulnerabilities long before developers. It goes without saying that better coding up front would help prevent the almost daily uncovering of a new vulnerability.

Configuration by inexperienced administrators could also lead to a higher level of exploitation by leaving unnecessary or often vulnerable services enabled. These services, if not configured properly, could lead to a system compromise from a source both internal and external. By establishing baseline builds for both Windows and UNIX environments, companies can reduce the risks associated with these unnecessary services. In addition, establishing or outsourcing penetration testing for your systems and networks will provide valuable insight to those applications and services that need to be evaluated by a risk assessment.

SERVICES

There is no prejudice when it comes to vulnerable services and operating systems. Just about every service available to an administrator has some sort of vulnerability attached to it. To make matters worse, services are necessary to allow the system to function, and to provide business functionality. Services can be exploited through a variety of methods during a penetration test. Prior to testing the systems for exploits, a clear understanding of the system's functionality is helpful to avoid testing services that shouldn't be running in the first place. In some cases, FTP may not be a required service to be running on a system, so the removal of it would be the recommendation instead of stating a specific exploit against the FTP service. Often the administrators of a large network are not sure what services are running on a system. For this purpose, the tester should run a tool against all the systems in question in order to clearly identify what services the system is running; such tools include NMAP, Nessus, and ISS scanner.

Services Started by Default

Many operating systems install and start unnecessary services by default. Although these services do serve a purpose, most are not needed for the system and applications to function properly. These services include sendmail, savecore, rpcbind, FTP, telnet for UNIX, and Internet Information Server (IIS) for Windows NT/2000/XP.

Every effort should be made to contain these services and disable them if not needed. We recommend the creation of a "standard" base build for both UNIX and Windows systems that has many of the security recommendations already configured. This will assist new administrators coming into the company, as well as simplifying security's task of identifying exactly which systems are running which services when new vulnerabilities are identified.

WINDOWS PORTS

Microsoft Windows allows systems to share files or folders across the network using Windows network shares. The Server Message Block (SMB) and the Common Internet File System (CIFS) protocols are the mechanisms that permit a system to modify remote files as if they were locally stored. The Sircam virus (CERT Advisory 2001-22) and Nimba worm (CERT Advisory 2001-26) were spread rapidly by discovering unprotected network shares and placing a copy of themselves there. Many systems, especially desktop users, open their systems up to co-workers for convenience, or sharing of files, when in fact they are opening them up to hackers that turn the convenience into malicious activity.

The tester should determine whether sharing is necessary before attempting any exploits. A scanning tool such as ISS, NMAP, or Nessus can determine which systems have file sharing enabled; then it is best to evaluate whether it is needed. If sharing files across the network is a business requirement then the tester can attempt to authenticate a system without being required to enter a username and password. They should be configured to require a user to authenticate before connecting. All ports used for Windows sharing should also be blocked at the network perimeter; these ports include TCP and UDP 137-139 and TCP and UDP 445. These ports should also be restricted internally through the firewalls, only permitted when a source and destination IP address is included, along with the user authentication.

Null Connection

Microsoft built an "administrator" backdoor, if you will, into their Windows products. This default "backdoor" is an anonymous connection called an interprocess connection share or IPC$. It is called a "null" connection because it is available for any Microsoft Windows machine to access that share. Why is this a "bad" thing to have? Because it allows any other Microsoft computer to access your "C:" drive; the main partition for your operating environment. Hackers can place Trojans and viruses and even obtain password files that are contained in this "default" share.

REMOTE PROCEDURE CALLS (RPC)

Remote Procedure Calls is a service that allows programs on one system to execute procedures on a second system by passing data and retrieving the results. It is a widely used service for distributed network services such as remote administration, NFS, and NIS. In most cases, RPC services execute with root privileges, therefore, when an RPC service is exploited, it can provide the hacker with root access to the system.

RPC services are usually exploited through buffer overflow attacks because the RPC services do not perform sufficient error checking or input validation. Some examples of RPC services include rcp.ttdbserverd, rpc.cmsd, rpc.statd, rpc.mountd, sadmind, cachefs, and snmpXdmid. In order to ensure exploitation is not possible, the tester should check to make sure that RPC TCP Port 111 and the RPC loopback TCP and UPD Ports 32770 to 32789 are blocked at the network perimeter.

Specifically on systems that require the use of NFS, the tester should ensure that host/IP-based export lists are implemented, file systems should only be read only, or no-suid, and "nfsbug" should be used to scan for vulnerabilities. If one of the above is not implemented, chances are the tester will find an exploit on the NFS server using the RPC service.

Simple Network Management Protocol (SNMP)

The Simple Network Management Protocol is used extensively in all organizations to remotely monitor and configure almost all types of TCP/IP-enabled devices. SNMP communication consists of exchanged messages between the management systems and the devices that run the SNMP agent. The method by which the messages are handled and the authentication mechanism both have significant exploitations associated with them.

SNMP is used by network management systems to determine the "health" of a networked device. These devices range from routers and switches to servers and desktops. SNMP is a cleartext protocol as discussed earlier. The information gathered by this protocol can be used by hackers to gain valuable knowledge such as the OS version, failed hardware, the managing NMS server IP, subnet mask, and internal and external IP information. There are two "default" network paths for SNMP, public (read only) and private (read/write). Because SNMP is a default service running on your network devices (routers and switches), you can bet that unless someone changed the default community strings, they are still set to public and private. Anyone with an SNMP tool can gain the information discussed earlier via the "public" community string. If they have the "private" string they now have write access on your device and can change information, and take control if you will, of your device.

To prevent these issues, SNMP needs to be configured properly. Change the names of the default community strings to something not easily guessed such as a polyalphanumeric character set. Then remove the default strings from the devices. Another suggestion, although not cost effective, would be to create a separate "management" network path for your SNMP traffic. Ideally, you don't want your user/information traffic over the same wire used for administration or management traffic. Of course, it goes without saying if you don't need the service, turn it off. If you do need it, make sure you keep it patched and updated.

Berkeley Internet Name Domain (BIND)

BIND is an application used to provide users and applications with domain name service. It is a very popular and common target for attacks because it is the most widely distributed DNS software and the servers running BIND are usually accessible from the Internet. Moreover, it does not help that a new vulnerability is exposed every three or four months, offering yet another form of access to attackers.

Many versions of BIND are vulnerable to exploits that allow attackers to gain control of the system or extract information to help them exploit the DNS server or another system on the network. These exploits typically involve buffer overflows and denial-of-service attacks.

BIND should not be installed on servers running applications other than DNS. For those needing to run BIND, system administrators should keep up to date on the latest versions and/or patches for BIND. BIND should also be configured to run as a nonprivileged account and in a secured environment such as "chroot."

COMMON GATEWAY INTERFACE (CGI)

CGI scripts are used by Web servers as a means to provide collecting Web user information, execution of programs, and accessibility to files requested by users of the Web site. CGI programs normally run with the same permissions as the Web server software. Sometimes, if not configured correctly, these permissions are of a privileged user such as "root." Hackers can exploit vulnerable CGI programs, most of which are installed by default.

CGI programs are readily available on the Internet and some companies even have internal developers to create these programs for custom Web applications. Developers are constantly challenged to include security practices when they are creating these programs. Elements such as running the programs with least-privilege or using valid buffers to prevent overflows are two examples of creating and implementing programs with slightly more resistance to attack. Another would be ensuring data arrays process their data correctly. All too often a program accepts data entry from a user, places it in an array or variable that stores the information in memory, and then proceeds to process the data without checking first if the entry was valid. An example of this would be a cross-scripting vulnerability that interprets the data input and forces it out to the shell for execution, thus allowing a user or attacker to execute other binary code available on the system such as an FTP session or a remote shell.

Programming a functioning system and ensuring security as considered throughout the process may seem difficult, but with standards, best practices, and policies supporting the process, it can be much less stressful. There are many sites and resources that provide information on known vulnerabilities in certain types of programming styles and on what should be avoided. Armed with supporting information, many development departments should have more than enough data to create sound applications.

CLEARTEXT SERVICES

Services that use unencrypted data present another challenge for administrators. These services transmit their data in the clear, which allows anyone "watching" on the same network the ability to retrieve that information, most importantly user IDs and passwords. These two key pieces of information will be used to log in to the system the valid user attempted to log in to when the information was gathered. Services such as FTP, telnet, and e-mail are frequently used by everyday users, especially e-mail. All it takes is a hacker with a sniffer tool to easily capture this data.

Consider using OpenSSH (freeware) or Secure Shell (commercial software) in place of FTP and telnet. This software set actually encrypts the data between the two points. Users should be reminded that e-mail is a very insecure means of transmitting very important data. There are tools available such as SMIME and the now defunct, yet still available, PGP to encrypt e-mail traffic containing important information.

Much of the adoption of VPN technology can be attributed to these types of exposures. Having the ability to communicate many different types of communication, including e-mail and internalized Web services, is a valuable reprieve from hackers gaining sensitive information or user credentials.

NETWORK FILE SYSTEM (NFS)

UNIX systems utilize NFS to share files and directories and drives across the network. NFS is insecure in its natural state. Most administrators allow read and write access to everyone rather than narrow down the list to a select few. The issue lies with NFS running on an Internet-facing server. This provides attackers, anyone really, with access to the files, directories, or drives on that system. The attacker is only limited to the actual permissions applied to the mounted system. Meaning, if the "world" or "other" group has write privileges, then so does your attacker. They can place any files or remove files from your NFS share. There are other vulnerabilities within an unpatched "nfsd," the daemon that runs NFS, that gives an attacker root privileges.

Your best defense is a good offense. Make sure your NFS is configured properly. Block access to your NFS server from the outside at the firewall. Make sure all your files, directories, and devices have the correct permissions. Most important, only allow users or servers that need access, access to the shares. And above all, make sure your administrators stay current on the patches.

DOMAIN NAME SERVICE (DNS)

DNS does the name resolution portion of BIND. It translates a domain name into an IP address and vice versa. Applications use DNS exclusively to look up address information when they need to send information over the Internet. Without DNS, users would have to know the exact IP address every time they wanted to surf the Web or send an e-mail. DNS is critical to the Internet.

Attackers realize how critically important DNS is with regard to information moving on the Internet. To this end, they have a variety of means by which they can deny access to or manipulate data from the DNS servers. Due to the fact that most DNS servers exist outside a firewall, it is very easy for attackers to employ a DoS attack by flooding the server with DNS requests. A poorly configured server will stop responding to legitimate requests to answer the bogus requests from the attacker.

Attackers can also "hijack" a DNS server IP address and respond to legitimate requests from unsuspecting users sending them to Web sites containing Trojans, or worse, they are able to obtain user names and passwords, credit card information, or bank account information. Moreover, DNS servers can be poisoned with alternate IP addresses to provide replies to users' requests with an alternate IP address to force them to a different site. There have been several instances of hackers defacing Web sites when in reality, they simply forwarded the requests to a different server altogether.

Another aspect of DNS that many hackers and testers alike will attempt to do is a zone transfer. Seeing that DNS has all the IP addresses associated with names of systems, it can be helpful for the attacker to have the IP addresses of systems accessible from the Internet. If not configured properly, the DNS system will provide all the IP addresses to a general request, revealing all the addresses of the systems supported by that DNS server. In the past, this was an enormous problem because many companies provided internal system IP addresses on their only DNS server that resided on the Internet. It was also typical for companies to provide external systems, such as remote access systems or intranet servers, to remote employees and attempt to hide in the tall grass of the Internet to avoid attack, assuming a hacker could not guess the name of the system and therefore would not have the IP address to attack. DNS information can be helpful in formulating an attack and assisting with the identification of the overall structure of the Internet connection. For example, there may be several IP addresses defined in DNS supporting systems behind a firewall. If some of the IP address ends up at a firewall, a hacker knows which systems are behind a firewall or directly accessible to the Internet.

FILE AND DIRECTORY PERMISSIONS

Files and directories are owned by users on a system. This means for other users to access or execute these files, the owner must assign the appropriate level of permission to his files and directories. Permissions are very similar between UNIX and Windows. There are three basics: read, write, and execute. Although there are many more in Windows, UNIX offers a "special" one called "setuid/setguid." Our three basics are self-explanatory. Read gives the owner and anyone in the group permission to "read" the file. Write gives the owner and anyone in the group permission to "write" to the file (Windows calls it modify). And last, execute gives the owner and anyone in the group permission to "execute" the file. These permissions, if not restricted, can lead to vulnerabilities.

You don't want everyone having access to read, write, or execute files without a certain level of trust being established, meaning, Bob in accounting has no need to see Jane's files in receiving and vice versa. Likewise, the CEO doesn't need to execute server cleanup scripts located in the system administrator's directory. This same logic holds true, maybe more so, with users outside your network.

Vulnerabilities exist in file and directory permissions. They can lead to elevated privileges, buffer overflows, and worse, the compromise of your server. Find a balance between keeping your servers secure and application/user functionality.

FTP and Telnet

Besides these two services sending information in cleartext, they are vulnerable to other attacks as well: buffer overflows and brute force password attacks to name just two. System administrators need to ensure the latest patches have been applied to those systems running these services. In most cases, patching your systems will close many of the vulnerabilities. In a brute force attack, however, the hacker will run through a dictionary containing common password combinations. They can guess quite accurately the privileged users on the system. So having one side of the pair combination already in the privileged user and combining that with the brute force attack, they have a very high success rate in compromising your systems.

Another issue with FTP is the fact that some administrators fail to remove or lock down the anonymous or guest account. These accounts, even with read-only access, can still provide some very valuable information about your system. If this service is not configured properly, administrators can give write privileges to these accounts as well, resulting in more serious consequences.

The most widely recommended practice would be to not use these services at all. Replace them with OpenSSH or Secure Shell. If they are required, consider using TCP Wrappers to secure the environment that the users of telnet and FTP will be using. This way your system is relatively secure and the users or applications can still function normally.

Internet Control Message Protocol (ICMP)

ICMP is used mainly by administrators as a quick way to determine if a server or, more appropriately, if an interface on a server is up or down. Ping provides a very simple answer and is one of the most common denial-of-service attacks. One of the first tools created to perform the denial-of-service attack is POD or ping of death. Traceroute on the Windows platform utilizes ICMP and actually provides the path a packet takes to reach that interface, usually in great detail. That detail is used by hackers to find out the IP of your firewall or Internet router. Other ICMP requests include timestamps, network masks, and other useful information. By disabling this protocol at the Internet router and firewall you prevent anyone, not just hackers, from being able to clearly identify your network. Throughout information security history, there have been a small number of tools that have been created to utilize ICMP by pushing malicious data through the encapsulated ICMP packets. Although there are many tools that can be used to scan your network, limiting ICMP is a step in the right direction.

IMAP and POP

Commonly used by Internet e-mail applications, these protocols allow remote users to access their e-mail over the Internet. This means ports have to be open on the firewall to permit this access. Hackers using a firewall scanning tool such as "fire-walk" can determine all the open ports and using known exploits for IMAP and POP can gain access to your network and/or e-mail systems. Also remember this traffic is not usually encrypted, unless you are using SSL.

Proper configuration of both the network and the servers running IMAP and POP can at a minimum lower your risk of compromise. Other steps include keeping current on application patches or updating to a newer version on the software.

NETWORK ARCHITECTURE

Although this might seem a bit obvious to most, this is actually one of the most overlooked flaws in network security. A poorly designed network can allow "unprotected" Internet access into your network. Multi-homed servers and servers in a DMZ are two of the most common sources for intrusion. This is due to the fact that these servers have interfaces that do not pass through a firewall. Servers in a DMZ might be DNS, Web proxy, or mail relays.

A company may only have one DNS server used by both internal and external users. If left inside the network, external users would not be able to resolve names internal to the company without opening DNS ports on the firewall. The same holds true for internal users if the DNS resides outside the firewall. The same principle applies for e-mail users.

It is very important that all angles and network diagrams be reviewed during the turn up of new equipment. Having a network and security engineer on hand during these meetings will help ensure new systems as well as existing systems are kept secure and functional.

13 The Deliverable

All the work from the engagement—materials collected, communications, tasks performed, results from tools, vulnerabilities, and any information about the target—culminate in a final document. Arguably, the company is effectively paying for the deliverable. The actions taken to this point were performed for the sole purpose of expressing the results, and that is where the tipping point of value can materialize: expressing the results.

All too often, the deliverable from an ethical hacking engagement is a collection of numbers, attributes, and cold assuming facts, the assumption of scientific survey results compiled in a manner that is no more insightful to the state of security than that of any other company suffering from the same vulnerabilities.

The deliverable must accomplish two challenges. The technical and pragmatic concerns must be clearly communicated elements of the test that are indisputable and not attached to interpretation of the type of test or actions of the tester. To elaborate, consider a tester exploiting a known weakness, a buffer overflow, in a Web server permitting unencumbered access to the files presented on the Web site. This attack represents a common threat to millions of servers and a typical avenue for hackers wanting to deface Web sites. The document can easily communicate the vulnerability and the potential impact because there is little room for interpretation within the test. If the tester were to use several tools and tactics in combination to pry the hole open to gain control over several business-critical applications, the test immediately falls under scrutiny, especially if the tactics used were not permitted.

This leads us into the second challenge of the deliverable: interpretation. During the initial phases of the test—planning, setting expectations, determining business objectives, and understanding the scope and granularity of the test—it would be sufficiently clear that the advantage of the test is not founded on mimicking a hacker, but rather the ability to operate in a structured approach to expose truly addressable security weaknesses. If planned and executed in a consistent manner, the challenge of interpreting the results, converting from hackerlike actions to business value, is simplified. Once there is a common understanding between the tester and company it is easy to delineate among the significant issues and the lesser points of concern no matter the preordained criticality associated with a vulnerability.

In addition to meeting these two challenges, the secondary role of the deliverable is to act as the catalyst for initiating the integration process. Everything about the deliverable, down to the format, will have an impact on the ability to take what was learned and apply it to have a positive impact on the security posture. Interestingly, the obvious concept of taking the test results and applying them to the realization of security is either overlooked or grossly oversimplified. Typically, the deliverable will list vulnerabilities and recommendations on fixing them. The document is then handed to the security team and exercised. Of course, this does very little to address the disease and treats the symptoms. The hope is to take the results from the test and find opportunities to develop more comprehensive solutions. For example, if the test reveals there are an excessive number of vulnerabilities associated with fixes over six months old, you may want to consider developing a patch management process.

The level of attention paid to creating an insightful deliverable is directly linked to the ability to ultimately realize value from the test. Therefore, a great deal of attention should be paid to the creation of the final documentation. For the company paying for the test, the deliverable should be scrutinized with the intent of converting the information into action.

All too often, companies look at the document in an effort to determine the technical success of the engagement with little concern for interpreting the results in a meaningful fashion. Not seeing the bigger picture of the test is the result of two very basic facts:

1. *Poor Information.* No interpretation is plausible because the only information in the document is a list of vulnerabilities: not very comprehensive when you consider all the intricacies of the test.
2. *Shock Factor.* Some companies are inexperienced in having tests and are shocked by the level of access the tester obtained, so much so that the entire focus is on the seemingly amazing depth the tester made into their network. Obviously, the level of success is based on hundreds of details (most introduced here) that when exposed would not be nearly as impressive. For example, it may be a shock to find that your prankster-friend sneaked into your house and stole your jewelry, until you find out that your alarm system was off and all your windows were open—kind of puts it into perspective.

Several features play an important role in the creation of a deliverable. Initially, you must perform a final analysis against the information collected, detail what was performed, and compare the original objectives to the results. Document the primary components of information provided by the company, such as the security policy, risk analysis data, or previous test results. Finally, the document must be formatted in a manner that presents the data in a form that is easiest to digest considering the focus of the test. For example, social engineering may have been performed, but thanks to the planning session the core reasoning was to find what kind of information was collected from dumpster diving, whereas the data collected about the wireless networks is much less important. Format will ensure the driving questions are answered without losing the overall picture of the test.

Additionally, the format can be based on the audience for the information. For example, highly technical details will not help the executives; they want the short and sweet version. In contrast, if the tester took over the E-commerce server, the developers are going to want to know every detail. Document format is an important characteristic for companies to be cognizant of when planning the test.

FINAL ANALYSIS

Throughout the engagement, analysis was being performed on the results of threads and groups to look for anomalies associated with inherent risks and vulnerabilities that may surface without being directly observed. Much in the same manner that the soft objective during the enumeration phase was performed to discover vulnerabilities based on information collected, the final analysis is an opportunity to take a broader look at the collection of information and provide some insights about the overall state of the company's security posture.

It is also important to begin to differentiate between high-risk and low-risk vulnerabilities. In many cases, this is not difficult, but has the potential to get very complex quickly if you are not prepared. A vulnerability that allows the changing of Web site data could be considered a moderate to high risk. However, this can only be assumed when the importance or value of the Web site is evaluated. Once again, this is representative of the importance of having asset value metrics prior to the test.

Depending on the complexity of the environment, the classification of the vulnerability in relation to risk can be challenging. Without the value of the data known, the overall risk a vulnerability symbolizes is left to interpretation.

Problems begin when there is no asset valuation to draw from or the business relies very heavily on all the systems that were exposed. In the latter case, the problem arises when trying to label one threat as more risk than another when the results of each have a negative impact on systems of equal value in the mind of the target.

Without asset valuation metrics, the depth of the attack thread, or layers penetrated, differentiate the final risk assigned to the vulnerability. To assign the level of risk based on depth introduces a level of interpretation of complexity of the attack and the number of systems that were involved in the target's demise. For example, in Figure 13.1 the systems (represented as circles) to the left are near the Internet,

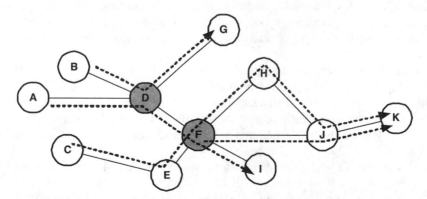

FIGURE 13.1 Establishing Level of Risk Based on Depth and Relationships within the Target

such as on the DMZ, and the systems on the right are deep within the target's network. Using systems A, B, and C as the entry points for three different threads, the tester finds a couple of paths to system K. The final K-attack group is made up of two primary threads: A-D-F-hijack F-J-K and C-E-F-H-J-K. To determine the level of risk to K, one has to consider the vulnerabilities in A, D, F, H, and J. Moreover, considering the thread starting at B and getting to D, there exists another potential launching point to get to F. The vulnerability in K, according to information on the Internet, is listed as critical and the one for F is listed as low, or informational. However, given that F is the tipping point for gaining access to K, the vulnerability, for this organization, is considered critical.

In this example, which system or threads of attack represent the greatest risk to the company? To answer this, you have to consider all aspects of the test. For example, there are thousands of script kiddies on the Internet that could successfully attack systems A and C, whereas only hackers could exploit system F. Moreover, given that the attack on system K was assisted by information collected via social engineering, the viability of internal threats must be weighed. When comparing only the vulnerabilities, the answer is that systems A and C represent the greatest risk. The vulnerabilities are easy to exploit and the likelihood of success is high. In addition, the downstream impacts have the potential to be damaging.

However, after including all the information from the test, system F appears to be a serious problem child given the links to other systems. To conclude F is a high risk with a vulnerability listed as low would not be possible without all this information taken into consideration.

By articulating the intensity of a vulnerability and the resulting attack thread, the company is made aware of the chain of events that led to a system's exploitation. If the tester uses a collection of vulnerabilities to dig deeper into a network only to penetrate a nonessential system, it cannot be readily assumed that there are no other similar systems on the same network segment that are not critical to the business. Therefore, systems K and F may be expendable, but once the threads and groups are detailed in a document, the company may determine there are other undetected and highly valuable systems at risk.

Ultimately, the goal of the classification is to provide a description of the vulnerability and how it relates to the computing environment, which will be compared to the associated business risks. Once the risk of the vulnerabilities is identified, a plan for mitigation can be created that best reflects the short- and long-term plans of the company.

Results are categorized as critical, warning, or informational to communicate the susceptibility the vulnerability represents to systems in the company's network. What's important is that the final analysis is designed to categorize the vulnerabilities identified and exploited (or assumed exploitable) based on the depth and overall impact on systems the hole represents to the company, not just the default ranking.

- *Critical.* Critical findings are those that place the enterprise at a high degree of risk. These types of threats are usually recommended to be corrected immediately, and can often be brought to the attention of the White Team during the test. The critical classification is usually assigned to vulnerabilities that have a high threat potential in the current environment.

- *Warning.* A warning is representative of a threat to the company that needs to be addressed in a meaningful timeframe. It is not a risk that poses an immediate threat to the enterprise; however, it could have grave repercussions if not corrected in the near future.
- *Informational.* Informational risks that are identified during a penetration test are those that pose a low level of risk to the organization, but in any case, need to be fixed just as the other two previously discussed. This classification of the analysis of the data collected during the penetration test is included in the final deliverable to provide additional remediation plans for the enterprise. These can sometimes include proactive measures to ensure the enterprise is protected on an ongoing basis after the penetration testing is completed. It also helps to ensure that if a third party were to come back to the enterprise, security controls would have improved within the enterprise and the same identical issues would not be discovered again.

POTENTIAL ANALYSIS

At the completion of the penetration test, all the results are gathered together and reviewed in their entirety with the goal of building containers that can be linked together to draw conclusions. There are several methods for doing this, but the best point to start at is collecting information in phases (representing the phase in which the information was obtained). In each phase there are areas representing the specific activity. For example, reconnaissance may have areas of collected data from trashcans or Web pages. Within the enumeration phase, areas may contain information detailing open ports on UNIX systems, open ports on Microsoft servers, and an area dedicated to applications identified. For the exploitation phase, areas are identified exploitations with the appropriate threads assigned. If groups were associated with any of the threads, they need to be added as well.

Demonstrated in Figure 13.2, the information—not just the tasks—is combined to evaluate the level of criticality associated with the entire act. By taking these elements and combining them, the tester can begin to construct the message that will ultimately appear in the documentation.

There are several points worth mentioning. First, the initial collection of data constructs a logical path from starting point to endpoint. Each area will have a risk associated with it in some form. For example, an advisory published by CERT may detail a vulnerability found by the tester. Based on CERT's definition, the level of risk is critical. However, to get to the point to exploit that vulnerability, given the specifics of the company's environment, the calculated risk may be much less. Therefore, each area within a phase may have a stated risk considering the unique environment of the company. When combined, the path to exploitation may reduce or increase the risk level based on the entire process for that company.

Another point is that once all the data is collected and assigned a risk (sometimes based on the tester's experience in exploiting that element) the different areas can

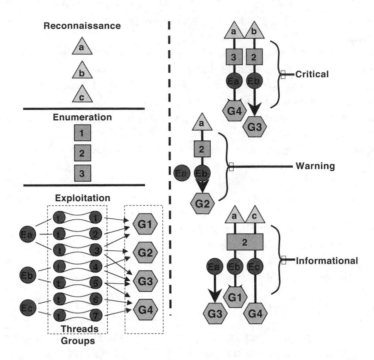

FIGURE 13.2 Collecting Information in Groups and Comparing to Determine Criticality

be combined in different ways to evaluate the level of severity associated with a given path a hacker *may* pursue. By far, this is one of the most valuable elements of the final analysis and one of the most difficult for some companies to grasp. Using Figure 13.2 as a guide, consider the combination on the right labeled "warning."

Triangle "a" may be a message board discussion captured by the tester, which offers some information about a server configuration. Enumeration square "2" is the result of scanning systems and listing a set of open ports. One of the ports was initially unidentifiable during the vulnerability analysis phase. Then in the exploitation phase, a server with certain characteristics was found and several threads were used to establish a group (G2) used to gain access. These combine to represent the primary attach "Eb." Later, it was concluded that exploitation "Ea" could have been used to get to the same point. The important factor in this example is that none of these were linked during the test. Only after the test is complete does the tester realize there is a potential path to a successful attack.

The best representation of this in other forms of security assessments is risk analysis. Some companies will define a level of importance to a business element. For example, the CEO of a hospital may state that patient health care information is classified as sensitive—the highest level—based on HIPAA requirements. After assigning levels of classification based on business demands, controls are defined, each with a set of metrics and supporting elements. Finally, risk is evaluated based on the level of threat. Finally, policies are used to merge all these components to determine the calculated risk based on applied controls for valued assets. The final

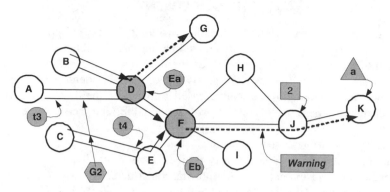

FIGURE 13.3 Potential Analysis Based on Identified Systems

analysis is very similar with a slightly different objective. Tasks, or acts of a hacker are rated, overlaid with information required to perform the task, then mapped against the specifics of the company's unique architecture. By interchanging these phases and their areas while maintaining the associated values, the "potential" of a threat and/or vulnerability can be more accurately determined, even if it was not directly tested.

To see how this relates back to the final analysis, Figure 13.3 depicts our earlier avenues of attack. Now we can relate the reconnaissance, enumeration, and exploit threads and groups from Figure 13.2 to the potential of attacks within the network.

Earlier, we determined the constructed potential vulnerability labeled "warning" was founded on threads "t3" and "t4" within "Eb" making group "G2." These can be translated to the viability of attack on system K thanks to "Ea," information "a," and collected data from "2." Therefore, the threads "t3" and "t4" allow the tester to get to system F, all represented as group G2. Based on pulling data from system J to F, the enumeration element "2" combined with an e-mail (a) found on a newsgroup about system K, the total exposure is rated as a warning.

The fact that you can base a level of risk on a system without directly testing that system is tough for many people to accept. Of course, conditions must exist that promote potential vulnerability analysis. First, a collaboration between the tester and the target company is required. Second, the security of the organization must be in good shape. To perform this on a poorly secured network would lead to dozens of potential vulnerabilities providing little value. Finally, the company must consider security as a core element to business success and realize the inherent limitations of the tester. At the end of a potential vulnerability analysis, the tester must ask himself, "If I had more time, could I have succeeded in attacking system J or even system K?" If the answer is "Yes," then you have to consider it a valid conclusion. Also, you can replace the word "time" in the question with all forms of limitations placed on the tester. For example, "I would have been successful if I could have used a certain tool, or been permitted to use a Trojan, or wardialing were allowed."

The goal of performing analysis at the conclusion of the test makes up for some limitations and missed opportunities. Final analysis is an opportunity to extrapolate untested options that a hacker may seek to gain access.

THE DOCUMENT

Every company formats their deliverables differently. They range from slightly modified versions of standard reports created from tools to a detailed analysis based on the information collected. Some professional services companies will categorize the information to communicate the level of risk for each identified vulnerability. Nevertheless, when employing a value-based framework, the deliverable will be a comprehensive perspective on security risk when taking into account the observed environment.

The deliverable represents the conclusion of the engagement, or at least the testing phase of a much larger security project. It is critical that the content of the final presentation of the data and the information structure clearly reflect the goals defined during the planning phase and be aligned with overall business objectives. Another aspect of the deliverable format is meeting the expectations of the company. For example, there are many situations where the format must meet specific requirements so it can be used effectively within the company.

Granted, some deliverables are simply the output of the tools and more than enough to be valuable to the company depending on the scope of the engagement and the original goals. It is not to insinuate you need 400 pages of detailed analysis to convey the results of the test, but there must be an association of the content to the reasoning of the test.

If the deliverable is not specifically structured to represent the findings in a manner that is representative of the stated objectives, not only will the organization be challenged to find value in the overall test, but it will also have great difficulty in integrating the results. Although the ethical hack may only last several days or weeks, the remediation process can last for months, even years. The deliverable can be a clear map to a successful security posture, or can lead the company down a misdirected path that does not provide any increase in overall security.

The deliverable, at a minimum, should convey each vulnerability, which ones were exploited, how they were exploited, and the results. This can also include assumed vulnerabilities based on the final analysis of the data collected.

After presenting the basic vulnerability information, the deliverable should present the findings in a matrix that ranks them based on specific attributes of the vulnerability and compares them to business demands and requirements. Once the matrix is complete, a mapping of recommendations can be formulated to support the company in investing time and energy into completing specific tasks to move to a secure posture in the straightest line.

Of course, the line to successful mitigation may not be the least expensive or the shortest, but it will be the most effective approach given the desired security posture of the company and the most critical risks. The recommendations should be respective of the costs, time to execute, and overall level of skill (or difficulty) required to accomplish them.

The difficulty in mitigating a vulnerability is usually associated with the skills required, scope of effort, and timeframe. For example, if it is recommended that the company needs to upgrade 120 firewalls in four countries in three weeks with only three skilled employees, it represents a significant level of difficulty in the remediation.

Other forms of difficulty arise when several departments within the organization require more collaboration and interdepartmental planning than traditionally experienced. A development department may meet with the networking and UNIX group once a quarter, but based on the remediation plan, they will have to work much more closely and regularly, possibly representing some difficulty in project management and extraneous project initiatives taking priority for one group leaving the others waiting.

The following is an introduction to the overall format of the deliverable:

- Executive summary
- Present findings
- Planning and operational summary
- Rank vulnerabilities based on business goals and needs
- Defining the processes and tasks employed during each phase
- Present recommendations based on a timeline founded on risk mitigation
- Outline any predetermined exceptions by the company
- Final analysis and potential analysis with levels of risk in not mitigating
- Conclusion

EXECUTIVE SUMMARY

A brief summary of the engagement outlining the top characteristics of the test's activities, findings, and high-level recommendations is very helpful in ensuring the most important areas of the test are communicated early. The executive summary highlights any major positive or negative findings. This section is usually a one-page summary of the entire document, which executive-level management can read to understand the overall "state of the union" from the perspective of the testers.

The key here is to ensure that positive findings as well as negative ones are listed in this section; the penetration test is not designed to be confrontational or critical of the company itself. It is meant to identify vulnerabilities to the organization and ways to remediate them. It is important for a firm to see what positive steps they have taken to protect themselves against a security breach. It also helps to identify what current practices are working well and compare those controls to unsuccessful portions of the test. Presenting the positive aspects of the company's security capabilities can be as valuable as presenting where there are problems.

All too often, the initial summary of the documentation is an introduction detailing the situation, how the engagement has come to pass, and other data that is, frankly, irrelevant. It should simply highlight points of interest and common attributes that existed during the entire process. The summary is for people who do not have the time or desire to read the entire document, but want a feeling of the situation.

PRESENT FINDINGS

Keeping in mind that the raw data from the test is provided in the appendix or on CD-ROM, the presentation of the findings is typically an explanation of technical issues in nontechnical terms. Many deliverables will have the list of vulnerabilities and their level of severity. Again, this is helpful, but is too analytical to ensure that business owners can readily translate them into meaningful concerns. The vulnerability information can be provided later, whereas this is an opportunity to explain issues identified within each phase of the engagement.

PLANNING AND OPERATIONS

It is recommended that the planning and operational aspects of the engagement be summarized at this point. For example, stating what information was provided at the beginning of the test, who participated in the scoping, and the members of the teams can be very helpful. Many of the details surrounding the planning and logistics of the test (e.g., e-mails, communications, faxes, phone calls, agreements, documentation, etc.) can be provided on a CD-ROM with the other raw data. This section is dedicated to ensuring that everyone is on the same page when discussing the test's results.

VULNERABILITY RANKING

During the planning of the engagement, it is hoped that ample information about the company was provided, allowing the consultant to know more about the organization than simply what the security vulnerabilities are. When armed with business-related information, the systems that have identified vulnerabilities become more than just boxes: they become parts of the business. Knowing a system's role can help create a realistic level of criticality of a given group, thread, and vulnerability.

PROCESS MAPPING

After the vulnerabilities are introduced, it is necessary to explain the tools, tactics, strategies, or any relevant process that was used to determine a vulnerability's existence and the potential exposure level. It is not necessary to explain how the tool was employed or other technical details. The goal is to explain what was performed to ensure that the exploitation of any vulnerability was within scope, a viable (fair) tactic, and there are no residual affects. Threads and groups make up much of the format. Presenting information in the same manner that the analysis was performed offers consistency of the message throughout the document. Therefore, if threads and groups were used during the exploitation phase the information collected will reflect those activities and the explanation of the process will coincide given their basic relation. Another important reason for this section is outlining the limitations later in the document. There will be the opportunity to explain the challenges facing the tester that a hacker may not be concerned with, all having an impact on the level of assumed insecurity.

RECOMMENDATIONS

It is always a good example of a well-thought-out deliverable when there is a collection of recommendations. It is one thing to be told what is wrong and left to your own devices, whereas it is completely another to be given some helpful advice, especially for critical vulnerabilities. Another aspect of value potential is receiving recommendations that reflect the current situation of corporate challenges. Throughout the engagement, more predominantly in the planning phase, there is the opportunity to share specific knowledge about the company with the tester. This will help everyone in understanding the challenges of mitigation and make for valuable recommendations. For example, a recommendation may be, "Upgrade to version X." However, the custom application will not run on "X" and the cost of an upgrade is significant given there are over 1000 seats. From an uninformed tester's perspective, the problem may be only on one system, therefore it would seem a trivial repair considering the limited scope. Albeit a simplistic example, the same holds true for any aspect of recommending solutions: the more you know, the better the recommendation.

EXCEPTIONS AND LIMITATIONS

At some point within the document the limitations and other controlling elements must be conveyed. Moreover, each limitation must be detailed as well as the impact of the restriction on the test. It is safe to say that the instant someone assumes the role of a hacker, limitations are implied or forced upon him; it is the nature of the beast. Therein lies the reason only limitations are defined as an constant. Unfortunately, many organizations do not fully comprehend the physiology of the test and how the framework of phases provides the countereffect to balance (and it is hoped exceed) the innate limitations. Therefore, it is necessary that these elements be documented. Some may conclude no limitations were put on the test, when in reality there was no acknowledgment of the reality of assuming a role that cannot be duplicated. It is also interesting when the process map section is referenced. Comparing the two sections offers enormous insight as to the effects of limitations and sets the foundation for explaining the potential analysis portion.

FINAL ANALYSIS

Every document has some form of final analysis. It is an opportunity to begin the conclusion and offer specific yet encompassing remarks that were not possible at the beginning of the document. This is also the opportunity to explain the potential vulnerabilities that could exist, and possibly be identified if there had been fewer limitations. No matter the limitation, it would be negligent not to offer insights of risk based on the entire experience of the test. Although some may assume this is simply FUD, the reality is a value-based process lends credence to the assumptions. When combined with previous experiences, understanding of the company's environment, and detailed phases resulting in a value-focused engagement, there is little room to contend many of the interpretations.

CONCLUSION

No document is complete without a conclusion. The best conclusions are short and provide references to other supporting documentation, such as an accompanying CD-ROM or links to more information on the Internet. In many cases, people feel

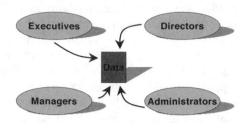

FIGURE 13.4 Organizing Data for the Audience

compelled to summarize the engagement all over again. For example, in more than half of these documents, the conclusion can be moved to the top and called the executive summary and the existing introduction removed.

OVERALL STRUCTURE

The final documentation cannot be everything to everyone, but knowing who the audience will be is certainly helpful, even when they may have very different needs (see Figure 13.4). Much of this can be managed by the overall structure of the information within the process mapping section, or can represent the entire document. Without a doubt, demonstrating value to the primary stakeholders is paramount, however, those paying the bill may not be aware of, or fully appreciate, the valuable details. Therefore, the specific components of the test should be uniquely expressed in order to help formulate a document.

The overall structure can be built founded upon the phases, the types of information, or the area affected. Of course, the best method for determining the structure is to start with what was planned, the breadth and depth of the test. If only e-mail-based social engineering was executed against the helpdesk, there is not much value in formatting the document based on phases and tasks within each phase. Conversely, formatting based on the data collected, vulnerabilities, ranking, recommendations, and final analysis within the single phase is more likely to have value.

All this becomes very complicated when several phases are specifically employed for many different target areas, such as applications or networks. Just when you think it's safe to start creating the document, there are departments, divisions, and other parts of the company that may have been targeted, possibly employing different phases. Given the potential for confusion in presenting the information, picking a structure and sticking with it throughout the document is important.

When in doubt, the best method is to use the threads as the common denominator of the structure. Therefore, you can take the related sequence of events, the vulnerabilities, the measured impact, the data that was collected or provided that played a role in the process, and any limitations that may have affected the outcome. By building on the lowest element, the information can be presented in several ways to accommodate various audiences with a predisposition toward, for example, applications in the marketing department.

Once the data structure of the deliverable is completed, the analysis section can be compiled. The analysis section can be presented in various ways. Risks can be broken down to high, medium, and low, which usually provides the most accepted format and sets the mold for the integration phase of the framework.

This way, the firm can address the high and medium risks first, and then move on to the low risks. If desired, each high, medium, and low risk can include such details as to whether it is a control, detection, or inherent risk, and in addition whether it is a critical, medium, or informational risk.

The section that offers recommendations is based on the company's current IT security policy, industry best practices, and industry standards, as well as any regulatory requirements. More often than not, the recommendations are too little, too much, or simply do not exist. Although the last is unacceptable—even in the most basic scenarios—too many recommendations are simply overwhelming. Moreover, in the face of piles of recommendations, the good intention will most certainly get lost in the confusion. Or worse, it may appear to have no value because the engagement was not long enough to justify the assumption of awareness to offer comprehensive counsel.

Once the deliverable is completed, the team responsible for conducting the penetration test would then present it to the company, specifically to the parties responsible for having the test performed. This allows the team to walk the management personnel through each phase of the test, ensuring that everything is being presented in a way they understand and feel they can move forward with once the project is over. For this reason, the final deliverable is not typically presented to the company until all data collection, analysis, and recommendations are included in a clear and concise manner. Because the deliverable is usually quite large, it can be very overwhelming for the company to review all at once. Therefore, a condensed presentation is usually more appropriate, not only to the persons responsible for conducting the penetration test, but also to upper-level management whom the penetration test affects.

In order to present the recommendations in a risk-related scenario, they are broken down into three groups: remedial, tactical, and strategic. To summarize, we have the risk (or severity) of the vulnerabilities—high, medium, and low—aligned with the phases of the framework or data, with a structure founded on threads, presented in the consolidated form of three groups. The next several sections begin to expand these thoughts and provide more information to ensure a sound deliverable.

ALIGNING FINDINGS

It cannot be readily assumed that a vulnerability should be immediately fixed based only on the ease or low cost in doing so, and comparatively it cannot be assumed that the most complex vulnerabilities have to be addressed for long-term initiatives. Holes come in all shapes and sizes with various degrees of impact, exposure, and the resources it takes to fix them. Without understanding the goals of the company and the desired security posture related to business threats, the deliverable would simply be a compilation of vulnerabilities ranked based on raw assumption without consideration for the unique environment.

ISS is one of many common, off-the-shelf products that many organizations use to perform vulnerability scans against their own or a customer's network. The results are categorized as high, medium, and low depending on the severity of the vulnerability, all of which are ranked based on common infrastructures. Although helpful in some of the cases, the majority are completely misaligned with the unique characteristics of the company's environment. To add to the malaise, Alan Paller, Director of Research at the SANS Institute, stated that the top three vulnerability scanning tools have roughly 20 percent overlap of high-ranked vulnerabilities. That means if you run ISS against your network and then FoundScan, there is the potential that only 20 percent of the problematic vulnerabilities in the report will actually be the same. If you combine the reports you could more than double your problems. The interpretation of vulnerability severity is very open to personal perspectives and many people know this already, but it is necessary to acknowledge this and use it to our advantage to squeeze value from the test. Otherwise, it's all for naught (well, at least 20 percent will be good).

Several years ago, during the initial explosion of ethical hacking as a service, it was not uncommon to see in deliverables the raw output of ISS with the logo of the consulting firm placed on the coversheet with a short executive summary. Unfortunately, this set in motion the acceptable "level" of information within a deliverable: black and white, technical to the core. Although this is OK and works pretty well, it does not come close to the potential value a business-aligned report can have.

There are companies that perform vulnerability scans against your network and present a listing of findings ranked based on predefined metrics. The popularity of services and deliverables is a reflection of poor alignment of vulnerabilities to the business demands and unique environmental characteristics. What we are seeing in the industry is ethical hacking service providers mimicking other popular services, such as Qualys, as the market moves towards commoditization. However, another level altogether can be attained when you move from scanning to controlled exploitation. Once the human interaction is made, the association with business challenges, geopolitical issues, regulatory requirements, customer pressures, and costs can be included in the evaluation of risk.

Initially, this can be frightening because the immediate assumption is people are getting skewed information. Companies are made aware of a new vulnerability labeled as "high" (as in high risk or severity) but based on their architecture it may simply represent an acceptable risk. The reality is that many companies do not have a clear mapping of business risks, goals, and architecture security to truly line up a vulnerability's risk to their environment. Many simply perform this on an ad hoc basis.

Seeing vulnerabilities appear in the dozens daily and many companies challenged with even the most fundamental security requirements, it is no surprise basic scans and services like Qualys are so popular and quite frankly, this is the time we live in, therefore these services can provide immense value. However, in the light

of a comprehensive ethical hacking engagement, there is understandably more consultative interaction. Therefore, it should be assumed there must be much more
attention paid to the business objectives, otherwise the company should seek Qualys'
services or buy a copy of ISS. Given the sophistication of today's technology, if a
company is looking for a professional services firm to perform a test, it can be rightly
assumed that they are seeking much more insight to the business needs.

There is always the challenge of effectively translating a vulnerability's assumed
impact to a custom infrastructure. To do so requires a certain level of knowledge
about the distinctive elements of the company's infrastructure, business drivers, risks,
and desired security posture. When a consulting firm becomes involved with a client
for the purposes of an ethical hack, the opportunity to collect the necessary information, if only through a handful of meetings, can go far in assuring there is an
acceptable association of a vulnerability to the business. Given the proliferation of
automated tools with comprehensive output and the availability of sophisticated
automated services, the human element of the consultative interactions weighs
heavily in the assumption of value and must materialize in the deliverable.

There are four characteristics that are used in combination to properly determine
if and when a vulnerability should be addressed. Throughout the deliverable, these
four characteristics are presented and finally used to recommend the best high-level
plan of attack for remediation. Each of the characteristics builds on the former,
establishing a chain of measurement to determine the breaking point where remediation is performed immediately or well into the future when time and money
permit. However, it is possible for one characteristic to outweigh all others depending
on the perspective and understanding of security by the company. To this end, the
four characteristics are split: two are technically related and based on measured
security, whereas the latter two are based on business-related decisions that may not
take into consideration the former pair.

TECHNICAL MEASUREMENT

Understandably, each vulnerability typically has a technical element, more often
than not. There are vulnerabilities related to process, awareness, and general inherent
risks associated with doing business and maintaining sensitive information. The
existence of door locks, fire extinguishers, and alarm systems are testament to
nontechnical security measures that are needed to protect against certain threats.
However, in a penetration test, the majority of vulnerabilities are technical in nature
and therefore have to be initially measured based on their digital attributes.

As introduced above, the business goals and risks communicated to the consultancy is the driving factor in producing the differentiating values of the deliverable
and these business elements provide the baseline for evaluating the technical characteristics of the vulnerabilities.

Severity

As vulnerabilities are discovered or published, they typically are assigned a level of
severity based on a typical infrastructure, application, or common environment. An

example is a weakness in a Web server that represents an opportunity for a hacker to perform a buffer overflow allowing malicious code to be injected into the system resulting in privileged access in the form of a command prompt. From the command prompt, the hacker can change security settings and modify data and configurations, effectively taking over control of the system. Given the popularity of the server throughout the industry and the ease of the attack, the vulnerability's severity is labeled high. A scanner may detect the vulnerability and, understandably, report the severity as high.

However, there are several pieces of information that would diminish the severity based on the architecture and required security. For example, a company may use proxy services that would stop the attack before it reached the vulnerable Web server. Or perhaps the company is employing only SSL services that are inherently resistant to the type of attack. There are several variations on this theme causing some difficulty in clearly mapping the level of concern.

Most notably, the degree of difficulty in exploiting the vulnerability in relation to the access or information attained can be a major element to determining the severity. Another attribute of a vulnerability is the scope of impact: the number of systems and their diversity are fundamental to determining the nature of the vulnerability. For example, if every server has the same vulnerability, the risk is increased because of the inflated exposure.

Severity is open to interpretation and is the fuel for many security debates. Even now there are many Information Sharing and Analysis Center (ISAC) applications that are designed to collect vulnerability information from companies, assign a level of severity, and recommend remediation solutions. Many of these are aligned to certain verticals, such as financial, utilities, and service providers that are used to share security information and findings with a similar community. These are in addition to and work in concert with public incident and vulnerability institutions such as BUGTRAQ. However, at least at the time of this writing, there is no agreed-upon standard for the assignment of severity. Overall, the severity is generally stated and assumed to be interpreted based on the company's understanding of its technical environment, once again introducing the difficulty of aligning threats with business-specific architectures.

Exposure

Exposure, by this definition, is based on the technical exposure of the system. For example, if a vulnerable server is sitting unprotected on the Internet, then anyone in the world connected to the Internet could feasibly approach the system, testing its resistance to attack. The same system residing deep within a company on a dedicated isolated network may not be accessible to anyone other than a handful of administrators, not only reducing the population of human exposure, but technical exposure as well. Given the extent of exposure to known and unknown entities, the severity of the vulnerability of the system can be evaluated, ultimately providing another layer of measurement to determine the overall remediation strategy.

Exposure can be a simple characteristic. As demonstrated above, this is most obvious when the Internet is involved. The Internet is massive and anyone with a computer (or a cell phone, PDA, etc.) can access the Internet and begin to attempt to hack into another system across the city, other side of the country, or halfway around the world; the proximity of the attack is transparent to the hacker. Therefore, it can be readily assumed that the exposure represented by the Internet is infinite and everything else is gauged based on this baseline of total exposure. From there, more and more restriction of technical access begins to appear.

Access can materialize in many ways when within the scope of technology, starting with the physical connectivity of the system to other networks. What network is the system connected to and who, or what, is sharing that network? It can also be categorized by logical access to the system or application. For example, a system may be exposed to a broad spectrum of influences but access may be controlled by another system based on a username and password, for example, a session-authenticating firewall. On the surface, this reduces the exposure, however, it is simply transferring the exposure to another system expected to be more secure and capable of protecting the lesser system.

Once the technical aspects of access are established, the population of the exposure is evaluated. Using the infinite exposure of the Internet as a starting point, each system's exposure—based on access—is appraised against the assumed trust of the elements that may have access. To illustrate further, a system may be on a protected segment of the network designated for use by partners. The exposure of the system is determined by the connectivity to other systems and users beyond the confines of the company's trusted employees and assets. It can be immediately assumed that the overall exposure of the system is much less than if sitting on the Internet because the partner networks represent a much smaller community. However, one of the risks in making this assumption is that the partner's network connection is shielded from the Internet. One of the most common security risks associated with partner connectivity is the exponentially increased exposure related to the connectivity the partner may have to the Internet or other organizations.

Lumeta is a company that provides a very comprehensive network discovery product that investigates every plausible avenue of the network, ultimately providing a map of connectivity of the network to other networks. By identifying known and trusted IP addresses, those that are part of your network and trusted partners, the map can clearly illustrate where unknown networks are connected, effectively defining exposure. When using Lumeta's network discovery tool on a relatively small network of a client, the map revealed over two dozen Internet connections and unknown networks all based on a single partner network connection. Up until this information was collected, the systems were assumed somewhat secure based on the limited access provided to the dedicated network.

Exposure eventually becomes translated into trust coupled to the internal or external entities. It is at this point where legal agreements between companies and even employee-acknowledged security policies come into effect, stipulating what is expected and the ramifications of not ensuring they are followed. Seeing that trust is impossible to completely define or measure and can only be assumed, the risk of establishing a trusted relationship is based on the consequences of breaking it. The result can be transference of risk anchored in financial restitution or legal actions to recoup the loss realized from the breach of trust. Nevertheless, there is rarely an equivalent of loss to compensation because of legal hardships, loss of brand value, or the destruction of irreplaceable data. In nearly all situations, the one assuming the level of trust and has the most to lose will typically not recover a fraction of what was lost or damaged. In this light, exposure can be used to determine trust and ultimately define a measurable level of risk that should be addressed, transferred, or simply accepted.

BUSINESS MEASUREMENT

Once the vulnerability is weighed against severity and exposure, the initial two fundamental characteristics of security, a business-related decision must take place. Without some form of investment management related to the demands placed on the company—the overall state of the organization, value of the affected assets, and the perception of security by the business owners—the weight of remediation cannot be accurately determined.

In the previous section, the importance of evaluating the technical attributes of vulnerabilities in relation to the unique technical personality of the infrastructure of the company was demonstrated. It was also noted that automated tools and popular services can provide valuable insights to vulnerabilities even when not considering the company's distinctive elements, adding to the criticality of the deliverable when a consulting organization is involved. The importance of the deliverable's content and structure cannot be understated, and this is epitomized by the ability to measure the vulnerability's impact on core business functions and requirements. In essence, all the planning and business requirements discovery in the initial phases of the project begin to materialize in the evolution of aligning the vulnerability to the business objectives.

To accomplish this task, the cost of risk becomes the foundation for determining the remediation plan for long-term success in applying security solutions. This may sound like an overstatement of value when compared to the assumed limited scope and involvement of a penetration test, but this is the critical aspect of security—risk—and the implied impact of testing security measures through exploitation.

Cost

Especially in today's economic times, the cost of doing anything is greatly scrutinized. This is more so when the investment is assumed to be in the form of insurance and without an immediate positive impact on revenue generation. Simply stated, if spending $50,000 does not have the potential to make the company more than the investment in a specific amount of time, it is usually not seen as a feasible venture. Of course, not all companies practice this tactic for spending, especially when there is substantial probability that money will be lost if the vulnerability is not rectified. Nevertheless, the cost of fixing a vulnerability can weigh heavily on the decision.

The cost of security has come under fire and has been growing in intensity over the last several years. The seeming inability to establish a return on investment for security endeavors has left the business community making conclusions simply based on available funds or perception of security. There are rare occasions where increased security is directly linked to business goals. For example, to do business with a large customer, the company may have to employ a comprehensive security policy and implement a certain type of IDS and VPN solution. However, in most cases, there is not a clear mapping from security to business-enabling solutions.

Historically, the determination to invest in security was based on the fear of being attacked and the potential of loss. Fear and concern have been the staple for many security firms in convincing their customers to invest in security. It has been fed by constant reports of major companies losing millions of dollars because of an attack, although, in the world of business, risks are taken every day to make money and for many the fear factor only works in times of prosperity or when there is a clear mapping to potential or previous losses. For example, if a company is hacked for $325,943 there is typically more than enough motivation to invest $30,000 to ensure it does not happen again. It is for this very reason security is still seen as an insurance policy, and in tough times risk is used as a leverage for greater business potential. In short, security is the first thing to go when survival of the business is at stake—interesting isn't it? To add to the malaise, ethical hacking is not used to present business-enabling security; in fact, it is sometimes used as fuel for the fear fire adding more difficulty in justifying cost for some.

The cost of repairing the vulnerability must be taken into consideration. To do so, the cost is based on the overall impact on the company, the level of skill required to fix the vulnerability, and if the company has the necessary skills in-house as well as the involvement of various attributes within the vulnerability. For example, a vulnerability may require several application changes or upgrades introducing unacceptable purchases, maintenance fees, and capital expenditures. Ultimately, the amount of cost will usually have a measurable effect on the focus management pays to the vulnerability. Cost less = more focus; cost more = less focus.

If the severity is high and the cost is low, the potential to make the necessary investment early is the usual conclusion. To continue with the earlier example, if all the Windows 2000 systems can be fixed by applying a freely available patch and the only cost is time of the administrators, then the hole should be fixed as soon as possible. If the severity is low or minimal but the cost is high, then the likelihood the vulnerability is going to be repaired anytime soon is questionable. For example, if a minimal Web site is vulnerable to a sophisticated attack that allows someone to only change the content—content that can be quickly replaced—but the cost of remediation is five times the cost of fixing the Web site 100 times a year, then there is little motivation for correcting it in the near future.

Risk

Unquestionably, without identifiable risk to the business, there is little incentive for eliminating a vulnerability. However, it is expected there is some form of risk when a vulnerability is identified, especially one found during a penetration test.

During the planning phase of the engagement, the results from a previous risk analysis were sought out or some form of metric was conveyed to the consulting firm to determine areas of specific value to the company.

By using the risk information, results can be organized to convey the impact of a vulnerability, sometimes even when the exploitation did not lead to discernable success. A vulnerability that on the surface does not appear to be a concern may actually affect a critical system based on the value of the application or data residing on the target. Moreover, the exploitation may have limited impact but, given other results, when compared to the overall state of the security, the vulnerability represents a measurable risk.

Of course, cost ultimately relates to risk. To expound on an earlier example, if the value of the Web server and the content is high, for example, brand recognition is paramount to the company's success, the risk cannot be accepted and must be transferred or rectified in a short timeframe. Risk takes into consideration all the above characteristics and provides the final decision-making milestone on the timing and level of investment of the remediation.

Each characteristic of exploitation, severity of the vulnerability, exposure of the susceptible system or device, cost of repairing, and the risk the threat represents all combine to establish a remediation plan to effectively address the weaknesses. If a consulting firm does not attempt to take every characteristic of information learned during the engagement, or does not effectively plan the test, the deliverable will not convey an effective roadmap to ensuring the holes most critical to the business are addressed.

In many cases, because some companies are not as secure as they may consider themselves to be or are leveraging a penetration test to obtain more funds for further security investments, the results are relatively scattered and the level of access obtained by the tester is so expansive that it is not feasible to construct a comprehensive deliverable. Given the number of vulnerabilities, poor security architecture, and the inability to determine which assets are critical, compared to those that are needed, or "used regularly," the final deliverable is typically nothing more than a list of vulnerabilities and how to fix them. On the other end of the spectrum, some tests have limited or no results that represent any threat to the company, and therefore cannot associate the test with critical business assets.

For a customer who may fall into the former example, the concern, beyond feeling incredibly insecure, should be, "Was the test too early or was there not enough asset information shared with the consulting firm to build a comprehensive roadmap to recovery?" The challenge for the customer will be to determine which vulnerabilities need the greatest attention and which ones she is willing to accept until there is time or money to fix them. A company that falls into the latter example should be concerned about the level of assumed security based on the consulting firm not finding any negative attributes about the security. One of the primary reasons for limited results are imposed limitations, or it was a zero knowledge test and a great deal of time was spent searching for data about the target as opposed to exploiting vulnerabilities.

Nevertheless, there is a substantial proportion of ethical hacks that fall clearly between too many results and not enough to construct a comprehensive document. Many tests end up with 15 to 40 vulnerabilities (I've seen in the thousands) ranging from low to high founded on a basic understanding of the weakness. Each one can be assessed, or each attack thread or group can be compared to the severity, exposure,

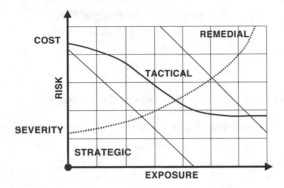

FIGURE 13.5 Aligning Cost in Relation to the Risk Will Assist in Prioritizing Remediation

cost, and risk represented by the test. As demonstrated in Figure 13.5, there must be a balance in the understanding of risk the vulnerability represents.

PRESENTATION

When weighing each of the test result's characteristics, the deliverable can be formatted to reflect the business' demands identified during the planning of the engagement. The company should be presented with a deliverable that provides information detailing the security issues in a manner that has taken into consideration the overall state of the business, security posture, and the risk to the company. The methodology of formatting the deliverable in this manner is the final realization of value to the company, which is the product of employing the framework. Every phase in the engagement, when properly executed to ensure value to the company, culminates in a clear path for them to follow that has taken into consideration business demands, asset valuation, threat types, and exposure.

To expound upon the defined security characteristics of the test, and to align them into a rationalized plan, the results are presented in the form of remedial, tactical, and strategic plans. Remedial recommendations are those that provide the company with immediate procedures to eliminate the risks threatening them. These are typically cost-effective fixes within the environment that will have the greatest impact on reducing risk in the shortest timeframe. Although the case in many scenarios, there are occasions when expensive and involved remediation plans are addressed as soon as possible given the level of risk associated with the threat. Tactical recommendations are those that can be employed within the mid-term plans of the company. For example, tactical recommendations can be defined to help formulate next year's budget for potential security spending, or to communicate there are investments that need to be made in people, process enhancements, or technology to eliminate the threat within the next six to twelve months. Finally, strategic recommendations are those that reflect the long-term goals of the company and the overall advancement of the security posture to meet planned business initiatives. Understandably, strategic plans are usually large, involving, or comprehensive security solutions that cannot be simply implemented based solely on the results of

FIGURE 13.6 Measurement of Valid Risks against Vulnerabilities

the ethical hack, but are revealed as a need for the company through the engagement process.

REMEDIAL

To determine what needs to be fixed today to eliminate a pending threat does not necessarily immediately include vulnerabilities with high severity or low cost to remediate. As detailed above, several factors must be considered to determine what can be fixed as soon as possible, rather than what should be fixed. The cost is used in combination with the severity to develop a baseline value to compare against risk and overall exposure. If the cost is low and the severity high, the risk may be high or low, and the decision will typically be to fix as soon as possible. When there are several vulnerabilities that fall into the remedial category, the prioritization is based on the nuances of exposure, which translates into some degree of risk. For example, a severe, low-cost vulnerability may be on an external Web server, and the same vulnerability exists within a file server deep within the organization's network; the greater exposure (hence increased risk) forces greater attention on the Web server (see Figure 13.6).

TACTICAL

There are scenarios where a vulnerability or group of related security weaknesses combines to represent a threat to the organization that either requires a great deal of involvement to rectify, or signifies an above-average cost that the client is not willing to invest without more planning and justification. Tactical remediation is an assignment of what to fix that is agreed to as needed, but is not the simple task of applying a patch, moving a server, or configuring some routers. It usually involves several groups to collaborate within the organization, costs more money than can be approved by a single manager, and includes security policy and procedure modification. There is only one problem that can occur, and that is when remediation projects are assigned as tactical and really should be rectified immediately. This is the result of poor interpretation of the results or the commitment to fix as much as possible in one pass. An example of the former is when the true risk and severity of the vulnerability are masked by the assumption of exposure (see Figure 13.7).

The risk to internal systems typically falls victim to this train of thought. The concept is that the exposure is limited to only internal employees and therefore assumes a greater level of trust, control, and detection. In some cases, this is farthest from the truth and a remedial fix becomes part of a mid-term plan. An example of trying to fix as much as possible in one project is when there are many different

FIGURE 13.7 Prioritizing Vulnerabilities and Their Fixes for Mid-Term Remediation

FIGURE 13.8 Prioritizing Vulnerabilities for Long-Term Consideration

types of vulnerabilities, and rather than implement minor, short-term changes to temporarily close the hole, organizations tend to develop large comprehensive projects that include completely repairing the issues without concern for the time between identification and remediation. For example, an entire group of servers is open to several types of vulnerabilities, with some based on simple software updates and others based on network architecture and configurations, each very different from the other. Rather than apply the patches to mitigate the initial risk, the company develops a comprehensive plan to redesign the architecture eliminating all the risks and negating the need for the patch application. This is when it is seen as more effective to fix all the vulnerabilities in one swing of the investment bat. Unfortunately, the reality is that many large projects become weighed down in bureaucracy or more people becoming involved, slowing the process and elongating the exposure related to a very small vulnerability. Eventually, items that are considered tactical should be reviewed to determine what parts should be included in the remedial phase even if those processes have to be duplicated later in the tactical plan.

STRATEGIC

As the definition would imply, strategic plans are long-term goals of security solutions to meet existing or planned changes in the business that can affect the security of the organization (see Figure 13.8). If a company acquires another, integrates the two networks, and makes some changes in security, they may opt for a penetration test to determine the level of risk associated with the new addition. If the business strategy is to acquire more and more companies in the future to support growth, identified vulnerabilities that were related to the merger of dissimilar systems and networks can promote changes to the existing security practices to support future business mergers. One of the less-used advantages of strategic plans is using them to help discern what should be done remedially and tactically to support the long-term objectives. For instance, I was working with a large organization that was moving their entire operations to a new facility being built several miles away that would be completed in 12 to 18 months.

The existing security was in shambles and in dire need of attention. The architecture of the network was overly complex and riddled with vulnerabilities to all types of threats with substantial risk related to each. The final remedial and tactical decisions were carefully planned, designed, and implemented to support the larger changes to be made during the move. Many of these introduced more products and unusual IP configurations with multiple layers of NAT and access controls that could be easily removed at the time of the move given the new architecture. Between the completion of the temporary network and the move, anyone assessing the network would find it more secure than before but it arguably looked worse from a design perspective if you were not aware of the final architecture. Ultimately, the cost of the temporary technology was less than half the cost of the penetration test and all of it had a role in the new architecture. This example demonstrates the true advantage of a well-planned test, constant focus on business needs and value to the customer, and a commitment to a sound deliverable (see Figure 13.9).

Sample Table of Contents

1 Executive Summary
2 Findings Summary
3 Planning and Operations
3.1 Team
3.1.1 Red
3.1.2 White
3.1.3 Blue
3.2 Timeframe
3.3 Meetings
3.4 Communication Protocol
3.5 Technical Preparation
3.6 Network
3.7 Systems
3.8 Applications
3.9 Tools List
4 Business Alignment
4.1 Business Risk Elements
4.2 Information Provided
4.2.1 Previous Test Results
4.2.2 Application Risk Analysis
4.3 Summary of Alignment
4.3.1 Remedial
4.3.2 Tactical
4.3.3 Strategic
5 Phases and Processes
5.1 UK Operations
5.1.1 London Network
5.1.1.1 Reconnaissance
5.1.1.2 Enumeration
5.1.1.3 Vulnerability Analysis
5.1.1.4 Exploitation
5.1.1.4.1 Specific Tool
5.1.1.4.2 Results Summary
5.1.1.5 Results
5.1.2 Bristol Network
5.1.2.1 Reconnaissance
5.1.2.1.1 Wireless Networks
5.1.2.1.2 E-mail
5.1.2.2 Enumeration
5.1.2.3 Vulnerability Analysis
5.1.2.4 Exploitation
5.1.2.4.1 Specific Tool
5.1.2.4.2 Results Summary
5.1.2.5 Results
5.1.3 London Applications
5.1.3.1 Reconnaissance
5.1.3.2 Enumeration
5.1.3.3 Vulnerability Analysis
5.1.3.4 Exploitation
5.1.3.4.1 Specific Tool
5.1.3.4.2 Results Summary
5.1.3.5 Results
5.2 North American Operation
5.2.1 New York Network
5.2.1.1 Reconnaissance
5.2.1.2 Enumeration
5.2.1.3 Vulnerability Analysis
5.2.1.4 Exploitation
5.2.1.4.1 Specific Tool
5.2.1.4.2 Results Summary
5.2.1.5 Results
6 Recommendations
6.1 Remedial
6.2 Tactical
6.3 Strategic
7 Exceptions and Limitations
7.1 Information Provided
7.2 Testing Format
7.2.1 Parallel Shared
7.3 Stated Restrictions
7.3.1 Application Restrictions
7.3.2 Timing of Test
7.3.3 Network Layer Restrictions
7.3.4 Social Engineering
7.3.4.1 E-mail
7.3.4.2 Physical Security
8 Final Analysis
8.1 Threads
8.2 Groups
8.3 Observations
8.4 Data Process
9 Conclusion

FIGURE 13.9 Sample Table of Contents

14 Integrating the Results

An ethical hack is the culmination of many activities resulting in the documentation of actions taken, their results, and recommendations. Many companies look to ethical hacking as an assessment service to gain better insight into their security posture. However, it can be just the beginning of establishing a comprehensive security program. Armed with information about the shortcomings of the environment, a company is well positioned to make good use of the results.

Possibly one of the greatest challenges at the completion of the test is translating insecurities identified by the test into functional solutions to address the exposures and reduce risk. Defining a solution is difficult because the perspective of the testers may not include all elements of the environment. It is for this reason that the most successful and valuable tests include a brief assessment at the end of the engagement to investigate unknown attributes.

Note 20: Fixing the Problem Cannot Always Be Done from the Outside

One of my first ethical hacking engagements was against a conglomerate of very large hospitals in the southern United States. I was provided two weeks, no information, and permitted to use any means of attack at my disposal. I identified several vulnerabilities with their Internet site and infrastructure that allowed the modification of sensitive information. At the conclusion of the engagement, I presented the findings and stated some very basic, best-practice recommendations. I explained that with a couple of days added to the engagement to allow me complete access to survey their internal systems and architecture, I would be able to provide much more assistance. After a short investigation of their internal controls, it was clear that the new perspective was incredibly valuable to proposing specific changes to accommodate not only my attack strategy, but others as well. From that point on, it seemed negligent not to include an internal assessment for every ethical hacking engagement.

To begin employing the results for a meaningful purpose, some companies continue to use the company that provided the ethical hack to assist with the remediation. Others may hire a different firm that they have experience with or want greater diversity in the solution, where some simply do it themselves based on the recommendations in the deliverable. A common misnomer is the concern for potential conflicts of interest. Many organizations do not permit the ethical hacking company to assist in the remediation. Unfortunately, this extinguishes any chance of gaining the tester's perspective and leaves the company and the selected consulting firm to make determinations based solely on the deliverable. Nevertheless, this example exemplifies the need for a detailed deliverable.

INTEGRATION SUMMARY

Integration comes in four phases and these phases can exist in their entirety or partially in remedial, tactical, or strategic planning, but must appear in some form within each characteristic of security. The one step common to each of the four areas is planning. At the onset of integrating the results of the test, a project plan should be developed for each of the four steps to ensure they are in alignment with the overall goals of the organization and the recommendations. The planning usually involves several departments, but should be owned by a single department or group, such as the IT group or security group, with executive management oversight. Once the planning is complete and a clear roadmap to recovery is established, the four areas can be addressed.

1. *Mitigation.* Dealing with the security vulnerabilities identified during the test is the obvious first step. Whether it is technical or procedurally related, small or large, at some point the known vulnerabilities must be addressed. During the mitigation process, the solution must be tested and piloted prior to implementation. Once implemented, the solution should be validated starting with the original vulnerabilities and weaknesses identified during the penetration test.

2. *Defense Planning.* As the security posture starts to take on a new look, the organization needs to establish a firm foundation to alleviate future shortcomings, such as those found during the test. This usually includes an architecture review to understand the results of poor networking and application development practices that may have led to the vulnerabilities and to establish guidelines for avoiding similar pitfalls in the future. Additionally, it provides the opportunity to review the existing architecture compared to the results to look for opportunities to reduce inherent risks that can be interpreted based on the results, even if not directly articulated in the deliverable. Defense planning includes a process review phase to look for breakdowns in incident response, or highlight and replicate good practices realized by the Blue Team during the test. Finally, it includes awareness training. Whenever a company learns something new about security and adjusts technically, procedurally, and culturally there must be some form of communication and awareness that follows the changes. Without raising the awareness of the expected security posture and the changes made, even if only to the IT department, the potential for new or old vulnerabilities to reemerge is substantial.

3. *Incident Management.* During the test, the Blue Team responded in one of three ways: identified the attack and responded accordingly, identified the attack but did not respond in a manner to thwart or reduce the attack's impact, or simply was not aware of the attack and consequently there was no response. No matter what the result, the incident response capability must be investigated to build it, refine it, or learn what was done correctly and enhance the process.

4. *Security Policy.* To fully integrate the results of the test and to ensure any remediation has long-term success within the company, the security policy must be modified to accommodate the changes. In this section we talk about the structure and content of a typical security policy and how it should be modified and where according to the results of the test. We also discuss what attributes of the policy will be affected the most and the end value to the customer the ethical hack will remain for some time to come.

MITIGATION

Depending on the two technical characteristics of the vulnerability, detailed above as severity and exposure, and the systems affected, the mitigation can be time consuming and quite involving. At the onset of the integration phase, a plan is constructed to manage the four areas of integration. The mitigation plan outlines the technical attributes required to rectify each of the vulnerabilities or other forms of risk that were identified. The plan would include each step and the associated time in completing the task, and would usually be aligned with the overall integration plan to ensure timely completion of the overall remediation. By doing this, several areas can be outlined, for example, hard costs associated with new applications, upgrades, or system modifications, downtime issues, and usage requirements.

TEST

The first step in the mitigation phase is testing the changes to the systems in a controlled environment, such as a lab. For example, a new version of software would need to be tested ensuring that the fix does in fact eliminate the vulnerability. If it does not eliminate the vulnerability, alternative solutions would need to be explored until the correct one is determined. Testing is usually done in a lab environment, which is separated from the rest of the corporate network. This is an important concept for testing environments: they should not be attached to a production network, and this is especially important if development work is occurring in the lab. Depending on the size of the organization and the number of systems running the susceptible software, sometimes the vendor will offer to do the testing at its site. Although this is dependent on the vendors themselves, it is a plausible workaround when the ability to accurately test the change is not feasible on the client's network. Another important aspect of the testing phase is the scale of the vulnerability, which the firm is trying to eliminate. If it is something rather minor, such as applying a patch, the test can be performed rather quickly on a duplicate system in the lab, a pilot and rollout plan created, and the patch ultimately applied to the entire environment. If it is a major fix or new software version, for example, moving from Windows NT 4 to Windows 2000, more detailed and complex testing would need to occur, taking months to complete.

The goal of the test is to make the changes in a controlled environment to ensure the changes not only eliminate the vulnerability, but also function in the normal operating environment. There are numerous examples of security fixes and patches being implemented in online environments only to bring the systems down. Once the systems are back up and running they are sometimes in worse security shape than when they started because the service pack applied overwrote a patch that may have been implemented long before the test.

PILOT

During the piloting phase of the mitigation plan, the new (or upgraded) software is tested in more detail, ensuring the accuracy of the upgrade. A system in pilot mode can be observed for various timeframes, again, mainly depending on the nature of the testing, the changes made, and the type of vulnerability. Usually, pilots are performed for large technical changes in diverse companies. For example, a vulnerability was found in the standard operating system used by the company. The changes may be tested in a lab and then rolled out to only one location for observation until the customer is satisfied there is no potential for system failure caused by the changes.

If a system is essential to the business, proper piloting of the new software should be completed in order to proceed into production rather seamlessly. In most large organizations, dedicated networks are established for piloting new or upgraded systems. These networks are connected to the rest of the production network; however, they are still isolated ensuring their protection. In some circumstances, a critical system could have a development network, a pilot network, and a production network. This is true in most financial institutions using database software, which can require constant upgrades improving its functionality. In these cases, establishing a separate network for the piloting phase is important to ensure a new system or version of software has been adequately tested and verified that it is ready for production.

IMPLEMENT

Once the testing and pilot phase of a mitigation plan is completed, it is ready to be put into production. At this point, the stability of the new or upgraded software is at a comfort level in which the organization feels it is ready to go live. This can be either the high point or low point of a mitigation plan. If the testing and pilot phases were completed accurately, and all scenarios assessed, then going into production should be seamless and provide the organization with a positive business outcome. If there were any discrepancies during the previous two phases, placing the new system into production can be detrimental to the organization.

VALIDATE

Once a system is placed in production, the final phase is validating that the changes have actually alleviated the vulnerability in the production environment. This phase exists to ensure that the system is properly implemented and operating as planned. The validation phase can last over several months, constantly monitoring the new system ensuring its stability. Of course, in some situations, the validation phase may occur in parallel with a new testing phase focused on a much larger portion of the remediation plan. There is no guarantee that once a system has been upgraded that another upgrade or security vulnerability will not be publicized. Each software version released and security vulnerability made publicly known should be closely assessed and a determination would need to be made on whether the firm's systems would need to reflect these new findings. The most important thing throughout the mitigation plan is ensuring that the current system in production is running as expected and achieving its business and security objective.

DEFENSE PLANNING

As the mitigation process starts and takes on a life of its own, the tactical and long-term strategic plans should be evaluated. One form of a plan falls under defense planning, which essentially is protecting the firm from any new risks or exposures. These are long-term strategic plans, which if implemented correctly can have a positive impact on future penetration tests. One thing a firm does not want is for each year, a third-party vendor to come in, perform a penetration test, and discover the same risks and exposures as in the previous years. A defense planning initiative can help to alleviate this issue. Defense planning can effectively help a firm increase its overall security posture, and benefit other areas of business security and operations through the evolution of a comprehensive security program.

Taking care to implement defense-planning tactics also guarantees that the firm has the appropriate security policies and procedures to meet its specific needs and business objectives. Because each company has a different business objective, it is important to tailor the policies and procedures to make certain they will realize the most rewards. Defense planning also entails implementing a structured framework to enable security and ensure that investments in policies and technology are realized and adaptable. It provides a cost-effective method to communicate sound practices to the user community within the organization and provides a central point of security control and management.

In order to ensure the risks identified in the penetration test are properly addressed, this section details the various subdivisions within a defense-planning initiative. It entails architecture reviews, which provide overall consistency and centralization in regard to implementing new infrastructures within the firm's network. It also entails process reviews, which ensure the processes that were effective yesterday are still effective today and in the future. The last piece of defense planning discussed is awareness training. This can be the most important defense tactic an organization can make today. An informed employee is more likely to protect the company's assets compared to an uninformed employee.

ARCHITECTURE REVIEW

After the test is complete and the mitigation plan is being enacted, there is a clear understanding of the changes that will occur. Given that the scope of the planned modifications to the environment is known, the company can begin to review the architecture of the network, specifically the areas that represented the greatest number of vulnerabilities or the highest degree of risk.

The architecture review is designed to accomplish many things. The ultimate goal is to determine what attributes and characteristics about the architecture lend themselves to inherent vulnerabilities and to establish a process for future changes to the architecture. However, there are many byproducts of performing a review. As mentioned in an earlier chapter, not all scenarios can be played out during the penetration test because of inherent or imposed restrictions. Nevertheless, the company can review the results of the test and virtually run scenarios against the information from the test to look for possible avenues for hackers and inherent risks. Combined with the architecture of the technical landscape, this practice can provide certain insights to the overall security of the organization, lending more value gained from the test performed weeks prior.

There are two forms of architecture review: technical and virtual. A technical review takes a high-level approach by looking at the primary technical areas of the network and assessing each element's role in providing security, even if the system in question is not normally associated with security, such as a switch. For example, you may review the perimeter network architecture by assessing the configuration of the Internet router, firewall, DMZ configuration, and the systems that reside on the DMZ. Each has attributes related to ensuring a secure environment. However, if they are not aligned, such as the firewall permitting a protocol onto the DMZ not being used by any of the servers, it could constitute a fundamental weakness in the relationship of the systems and networking elements. Although this is an oversimplified example, the same concern holds true regardless of what area of the network is being reviewed. The value to the customer is severalfold. The technical architecture review provides an opportunity to test the network configuration against hypothetical attacks based on the information gleaned from the test results. In addition, there are many cases where the tester may have stopped because to go any further had the potential of harming the network. The review can compare the system's configuration to what could have been the result if the tester were to have completed the test. Another reason a tester may have stopped was because the next hole to crawl through was not discovered. The results of the test may state that if there were more time to look for more vulnerabilities that were expected, the impact could have been greater. The review provides an interesting opportunity to extend the life of the test to make educated assumptions about the "what if" of network security.

Second, the architecture review can be against the virtual architecture. Detailed early in the book, a virtual architecture is the logical segmentation of security elements and resources to establish a foundation of understanding of how security is realized within the organization. By using the results of the test, a very high-level assessment can be completed that may expose fundamental weaknesses about the logical interaction between technical solutions and business requirements.

Beyond the value of an architecture review, there is the structure of a review process. The next section discusses some of these characteristics.

Architecture Review Structure

Perhaps the results of the penetration test concluded that the firm had implemented three different versions of database software, which the company relies on for credit card transactions. Perhaps each flavor of the database software is old, outdated, and susceptible to various known security vulnerabilities. Creating a remediation plan to address each of these systems could be a complicated and time-consuming task. What if the organization had one architecture committee within the IT department responsible for all database servers, and maintained them all. It would be simpler to remediate them from this perspective. This is why having an internal architecture review within an organization's IT department can be greatly beneficial.

An architecture review is helpful for a plethora of reasons. The main reason and the most important is consistency. Consistency within the network infrastructure is beneficial both from an ease of use and administration as well as from a security perspective. One router type, or routers from multiple vendors, each configured, administered, and maintained by a different group, would be nearly impossible to ensure the risks associated with each vendor, platform, or device are eliminated, let alone reduced. If a vulnerability that needs to be repaired was identified during the penetration test, one group would need to implement this fix on all systems affected, instead of multiple fixes on multiple vendor applications.

With a centralized architecture review board put in place within the IT department, control of what goes into the infrastructure is monitored and approved by those with the proper authority to do so. Marketing may come up with a great idea and want to implement a new Web server somewhere in the network. They could go out and buy their own hardware, configure it themselves, and plug in into any network connection within the building. Would the IT staff be aware of this? And who would be responsible should something occur? Now an architecture review board or just an architecture review process would ensure that the marketing department gets their idea implemented, benefiting the company, perhaps even financially, but better yet, it would be a system aligned with the security program.

Organizations can grow very large and dispersed in a short period of time. If all new implementations are centralized from the start, growth can occur rather seamlessly. Centralization not only encompasses data center locations, but also implementation teams, administration, and maintenance or network operations centers (NOC). If one NOC is responsible for all of the organization's systems, it is easier to ensure they are all running as planned, and if an issue occurs, there is someone that sees an issue, and can mitigate it immediately.

Architecture reviews can also ensure that each system being implemented within the network infrastructure is implemented in a standardized manner. This can be in the context of not only hardware, but also software, and application builds. In the simplest form, a standard build is defining what all new servers must have installed. This ensures the integrity of the system and protects it from known security vulnerabilities. If an upgrade to a standard build must occur, all systems would be upgraded in the same fashion. Not only does this alleviate the risks to the organization, but also allows for quick implementation of new infrastructures, constantly growing the business at a much faster rate than if it were decentralized.

Architecture reviews can take many forms, whether it's the same group of people, or a committee chosen by their position and experience. A department within an organization can go to the group, or committee, and for the most part, state its case. Perhaps a new customer needs a VPN connection established for financial transactions, or a new HR service is going to be introduced to the employees. Regardless of the need, each request would be filtered through a specific committee. This committee would then determine whether there was enough bandwidth through an existing leased line, which the new VPN tunnel could use, or whether HR's current Web server has enough CPU power to maintain another Web site. A person within the committee would then be responsible for heading up this new initiative, ensuring that it meets corporate standards and passes through all the appropriate review boards prior to being implemented.

An architecture review covers another major area highly important with any new infrastructure or business function, and that's security. Centralizing IT responsibilities, and consistency within hardware and software builds, allow the level of security to be raised above the bar and fully comply with the security policy put in place. If one group or team of people is responsible for implementation, they are fully knowledgeable in the hardware they are implementing, and know the best way to secure it. Yet, they are also aware that the business function of the infrastructure plays an important role; therefore, they can provide the balance between the two. Establishing this level of balance between security and business can take many years to accomplish.

With an architecture review implemented within an organization, a penetration test would then simply become a sanity check for the IT department. It would ensure them that the processes they have in place are effective and providing a benefit to the organization. This would come back to them in the results of the penetration test, if by each year the amount of threat or risk is reduced due to their ongoing diligence.

AWARENESS TRAINING

Awareness training is a simple concept but it can be difficult to employ. It requires constant vigilance on the part of management to not only keep it consistent and comprehensive, but interesting as well. Security can be incredibly boring for people who have little or no comprehension of security or even technology. The goal is to provide many different flavors of awareness that clearly reflect the needs of the organization and present them in a manner that is informational, interesting, and unobtrusive.

In an effort to meet these requirements, an awareness program should be tailored to the organization in addition to presenting information specific to the activities of the various roles within the organization. All too often awareness programs are general and all-encompassing, broadcast to the company, and in many cases these get filtered into the trash folder. When security is communicated that has relevance to the daily challenges of the employees, they are more apt to read it. This is not to state that global e-mails and Web sites focused on information security are not valuable, but when combined with focused communications, the impact is certainly greater. For example, the marketing department will not digest an e-mail that speaks to the challenges of the IT group, finance department, or sales. People are critical to the security of an organization and they are just that—people. It is the responsibility of the company and the process to speak to them in terms they can relate to and that supports their perspective. This basic concept can be used to format the security campaign to increase the effect of the media being used. To illustrate, a company may have three departments, each with a unique need to comprehend the challenges of information security. Each department has its own floor in an office building. Therefore, posters, e-mails, presentations, classes, and announcements can be based modified from a standard template and message to meet the distinctive needs of the group.

As stated, user awareness can be the most beneficial in a proper defense plan against attack. The social engineering phase of a penetration test can represent a substantial risk to the organization. It is usually not the fault of the employees, but instead, the fault of the mis- or uninformed employee. Most firms want to protect their assets, but through employee lack of knowledge, they can be compromised. An employee security awareness program can minimize the problem of employee-based security breaches by educating them on the importance of security and the need for controls. The process of implementing user awareness training specifies the details of the program including the content and method of delivery. The method of delivery includes media and whether internal or external trainers will be used.

There is a variety of elements within a user awareness training program. For instance, all users should be made aware that security is their responsibility, both as an employee and as an individual. Different types of training should be provided, such as a training class with an experienced instructor, videos that can be watched in a classroom-style atmosphere, and online documentation that can be accessed any time a user has a concern or question. Perhaps during the penetration test it was discovered that during the new-hire process there is no mention of security awareness in the new-hire packet, or that training only occurs during the new-hire process and then is forgotten about.

Training should include clear steps on how a user should report a security problem if one arises. An organization may have a strong user awareness program in place; however, it may also be ten years old. In this case, it is not as effective as it once was. A recommendation would be to consistently review the training plans to make sure they are up to date and effective on a routine basis and make modifications as required.

There are three basic phases to develop an effective security awareness program:

1. *Introduce Security Awareness to Employees and Contractors.* Add security awareness to the employee handbook, include security awareness in new-hire orientation, and deliver security awareness to existing employees.
2. *Continually Improve Security Awareness.* Place security topics on the agenda in IT staff meetings, include security articles in client newsletters and publications, provide security information on client intranet, display security awareness posters and change them periodically, and distribute security responsibility booklets.
3. *Measure Security Awareness.* Review trends in user-related security issues and prepare a "quiz" on security awareness and analyze responses.

There is a variety of security awareness training programs available to organizations today. However, they should be tailored to meet the needs of the organization and its user community. Some of the common security awareness training topics include:

- Physical security, access controls, and visitors
- Acceptable use of resources such as Web, e-mail, and software
- Recognizing and handling social engineering
- Safeguarding printouts and files (storing, distributing, and destroying)
- Choosing and maintaining a strong password
- Protecting portable computers, PDAs, and cell phones
- Taking action in an emergency or disaster situation
- Protecting yourself from viruses
- Backing up important files and safeguarding the backup copy
- Complying with legal and regulatory issues, including copyright and privacy

Although each of the above items is important, the first step is to determine what you are trying to accomplish, and then customize the training program accordingly. Third-party instructors can also present the training curriculum to the firm's employees. In some cases, bringing in a third party will have a positive impact on the training because it is coming from someone experienced in this area, instead of just another co-worker. After the penetration test, the security awareness training can be evaluated, if one is present, and recommendations made based on the needs of the organization.

Awareness Program

To establish an awareness training program one must develop a curriculum that provides information in a manner that is useful and understandable to the focus group. In addition, the information must represent the requirements for the group's role and responsibilities.

The first step is to define focus groups and define subjects (see Table 14.1) to be presented. The best starting point is with everyone in the organization. This is founded on the assumption that any security awareness training, no matter the role

TABLE 14.1
Awareness Program Groups and Subjects

Role	Subject(s)	Description
Everyone	• *Passwords:* Their use, selecting a strong password, good password management. • *Information sharing:* Know what you are providing to whom. • *E-mail:* Downloading e-mail, viruses, worms, suspicious e-mail. • *Reporting:* When and to whom do you report potential security issues. • *Using controls:* How to use the security tools available to you as a user. • *Computers:* How to use systems in a secure manner.	• Every user and/or employee in the company should receive regular security awareness training.
Data Management	• *Applications:* Their security features, information sensitivity, system access controls. • *Backups:* Data backup, storage, rotation, restoration, and identifying changes. • *Information sharing:* Data classification and associated controls.	• Anyone involved with the creation or management of sensitive information. This represents employees in HR, finance, R&D, or legal. Although they may handle sensitive data, one cannot assume they are employing effective security practices regularly.
IT Staff	• *Access tools:* Using access tools, such as SSH or Kerberos enabled tools, for system access and administration. • *User management:* Secure directory management, new/updating credentials, user change management. • *System security:* Operating systems, patches, updates/upgrades, maintenance, backup.	• Individuals who interact with the technical infrastructure as part of their job must receive specific awareness training and more regularly.
Security Management	• *Technical security controls:* Network security, firewalls, VPN, IDS, switches (VLANs). • *Procedural security controls:* Policies and procedures, risk management, incident management, quality control, operations. • *Monitoring:* System activity awareness, logging, reporting, system analysis, forensics, backup.	• Although in most cases the security group is providing the training, they should not be overlooked. Training for security professionals is focused at keeping them abreast of industry changes, internal environment, and reiterate to them good security practices.

within the company, is a good practice. Once the basis of the program is initially defined, more specific groups should be defined to communicate security practices that relate to daily interaction with information, systems, and potential threats.

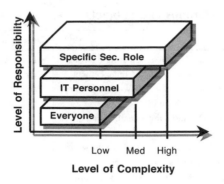

FIGURE 14.1   Awareness Training Model

As shown in Table 14.1, there are common subjects from one group that can be shared with the next group with more information to accommodate particular needs. However, it should be noted that although a subject may be repeated, the level of sophistication is substantially increased to ensure the audience's skill level is reflected. As demonstrated in Figure 14.1, the content's complexity keeps pace with the group's skill set.

It is recommended that anyone pursuing the development of an awareness program refer to SP 800-50, *Building an Information Technology Security Awareness and Training Program*, published by the Computer Security Resource Center of NIST (csrc.nist.gov) for a complete program definition.

INCIDENT MANAGEMENT

Incident management is a methodology for reacting to and resolving unexpected information security events. The time to plan a network incident response operating procedure is before the incident occurs. Incident response procedures, when integrated into an organization's network operating procedures, can mitigate loss, damage, and downtime, and can help preserve evidence during a network incident. The tools and processes used to effectively handle and recover from a security incident should be incorporated into the firm's security program. It is a key element of an organization's incident response strategy.

The benefits of an incident response plan include:

- Minimize the damage from network intrusions by having a well-established plan in place.
- Decrease network downtime from security incidents.
- Preserve evidence from attacks.
- Increase the firm's overall security posture and awareness.

Once an incident has occurred, it is important to ensure the situation is handled in the proper manner. However, for many organizations, the thought of an incident response process does not come to light until their first security breach. It is at that point they realize how the situation could have been handled better, with less of a business impact to the organization. It allows them to assess what happened, and take steps to ensure it does not repeat. There are six main steps in an incident response process: detecting a security breach has occurred, identifying what exactly occurred, isolating the breach, eradicating it, recovering from the incident, and most important, learning from the process. Each of these steps is discussed below in more detail. (The following discussion does not take into account computer forensics. Forensics on computer systems is an incredibly convoluted subject that would take much more than a few bullets to describe.)

- *Detect.* Detection of an incident is the obvious first step. The inability to detect an attack is occurring will impede any of the processes associated with stopping and recovering from the attack. Detection is arguably one of the most difficult parts of incident management and there is a plethora of products out there to help in the process. Intrusion detection and prevention systems are all the rage today and once they are properly implemented, tuned to the environment, and maintained, they can be incredibly effective. However, there are many other attributes to detection: log files, changes in system and data files, increased activity on a system, network, or even a protocol, and the existence of Trojans on the system. An incident management program is founded on the identification and alignment of technology and practices to detect an event.
- *Identify.* Once the intrusion is detected, there is the challenge of under-standing what is under attack, why, and what is being exploited. This is where the ability to detect can play a role. Many IDS systems will not only tell you there is an anomaly, but what is happening and the targeted system. Once the attack tactic is identified, measures can start to take form in defending yourself.
- *Isolate.* An attack can present itself in many ways and does not have to be a single source point or a single target. As the picture of the attack becomes clearer, its scope has to be evaluated. Determining the overall impact will set the groundwork for eliminating the negative affects. However, doing so is easier said than done. You have to evaluate all things that could be related to the identified attack and this can feel a great deal like looking for a light switch in the dark. The best method is to leverage the information you have to this point and use it to make logical deductions on where else to look for other related activities.
- *Eradicate.* Once the attack is understood and the scope of the impact is known, the process of stopping the attack can begin. At this point, many activities have been executed to stop the attack, understandably, but it is at this point all the information to address the entire attack has been collected and evaluated.
- *Recover.* After the attack has been thwarted, the arduous task of repairing the damage begins. In most cases, you know which vulnerabilities were exploited, the tactic used, and what part of the system was affected. At

this point, you start evaluating the system and data status and searching for any remnants left over from the tools that may have been used. Finally comes the act of addressing the vulnerabilities through the application of patches and fixes, configuration changes, and infrastructure modifications. This can become challenging when the fix has a negative impact on the operation of the system or application increasing the impact of the original attack. Many companies that have a robust incident management program have a lab prepared for testing patches to quickly implement a fix.

- *Learn.* Arguably the most important aspect of incident management is learning from the event and using the experience to your advantage by refining and updating the program practiced. This instills a cyclic process that builds upon itself to ensure the next attack is addressed more efficiently. Typically, this includes a debriefing meeting to discuss all the actions that were taken, review e-mail conversations, review the track of the attack, and look for opportunities to build a better mousetrap.

In nearly every penetration test there has been some form of incident management capability of the customer, however, it is difficult to recall a time when the attack was thwarted. Penetration testing is one of the most effective tools to test a company's ability to respond appropriately to an attack. It is this point that makes the need for teaming so critical. The Blue Team is none the wiser that an attack is being planned and is surely being monitored during the attack. Some have argued the test is designed to seek vulnerabilities and to exploit them to determine the exposure and difficulty of the entire process, therefore having an employee identify the attack and stop it before the test reaches its completion defeats the purpose. If a test is purposely focused on certain characteristics of the test, such as testing the network, applications, services, users, from inside or out, it is plausible to limit the response of the attack if it is in alignment with the original planned objective and expectations. However, allowing the natural flow of attack and response promotes greater awareness of real capabilities rather than those that may be assumed.

What should be considered is you're ultimately concerned with the ability of your environment to survive an attack and not have any valued assets put in harm's way or be exposed. Even though a vulnerability may exist and the test was thwarted by an employee, the results are much more valuable to the organization than any other scenario. It could be stated that, even without successfully stopping the attack, one could gain more value than simply exploiting a hole and reporting on it.

Building a Team

A Computer Emergency Response Team is an essential requirement for managing an incident response capability. Several steps are needed to define the team, establish policies and procedures, and implement the necessary technology required to respond to a threat. Ethical hacking can play a significant role in the development of a CERT. In the following sections, each ingredient of a CERT is introduced and the positive impacts of a test highlighted.

People

Creating a team of people is only the first hurdle. The CERT should have security experts in addition to legal, administrative, and executive representation from various departments. Each company has a different approach to identifying resources to include on the team. The best approach is to ensure the appropriate security skills are represented, followed by people who can make command decisions confidently. Although the CERT performs regular tasks between events, during an attack critical decisions have to be made quickly and closely managed.

The next consideration is selecting representatives from different departments of geographical regions in an effort to establish an operational hierarchy. Also, by spreading the team throughout the organization, the likelihood of obtaining broad support for CERT activities is greater.

The role ethical hacking plays in determining who should be on the team is slight. Depending on the scope of the engagement, the actions of the White and Blue Teams can assist in selecting people who have a predisposition for responding to adverse conditions.

Note 21: Food and Beverage

Working with a large company in California to assist in the creation of a CERT, the CEO wanted to look for people within the predefined group who had previously worked in the food and beverage industry. Her seemingly odd request began to make sense when considering the extreme fluctuation of stress associated with serving the public. Employees of the service trade are typically faced with challenges that must be addressed in a very short amount of time and remain calm throughout. There are several other lines of stressful work many people have tried at some point in their lives that can be leveraged in a CERT. Dealing with stressful situations and having the ability to stay calm is a valued quality in a CERT. By looking to other industries that employees have worked in, it may be surprising to see who can take the heat.

Mission

In defining any group or committee that is to serve a specific purpose, a mission statement is the place to start. A mission statement is a clear, agreed-upon collection of statements that can be easily translated by others. Unfortunately, many CERTs have overlooked creating a mission statement resulting in a lack of a clear understanding of their goals and objectives. Additionally, this translates into ineffective communication to the departments and organizations they interact with about their role and services. A mission statement should establish the overall type and quality of services and describe whom they serve. Although this may seem overly simple, it can go a long way in ending debates over various activities and roles.

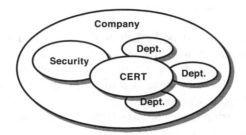

FIGURE 14.2 CERT Organizational Structure

Constituency

The CERT serves as a hub of information and processes that exist to serve many different people and organizations. The most obvious is the company that has established the team. However, additional groups include other CERTs in other companies, law enforcement, and the industry as a whole. By defining who the CERT interacts with the team can begin to define services, tracking mechanisms, and information flows. Fundamentally, when combined with the mission statement, this creates a basic operational framework for the CERT.

Organizational Structure

We've discussed the types of people who should be members of the team, but it is also helpful to create a high-level representation of the CERT structure. The placement of the CERT within the organization will greatly affect the capabilities of the CERT. Coupled with the mission statement and constituency, the role within the organization (see Figure 14.2) and the interaction required with other entities must be established.

Alluded to above, a more detailed representation of the hierarchical structure of the CERT is helpful, especially in large or diverse organizations, to better understand the team's internal relations. Defining the team's organizational structure can be critical for being certain the correct information is shared within the service-specific period. As demonstrated in Figure 14.3, there can be levels of CERTs within the company to accommodate the environment and to overcome limitations in diverse companies.

For example, a CERT may be divided up geographically to accommodate time zones, languages, varying degrees of exposure, or business units. The division may be founded on levels of risk and sensitivity of assets maintained at the site. No matter the architecture of the CERT, once separated there must exist levels of involvement in the process. For example, a top-level team that provides coordination and primary services must exist, with regional CERTs providing the much-needed information and acting on directions received by the coordinators.

Not all CERTs must have separation of duties or focus. In fact, the increase in segmentation can hinder the team's ability to appropriately respond to incidents. For every level of granularity, the policies and communications plans must be enhanced exponentially to accommodate the diversity.

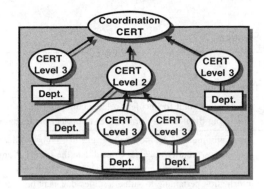

FIGURE 14.3 CERT Interaction with Other Departments and CERTS within the Company

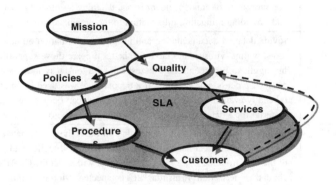

FIGURE 14.4 CERT Service and Quality Framework

Ethical hacking can help identify areas for segmentation based on risk and exposure. For example, if a test were performed against every Internet connection of a company resulting in a broad spectrum of results, one can begin to determine the types and skills required at each location. Although it is not required to have a strong response resource at the most insecure sites, knowing the level of exposure, the potential risk, and the type of threats that may be unique to a region can help in defining the CERT architecture.

Defining Services and Quality

For each service provided, the CERT must provide its organization with service descriptions, or SLAs, in as much detail as necessary so the organization is clear on the role and responsibility of the CERT. The description of services includes specific features, expectations, and the quality expectations of the services. It defines the primary organizations that are most interested (affected) by the service, communication standards, and priority rating of the service (see Figure 14.4).

Each organization and CERT will have unique approaches to services and the level of quality for each. No matter the approach, many services are fundamental

TABLE 14.2
Common CERT Services

CERT Services	
Service	**Description**
Incident Response	Provide focal point for incident-related communications, coordination, and employing the necessary procedures to protect organizational assets.
Vulnerability Awareness	Continually monitor the industry for information on vulnerabilities, incidents, and various security updates. Consolidate the information that is applicable to the organization and communicate. The results from the test should include information pertaining to vulnerabilities that may be specific to the organization based on engagement research.
Communications	Provide regular announcements regarding security activities, internal or industrywide, that will assist others in addressing security concerns. The most common form of announcement is one detailing a vulnerability or incident and providing mitigation information to the organization.
Threat Analysis	Provide detailed documentation and insightful information on new malicious tools, worms, viruses, and tactics to better prepare those supporting and managing security controls. The test can go a long way in assisting in the analysis process. For example, if a popular tool was used by the testers that is readily available to hackers, the information can be used as foundation material for a detailed analysis on the impacts to the organization.
Incident Tracking	The CERT is responsible for identifying all the activity associated with an intrusion. The ethical hacking deliverable will detail tactics and progression of the test, from the tester's perspective, that will assist the CERT in learning about their network from an attacker's perspective. Moreover, if the Blue Team was never alerted to the test, or could only identify an attack was occurring, the results and conclusion will assist in selecting the appropriate technology to support incident tracking.
Collaboration	An essential element of the CERT is to act as a central command and communication platform for the entire organization. Given the importance of the role and the necessary duties, collaboration with the rest of the organization is paramount. Much of the information the CERT requires to accomplish their stated goals will come from other departments. Interestingly, the actions of the Blue Team during the test should provide a great deal of insight to the collaboration practiced within an organization in the face of an attack.
Coordination	Any adverse event, physical or technical, in the realm of security should be coordinated by the CERT. There are certain situations (e.g., fire, flood, explosion, etc.) when the CERT is not the primary group sought out to manage the response. Nevertheless, they should be included in all events to ensure data protection is not threatened.

to a CERT. Demonstrated in Table 14.2, services provided by the CERT should be outlined and detailed for the organization as well as the CERT itself.

Once the services are defined and communicated, the CERT can start doing its job. Of course there is much more information that can be shared about the inner workings of a CERT, but the goal was to demonstrate that something considered unrelated—such as ethical hacking—can go a long way in creating a team.

CERT Forms

Another aspect of a CERT is procedure. In the face of an event, documentation is incredibly important. It provides a record of activities and offers the opportunity to perform an analysis of the team's actions once the problem is resolved.

Tables 14.3 and 14.4 demonstrate examples of forms that can be used to report on an incident and gain better insight into exactly what happened. The examples are provided to demonstrate how an ethical hack can be used to focus the efforts of the CERT in collecting information. An ethical hack exposes weaknesses in technology, people, and processes. Of course, these change with time and if a test is performed regularly, the results of the test can be used to modify the forms to accommodate changes in the dynamics in the relationship among threats, vulnerabilities, and the security control. Every CERT should regularly update the forms to ensure information—support by the test—is accurately collected. Forms should be updated, or at least reviewed for potential changes:

- When each test is performed
- When changes in the environment occur
- When an event or incident is responded to
- At regular intervals (i.e., annually, quarterly, etc.)

One may ask how these events can affect the format of a questionnaire. When investigating and collecting information about an event it should be recognized that people can interpret the same event differently. If a potential risk to a threat has not been mitigated, the form can present questions in a manner that will help in isolating the event. If the form is too generic, as many are, the resulting information is usually compressed into comments from the witness, which are left to interpretation. By asking questions of a specific nature in many ways, a skilled CERT member can quickly surmise, or at least reduce, the number of options that represent what actually happened.

SECURITY POLICY

To integrate the results of the test and to ensure any remediation has long-term success within the company, the security policy must be modified to accommodate the changes in perception of security based on the results of the test. Understandably, certain sections of a policy will not change and others may be drastically modified or complete sections added to accommodate what was learned from the test.

It is the security policy that binds the value of the test to the organization, closes the life cycle of the entire experience, and helps prepare for the next challenge. The policy was used as an input to formulate a plan for executing the test and it should be no surprise that the test's results will have an impact on that policy, eventually changing the perspective of security, practices, and management, and better preparing for the next test.

TABLE 14.3
Sample CERT Incident Reporting Form

Tracking Number # (internal use only)
CERT Point of Contact Information
Date Reported: _____ Contact: _____ Title: _____
Program Area: _____ Telephone Number: _____ E-mail: _____

Background Information
Computer Model: _____ Computer IP: _____ Computer Name: _____
Date Incident Occurred: _____ Time Incident Occurred: _____ Duration of Attack: _____
Physical Location(S) Of Affected Computer System/Network:
How Was The Incident Detected?
Is The Affected System/Network Critical To The Company's Mission? (Yes/No)

Description of Intrusion/Attack

☐ Misuse of system (internal or external)	☐ Theft
☐ Account sharing	☐ Fraud
☐ Malicious code (virus, worm)	☐ Exploitation of trust
☐ Account compromise	☐ Website defacement
☐ Unauthorized software use	☐ Denial of service
☐ Copyright infringement	☐ Distributed denial of service (caused by
☐ Loss or damage	employee)
☐ Suspected violation of special access	☐ Intrusion/hack
☐ Unfriendly employee termination	☐ Probe/Scan
☐ Unauthorized release of confidential or	☐ Unauthorized electronic monitoring (sniffers)
sensitive information	☐ Unauthorized access to a security area
	☐ Unknown/other (explain below)

Other\Remarks:

Experienced this problem before? (Yes/No; If yes, explain)

Suspected Method of Intrusion/Attack

☐ Virus (provide name below, if known)	☐ Worm
☐ Vulnerability exploited (explain below)	☐ Spam
☐ Denial of service	☐ Inside attack
☐ Trojan horse	☐ Outside attack
☐ Distributed denial of service	☐ Unknown/other (explain below)

Did the Incident Result in Damage to System(s) or Data?
☐ No ☐ Unknown ☐ Yes (Explain below)

Other/Remarks:

What Actions and Technical Mitigation Have Been Taken?

☐ System(s) disconnected from the network	☐ Patches installed if so, list_____
☐ System binaries checked	☐ IOS upgraded if so, list_____
☐ Backup of affected system(s)	☐ Switch configurations modified
☐ Log files examined	☐ Firewall configurations modified
☐ Other (Please provide details in remarks)	☐ Router configurations modified
☐ No action(s) taken	

TABLE 14.3
Sample CERT Incident Reporting Form (continued)

Other/Remarks:

Law Enforcement Notified?
☐ Yes-Local law enforcement
☐ Yes-State Highway Patrol
☐ Yes-FBI field office
☐ No
Other (Explain below)
Other/Remarks:

Suspected Perpetrator(s)/Motivation(s)
☐ Insider/disgruntled employee
☐ Former employee
☐ Hacker
☐ System generated
☐ Unknown/other (explain below)
Other/remarks:

The apparent source (IP address) of the intrusion/attack:
Evidence of spoofing (Yes/No/Unknown)
What computers/systems (hardware and software) were affected

☐ Unix version _____	☐ Windows 2000 version_____
☐ OS2 version _____	☐ Windows ME version _____
☐ Linux version _____	☐ Windows XP version _____
☐ VAX/VMS version _____	☐ Sun OS/Solaris version _____
☐ Windows/98 version _____	☐ Other (explain below)
☐ NT version _____	

Other/remarks:

Affected Security Infrastructure Controls

☐ Encryption	☐ Warning banners
☐ Firewall	☐ Packet filtering
☐ Secure remote	☐ Access control lists
☐ Access/authorization tools	☐ Authentication
☐ Intrusion detection system	☐ Specific switch configurations available/in place
☐ Security auditing tools	☐ Other (explain below)

Other/remarks:

Did Incident Result in a Loss/Compromise of Sensitive or Confidential Information?

☐ No
☐ Unknown
☐ Yes (explain below)
Other/remarks:

TABLE 14.4
Sample Incident Response Postmortem Report

Tracking Number # (internal use only)

Form Completed By

Contact: _____ Title: _____ Date: _____

Email: _____ Phone: _____

Background Information

Has a CERT Incident report form been completed (Yes/No):

Date Incident Occurred: _____ Time Incident Occurred: _____ Duration of attack: _____

Closure Information

Did your detection and response process and procedures work as intended? If not, where did they not work? Why did they not work?

Explain methods of discovery and monitoring procedures that would have improved your ability to detect an intrusion:

Explain improvements to procedures and tools that would have aided you in the response process:

Explain improvements that would have enhanced your ability to contain an intrusion:

Describe correction procedures that would have improved your effectiveness in recovering your systems:

Describe updates to policies and procedures that would have allowed the response and recovery processes to operate more smoothly:

List areas for improving user and system administrator preparedness:

List areas for improving communication throughout the detecting and response processes:

Give a description of the costs associated with an intrusion, including a monetary estimate if possible:

Give a summary of postmortem efforts:

Some of the elements that may change, or be added, typically have to do with information classification, processes, and standards. Understandably, many aspects of a security policy may not change, but it is not uncommon to rework an entire policy to accommodate what was learned.

Once the test is complete, the results will promote an awareness of security-related activities that will certainly demand some form of change to the overall approach to security within the organization. Because a security policy is management's method for communicating security expectations and accepted practices, any change to the operations to accommodate greater security will appear in the policy or be driven by it.

A security policy by itself is not a solution; it is, however, the foundation for ongoing security improvement within an organization. Modifying the security policy increases the foundation an organization's security is built on and continuous modifications to the policy are a fundamental characteristic of a well-planned and structured policy. Implementation of a security policy and its supporting mechanisms is critical, and is often one of the most challenging aspects of running a successful firm. Consistently updating it to meet an organization's growing needs and threats is even a more challenging task.

DATA CLASSIFICATION

Information is clearly one of the organization's most valuable assets if not *the* most valuable asset. During the penetration test, it may have been determined that the organization's information is one of its most highly vulnerable assets and exposed to outside influences. If the information is compromised, corrupted, or lost it would negatively affect the company.

Given the results of the test, it may be clear that an attacker can obtain, manipulate, or destroy valued digital assets. However, without some form of data classification, the true impact of such a threat would remain speculative. It is no surprise many companies have a difficult time determining the true impact of the results unless an obvious breach is realized. For example, a tester may gain access to the DMZ and collect application code under development. The initial interpretation may be to reduce the exposure, but the priority assigned to the repair may be very low because of the assumed limited value of the information. In addition, the primary driver to repair the hole is concern for greater impact if a real hacker, with more time, were to leverage the same weakness for deeper access. If the value of data is based on the interpretation of the attack and not the actual value of the information or system, the company is relegated to making a judgment call or, simply put, a guess on where to start and how much to invest. Data classification, although a difficult policy to define and employ, can be a valuable commodity when dealing with an incident or creating a remediation plan after an ethical hack.

By applying a data classification scheme, information is afforded a level of protection equal to its sensitivity, providing an efficient tradeoff between security and usability. Data classification provides an accepted methodology for securing data with different levels of sensitivity, value, or use. Because the classification not only defines the practices used to protect identified data types, it inherently provides a means of auditing the results of the test. If a tester manages to obtain access to a general directory full of many different types of files, the data may be simply collected and stored to prepare for the final presentation and deliverable. When the findings are presented, the customer may not be aware that very sensitive data was included in the directory and it will not have the same level of urgency if it were known.

Classification of data is typically broken into levels, such as sensitive, confidential, restricted, and unclassified. However, there are many schemes that can be implemented to best meet your data requirements. Nevertheless, each classification is afforded standards and guidelines for managing the data.

- *Classification Authority.* Who has the authorization to classify data? For example, you don't want any employee with the ability to classify the HR data as unclassified and put it up on the Web.
- *Marking.* How the data is identified: this can be as simple as a marking in the header of a printed document, coversheet, or digital watermarking to ensure the data is clearly marked for human as well as computer identification.
- *Access Control.* If unclassified data is accessible to anyone, it is safe to assume that sensitive data is accessible only to a select few. Therefore, one of the primary attributes of data classification schemes is the access requirements. This can include the types of technology in addition to how they are implemented. For example, unclassified data is accessible to anyone, with anonymous access, whereas restricted data requires a user-name and password with a length of 6 to 8 characters. Confidential data may require a username and password, but with a length of 12 to 15 characters and has to be changed every 30 days.
- *Handling Hard-Copy Documents.* At some point in the life of a digitized document, it will get printed. It is necessary to tell people how to store, destroy, and share the document. A sensitive document may have to be bound, labeled, and stored in a locked fireproof cabinet in the basement and require sign-in and out access, whereas restricted may simply need to be placed in the locked file box under the HR director's desk.
- *Transmission.* How information is transmitted from one location to another is accepting a certain level of risk associated with the transmission. Over the Internet, fax, postal service, UPS, FedEx, you name it, when you move data from one person or system to another, how it is performed must be questioned. This is most evident with digital assets, mostly because they are always being moved from one point to another and being shared. Confidential data may require a VPN connection employing a high level of encryption and certificate-based authentication, whereas restricted can use less stringent encryption over the same virtual network. In contrast, unclassified data needs no protection (typically) and sensitive data is never transmitted across an untrusted medium.
- *Storage.* When data is not being processed or moving from server to workstation to Mary's PDA it is being stored. With the advent of complex storage solutions, data is being collected from thousands of different points and being maintained in a single location. With the mixture of data types, different classifications, varying access, and application uses, storage represents a challenge. Of course, this problem applies to something as simple as a floppy disk, CD, or backup tape. How data is stored (i.e., the technology used, such as a file system), what it is stored on (a CD will last longer than a floppy, and a steel tape will last longer than a CD), and access to the medium needs to be defined and controlled.
- *Disposal.* Data will eventually grow old, become too expensive to maintain, or become a liability (just ask Enron) and when that point is reached

it needs to be destroyed. In reality, you don't actually destroy data, but rather the medium containing it. Paper, hard drives, CDs, PDAs, memory cards, tapes, MO drives, even images burned into monitors represent the medium of data. Therefore, a standard for destroying each type of medium classified data may reside on must be defined. For example, sensitive and confidential data may only exist on hard drives, CDs, tapes of a certain type, and paper. Destroying a hard drive that has confidential data on it requires disassembly and demagnetization. Sensitive data requires that plus shredding and incineration.

The results of the penetration test could have shown that information was not accurately rated; therefore, stringent controls were not placed on this data allowing it to be proven vulnerable to disclosure. In some of these cases the security policy may not need to be modified, but the data classifications may need to be examined ensuring they were given the correct level of classification. To this point, in nearly every case where an attack proved to have more impact than first thought, the data was not properly classified. What is even more interesting is there is a logical process that usually takes over in an organization that doesn't have a classification scheme. In short, people know when they are looking at something they shouldn't. Nevertheless, penetration tests continue to gain access to information that just shouldn't be that easy. For example, a password file is put on a DMZ server because the admin wanted to play with a password cracker without getting discovered. He may not have cracked it, but the tester that found it did, and gained root access to the entire network.

The access control section of the policy simply states that employees should only have access to data they are authorized to use. It is based on the well-known "need-to-know" statement, also known as the principle of least privilege. Users should only have access to that which they need to perform their job functions, and no more. Access control can be based on many elements, such as job title, classification, and whether they are an employee, contractor, partner, or even a customer. Employees' levels of access can increase or decrease during their time with the firm, therefore, access control must be constantly monitored, ensuring that if an employee no longer needs access to a set of documents, or a system, the access is disabled.

More than likely after a penetration test, the data exposed during the attack will have to be evaluated against the classification, or the controls associated with the path the test took to gain access will have to be reviewed to see if they meet policy, or if the classification definition needs to be changed. Pretty much everything can fall into one of these three areas. In the cases where a classification scheme exists, it is—at least in my experience—never the fault of the policy defining the requirements for the classification. It is always poor implementation of the policy or the data was not properly classified.

An aspect of penetration testing that continues to raise concern is the utter lack of classification practices in organizations that practice regular penetration testing. They will have a test annually, biannually, quarterly, and in some cases monthly without ever using the information to apply a standard approach to data management.

Companies who use penetration testing as a tool will never truly reap the overall business value an ethical hack has the potential of providing because there is no fundamental change in the measuring device. From test to test you're being compared to the same template and without escalating the measuring device, you're doomed to remain stagnant and locked into a vicious cycle. Data classification is the first step in raising the bar. It requires an understanding of risk, access management, technology, policy, and practices. Once these have been defined, the classification is comparatively simple and the definition of controls obvious. Once armed with this information, a penetration test is now a validation of implemented security posture rather than simply identifying vulnerabilities; it is now more.

Organizational Security

Controlling access, as expected, has been addressed in several discussions throughout this book. Organizational practices are included in the organization's security policy in order to support employees in operating according to expectations. These are important aspects within the security group's responsibilities: because employees are afforded a certain level of trust, sound practices must be established and maintained to support them.

Fraud management is included in organization security to ensure that the company employs prudent controls that reduce the opportunity for employees to commit fraud. With the onslaught of organizational layoffs and downsizing, disgruntled employees are plentiful today. This includes setting specific roles and responsibilities when it comes to handling data, systems, and networks. For example, in a smaller organization there may only be one system administrator responsible for user account management. If this position were to be eliminated due to a reduction in staff, that administrator holds the key to the kingdom. Prior to her departure, she would have access to any or potentially all systems using a user account of choice to implement some type of fraudulent attack.

Defining roles and responsibilities can be difficult depending on the internal structure of the organization. More often than not a company has too many levels of employee status that make it difficult to align to an existing standard. Therefore, many define their own roles and responsibilities, but do not implement the necessary controls to manage them or do not apply separation of duties properly, providing a loophole for certain individuals to make changes to the environment and have the power to cover their tracks.

Essentially, you have to define roles, much like levels of classification, and responsibilities, like policies and practices for each level. However, the actions permitted by a role may need to be counterbalanced with a separate role to ensure one role is not permitted to make critical changes.

A person's ability to make changes to systems, such as firewalls, and place sensitive data in harm's way is directly related to the access and management controls afforded to that user or role. These controls will help defend against a single role or individual having the capability to have a direct impact on the security of the entire organization.

CONCLUSION

Hackers, phreaks, terrorists, script kiddies, pranksters, criminals, extortionists, or spies are real threats to all types of organizations. People who attack computer systems, their motivations, and social physiology have been the focus of much research and debate.

Nevertheless, the world is under a constant deluge of attacks ranging from seemingly harmless scans that fill logs to highly sophisticated tactics that render security controls useless. Hackers are a real threat because they have time, resources, skills, motivation, community, and an element of exciting risk driving them.

Ethical hacking has become the 21st century's security workhorse. In an effort to address security in the seemingly most logical manner, thousands have sought to understand their security from the hacker's perspective. Understanding the technical and human capability to withstand a direct assault can be a powerful advantage in ensuring the investment in security measures is appropriate and functioning as expected. For some, the security requirements are to ensure a safe environment for employees and protect essential systems. Others may have more complexity, introduced by Internet applications, extensive partner interaction, customer demands on information security, and vast exposures to various forms of threat. In any event, performing a penetration test can be an enormous asset in formulating a sound security posture.

However, as we have learned, without an established set of goals and objectives married to a comprehensive plan, the value of the test will not reach its full potential. It is no surprise many feel impersonating a hacker is the best method for duplicating the threat and clearly represents the exposure and impact of exploiting vulnerabilities. Yet this common belief has tainted the practice of ethical hacking and has set the bar of value far below what can be realized. The issue of reduced value stems from assuming a hacker can be truly mimicked, and not leveraging the opportunity for structure to overcome the inherent limitations. By employing a framework around the technology, focused on the business goals, organizations can extract an abundance of value from the exercise.

The excitement and awareness throughout the industry over ethical hacking is unparalleled. Only the advent of the firewall has challenged the volume of interest in security. However, the test's format is reaching a technical barrier and more and more companies are seeking greater value from the process. Many consultants and professional service organizations alike are tweaking the tactics and refining skills in an effort to be proactive in providing more than a list of vulnerabilities.

However, this has just begun and ethical hacking is beginning to evolve from one-off tests to becoming a fundamental component of a broader security program. Yet to make the leap from technical prowess to becoming an integral part of business strategy, one must take a deeper look into the structure of the test and its relationship to security goals. By employing a framework that stimulates sound practices and introduces opportunities to manipulate the test to overcome the inherent limitations, ethical hacking will evolve from being a popular activity to becoming a significant value to all types of organizations.

It is hoped that the framework and processes discussed herein raised awareness of the "gives and takes" of security in the light of ethical hacking. More so than in any other area of security, the value gained from a test can be greatly affected by apparently innocuous decisions. Any effort to test security without specific goals and objectives and a framework to operate within can become a fruitless exercise in futility, destined to repeat itself.

The value of security to businesses will become exceedingly more important as time passes. Today ethical hacking is an established practice that is used worldwide to evaluate security controls of all types. Nevertheless, we have only experienced the beginning of the potential value that can be realized. By integrating a framework that allows for all options to be explored, addresses the realities of the test, and uses apparent disadvantages as leverage, it is only a matter of time before it becomes essential to business as opposed to remaining a simple test.

Index